ORTHODOX READINGS OF AUGUSTINE

T0373275

Orthodox Christianity and Contemporary Thought

SERIES EDITORS
Aristotle Papanikolaou and Ashley M. Purpura

This series consists of books that seek to bring Orthodox Christianity into an engagement with contemporary forms of thought. Its goal is to promote (1) historical studies in Orthodox Christianity that are interdisciplinary, employ a variety of methods, and speak to contemporary issues; and (2) constructive theological arguments in conversation with patristic sources and that focus on contemporary questions ranging from the traditional theological and philosophical themes of God and human identity to cultural, political, economic, and ethical concerns. The books in the series explore both the relevancy of Orthodox Christianity to contemporary challenges and the impact of contemporary modes of thought on Orthodox self-understandings.

Orthodox Readings of Augustine

Edited by

GEORGE E. DEMACOPOULOS

and

ARISTOTLE PAPANIKOLAOU

FORDHAM UNIVERSITY PRESS

NEW YORK

2020

Copyright © 2020 Fordham University Press

Orthodox Readings of Augustine was previously published by St. Vladimir's Seminary Press. © 2008 St. Vladimir's Seminary Press.

Fordham University Press has no responsibility for the persistence or accuracy of URLs for external or third-party Internet websites referred to in this publication and does not guarantee that any content on such websites is, or will remain, accurate or appropriate.

Fordham University Press also publishes its books in a variety of electronic formats. Some content that appears in print may not be available in electronic books.

Visit us online at www.fordhampress.com.

Library of Congress Cataloging-in-Publication Data available online at https://catalog.loc.gov.

Printed in the United States of America
22 21 20   5 4 3 2 1
First Fordham University Press edition

Table of Contents

Acknowledgments

The papers that follow were initially delivered at the Orthodox Readings of Augustine Conference, June 14–16, 2007, at Fordham University. This was the first conference of Fordham's Orthodox Christian Studies program. We would like to begin by acknowledging Rev Joseph McShane, SJ, President of Fordham University, who has offered unswerving support of the program and its mission since the creation of the Orthodoxy in America Lecture Series (the first initiative of the program) in 2004. Along with Fr McShane, we would like to thank Rev Gerald Blaszczak, SJ, who was the Vice President of Fordham's Office of Mission and Ministry in 2004 and who first encouraged us to develop the program.

The Kallinikeion Foundation provided the single largest grant for the conference. Other external benefactors included the Augustinian Institute of Villanova University, Mr and Mrs Constantine Poulopoulos, and Mr and Mrs Kenneth Hickman. Within Fordham, Rev Patrick Ryan, SJ, Vice President of Mission and Ministry; Robert Himmelberg, the Dean of Faculty; Nancy Busch, the Dean of the Graduate School of Arts and Sciences; Brennan O'Donnell, the Dean of Fordham College at Rose Hill; Rev Robert Grimes, SJ, the Dean of Fordham College at Lincoln Center; the Department of Theology; and the Center for Medieval Studies all contributed resources. An AMES grant, provided by the Graduate School of Arts and Sciences, has covered the cost of the index and of licensing the cover art. The Center for Medieval Studies provided critical logistical support for the conference and we would especially like to acknowledge Dr Maryanne Kowaleski (the Director of the Center) and her assistants, Dr Janine Peterson (now an assistant professor at Marist College) and Kerri Kupec.

Rev Thomas Martin (Augustinian Institute of Villanova University), Dr Tia Kolbaba (Rutgers University), Dr Peter Bouteneff (St Vladimir's Orthodox Theological Seminary), Dr Demetrios Katos (Hellenic College), and Dr Terrence Tilley (Fordham University) each chaired one of the five sessions of the conference. Reginald Kim, Matthew Lootens, Jason Stevens, Jennifer Jamer, and Kate DiGeronimo provided unfailing staff support throughout the event.

Erica Olson has provided keen editorial assistance during the preparation of the manuscript. We would also like to acknowledge Dr Helen Bender, Professor of Law at Fordham, who, in many unpublicized ways, has contributed greatly to the Orthodox Christian Studies program.

Texts and Abbreviations

De prae. sanc.	*De praedestinatione sanctorum* (On the Predestination of the Saints)
De serm. dom.	*De sermone Domini in monte* (The Sermon on the Mount)
De symb. ad cat.	*De symbolo ad catechumenos* (On the Creed for Catechumens)
Trin.	*De Trinitate* (On the Trinity)
De util. cred.	*De utilitate credendi* (On the Usefulness of Believing)
De vera rel.	*De vera religione* (On True Religion)
En. in Ps.	*Enarrationes in Psalmos* (Enarrations on the Psalms)
Ench.	*Enchiridion ad Laurentium* (Enchiridion)
Ep.	*Epistulae* (Epistles)
Tract. ep. Jo.	*In epistulam Johannis ad Parthos tractatus* (Tractates on the First Epistle of John)
Tract. Ev. Jo.	*In Evangelium Johannis tractatus* (Tractates on the Gospel of John)
Opus imp.	*Opus Imperfectum . . .* (Unfinished Work against Julian)
Serm.	*Sermones* (Sermons)
Sol.	*Soliloquiorum* (Soliloquies)
Reg.	*Regulae* (Rule for Monks)
Retr.	*Retractiones* (Retractions)

OTHER WORKS

Vita	Possidius' *Vita*
CCSG	Corpus Christianorum: Series graeca, Turnhout, 1977–
CCSL	Corpus Christianorum: Series latina, Turnhout, 1953–
CSEL	Corpus scriptorum ecclesiasticorum latinorum
PL	Patrologia latina
PG	Patrologia graeca
SC	Sources chrétiennes
BA	Bibliothèque augustinienne
SVTQ	*St Vladimir's Theological Quarterly*

Augustine and the Orthodox:
"The West" in the East[1]

GEORGE E. DEMACOPOULOS AND
ARISTOTLE PAPANIKOLAOU

It remains one of the most surprising facts of Christian history that St Augustine became so influential for each of the subsequent western theological traditions, yet remained largely unread in the Christian East until the modern era. While it is true that the Greek fathers, in general, had a much wider readership in the West than the Latin fathers had in the East during the middle ages, it is still surprising that no part of Augustine's enormous corpus, apart from florilegia, seems to have circulated in the East prior to the thirteenth century.[2] This was not for a lack of effort. During his lifetime, Augustine labored to gain the attention of the eastern Church, particularly during the Pelagian controversy.[3] He may

---

[1] We would like to thank Fr John Behr and Bradford Hinze, who read and offered many useful comments on an earlier version of this paper.

[2] The two Latin fathers who were read in translation in the Greek East were John Cassian, whose *Institutiones* and *Conlationes* were excerpted, translated, and included in the wildly popular *Apophthegmata Patrum* (PG 65.71–440), and Pope Gregory I (the Great), whose *Liber Regulae Pastoralis* (SC 381–82) and *Dialogorum* (SC 251, 260, 265) were translated during his lifetime and circulated by imperial order throughout the Byzantine empire. On the meager circulation of Augustinian florilegia prior to the time of Photius, see Berthold Altaner, "Augustinus in der griechischen Kirche bis auf Photius," in his *Kleine Patristische Schriften* (Berlin: Akademie Verlag, 1967), 76–98.

[3] See his *Ep*. 179 to John of Jerusalem and *Ep*. 4* and 6* to Cyril of Jerusalem and Atticus of Constantinople, respectively. For more on this, see Robert Eno's comments in his translations of the newly discovered letters. Eno, *Saint Augustine: Letters Volume VI (1*–29*)* (Washington, DC: Catholic University Press, 1989), 38–40, 49–53. The "*" designates that the letter belongs to the new letters collected and edited by J. Divjak (CSEL 88).

have even commissioned translations of his work into Greek to assist in the effort.[4] But despite these initiatives, and despite the unparalleled importance of Augustine for the subsequent western traditions, knowledge of his corpus in the East was virtually nonexistent until the thirteenth century, when his *De Trinitate* (*On the Trinity*) was first translated into Greek.[5]

This is not to say, however, that Augustine was unknown in the East—he was known, but mostly by reputation. Before news of his death reached Constantinople, the emperor, Theodosius II, invited Augustine to attend the Council of Ephesus, which convened in 431. The council was primarily concerned with the christological questions reflected in the protracted debate between Cyril of Alexandria and Nestorius. Nevertheless, there was time enough for the delegates to include a censure of the errors attributed to Pelagius.[6] This condemnation of the Pelagian teaching by an ecumenical synod was due, in large part, to Augustine's lobbying efforts in the final fifteen years of his life. Although Augustine is not mentioned by name in the *acta* of the Council of Ephesus, his reputation as a saint and father of the Church was preserved in the East long after his passing.

Byzantium

There is little doubt that pockets within the Byzantine Church vaguely remained aware of the theological contributions of Augustine. The *acta*

---

[4]Josef Lössl, "Augustine in Byzantium," *Journal of Ecclesiastical History* 51 (2000): 267–73. See also Altaner, 73–76; and Alfons Fürst, "Augustinus im Orient," *Zeitschrift für Kirchengeschichte* 110 (1999): 294–303.

[5]There is an interesting (partial) treatise attributed to Theodore of Mopsuestia (350–428), *Ex libro contra defensores peccati originalis* (*From the Book against the Defenders of Original Sin*), which survives in Latin translation (PG 66.1005–12). Migne believed that Theodore responded directly to Augustine's works of the early 420s (PG 66.1010), possibly in 423, but Augustine is not actually named in the text.

[6]Technically, Pelagius was not named; rather, the council named one of his chief early supporters—Celestius. See canons 1 and 4 of the Council of Ephesus in *Decrees of the Ecumenical Councils*, vol. 1: *Nicaea I to Lateran V*, ed. Norman Tanner (London: Sheed & Ward Limited, 1990), 63–64.

of the Fifth Ecumenical Council (meeting in Constantinople in 553) acknowledges Augustine in three ways: it lists him among the "holy fathers and doctors of the Church";[7] it includes excerpts from his writings among the florilegia;[8] and it documents that some of his letters were read publicly during the deliberations of the fifth session.[9] What is perhaps ironic with respect to the present East/West dichotomy concerning Augustine is that this appropriation of the bishop of Hippo in 553 was used to convince Pope Vigilius to accept the condemnation of the *Three Chapters*.[10] In other words, the Greek and African delegates at the council used the authority of Augustine to convince Pope Vigilius to accept the consensus of the assembly![11] Subsequent eastern councils similarly acknowledged the authority of Augustine and, in at least one case, cited a florilegium taken from the *In Evangelium Johannis tractatus* (*Tractates on the Gospel of John*).[12]

There may be no better example of the Byzantine Church's high regard for Augustine than Photius' defense of him in the midst of the *filioque* controversy. Photius entered the trinitarian maelstrom in the late 860s when he included an attack on the *filioque* as part of a larger campaign to protect the Byzantine Church (and his own position as patriarch) from

---

[7] *Acta Conciliorum Oecumenicorum* (hereafter ACO), ed. Johannes Straub, tome 4, vol. 1 (Berlin: Walter de Gruyter & Co, 1971), 37.

[8] ACO 4.1.102–03.

[9] ACO 4.1.212: "Augustini religiosae memoriae, qui inter Africanos episcopos splenduit, diversae epistolae recitatae sunt significantes quod oportet haereticos et post mortem anathematizari." According to the *acta*, these letters were read by a delegate from North Africa.

[10] *Sententia adversus "tria Capitula"* (*Sentence against the Three Chapters*) in *Decrees of the Ecumenical Councils*, 110–11. Among other reasons, Vigilius did not want to condemn the three clerics because they were already deceased. The delegates pointed to the fact that Augustine had, in his lifetime, sanctioned posthumous condemnations.

[11] Ultimately, he did so and even used Augustine's *Retr.* as a precedent for his own change of position. Virgilius, *Epistula II ad Eutychium*, contained in ACO 4.1.245–47.

[12] For example, the *acta* of the Sixth Ecumenical Council (Constantinople, 680–681) refers to him as the "most excellent and blessed Augustine." Perhaps even more surprisingly, the *acta* of the Comnenian Council of Constantinople (1166–1167) inserts him in the florilegia between Gregory of Nyssa and John Damascene as Ὁ ἅγιος Αὐγουστίνος and includes a paraphrase of his *Tract. Ev. Jo.* 78.3. See PG 140.217.

the encroachments of Pope Nicholas I.[13] For our purposes, what is significant about this confrontation is Photius' method for dealing with the possibility that someone of Augustine's stature could have authorized a teaching as flawed as the *filioque.* Twice Photius responded to the fact that the Franks supported their teaching with the authority of Augustine: in his famous *Mystagogia,* and in *Ep.* 291, written to the archbishop of Aquileia.[14]

Although it provided the content for nearly all subsequent Byzantine critiques of the *filioque,* Photius' *Mystagogia* was not a systematic treatise. He prepared it in haste, without access to his library, and it reads like a collection of overlapping arguments rather than a sustained thesis. Because he did not have the actual Latin texts at his disposal, Photius relied upon alternative methods when he addressed the fact that the Franks claimed to ground their position in the teachings of Ambrose, Jerome, and Augustine. For example, he proposed that the original texts of these saints might have been corrupted or that more pressing reasons, now unknown, required these fathers temporarily to resort to an exaggeration of the Orthodox teaching in order to prevent some other, more dangerous, alternative.[15] Another of his strategies, however, might be the most compelling for modern readers. Photius argued that if Augustine taught something only slightly divergent from the rule of faith, without any malicious intent and without the foreknowledge of a subsequent error, he cannot be held accountable for the later provocateurs of heresy who would use his teachings illegitimately to promote their own error.[16] He also insisted that the conscientious Christian is the one who hides the human flaws of their "fathers" (like the sons of Noah who covered their father's nakedness) rather than expose them for their own purposes.[17]

In the letter to the archbishop of Aquileia, Photius was less thorough in his defense of Augustine but equally scandalized that the Franks would

[13]For a general overview of the controversy, see Henry Chadwick, *East and West: The Making of a Rift in the Church* (Oxford: Oxford University Press, 2003), 124–92.

[14]The dating of the *Mystagogia* is complicated. Its revised form may well stem from his second exile, near the end of his life, c. 886–893. *Ep.* 291 dates to either 883 or 884.

[15]Photius, *Mystagogia* 71–72 (PG 102.352–53).

[16]Ibid., 68 (PG 102.345–48).

[17]Ibid., 70 (PG 102.349–52).

dare to soil the saint's reputation by including him among those who reject both the gospel and the teaching of the Church's ecumenical councils.[18] That Photius was willing to go to such lengths to defend the sanctity of a saint that he appears to have never read offers a clear testimony of two overlapping concerns: (1) he knew the importance of Augustine to the western Church; and (2) he felt that it was critical to retain Augustine among the canon of Orthodox fathers. The elaborate excuses Photius offered in defense of Augustine were ultimately designed to protect the dignity of Augustine and to retain him as an authority for the Orthodox. In short, Photius' defense of Augustine suggests that he remained well respected, if rarely read, in ninth-century Byzantium.

In the later part of the thirteenth century, more than eight hundred years after his death, Augustine's *De Trinitate* was, for the first time, translated into Greek as part of the wide-ranging pro-union agenda of the emperor Michael VIII Palaiologos.[19] The translation was conducted by Maximus Planoudes in a complex and highly charged theological environment. This translation was subsequently employed by some of the most prominent members of the Byzantine Church, including Gregory Palamas.[20]

Following Planoudes' translation of *De Trinitate*, other works of Augustine appeared in Greek. The fourteenth-century brothers, Demetrios and Prochoros Kydones, translated several texts into Greek—the latter having better fortune than his brother in avoiding pseudonymous works. A list of these translations have been provided in recent essays by Aidan Nichols

[18]Photius, *Ep.* 291.245f. *Photii Patriarchae Constantinopolitani Epistulae et Amphilochia*, vol. 3, ed. B. Laourdas and L.G. Westerink (Leipzig: BSB G.G. Teubner Verlagsgesellschaft, 1985), 146–47.

[19]Michael assumed the throne of the Empire of Nicaea in 1261 and of Byzantium (upon his successful capture of Constantinople) in 1263. He held that position until his death in 1282. As one of the stipulations for lasting union pronounced at the Second Council of Lyon in 1274, the Latin fathers were to be translated into Greek so that the eastern Church could conform to the teachings of the West. See Aidan Nichols, "The Reception of St Augustine and his Work in the Byzantine-Slav Tradition," *Angelicum* 64 (1987): 443–44.

[20]See R. Flogaus, *Theosis bei Palamas und Luther. Ein Beitrag zum ökumenischen Gespräch* (Göttingen: Vandenhoeck & Ruprecht, 1997); and "Der heimliche Blick nach Westen. Zur Rezeption von Augustins De trinitate durch Gregorios Palamas," *Jahrbuch der Österreichischen Byzantinistik* 46 (1996): 275–97.

and Alfons Fürst.[21] The small circle of pro-western intellectuals in Constantinople certainly drew upon these texts as they sought to forge a theological bridge to the West in the final century of the Byzantine empire. But they were not alone. Manuscripts of Planoudes' and the Kydoneses' translations survive on Mount Athos (never a hotbed of pro-unionist sentiment) and in Jerusalem. What is more, Mark of Ephesus, the fifteenth-century leader of the anti-unionist cause, accepted the authority of Augustine at the Council of Florence (1438–39) and even quoted from his *Epistulae* (*Epistles*), *Soliloquiorum* (*Soliloquies*), and *De Trinitate* during the debates on purgatory.[22] Mark repeatedly referred to Augustine as ὁ μακάριος Αὐγουστῖνος (Blessed Augustine) and concludes one lengthy collection of proof-texts (which included several references to Augustine) by noting that all of these statements were offered by teachers (διδασκάλοι) of the Church.[23] That Mark openly accepted the authority of Augustine and, like Photius, deflected the possibility that his teachings could be used to endorse subsequent western errors[24] is conclusive evidence that Augustine, the individual, remained an authority for leading members of the eastern Church until the end of the Byzantine empire.[25]

[21]Nichols, "The Reception of St Augustine," 444–45; and Fürst, "Augustinus im Orient," 304–9.

[22]For his use of Augustine's *Ep.* (*Ep.* 82 and 148), see Marci Epesii, "Oratio altera de igne Purgatorio," in *Concilium Florentinum: Documenta et Scriptores*, vol. 8, pars 2: *De Purgatorio disputationes*, ed. L. Petit and G. Hofmann (Rome: Pontificum Institutum Orientalium Studiorum, 1969), 76 (beginning at lines 18 and 27 respectively). For his use of the *Sol.* (ch. 31), see his "Responsio quibusdam quaesitis Latinis," in op. cit., 110 (line 32)–11 (line 17). And for his use of *Trin.* (14.19), see ibid., 113 (lines 4–17).

[23]Ibid., 112.

[24]According to the Greek *acta*, Mark believed that Augustine's corpus has been deliberately corrupted by western scribes. See *Concilium Florentinum: Documenta et Scriptores*, vol. 5, pars 2: *Acta Sancti et oecumenici concilii Florentiae Habiti*, ed. J. Gill (Rome: Pontificum Institutum Orientalium Studiorum, 1953), 259.

[25]It should not go unnoticed that each of the three "Pillars of Orthodoxy" (Ss Photius, Gregory Palamas, and Mark of Ephesus) who are frequently promoted by modern opponents of engagement with the West embraced Augustine as an authoritative father of the Church. Photius did so by reputation alone; Palamas carefully extracted what he found useful from *Trin.*; and Mark took advantage of additional, more recently translated, materials in his campaigns against the innovations of the post-Augustinian West.

The Greek Church in the Ottoman Period

Following the conquest of Byzantium by the Ottoman Turks in 1453, the Christian East suffered a prolonged economic and intellectual decline. During the same period, three distinct forces combined to inject a new level of western influence into the vacuum. The first was the Ottoman government's promotion of the Uniate Church, a measure designed to spread division among the Christian subjects of the empire. The second was the government's restrictions placed upon the printing of Orthodox materials.[26] These restrictions led to the establishment of Orthodox printing houses in the West, especially in Venice, where the majority of the Orthodox ecclesial books were printed for the first time. The third was the closing of most Orthodox schools, resulting in a migration of clerics to the Catholic seminaries in the West.[27] Not surprisingly, the resulting interaction between Orthodox and Catholics produced a variety of results (ranging from peaceful coexistence to open hostility) and led to fiercely ambivalent reactions to the West among those Orthodox communities that remained under Ottoman control.

For our purposes, it is worth noting that during this period the Byzantine translations of Augustine's works (as well as several pseudonymous texts attributed to him) continued to circulate, especially on Mount Athos, the last great bastion of Orthodox identity and culture within the Ottoman territory. St Nicodemus the Hagiorite (1749–1809), an Athonite monk and prolific author, was perhaps the most significant theological mind from the Ottoman period, and his own ambivalence toward the West well characterizes the attitudes of many within the Greek Church of

[26]Ecclesiastical printing was not completely prevented, but it was limited. For example, when the patriarch of Constantinople Cyril Loukaris attempted to open a print shop in the early seventeenth century, the Ottoman government had it closed. See H.A. Hodges' introduction in *Unseen Warfare* (Crestwood, NY: SVS Press, 1987), 41.

[27]We would like to acknowledge that the situation in Turkey is even more oppressive for the Orthodox community today than it was during the Ottoman period. The last Orthodox seminary, the Halki School of Theology, was closed by the Turkish government in 1971 and remains at the center of an international dispute over the lack of religious freedom in Turkey. For more on the campaign to promote religious freedom in Turkey, visit the website of the Archons of the Ecumenical Patriarchate, www.archons.org.

his time.[28] For this reason, it is all the more important to see the extent to which Nicodemus embraced Augustine.

In 1799, Nicodemus edited and published Demetrios Kydones' translation of Augustine's *Soliloquiorum,* which had been circulating under the title *Monologia.*[29] Perhaps more significantly, he included Augustine's name among the saints to be commemorated on June 15, when he completed his monumental revision of the *Synaxarion* (a calendar of saints' feastdays) between 1805 and 1807 (published for the first time in Venice, 1819).[30] Following Nicodemus' lead, the Russian Church added Augustine to their own *Synaxarion* later that century.[31] These *Synaxaria* remain in use today. Although Nicodemus did not offer a *vita* or publish hymns for liturgical veneration, the latter was produced by Fr Ambrose Pogdin of the Russian Orthodox Church in 1955.[32]

When Nicodemus compiled the *Pedalion* (*Rudder*), the first printed collection of Orthodox canon law, in 1793, he added a fascinating footnote

[28]Although he translated and appropriated many contemporary western texts (including his famous *Unseen Warfare* and *Spiritual Exercises*), Nicodemus remained openly critical of western errors. He wrote, "[w]e must hate and detest the misbeliefs and unlawful customs of the Latins and others who are Heterodox; but if they have anything sound and confirmed by the Canons of the Holy Synods, these we must not hate." Cited by George Bebis in his introduction to *Nicodemus of the Holy Mountain: A Handbook of Spiritual Counsel* (Mahwah, NJ: Paulist Press, 1989), 26. For more on Nicodemus' appropriation of western writers, see Hodges, *Unseen Warfare,* 41–56. See also Bebis, *Nicodemus,* 14–15 and 26–30.

[29]The original printing was done in Constantinople with the title Ἐπιτομή ἐκ τῶν προφητανακτοδαβιτικῶν ψαλμῶν. We would like to thank Fr Maximus Constas, the librarian of the monastery of Simonopetra (Mount Athos), who informed us of this and other holdings in Simonopetra's library. Also of note is the so-called *Kekragarion,* which was translated by Eugenios Voulgaris (1716–1806). Of this, the library at Simonopetra has five editions (Leipzig, 1804; Moscow, 1824; Athens, 1910 [edited by St Nektarios]; Thessaloniki, 1973; and Athens, 2002).

[30]Nicodemus added hundreds of names to the existing *Synaxarion,* the great majority of which were the "neo" martyrs of the Ottoman period.

[31]Seraphim Rose, *The Place of the Blessed Augustine in the Orthodox Church,* rev. ed. (Platina, CA: St Herman of Alaska Brotherhood, 1996), 78.

[32]See the appendix to Rose, *The Place of the Blessed Augustine,* 117–38. For an excellent discussion of the liturgical commemoration of Augustine in the Christian East, see Peter Galadza, "The Liturgical Commemoration of Augustine in the Orthodox Church: An Ambiguous *Lex Orandi* for an Ambiguous *Lex Credendi,*" *SVTQ* 52.1 (2008): 111–30.

to canon 81 of the Council of Carthage. He observed that in North Africa at that time was "St Augustine, that wonderful man . . . who was so great a theologian of the Church, . . . [and whose writings] were preserved despite the fact that thereafter they were garbled by heretics. That is why Orthodox Easterners do not accept them *in toto* and as a matter of course, but only whatever agrees with the common consensus of the catholic Church."[33] Note that Nicodemus, like Photius and Mark of Ephesus, did not attribute the possible errors in Augustine's corpus to the saint himself, but rather presumed that any errors that they contained had been inserted by others. Nevertheless, unlike Photius or Mark, Nicodemus seems to have had a personal knowledge of the actual "errors" and therefore cautions his reader that the Church does not endorse the entire corpus. By the end of the nineteenth century, Orthodox theologians would begin to identify specifically what it was that they found to be unacceptable in the Augustinian corpus.

Tsarist Russia

Students of early-modern European history know well the attempts of Peter I (1672–1725) and Catherine II (1729–1796) to modernize (i.e., westernize) Russia. One important aspect of their program was the creation of an educational system that was designed to establish and sustain a submissive and patriotic populace that would, in turn, fuel the desired modernization.[34] For our purposes, it is important to note that these educational reforms included the creation of the first unified seminary system in the Orthodox world. In part, because Peter and Catherine's priority for these seminaries was to train an elite bureaucratic corps (rather than an educated priesthood) and, in part, because they saw the seminary program as a means to further other pro-western agendas, these schools

---

[33] *The Rudder*, trans. D. Cummings (Chicago: The Orthodox Christian Educational Society, 1983), 652.

[34] J.L. Black, *Citizens for the Fatherland: Education, Educators, and Pedagogical Ideals in Eighteenth-Century Russia* (New York: Columbia University Press, 1979).

adopted a decidedly western curriculum, which replaced the traditional Orthodox canon with scholastic and enlightenment authors.[35] What is more, by 1700, Latin replaced Old Slavonic and Greek as the intellectual language of Russia,[36] and the most respected of the theological academies (Kiev) taught in Latin rather than Russian for much of the eighteenth century.[37] While it would be impossible to quantify the impact of these educational reforms for subsequent Russian theology, it is certain that the push for westernization by Peter I and Catherine II fueled the nineteenth century's reactionary movement against the West and, especially, the western Christian traditions.[38]

This attempt at the westernization of Russia would not go unchallenged and would contribute to a revival of interest in the ascetic and patristic sources of the Orthodox tradition begun by Nicodemus of the Holy Mountain. A sign of this revival is the translation into Russian of the *Philokalia* (originally compiled by Nicodemus), which was followed by a series of translations of eastern patristic texts. A more extreme response to this westernization was the Slavophile movement, which interpreted the theology and the cultural ethos of the Christian "West" as mutually exclusive to the Christian "East." As a result of this hermeneutical lens, Augustine, for the first time in the history of the Orthodox Church, was categorically condemned as the one who initiated western Christianity's slide into heresy. Although the Slavophile critique was not pervasive in Russian intellectual circles, it did anticipate what would become the three central theological concerns for Orthodox readers of Augustine in the

---

[35]The tsars believed it was important for the clerical class to be subordinate to the state, and the creation of the seminaries was thought to advance this objective. See Gregory L. Freeze, *The Russian Levites: Parish Clergy in the Eighteenth Century* (Cambridge: Harvard University Press, 1977).

[36]Black, *Citizens for the Fatherland*, 17.

[37]See Alexander Sydorenko, *The Kievan Academy in the Seventeenth Century* (Ottowa: University of Ottowa, 1977).

[38]See Miroslaw I. Tataryn, *Augustine and Russian Orthodoxy: Russian Orthodox Theologians and Augustine of Hippo: A Twentieth Century Dialogue* (Lanham, MD: International Scholars Publications, 2000), 27–30, for a summary of the late nineteenth-century reaction against the westernizing seminaries and academies in Russia. Many of these protagonists advocated replacing the seminaries with a monastic "education."

twentieth century: theological epistemology, sin and grace, and trinitarian theology.[39]

For the most part, however, the Russian intellectual response to Augustine was a generous critical engagement.[40] The middle of the nineteenth century saw the first systematic attempt to translate patristic texts into Russian. Of significance is the translation of the entire corpus of Augustine's works, which was completed between 1879 and 1895. Paralleling this translation project were twelve distinct studies of Augustine that were published in Russia between 1870 and 1914.[41]

Russian Sophiology

One of the most sustained theological engagements with Augustine occurs in the work of Sergei Nikolaevich Bulgakov (1871–1944).[42] Bulgakov focused on two theological themes: Augustine's teachings on sin and grace and his trinitarian theology. The latter was already a focus of some discussion in Byzantine theology because of the *filioque* controversy, but there is a lack of any sustained discussion of the former prior to Nicodemus. It may well be that the central role of Augustine's understanding of sin and grace in post-reformation debates between Protestants and Roman Catholics may have contributed to turning the attention of the Orthodox to this aspect of Augustine's theology.[43] Much of Bulgakov's

[39] For a good overview of the reception of Augustine in Russia, see Tataryn, *Augustine and Russian Orthodoxy*.

[40] In fact, the *Orthodox Theological Encyclopedia* (St. Petersburg, 1900), 108, asserted that "the teaching of Augustine can be accepted as the image of true Orthodox Christian teaching."

[41] Tataryn, *Augustine and Russian Orthodoxy*, 15.

[42] For a general overview of contemporary Orthodox theology, see Aristotle Papanikolaou, "Orthodox Theology," in Erwin Fahlbusch, Jan Milič Lochman, John Mbiti, Jaroslav Pelikan, Lukas Vischer, eds.; Geoffrey W. Bromiley, English-language ed.; David B. Barnett, statistical ed., *Encyclopedia of Christianity*, vol. 5 (Grand Rapids: William B. Eerdmans Publishing Co.; Leiden: Brill, 2007), 414–18.

[43] Although the Russian intellectual response to Augustine was generous, his understanding of sin and grace was generally criticized. See Tataryn, *Augustine and Russian Orthodoxy*, 22–24, 81–84, 107–16.

discussion of Augustine occurs in his dogmatic trilogy, *On Divine-Humanity*,[44] which he wrote after his exile from Russia and while he was dean of St Sergius Orthodox Theological Institute in Paris, the first Russian Orthodox theological academy outside of Russia. His thought represents the most sophisticated and coherent culmination of the intellectual tradition in late nineteenth- and early twentieth-century Russia known as sophiology. Vladimir Sergeevich Solovyov (1853–1900) is considered the father of sophiology, and his thought would exercise considerable influence on the Russian intellectuals of the Silver Age, especially Pavel Florensky (1882–1943).[45] It would be Bulgakov, however, who would explicitly relate Solovyov's sophiology to the dogmatic tradition of the Orthodox Church.[46]

Bulgakov argued that Augustine's trinitarian theology begins with the divine essence, in contrast to the Cappadocians, who begin with the trinity of persons—an interpretation of Augustine that would become common in the twentieth century.[47] This starting point would allow Augustine to offer what Bulgakov thinks is his most distinctive and important contribution to trinitarian theology: the understanding of the Holy Trinity as Love, and, specifically, the Holy Spirit as the love that binds the Father and the Son. Bulgakov argues that:

[44]All three volumes have recently been translated and published by William B. Eerdmans Publishing Company: vol. 1, *The Lamb of God* (2008, orig. pub., 1933); vol. 2, *The Comforter* (2004, orig. pub., 1936); vol. 3, *The Bride of the Lamb* (2002, orig. pub., 1945, though it was submitted to the publishers in 1939).

[45]For more on Florensky's attitude toward Augustine and his influence on Bulgakov, see Tataryn, *Augustine and Russian Orthodoxy*, 45–52.

[46]For a good discussion of Solovyov and Bulgakov, see Paul Valliere, *Modern Russian Theology: Bukharev, Soloviev, Bulgakov—Orthodox Theology in a New Key* (Grand Rapids: William B. Eerdmans Publishing Co., 2000).

[47]Bulgakov, *The Comforter*, 41. The critique would be repeated especially by Zizioulas, who judges it as problematic for reasons different than those of Bulgakov. This understanding of Augustine, and western trinitarian theology in general, as beginning with the notion of the one God and proceeding to an understanding of the doctrine of the Trinity was probably influenced by Théodore de Régnon's *Études de théologie positive sur la Sainte Trinité* (Paris: Retaux, 1892–1898). For a discussion of de Régnon's influence in shaping contemporary discussions on eastern and western trinitarian theologies, see Sarah Coakley, "Introduction: Disputed Questions in Patristic Trinitarianism," *Harvard Theological Review* 100 (2007): 125–40. For further analysis of de Régnon's work, see the papers by Ayres, Behr, and Hart (*intra*).

Augustine's point of departure in the doctrine of the Holy Trinity gives him a greater grasp than the Eastern theologians have of the problem of the *connection* of the Holy Trinity with respect to the interrelations of the hypostases; the Eastern theologians replace this connection to a certain degree by the mere *juxtaposition* of the hypostases. On this pathway, Augustine makes a true discovery in the trinitarian and pneumatological theology: he is the first to express the idea, wholly foreign to Eastern theology, of the Holy Trinity as Love. Here he clarifies a special significance of the Third hypostasis, namely, that this hypostasis is love itself, the connection of love, *amor* or *dilectio*.[48]

Implicit here is the claim that Augustine offers a more adequate account of the unity of the Trinity than anything found in the Cappadocian fathers. Beginning with the divine essence, however, would also lead Augustine to the fateful formulation of the *filioque*—the claim that the Holy Spirit proceeds from the Father and the Son.

It is worth emphasizing several points in Bulgakov's treatment of Augustine on the Trinity that are especially relevant to contemporary Orthodox portrayals of Augustine. First, Bulgakov did not treat Augustine's "beginning with the essence" as a betrayal of the Cappadocian approach to the Trinity and, hence, the start of the demise of the doctrine of the Trinity. The relation is not one of mutual exclusivity but of complementarity, as Bulgakov credited Augustine for a contribution not found in the Cappadocians. What is also striking is the way that Bulgakov treated Augustine as equal to the Greek fathers, i.e., as one who made significant advances on dogmatic questions but whose answers can be criticized as in some respect inadequate. This equality is especially clear on the *filioque*

---

[48]Bulgakov, *The Comforter*, 42. For a fascinating discussion of the influence of Augustine's "love analogy" on Russian thought, see, Michael Aksionov Meerson, *The Trinity of Love in Modern Russian Theology: The Love Paradigm and the Retrieval of Western Medieval Love Mysticism in Modern Russian Trinitarian Thought: from Solovyov to Bulgakov* (Quincy, IL: Franciscan Press, 1998). For a general overview of trinitarian theology in contemporary Orthodox theology, see Aristotle Papanikolaou, "Sophia, Apophasis and Communion: Trinity in Contemporary Orthodox Theology," in *Cambridge Companion to the Trinity*, ed. P. Phan (Cambridge: Cambridge University Press, forthcoming).

issue, where Bulgakov was critical not simply of Augustine but of the Greek formulation of διὰ Υἱοῦ (through the Son).[49] More specifically, Bulgakov rejected the Greek patristic interpretation of the monarchy of the Father in terms of causality. As an issue that divides eastern and western Christians, Bulgakov actually placed more blame on Photius, who, Bulgakov argued, would establish the terms of the theological debate for future generations in a way that would preclude the possibility for any real advancement in dogmatic clarity. The problem for Bulgakov was not Augustine's theology per se, but the more extreme interpretations of Augustine's formulation of the *filioque* that would be used theologically and politically to harden Christian divisions.

A similar attitude is found in Buglakov's understanding of sin and grace. Bulgakov was part of a consensus among contemporary Orthodox theologians in rejecting Augustine's teachings on sin and grace, which he had articulated during the Pelagian controversy. For Bulgakov, Augustine claimed that original sin corrupted human nature to the point of denying free will.[50] Although Augustine did not support the doctrine of double predestination, his understanding of sin, grace, and free will would be taken to its most extreme conclusion in the Reformation theologians associated with John Calvin. Even if Augustine did present theological ideas on sin and grace that were not present in the eastern patristic texts, for Bulgakov, Augustine should not be held responsible for the more extreme formulations that ultimately divided Orthodox, Catholic, and Protestant Christians.

The Neo-patristic School

Although currently experiencing a revival of interest with the recent translation of his work into English, after his death, Bulgakov's sophiology was

---

[49]See Bulgakov, *The Comforter*, 75–152, for an extensive discussion of the *filioque*.

[50]See Bulgakov, *The Bride of the Lamb*, esp. 212–19. Unfortunately, the translator decided not to include what he describes as a "book-length 'excursus' on Augustinianism and predestination" (xiv). For a discussion of this "excursus" in *The Bride of the Lamb*, see Tataryn, *Augustine and Russian Orthodoxy*, 75–81.

not the most influential form of Orthodox theology both within and out-side Orthodox intellectual circles. The Russian Orthodox diaspora would give birth to an alternative vision for Orthodox theology that Georges Florovsky (1893–1979) coined as a "neo-patristic synthesis," one that, at least in its initial phases, would self-identify itself against Russian sophiology. This neo-patristic school of Orthodox theology can also be seen as "neo-Palamite" because of its emphasis on apophatic theology and the essence/energies distinction, i.e., the notion that even though God's essence is incomprehensible, humans were created for deification, which is given through a participation in the divine energies, which are fully God.

Together with Florovsky, Vladimir Lossky (1903–1958), a Russian émigré to Paris, would become one of the most influential representatives of this neo-patristic school.[51] Though he was far from being a Slavophile, Lossky echoed their understanding of the causes of division within Christianity in terms of a western rationalization of theology versus an eastern emphasis on a knowledge of God as mystical experience. For Lossky, the culprit of this rationalization of theology was not so much Augustine as it was Aquinas and, more specifically, the modern interpreters of Aquinas. The failure of scholasticism, for Lossky, was its misinterpretation of Dionysian apophaticism, which would lead to the western rejection of the essence/energies distinction and the understanding of grace as created. The essence/energies distinction, Lossky would argue, is rooted in the affirmation of the realism of divine-human communion, i.e., that God *is* so as to allow for a communion with what is not God (creation). Put another way, the only way to adequately conceptualize *theosis* (deification) is through the antinomic distinction between God's essence and God's energies, even if such a distinction is judged nonsensical by certain philosophical criteria. The rationalization of theology by scholasticism obfuscates the truth of human existence as created for union with God by affirming a propositional notion of truth, thus constructing idols out of human concepts, and by attempting to justify Christian beliefs in philo-

---

[51] For Lossky's theology, see Aristotle Papanikolaou, *Being with God: Trinity, Apophaticism, and Divine-Human Communion* (Notre Dame, IN: University of Notre Dame Press, 2006).

sophical categories that cannot adequately conceptualize the patristic notion of theosis.

Apart from Bulgakov, Lossky was one of the few Orthodox theologians to offer a sustained analysis of Augustine, but one that focused on the apophatic strain in his work. In "Elements of 'Negative Theology' in the Thought of St. Augustine,"[52] Lossky asserts that apophaticism functions differently in Augustine than it does with Dionysius. Lossky did not exploit this difference, however, to fault Augustine for laying the foundation for the theological mistakes of the West. In fact, the difference was not so great as to prevent it from being integrated in a Dionysian form of mystical theology. It took the Latin translations of Dionysius and John Scotus Eriugena "in order for elements of St Augustine's negative theology, set in new contexts, to receive the somber light of mystical apophasis."[53] The thrust of the article, especially in light of Lossky's other writings, is an implied discontinuity between Augustinian and scholastic understandings of apophaticism, and a linking of Augustine with more authentic interpretations of Dionysius in the mystical tradition of the West.

The other father of the neo-patristic school, Georges Florovsky, offered a more ambivalent attitude to Augustine, though his work only contains scattered references to Augustine's writings. Florovsky echoed the critique of Augustine's understanding of sin and grace, which ultimately painted too bleak a picture of human nature and denied human freedom. For Florovsky, such an understanding of sin and grace was incompatible with the core of the eastern Christian tradition—theosis—insofar as such a union with the divine energies was achieved through a free cooperation with God. If, for Lossky, the West's mistaken rejection of the essence/energies distinction occurred with scholasticism, Florovsky extended this rejection back to Augustine.[54] The attribution of this rejec-

---

[52]First published in French in *Augustinus Magister,* vol. 1 (Paris: Editions des Études Augustiniennes, 1954), 575–81; reprinted in English in *SVTQ* 21 (1977): 67–75.

[53]Ibid., 75.

[54]Florovsky, "Creation and Creaturehood," in *Creation and Redemption,* vol. 3 in The Collected Works of Georges Florovsky (Belmont, MA: Nordland Publishing Company, 1976; orig. pub. in *Studies of the Orthodox Theological Institute* [Russian] 1 [1928]: 176–212), 274, n. 68: "The Eastern patristic distinction between the essence and energies of God has

tion to Augustine, however, was only asserted in a footnote; that, together with the fact that Florovsky never presented a sustained analysis of Augustine's theology, can only indicate that Florovsky did not hold Augustine responsible for the theological divisions between eastern and western Christianity. Otherwise, it would be difficult to imagine Florovsky referring to Augustine as "a Father of the Church Universal."[55]

Theology in Greece: The 1960s Generation

The neo-patristic school would exercise a decisive influence on Orthodox theology in the twentieth century through a group of young theologians in Greece in the late 1950s and throughout the 1960s.[56] This new generation of Greek theologians wanted to break with their professors, whom they perceived as simply imitating the theological manuals of the West. This theological imitation is not surprising, and perhaps even understandable, given the fact that Greece suffered more than four hundred years under Ottoman oppression. The post-colonial situation in Greece was such that, given the decimation of a once vibrant intellectual tradi-

always remained foreign to Western theology. In Eastern theology it is the basis of the distinction between apophatic and cataphatic theology. St Augustine decisively rejects it." It is important to note that in this footnote, Florovsky refers the reader to I.V. Popov's work, *The Personality and Teachings of the Blessed Augustine*, which was published in Russian in 1916. It indicates that already in early twentieth-century Russia there was emerging an explanation of the divisions between eastern and western Christianity in terms of the latter's rejection of the essence/energies distinction that is rooted in Augustine's theology of sin and grace.

[55]"St Cyprian and St Augustine on Schism," in *Ecumenism II: A Historical Approach*, vol. 14 in The Collected Works of Georges Florovsky (Vaduz, Europa: Büchervertriebsanstalt, 1989), 50.

[56]For the influence of the neo-patristic school in Greece, see Christos Yannaras, *Orthodoxy and the West*, trans. P. Chamberas and N. Russell (Brookline, MA: Holy Cross Orthodox Press, 2006). For Lossky's influence on Greek theologians, especially their theologies of personhood, see Basilio Petrà, "Personalist Thought in Greek in the Twentieth Century: A First Tentative Synthesis," *Greek Orthodox Theological Review* (forthcoming); and Aristotle Papanikolaou, "Personhood and its Exponents in Twentieth-Century Orthodox Theology," in *Cambridge Companion to Orthodox Christian Theology*, ed. E. Theokritoff and M. Cunningham (Cambridge: Cambridge University Press, 2008), 232–45.

tion that reached back to the Byzantine period, in the rush to reestablish
institutions of higher learning, theological education would rely on the
forms of Christian thinking dominant in the non-Orthodox Christian
world, especially those forms of thinking that were most consistent with
the general outlines of Orthodox belief. For many of these young Greek
theologians, the shedding of one colonizer from the Muslim East only
allowed for the surreptitious colonization of the intellectual life in Greece
by the Christian West. The return to the fathers was an attempt to liberate theology from all colonization.

Given this context, most Greek theologians of this new generation
interpreted the "West" as diametrically opposed to the "East," both theologically and in terms of its cultural ethos. One of the most vociferous
spokespersons for this dichotomous juxtaposition between West and East
was John Romanides (1926–2001). It is generally agreed that Romanides
was the most important in a series of Orthodox writers who unapologet-
ically condemned Augustine. Romanides not only unequivocally faulted
Augustine for the theological mistakes of western Christianity but also
attributed to him a mode of thinking that would serve as the foundation
for a cultural ethos in the West that would be diametrically opposed to
that embodied in Christian antiquity and the Byzantine empire—what
Romanides refers to as Ρωμιοσύνη.[57]

Romanides was a student at St Sergius, where he no doubt came into
contact with the work of Lossky and Florovsky, the two most influential
Orthodox intellectuals of the time. Like Lossky, Romanides argued that
the West's key theological error was the rejection of the essence/energies
distinction, which was also a rejection of theosis, since the essence/ener-
gies distinction is necessary for conceptualizing theosis. The rejection of
the essence/energies distinction is rooted in Augustine's approach to theology, which "is based on the method [that]is summed up in the dictum,
'*I believe in order to understand.*'"[58] Augustine lays the foundation for a
"Franco-Latin" approach to theology that uses "the categories of philoso-

[57]See his Ρωμιοσύνη, Ρωμανία, Ρούμελη (Thessaloniki: Pournara, 1975).
[58]John Romanides, *An Outline of Orthodox Patristic Dogmatics*, ed. and trans. G. Dra-
gas (Rollinsford, NH: Orthodox Research Institute, 2004), 35.

phy to examine the essence of God" and employs "certain philosophical systems in order to understand the dogma of the Holy Trinity."[59] As a result of his theological method, which gives understanding to faith, Augustine interpreted the God-world relation in terms of the philosophical category of divine essence and, thus, mistakenly identified God's being with God's activity. This identification laid the foundation for the scholastic conceptualization of God in terms of *esse*, which affirms that God's essence is God's existence:

> St Augustine himself does not appear to have accepted this (essence/energies) distinction. Speaking about the procession of the Holy Spirit, he makes a clear confusion between essence and energy in God. This identification of essence and energy in the West led Western theologians to articulate the thought that God is "*pure energy.*" The articulation of the above thought is also due to other philosophical presuppostions of Augustine, such as his faith concerning knowledge of the essence of God.[60]

This identification, however, makes theosis impossible and accounts for why, "[i]n the theological tradition of the Franks, beginning with Augustine, there is no doctrine of deification."[61] The absence of the essence/energies distinction means, according to Romanides, that there can be no bridge between two ontological others, God and creation. The latter can only relate to God through the created effects of God's activity, i.e., created grace; precluded is any real union with God, i.e., uncreated grace, which is what is necessary for salvation from death. Romanides essentially extends Lossky's critique of scholasticism back to Augustine, to whom he attributes its foundations.[62] Although Florovsky also admit-

[59]Ibid., 37 and 39.

[60]Ibid., 5.

[61]Ibid., 39.

[62]For the most sophisticated philosophical defense (much more developed than Romanides') of the position that Augustine's rejection of the essence/energies distinction is the source of the theological differences between East and West, and for a good overview of the contemporary debate on the essence/energies distinction, see David Bradshaw, *Aris-*

ted that Augustine rejected the essence/energies distinction, Romanides went beyond Florovsky in labeling Augustine's thought as the source for subsequent western theological errors. One could say that for Romanides, the theological schism begins with Augustine, and he would not agree with Florovsky's referring to Augustine as a "Universal Father of the Church."

Romanides' 1957 doctoral dissertation, Τό Προπατοπικόν Ἀμάρτημα (*The Ancestral Sin*) was the first systematic attempt to compare Augustine's doctrine of grace, free will, and predestination to the first- and second-century Orthodox writers (mostly Greek) who had written on the same topic.[63] Despite the many criticisms of Augustine's teaching on original sin, human freedom, and predestination by earlier Russian theologians, no one, prior to Romanides, had offered a textual comparison of Augustine and the Orthodox fathers on these points. That modern scholars almost universally hold Augustine's views on these matters to have been so innovative among the church fathers is a testament to Romanides' ground-breaking work. For example, Romanides distinguished between the ancient Church's idea of an "ancestral sin" and Augustine's concept of an "original sin."[64] Although Romanides' assessment of Augustine's position was not especially systematic, we can now see that Augustine's teaching on original sin came to comprise five principal tenets: (1) the actual sin of Adam, as well as its punishment, was inherited; (2) the post-lapsarian condition left every dimension of the human person subject to sin; (3) original sin was transmitted from parent to offspring through the concupiscence associated with procreation; (4) the infant soul was guilty; and (5) salvation required baptism even for infants.[65]

totle East and West: Metaphysics and the Division of Christendom (Cambridge: Cambridge University Press, 2004), 263–77. For a less persuasive defense of the Romanides thesis, see Michael Azkoul, *The Influence of Augustine of Hippo on the Orthodox Church* (Lewiston, NY: The Edwin Mellen Press, 1991). Azkoul wonders whether it might be better to call Augustine "an outlaw" (265).

[63]In addition to biblical authors, Justin Martyr and Irenaeus of Lyons feature prominently in the text.

[64]John Romanides, *The Ancestral Sin*, trans. G. Gabriel (Ridgewood, NJ: Zephyr Publishing, 1998), 155–75.

[65]The scholarly output on this subject is endless. For a concise overview of Augustine's

With few exceptions, Romanides' study does not engage eastern texts later than the third century. Nor does it deal with the historical circumstances of the Pelagian controversy, which had prompted Augustine's advanced thinking on the subject. Throughout the controversy, Augustine's aim had been to counter an inflated optimism that he believed would lead to arrogance and a failure to appreciate God's generous gifts. But these positions were vehemently critiqued by Pelagius' supporters, such as Julian of Eclanum, and they remained unique within the Christian tradition to that point. Even by 600, leading theologians in the West continued to advocate a soteriology that was more consistent with that of Athanasius, the Cappadocians, and John Chrysostom than that of Augustine.[66] With the exception of the fifth tenet of Augustine's teaching (salvation required baptism), most eastern writers of the patristic period would not have shared Augustine's teachings on original sin.[67]

Following Romanides' thesis to a more exhaustive conclusion, we are now able see that the eastern fathers of the late fourth century believed that the fall brought corruption to humanity and inaugurated a cycle of death, but they did not believe (as Augustine, at the end of his life, had) that the post-lapsarian human condition prevented the possibility of human participation in the process of salvation. For example, the ascetically inclined Cappadocians consistently taught that salvation required acts of almsgiving, fasting, and worship.[68] Through ascetic discipline and active participation in the sacramental life of the Church, Christians united their own efforts to God's grace-filled economy—the

teaching, see Paul Rigby, "Original Sin," in *Augustine through the Ages: An Encyclopedia*, ed. A. Fitzgerald (Grand Rapids: William B. Eerdmans Publishing Co., 1999), 607–14.

[66]See George Demacopoulos, "The Soteriology of Pope Gregory I: A Case against the Augustinian Interpretation," *The American Benedictine Review* 54 (2003): 313–28; and *Five Models of Spiritual Direction in the Early Church* (Notre Dame: University of Notre Dame Press, 2007), 100–105.

[67]Romanides had carefully distinguished between the Augustinian "original" sin and the Orthodox teaching of the "ancestral" sin, which implied that whereas Adam alone was guilty, each of Adam's descendents shared in the punishment—namely death.

[68]See, for example, Basil's various ascetic treatises, such as the *Moralia* and *Regulae fusius tractate* (*Longer Rules*) (PG 31), or Gregory Nazianzen's *Orations* 11, 14, and 32 (SC 405, PG 35, and SC 318, respectively).

Augustinian/Pelagian dichotomy between grace and free will was simply not part of the Cappadocians' theological imagination. The same was also true of Augustine's teaching on predestination, which even the western Church did not accept at the pivotal Second Council of Orange in 529.

And yet despite the appeal of his basic thesis (i.e., that Augustine's anthropology was not consistent with the eastern tradition before or after), by today's academic standards, Romanides' study is somewhat superficial and anachronistic. For example, although there is plenty of textual evidence for his treatment of biblical and eastern authors, Romanides' work has very little engagement with Augustine's actual writings. Footnotes rarely point to specific passages in Augustine's corpus, and when they do there are frequent mistakes and/or false attributions.[69] Moreover, like Florovsky, Romanides read the Augustinian material on grace and free will through the lens of the fourteenth-century Palamite distinction between God's essence and his energies. As more than one of the speakers at the Orthodox Readings of Augustine conference noted during the discussion, Romanides essentially accused Augustine of being a poor hesychast.

Through this and subsequent writings, Romanides inaugurated a movement in Greek theological circles to expunge the well-established Roman Catholic and Protestant academic perspectives that prevailed in the Greek universities of his day.[70] One can read much of Romanides' historical work as a post-colonial search for an authentic Orthodox identity in the midst of what he took to be a poisonous western influence in the theological academies of the Christian East.[71] Romanides was, of course,

[69]We would like to acknowledge Jason Stevens, a doctoral student at Fordham, who identified the latter point.

[70]Another important example of Romanides' criticisms of western innovation in the early middle ages is a collection of his public talks, entitled *Franks, Romans, Feudalism and Doctrine* (Brookline, MA: Holy Cross Orthodox Press, 1981). Here too, he attacks Augustine specifically. See 53, 72–90.

[71]Romanides was especially critical of the two main dogmatic theologians in Greece in the twentieth century, Christos Androutsos and Panayiotis Trembelas, for falling under western influence. As a result, his *The Ancestral Sin* was an indirect attack against the leading twentieth-century theologians in Greece, which prompted a negative reaction to his dissertation. For more on the debate *The Ancestral Sin* caused in Greece, see Yannaras, *Orthodoxy and the West*, 275–78.

not the only Orthodox writer of the twentieth century to point to Augustine as the cause for most of what went wrong with the West in the middle ages, but it was his work that first articulated and likely informed the sentiments espoused by later authors, including Christos Yannaras (b. 1935) and John Zizioulas (b. 1931).

Yannaras would agree with Romanides that Augustine's rejection of the essence/energies distinction was the beginning of the emergence of a distinct western theological and cultural ethos, but he would amplify this claim by arguing that the sources of the absence of this distinction lie in Augustine's rejection of apophaticism. The problems of the West do not begin with the misinterpretation of Dionysius, as Lossky had claimed of the scholastics, but with Augustine's rejection of apophaticism: "The first heretical differentiation which not merely survives historically, but has transformed radically the course of human history is one which denies the fundamental presupposition of orthodoxy, the apophaticism of truth . . . Augustine is surely the first great stage in the theoretical foundation of the rejection of apophaticism."[72] Elsewhere Yannaras adds, "Augustine's theology was decisive, offering an ideal basis for a differentiated Western version of Christianity."[73] Following Lossky, apophaticism for Yannaras is not simply defining God in terms of what God is not, but the affirmation that true knowledge of God occurs in mystical union with God. Although apophaticism does assert the incomprehensibility of God's essence, it does not deny that God is known. Apophaticism points to a limit in the adequacy of human conceptualization of God not to silence theology, but to indicate that true knowledge of God is an *ekstatic* going beyond human reason in the experience of mystical union. The logic of divine-human communion, theosis, thus demands an apophatic method in theology, in the sense that it asserts the incomprehensibility of the divine essence; but this incomprehensibility implies that knowledge of God lies beyond reason in an *ekstatic* movement of participation in the divine energies.

---

[72]Yannaras, *Elements of Faith: An Introduction to Orthodox Theology*, trans. K. Schram (Edinburgh: T&T Clark, 1991), 154–55.
[73]Yannaras, *Orthodoxy and the West*, 16.

Yannaras follows Romanides in identifying Augustine's fatal flaw as understanding knowledge of God as an intellectual activity, which caused him to prioritize the essence of God and reject the notion of the divine energies. Augustine ultimately attempted to weld together philosophical notions of the divine essence to the tenets of Christian faith and, in so doing, allowed the content of Christian faith to be determined by the logic of philosophical rationalism. The rationalization of theology by Augustine would be a fateful move that would determine western thinking about God, through Descartes and, ultimately, ending in the atheistic nihilism of Nietzsche:

> Hence, the proclamation of the "death of God" is revealed as the historical outcome that makes clear the whole theological development of Western Christianity. The replacement of ecclesial experience with intellectual certainty prepares for rational argument over this certainty. Rationalism, freed from the metaphysical guarantees provided by scholasticism, assumes the role of the historical preparation for the dominance of an empiricism centred on the individual. And an empiricism centred on the individual is the "open door" at which nihilism reappears.[74]

Like Romanides, Yannaras argues that Augustine instituted a way of thinking that would define a western cultural ethos that is diametrically opposed to that formed within the Byzantine East.

Theologically, one could summarize the critique of both Romanides and Yannaras of Augustine in one word: distance. What both see occurring in Augustine is the foundation for a theological method that would ultimately deny theosis, the realism of divine-human communion, and reinforce a distance between the God-world relation in terms of a propositional understanding of theological knowledge, an understanding of

---

[74]Yannaras, *On the Absence and Unknowability of God: Heidegger and the Areopagite,* ed. with introduction Andrew Louth, trans. H. Ventis (New York: T&T Clark International, 2005; orig. pub. 1967), 46. For an account of how this historical trajectory begins with Augustine, see 21–37.

grace as "created" and, hence, a legalistic, Anselmian understanding of salvation. The question must be raised, however, whether Romanides and Yannaras were judging Augustine anachronistically through a hesychastic framework. It might also appear that they were injecting neo-scholastic-manual understandings of theological epistemology and salvation, albeit in their filtered, imitative Greek form, into Augustine.

Of the new generation of Greek theologians, the most influential both within and outside Orthodoxy has been John Zizioulas.[75] Zizioulas follows Romanides and Yannaras in attributing to Augustine's thought the basis for theological errors in the West. Surprisingly, however, Zizioulas does not locate Augustine's mistakes in a rejection of apophaticism or the essence/energies distinction. In fact, even though Zizioulas would identify his theology as a response to the call for a neo-patristic synthesis (Florovsky was his teacher), his own version of such a synthesis is distinctively non-Palamite: apophaticism and the essence/energies distinction do not play a central role in Zizioulas' theology.[76] Instead, the problem with Augustine is his trinitarian theology, specifically his prioritizing the essence of God over the trinitarian hypostases: "There can be no doubt that Augustine makes otherness secondary to unity in God's being. God *is* one and *relates* as three. There is an ontological priority of substance over against personal relations in God in Augustine's Trinitarian theology."[77] For Zizioulas, Augustine's trinitarian theology is based on a substance ontology that attempts to understand how the one God can be Trinity, and which has affinities with the substance ontology of the ancient Greeks. It is because of Augustine that dogmatic manuals in the West always began with a consideration of the one God, the God of philosophy, before discussing the Christian doctrine of the Trinity.

---

[75]Zizioulas' influence, including his interpretation of western trinitarian theology, particularly that of Augustine, is evident in Catherine Mowry LaCugna, *God for Us: The Trinity and Christian Life* (San Francisco: HarperSanFrancisco, 1991); and Colin Gunton, *The Promise of Trinitarian Theology* (Edinburgh: T&T Clark, 1991).

[76]For more on why, see Papanikolaou, *Being with God*, 106–27.

[77]Zizioulas, *Communion and Otherness: Further Studies in Personhood and the Church* (New York: T&T Clark, 2006), 33.

Zizioulas contrasts such an approach to the Trinity with that of the Cappadocians, whose trinitarian theology initiated a "revolution in Greek philosophy."[78] The revolution in ontology consists primarily in prioritizing personhood over substance; such an identification means that being is identified with relationality, particularity, otherness, and communion. Augustine's attempt to justify philosophically how the one essence of God can be three betrays the ontological implications of the Cappadocian trinitarian theology. These implications include an understanding of personhood as freedom and uniqueness that is constituted in relations of communion. In contrast to this trinitarian understanding of personhood, Augustine lays the foundation for a definition of personhood in terms of self-consciousness, which is ultimately individualistic and solipsistic. Augustine's trinitarian theology, thus, represents a radical break with the Cappadocian approach, even if unintentional—and one that would have repercussions throughout the history of western philosophy.[79]

"The West" in the East

What began in nineteenth-century Russia as a general rejection of the Augustinian understanding of sin and grace developed into a more sweeping condemnation of Augustine's theological method. In fact, his understanding of sin and grace is eventually attributed to his approach to theology. The common thread in the contemporary Orthodox critique of Augustine is the perception that Augustine prioritizes philosophy over theology. This particular critique, however, only began to take shape in the

[78]Zizioulas, *Being as Communion* (Crestwood, NY: SVS Press, 1985), 36.

[79]It should be noted that not all Orthodox theologians agree with this condemnation of Augustine's trinitarian theology. As we saw, Bulgakov certainly did not, but more recently, Dumitru Staniloae appropriates Augustine's "love analogy" in his own trinitarian theology. See his "The Holy Trinity: Structure of Supreme Love," in *Theology and the Church*, trans. R. Barringer (Crestwood, NY: SVS Press, 1980), 73–108; also, *The Experience of God*, vol. 1, *Orthodox Dogmatic Theology*, trans. I. Ioanita and R. Barringer (Brookline, MA: Holy Cross Orthodox Press, 1998), esp. 245–80. Interestingly, Stanilaoe does not cite Augustine. For Stanilaoe, the source for the love analogy appears to be Pavel Florensky, whose work also was decisively influential for Bulgakov.

generation of Greek theologians of the 1960s. For them, the prioritization of philosophy was evident in Augustine's attempt to understand Christian doctrines in terms of the Greek philosophical category of essence, which either prevented him from accepting the necessary essence/energies distinction and thus resulted in a denial of divine-human communion (Romanides/Yannaras), or led him to a trinitarian theology antithetical to the Cappadocian trinitarian ontology (Zizioulas). Either way, the result was the same: the foundation for a western Christian understanding of the God-world relation is legalistic and, thus, ultimately nominalistic; and as a consequence, it makes possible an Anselmian atonement theory of salvation rather than the eastern patristic notion of deification. Even the evils of a secularized, unfettered individualism have their roots in Augustine's *Confessiones* (*Confessions*). Prior to this generation of Greek theologians, Augustine's status as a father of the Orthodox Church was never questioned, though aspects of his theology were critiqued, especially his understanding of sin and grace. The latter, however, first appears in the early nineteenth century primarily due to the central role of Augustine's theology in post-Reformation debates. Prior to the Reformation, eastern Christian concerns with Augustine's theology related entirely to his supposed endorsement of the *filioque*. These concerns, however, never led to the condemnation of the man or his work in the Byzantine period, and did not preclude the appropriation of his writings once they were translated.

It is illuminating that the unequivocal condemnation of Augustine by Orthodox theologians first appears in early nineteenth-century Russia in its Slavophile form and then reappears in the late 1950s among Greek theologians. In both situations, the anti-Augustine sentiment emerges together with a reaction against what is perceived to be western influences that are incompatible with the intellectual and spiritual tradition in Russia and Greece. The move toward a restoration of a more authentic national, intellectual, and spiritual identity in these Orthodox countries was based on a construction of a particular set of categories, namely "the West" and "the East," and an understanding of these categories in terms of diametrical opposition. Anything falling on one side of the divide was judged as opposed to the other. Augustine, one could say, simply lived on the wrong side of the tracks. The contemporary Orthodox response to Augustine, coupled with an anachronistic emphasis on the essence/energies distinction as the hermeneutical key for interpreting an East/West dichotomy, may have as much to do with Orthodox identity formation vis-à-vis "the West" as it does with genuine theological differences.

The Conference

The articles presented here offer for the first time an ecumenical engagement with the history of the reception of Augustine, both the man and his work, in Eastern Orthodox Christianity. Elizabeth Fisher illuminates with unprecedented clarity the context surrounding Planoudes' translation of Augustine's *De Trinitate*, while Reinhard Flogaus evinces convincingly that Gregory Palamas not only knew of this translation, but extracted from it lengthy quotations. Flogaus also shows how this appropriation of Augustine by Palamas has gone unnoticed in contemporary scholarship on Palamas and may have something to do with an inability on the part of eastern Christian scholars to admit of any western influence on the person whose work is perceived to be the culmination of the eastern patristic tradition.

Not surprisingly, many of the essays in this volume tackle the problem of Augustine's trinitarian theology. Joseph Lienhard, SJ, traces the extent of Augustine's knowledge of the Cappadocians. David Bradshaw offers a sophisticated defense of the Romanides/Yannaras thesis that Augustine rejects the essence/energies distinction and, as a result, initiates a way of doing theology unknown in the East. Lewis Ayres challenges specifically the charge that Augustine's trinitarian theology begins with an identification of the one God with the divine essence. Though rejecting a Zizioulian interpretation of the Cappadocians, John Behr argues that the Augustinian approach to the doctrine of the Trinity is one that is not discernible in the eastern patristic texts of the fourth century. David Bentley Hart disputes the diametrical opposition between Augustine and the eastern fathers established by contemporary Orthodox theologians, and instead of arguing for how Augustine is continuous with the Greek fathers, evinces how the Cappadocians are closer to Augustine than previously imagined. Against the criticism that Augustine's understanding of God is non-apophatic, Jean-Luc Marion posits the thesis that Augustine's notion of "being" is analogous to that of Pseudo-Dionysius and, more forcefully than Lossky, situates Augustine in the Christian apophatic tradition rather than the Christian metaphysical tradition of the scholastics.

Brian Daley, SJ, is the sole author in this volume to explore Augustine's theology of sin and grace. Daley shows that though it cannot be determined to what extent Maximus the Confessor knew of Augustine's work, there are affinities between Augustine's and Maximus' soteriologies, implicitly questioning whether Augustine's soteriology in its entirety is mutually exclusive with the eastern Christian patristic tradition. Though the contemporary Orthodox theologians were united in rejecting Augustinian notions of sin and grace, it is worth noting that the same criticism is evident in twentieth-century Roman Catholic theologians such as Karl Rahner, Hans Urs von Balthasar, Henri de Lubac, and Gustavo Gutiérrez. Since Vatican II, Augustine's view on sin and grace can no longer be isolated as a major point of dispute between the Orthodox and Roman Catholic traditions.[80]

The essays of David Tracy, Andrew Louth, and Carol Harrison challenge Christians of all traditions to go beyond the usual suspects of Augustine's corpus, which include *Confessiones, De Trinitate*, and *De civitate Dei* (*City of God*), and to look at ignored or forgotten aspects of Augustine's work, especially his sermons. Augustine "as pastor" does not mean Augustine has stopped being a theologian, and these unexamined works of Augustine's corpus may serve as a point of departure and point of unity for the Christian reassessment of the value of Augustine's thought. David Tracy implicitly disputes the notion that Augustine is primarily a philosopher by showing how Augustine's sermons reveal a theocentricism that is informed by Augustine's affirmation of the divinity of Christ.

---

[80]See Roger Haight, "Sin and Grace," in *Systematic Theology: Roman Catholic Perspectives*, ed. Francis Schüssler Fiorenza and John P. Glavin (Minneapolis: Fortress Press, 1991), 75–142.

The title, *Orthodox Readings of Augustine*, can be interpreted in several ways: it could indicate a reassessment of responses to Augustine by Orthodox theologians; or, it may refer to an attempt at readings of Augustine that illustrate his continuity with the dogmatic tradition shared by the Christian West and East. We hope this volume initiates a conversation that speaks to both these concerns. There can be no question that Augustine exercised an influence on western Christianity that is not discernible in the East. In fact, it is difficult to locate anyone in the East who was as influential as Augustine was in the West. In the East, the writings of one patristic writer were always read in the light of the other patristic texts. The language divide may have prevented Augustine from being read together with the Greek fathers, but there is nothing to prevent that from happening today.

Planoudes' *De Trinitate*, the Art of Translation, and the Beholder's Share

Elizabeth Fisher

I am doubly grateful for the opportunity to participate in this cooperative venture between the eastern and western Churches, and for the occasion to examine the translation into Greek of Augustine's *De Trinitate* (*On the Trinity*) by Maximus Planoudes. This topic seems especially appropriate in the context of "Orthodox Readings of Augustine," for Josef Lössl has termed Planoudes' translation "the pioneering effort towards bridging the huge gap between Augustine's paramount role in the West and near oblivion in the East."[1]

My assessment of this "pioneering effort" will be from the standpoint of a philologist focusing upon Planoudes' role as a translator and upon the reception of his work by both Byzantine and western readers. I must note from the outset that neither my training nor my research qualifies me as a theologian. However, many other contributors to the present volume fill that important role.

It is generally agreed that Planoudes made his translation of the fifteen-book *De Trinitate* around the year 1280 in the context of strenuous measures taken by the Byzantine emperor Michael VIII Palaiologos (1261–1282) to secure union with the western Church.[2] Ecclesiastical union was a contentious issue in Byzantium. Some Greeks supported uni-

---

[1] Josef Lössl, "Augustine in Byzantium," *Journal of Ecclesiastical History* 51 (2000): 275.
[2] Gianpaolo Rigotti, in Αὐγουστίνου περὶ Τριάδος βιβλία πεντεκαίδεκα ἅπερ ἐκ τῆς Λατίνων διαλέκτου εἰς τὴν Ἑλλάδα μετήνεγκε Μάξιμος ὁ Πλανούδης, ed. Manolis Papathomopoulos et al. (Athens: Kentron Ekdoseōs Ergōn Hellēnōn Syngrapheōn, 1995), liv.

ate measures, either recognizing union as a political necessity to maintain Byzantine control of Constantinople or regarding it as a desirable ideal for the Church. Most of Michael's subjects, however—monks, clergy, and laity alike—despised the idea of surrendering to what they considered foreign ideological/theological domination, famously summarized in the western *filioque* clause that specified the procession of the Holy Spirit.

In the theological debates between the eastern and western Churches, Augustine's *De Trinitate* had special merit. As a theological bridge to the East, Augustine's writings were attractive because the bishop of Hippo was eager to present his theology in accord with Greek patristic texts.[3] *De Trinitate* was, however, little known in the East, although it was regarded in the West as basic to trinitarian theology.[4] The work admittedly presented exceptional difficulty for the reader, as Augustine himself acknowledged. While engaged in writing it, he complained that its fifteen books "involve too much hard work and are understandable, in my opinion, to only a few."[5]

Therefore, Michael's project to make Augustine's *De Trinitate* accessible to a Greek audience represented a significant challenge. The emperor needed a translator who was not only able to understand correctly the theological content and Latin syntax of Augustine's Latin text but who was also well trained in the artificial and archaizing "Attic" register of the Greek language that Byzantine readers considered appropriate to a serious work of literature.[6] To appreciate the challenge faced by Michael VIII, it will be useful to examine briefly the tradition of Latin translation inherited in thirteenth-century Constantinople.

[3]For a detailed examination of Augustine's use of Greek patristic authors, see Joseph Leinhard's contribution in this volume; see also Lössl, 268–71.

[4]Lössl, 271–73.

[5]"Nimis operosi sunt et a paucis eos intelligi posse arbitror." Augustine, *Ep.* 169.1.1. *S. Aureli Augustini Hipponiensis episcopi Epistulae,* ed. Alois Goldbacher, CSEL 44 (Vienna: F. Tempsky, 1895), 612.

[6]For a lucid description of the artificial "Attic" dialect favored in Byzantium, see Robert Browning, "The Language of Byzantine Literature," in *The Past in Medieval and Modern Greek Culture,* ed. Speros Vryonis (Malibu: Undena Publications, 1978), 103–33 (repr. in Robert Browning, *History, Language and Literature in the Byzantine World* [Northampton, England: Variorum Reprints, 1989], as XV [same pagination]).

For Byzantium, the Latin language was reserved exclusively for diplomatic and commercial contacts. Secure in the possession of their own rich Greek cultural heritage, educated Byzantines saw no necessity to translate Latin literary texts surviving in a western culture they considered inferior; this prejudice began to erode only in the final decades of the thirteenth century.[7] Up until that time, translation was a matter of practical necessity, and translators in the chancery of the emperor and of the patriarch were functionaries who provided Latin translations to accompany Greek documents sent to western powers. The first evidence of such a dual-language document survives from the reign of Basil I in correspondence with Ludwig II (871); in the following century, an Arabic translation accompanied the correspondence of Romanos I Lecapenos with the caliphate of Baghdad (938).[8] By the mid-twelfth century the activities of translators in the imperial chancery included not only providing written translations of documents but also interpreting for western diplomatic missions to Constantinople; their work was sufficiently complex and extensive to warrant the creation of a new chancery official, the μέγας διερμενευτής, who supervised translation under the general purview of the λογοθέτης τοῦ δρόμου.[9] Several translators served in the Latin translation office, both native speakers of Latin and of Greek; an accomplished Latin translator might also be borrowed from the imperial chancery by the patriarch. On occasion, the imperial chancery "outsourced" a document, as in the case of the Armenian translation provided by the monastery in Philippopolis.[10] After 1204 the Laskarid empire of Nicaea continued these practices, as did Michael VIII in his Constantinopolitan chancery.[11] Unlike his Nicaean predecessors, however, Michael VIII emphasized relations with

[7]See Elizabeth A. Fisher, "Planoudes, Holobolos, and the Motivation for Translation," *Greek, Roman, and Byzantine Studies* 43 (2002): 77–104.

[8]Christian Gastgeber, "Die lateinische Übersetzungsabteilung der byzantinischen Kaiserkanzlei unter den Komnenen und Angeloi," in *Byzance et le Monde extérieur*, ed. Michel Balard, Elisabeth Malamut, Jean-Michel Speiser (Paris: Publications de la Sorbonne, 2005), 121.

[9]Gastgeber, 105–7.

[10]Gastgeber, 107–11, 122.

[11]Luca Pieralli, "La corrispondenza diplomatica tra Roma e Costantinopoli nei secoli XIII e XIV," in *Byzance*, 151–63.

the West in his foreign policy and placed westerners in positions of responsibility within the Latin translation office.[12]

Michael VIII could therefore look to his own chancery for Latin translators, to the chancery of the patriarchate, or to reliable Latins or Byzantines competent in both Latin and Greek. Who, then, was not only available to accept Michael's commission but also competent to undertake the translation of so lengthy and difficult a text as Augustine's *De Trinitate*? I know of only a handful of such individuals: John Parastron, Simon of Constantinople, Manuel Holobolos, Ogerius the Protonotarius, and Manuel (later Maximus) Planoudes.

In order to suggest how Manuel Planoudes, the youngest and least experienced of this group, became Michael's translator of *De Trinitate*, it is necessary to make a brief excursus into the complex ecclesiastical and political circumstances of the mid-thirteenth century.[13]

When the Fourth Crusade expelled the "schismatic" Byzantines from their capital and installed a Latin king and a Latin patriarch, Constantinople fell under Latin domination. Under papal mandate, mission houses of Franciscans and Dominicans worked zealously to convert the Greeks of the East and restore them to union with the western Church. In 1259, Michael Palaiologos assumed power at the exiled Byzantine court of Nicaea, and in 1261 his forces captured the city of Constantinople. Michael blinded John IV Laskaris (1258–1261), the legitimate heir to the throne, and as emperor, Michael VIII Palaiologos (1261–1282) expelled the Latin king Baldwin II, the Latin patriarch, and the Latin monastic houses from the city. Although threatened from the east by the Ottoman Turks and from the north by the Slavs, Michael's greatest fear was of the ambitious and skillful politician Charles of Anjou, King of the Two Sicilies (1266–1285). Michael's political enemies, Baldwin II and John IV Laskaris, joined Charles at his court and provided him with some pretext to legiti-

[12]Nicolas Oikonomides, "La chancellerie impériale de Byzance du 13e au 15e siècle," *Revue des Études byzantines* 43 (1985): 171–73, 193.

[13]For my discussion of this period and its complexities, I have relied upon the clear and concise narrative in the classic survey by A.A. Vasiliev, *History of the Byzantine Empire,* vol. 2 (Madison: University of Wisconsin Press, 1952), 592–99, 656–63.

macy in his plans to overthrow Michael and restore Constantinople to Latin control. In such a climate, Michael VIII, no less adroit in politics than Charles, used the prospect of ecclesiastical union to solicit aid from Charles' enemies in the West and neutralize the threat from Sicily. He dispatched an embassy to Louis IX ("the Pious") of France in 1270 and opened discussions with Pope Gregory X (1271–1276) in 1272 to unify the eastern and western Churches. Michael ensured that the pro-union patriarch he installed would accept the terms for ecclesiastical union ratified at the Second Council of Lyons in 1274 and enforce the union harshly, exiling, imprisoning, and publicly humiliating those who opposed it, including members of his family, his court, and his military.[14]

With the single exception of Planoudes, the known potential translators of Augustine's *De Trinitate* were each associated in some way with the contentious politics of Michael's reign.

John Parastron/Parastos was a Franciscan, born probably in the Latin kingdom of Constantinople and perhaps in the Greek/Venetian community.[15] Although John Parastron's origins and early career are obscure, Michael VIII commended him for his perfect fluency in Latin as well as in Greek and dispatched him as imperial envoy to Louis IX and to the papal court; he also served as a legate to the Second Council of Lyons and brought the signed union agreement back to Constantinople, where he participated in the public celebration of ecclesiastical union. No evidence suggests that he extended his expertise as an accomplished bilingual negotiator into the field of literary or even documentary translation during his diplomatic service to Michael. In any case, his death in 1275 removed John Parastron from the list of potential translators of *De Trinitate*.

---

[14]Michael VIII expressed his frustration over this situation in a detailed and confidential letter addressed to the messengers he dispatched in 1278 to Pope Nicholas III; see R.-J. Loenertz, "Mémoire d'Ogier, protonotaire, pour Marco et Marchetto nonces de Michel VIII Paléologue après du pape Nicolas III (1278, printemps-été)," *Orientalia Cristiana Periodica* 31 (1965): 374–408.

[15]I have relied for this account upon Gualberto Matteucci, *La mission francescana di Costantinopoli*, vol. 1 of *La sua antica orgine e primi secoli di storia (1217–1555)* (Florence: Edizioni Studi francescani, 1971), 111–36.

Like John Parastron, Simon of Constantinople (c. 1235–c. 1325) was born probably in Constantinople, where he joined a western monastic order and lived at the Dominican monastery in the city until the community relocated to Negroponte after 1261. His fellow Dominican and student Philip of Pera described him as "steeped to an even greater degree in Greek learning than in Latin."[16] In Negroponte, Simon was an active and energetic scholar. He consulted ancient manuscripts of patristic texts in the libraries of nearby Greek monasteries and conducted a lively but undated correspondence promoting ecclesiastical union with several notable Byzantine figures back in Constantinople, among them Michael VIII's son and successor Andronikos II and Manuel Holobolos. Simon's language, citation of scholarly sources, and pattern of argumentation were impeccably Greek in style and design, although his theology was undeniably Latin. Like John Parastron, Simon of Constantinople does not seem to have translated Latin texts into Greek, although he had ample opportunity to do so during his long career; he died c. 1325 and would surely have qualified for any list of candidates capable of producing a Greek version of *De Trinitate* for Michael VIII.

Available within Michael's own imperial court circle was a highly qualified candidate for the commission to translate Augustine's *De Trinitate*, Manuel Holobolos (1245–c. 1312). Although a talented and precocious scholar, Holobolos was combative by nature and undeterred by the drastic consequences of imperial displeasure. Because he vigorously protested Michael VIII's mistreatment of John IV Laskaris, the angry emperor ordered Holobolos mutilated and confined to a monastery in 1261/62, where he translated two Latin rhetorical treatises of Boethius.[17] Rehabilitated at the request of Patriarch Germanos III in 1265, Holobolos was

---

[16]". . . imbutus scientia graeca magis etiam quam Latina." For this discussion of Simon, I have followed Marie-Hélène Congourdeau, "Frère Simon le constantinopolitain, O.P. (1235?–1325?)," *Revue des Études byzantines* 45 (1987): 165–74; Philip of Pera quoted on 165, n. 3.

[17]For a discussion of Holobolos' translations, see Fisher, "Planoudes, Holobolos, and the Motivation for Translation," 77–104; and Börje Bydén, "'Strangle Them with These Meshes of Syllogisms!': Latin Philosophy in Greek Translations of the Thirteenth Century," *Interaction and Isolation in Late Byzantine Culture*, ed. J.O. Rosenqvist (Stockholm: Swedish Research Institute in Istanbul, 2004), 137–46.

appointed professor of rhetoric in the patriarchal school, although he was only about twenty years old at the time.[18] In his official capacity as "rhetor of the rhetors," Holobolos delivered public panegyrics for Michael VIII and may have been the clever writer who drafted the imperial letter of 1265 that proposed to the pope a discussion of ecclesiastical union.[19] The period of his imperial favor, however, was brief. In 1273 Holobolos openly declared fervent opposition to the proposed Union of Lyons and found himself first exiled to a Bithynian monastery and then cast as the chief miscreant in a humiliating and disgusting procession through the streets of Constantinople.[20]

In the 1270s the translation section of Michael VIII's imperial chancery included a westerner euphoniously known as Ogerius the Protonotarius or Ogerius Boccanegra, related to a prominent Genoese family.[21] Pieralli traces the chancery career of Ogerius back to the Treaty of Nymphaeum (1261) and through various documents exchanged between 1272 and 1279 by the Byzantine and papal courts concerning the Union of Lyons. Despite his extensive experience in the chancery and skill as a translator, Ogerius did not have sufficient command of Latin theological terms to avoid complaints from the papal court regarding vocabulary choice.[22] In this respect, Ogerius was clearly not the ideal translator to undertake Augustine's *De Trinitate*.

At this point, let us recapitulate the inventory of potential translators for *De Trinitate* remaining in 1275, after the Union of Lyons and the death of John Parastron. Manuel Holobolos was a bitter enemy of the emperor

---

[18]*Oxford Dictionary of Byzantium* (Oxford: Oxford University Press, 1991), s.v. "Holobolos, Manuel."

[19]Pieralli, "Corrispondenza," 155, 161; also discussed by Bydén, 145.

[20]Michael VIII ordered ten opponents of the union to be roped together, laden with sheep entrails and dung, and led through the city, with Holobolos as their leader. Holobolos was further humiliated by blows to the mouth with sheep's livers. See *Relations historiques/Georges Pachymérès*, vol. 2, ed. Albert Failler (Paris: Belles Lettres, 1984), 502.25–505.4. I am grateful to Tia Kolbaba of Rutgers University for this vivid citation.

[21]Luca Pieralli, "I Rapporti diplomatici tra Roma e Costantinopoli negli anni 1274–1279 attraverso le varianti introdotte nel testo della professione di fede imperiale," in *Documenti medievali greci e latini. Studi comparativi*, ed. Giuseppe de Gregorio, Otto Kresten (Spoleto: Centro italiano di studi sull'alto Medioevo, 1998), 396.

[22]Pieralli, "Rapporti," 396.

and the union, and Simon of Constantinople was in Negroponte living in
the Dominican community that had attempted under the Latin kingdom
of Constantinople to convert the Greeks of the East. This association
made Simon suspect in the view of the anti-unionists Michael hoped
to persuade with a translation of Augustine's *De Trinitate*. Moreover,
Michael was on very poor terms with the Latins of Negroponte. Confronted with further intrigues against him by Charles of Anjou, Michael
sent an expedition against Negroponte in 1276.[23] As a potential translator
in such a highly charged political atmosphere, Simon occupied the unen-
viable status of an untrustworthy "in-between" from the perspective of
the Latin and Greek communities, rather than that of an honest "go-
between."[24] Similarly compromised because he was a Latin, Ogerius
Boccanegra was in any case fully engaged in the complexities of Michael
VIII's Latin diplomatic correspondence and does not seem to have
attempted any sort of literary translation from Latin during his career.
Moreover, as we have seen, Ogerius had little aptitude for translating a
lengthy and complex theological treatise like Augustine's *De Trinitate*.
Since Ogerius the Protonotarius, Simon of Constantinople, and Holobolos were all either unavailable or undesirable as translators, only Planoudes remained.

In 1275 Planoudes was about twenty years old and perhaps already
employed in the imperial chancery as a Latin translator.[25] Like Holobolos,
he must have been a precocious student of both Latin and Greek, for
around 1280 he appeared as one of the principal scribes in a manuscript
copied in Constantinople (Florence, Laurenziana ms. Plut. 32.16) that dis-
plays his facility with both classical Greek and Latin literary texts.[26]

[23]Loenertz, 399.

[24]I owe this provocative distinction to Sylvia Molloy in her paper "Reading Bilingual:
An Uneasy Reflection on Cultural Encounters," delivered at The George Washington University, April 27, 2007; to illustrate the ambivalent position of current translators in a conflicted political situation, she cited George Packer, "Betrayed: The Iraqis Who Trusted
America the Most," *The New Yorker* (3/26/2007), 52–73.

[25]Cf. Carl Wendel, "Planudes, Maximos," in *Paulys Real-Encyclopädie der classischen
Altertumswissenschaft* 20. 2 (Stuttgart: J.B. Metzler, 1950), col. 2203–05.

[26]Alexander Turyn, *Dated Greek Manuscripts of the 13th and 14th Centuries in the
Libraries of Italy,* vol. 2 (Urbana, IL: University of Illinois Press, 1975), 28–33; discussed by

Manuel Planoudes undertook Michael's commission to translate Augustine's *De Trinitate*. Precisely when Planoudes began to work is unknown, but given his relative youth scholars suggest that he made the translation about 1280, as noted above. If so, Planoudes evidently worked quickly at his task, because the political and ecclesiastical landscape in Byzantium was shifting rapidly. In 1281 the new pope, Martin IV, a partisan of Charles of Anjou, abrogated the Union of Lyons. In 1282 Michael VIII died, and his successor Andronikos II abandoned his father's policy of ecclesiastical union.[27] Supporters of union were disgraced and its opponents, such as Holobolos, returned to Constantinople and to imperial favor.[28]

The first complete critical edition of Planoudes' *De Trinitate* appeared in 1995, when Manoles Papathomopoulos, Isabella Tsavari, and Gianpaolo Rigotti presented the Greek text accompanied by Augustine's Latin original on facing pages. Rigotti provided a very substantial introduction describing the career of Planoudes, his other translations from Latin, the reception of his *De Trinitate* translation, its style, and its manuscript tradition. His work is indispensable, and I have drawn heavily from it. Rigotti characterizes the translation as accurate but not mechanical nor slavishly literal.[29] Planoudes' translation is a work of Greek literature that readers could appreciate as both idiomatic and stylish. To accomplish this, some omissions, expansions, syntactic adjustments, and variations in vocabulary were necessary. Rigotti insists, however, that Planoudes did not deliberately misrepresent Augustine's text in any way. A brief passage from Planoudes' version of *De Trinitate* 15 (with critical apparatus) followed by Augustine's original Latin text will provide the basis to illustrate and expand upon Rigotti's characterization of the translation:

Elizabeth A. Fisher, "Ovid's *Metamorphoses,* Sailing to Byzantium," *Classical and Modern Literature* 27.1 (2007): in press.

[27]Vasiliev, 596–97, 663.

[28]Constantine N. Constantinides, "Byzantine Scholars and the Union of Lyons (1274)," in *The Making of Byzantine History, Studies Dedicated to Donald M. Nicol,* ed. Roderick Beaton and Charlotte Roueché (Brookfield, VT: Variorum, 1993), 92.

[29]Rigotti, lix–lxxix.

(60) . . . οὐδὲ ἐξ
οὗ ἐγεννήθη ὁ λόγος καὶ ἐξ οὗ ἐκπορεύεται ἀρχοειδῶς τὸ Πνεῦμα τὸ
ἅγιον, εἰ μὴ ὁ Θεὸς καὶ Πατήρ. Διὰ τοῦτο δὲ προστέθεικα, ἀρχοειδῶς,
ἐπειδὴ καὶ ἐκ τοῦ Υἱοῦ [τοῦ Θεοῦ] τὸ Πνεῦμα τὸ ἅγιον εὑρίσκεται
ἐκπορευόμενον. Ἀλλὰ [ἐπειδὴ] καὶ τοῦτο αὐτῷ ὁ Πατὴρ ἔδωκεν (οὐκ
ἤδη
(65) ὑφεστηκότι καὶ μήπω ἔχοντι), ἀλλ᾽ ὅ τι ποτὲ τῷ μονογενεῖ λόγῳ
δέδωκεν, ἐν τῷ γεννᾶν δέδωκεν. Οὕτως ἄρα αὐτὸν ἐγέννησεν ὡς κἀξ
αὐτοῦ τὸ δῶρον κοινὸν προέρχεσθαι καὶ Πνεῦμα ἅγιον <Πνεῦμα>
εἶναι ἀμφοῖν.

63 τοῦ Θεοῦ seclusimus ex Aug ‖ τὸ ἅγιον **α**, *spiritus sanctus* Aug: om.
β 64 ἐπειδὴ seclusimus ex Aug 66 κἀξ nos, *etiam de* Aug: ἐξ codd. 67
Πνεῦμα suppleuimus, *spiritus* Aug

(Planoudes, Περὶ Τρίαδος Βιβλίον Πεντεκαιδέκατον,
ed. Papathomopoulos et al., 2.933, lines 60–68)[30]

(61) . . . nec de quo genitum est uerbum
et de quo procedit principaliter spiritus sanctus nisi deus pater. Ideo
autem addidi, principaliter, quia et de filio spiritus sanctus procedere
reperitur. Sed hoc quoque illi pater dedit (non iam exsistenti et nondum (65) habenti), sed quidquid unigenito uerbo dedit gignendo
dedit. Sic ergo eum genuit ut etiam de illo donum commune procederet et spiritus sanctus spiritus esset amborum.

(Augustine, *De trinitate liber quintus decimus*,
cited by Papathomopoulos et al., 932)

The editors of Planoudes' translation have followed a modern edition
of Augustine's text in marking additions (i.e., [τοῦ Θεοῦ] and [ἐπειδὴ]

---

[30]". . . (and there is no one) from whom the Word was begotten and from whom the Holy
Spirit proceeded principally except the God and Father. For this reason I have added 'principally,' since also from the Son [of God] the Holy Spirit is found to proceed. But [since] the
Father also gave this to him (not as already existing and not yet having it), but anything he
ever gave to his only begotten Son he gave in his begetting, thus then he begot him so that
also from him the common gift goes forth and the Holy Spirit is [Spirit] of both."

lines 63–64) and omissions (i.e., <Πνεῦμα> line 67) in the Greek translation. Since the textual tradition of Planoudes' translation is strong,[31] I consider its deviations from a modern Latin text of Augustine to be authentic and intentional, representing either Planoudes' deliberate alterations or an accurate translation of the unidentified Latin manuscript he was using.

A superficial comparison of the Greek translation with its Latin original demonstrates that Planoudes devised a more sophisticated sentence structure in lines 64–66 by adding [ἐπειδὴ] (line 64) in order to combine two of Augustine's fairly straightforward Latin sentences (*Sed hoc... dedit,* lines 64–65, and *Sic ergo... amborum,* lines 65–66) into one complex Greek sentence and at the same time preserve the subordinate clauses from Augustine's original text (*quidquid... dedit,* line 65: ὅ τι... δέδωκεν, lines 65–66; and *ut... amborum,* lines 66–67: ὡς... ἀμφοῖν, lines 66–68). In general, Planoudes preserves the structure of the original Latin constructions, although the rules of Greek syntax require some adjustments: the infinitive with *reperitur* (line 64) becomes a participle with εὑρίσκεται (line 63), the ablative gerund *gignendo* (line 65) becomes an articular infinitive in a prepositional phrase (ἐν τῷ γεννᾶν, line 66), the Latin subjunctive in a result clause (*procederet,* line 66) becomes a Greek infinitive (προέρχεσθαι, line 67), and the perfect tense of verbs indicating simple past action, so comfortable and frequent in Latin, sometimes yields to the Greek aorist (*genitum est:* ἐγεννήθη, line 61; *genuit:* ἐγέννησεν, line 66).[32] Planoudes regularly translates a Latin compound word with a Greek compound, not awkwardly nor automatically calqued from Latin but each appropriate in its Greek connotation: forms of *pro/cedere* (lines 62, 63, 66) with forms of ἐκ/πορεύεσθαι (lines 61, 64) or προ/έρχεσθαι (line 67), *ad/didi* (line 63) with προσ/τέθεικα (line 62), *ex/sistenti* (line 64) with ὑφ/εστηκότι (line 65), and *uni/genito* (line 65) with μονο/γενεῖ (line 65).

---

[31]Ten manuscripts of the fourteenth century, ten of the fifteenth, two of the sixteenth, four of the seventeenth, and one of the nineteenth; Rigotti, lxxx–lxxxiv.

[32]In this period the aorist and perfect tenses of Greek were functionally interchangeable. See Robert Browning, *Medieval and Modern Greek* (New York: Cambridge University Press, 1983), 30, 64.

Planoudes' compound words, perfectly idiomatic in context, elevate the tone of his Greek text as does his use of the perfect tense, of the dative case (αὐτῷ, line 64; ὑφεστηκότι, line 65; τῷ μονογενεῖ λόγῳ, line 65; and τῷ γεννᾶν, line 66), and of the dual form (ἀμφοῖν, line 68). These forms, obsolete in the spoken Greek of Planoudes' time, characterize the translation as a properly literary and "Attic" text.[33] Considerations of pleasing "Attic" style may also have induced Planoudes to replace the repetitive phrase *spiritus sanctus spiritus* (line 67) with a simple Πνεῦμα ἅγιον (line 67) and to construct *donum commune* (line 66) with an emphatic predicate adjective τὸ δῶρον κοινὸν (line 67). Further, Planoudes translates Augustine's significant adverb *principaliter* (line 62) with its exactly equivalent Greek adverb ἀρχοειδῶς (lines 61, 62), a *vox propria* rare in Christian texts before the time of Planoudes but frequent in *TLG* citations thereafter.[34]

In closing, it is important to note that Planoudes chose to incorporate in his translation some features of vocabulary and syntax that echo the Constantinopolitan Creed and place the Greek version of Augustine's *De Trinitate* into the linguistic framework of this fundamental Christian text:[35] μονογενεῖ (line 65) recalls Ἰησοῦν . . . μονογενῆ (Creed line 3), forms of γεννᾶν (lines 61, 66) reflect γεννηθέντα (Creed lines 3, 4), the emphatic positioning of the attributive adjective in τὸ Πνεῦμα τὸ ἅγιον (line 63) is identical to the phrase appearing in line 13 of the Creed, and forms of ἐκπορεύεσθαι (lines 61, 64) recall the formulation τὸ πνεῦμα τὸ ἅγιον τὸ κύριον καὶ ζωοποιὸν τὸ ἐκ τοῦ πατρὸς ἐκπορευόμενον (Creed lines 13–15). Planoudes uses a form of ἐκπορεύεσθαι to translate two of the three occurrences of *procedere* in Augustine's Latin text (*procedit,* line 62; and *procedere,* line 63), but in the third instance he chooses to vary his

[33] Ibid., 45–50, 58 (dative case).

[34] The *Thesaurus linguae graecae* (on-line version available under license at http://stephanus.tlg.uci.edu) cites ἀρχοειδῶς in act 3 of the Lateran Council of 649 (see R. Riedinger, *Acta Conciliorum Oecumenicorum,* 2d series, vol. 1: *Concilium Lateranense a. 649 celebratum* [Berlin: De Gruyter, 1984] 122, l. 10) and in document 13 of the Third Council of Constantinople of 680–81 (see R. Riedinger, *Acta Conciliorum Oecumenicorum,* 2d series, vol. 2: *Concilium universale Constantinopolitanum tertium, pars 1–2* [Berlin: De Gruyter, 1990, 1992], pars 1, 604, l. 10).

[35] References to the text of the Constantinopolitan Creed are from Guiseppe L. Dossetti, *Il simbolo di Nicea e di Costantinopoli* (Rome: Herder, 1967), 244–51.

vocabulary, perhaps for stylistic effect. He translates *procederet* (line 66) with προέρχεσθαι (line 67), an equivalence he later favors in his version of Ovid's *Metamorphoses* when the subject of the verb is a person;[36] when a form of *procedere* refers to an animal, a collective, or an inanimate noun, Planoudes prefers a compound of the verb χωρεῖν. In no other occurrence of *procedere* in the Latin texts translated by Planoudes does he equate the verb with a form of ἐκπορεύεσθαι;[37] that usage is distinctive to his translation of Augustine's *De Trinitate*.

It is interesting to note that Planoudes' translation style and methodology in *De Trinitate* are consistent with his practices in his other Greek translations of Latin literature—Ovid's *Metamorphoses* and *Heroides* and Boethius' *De consolatione philosophiae*, to name only the most substantial.[38] The same style and methodology also characterize the translations of Manuel Holobolos.[39] Gastgeber notes that twelfth-century chancery translations from Greek into Latin attempt to reflect a compound word in the original text with a compound in the Latin translation, just as Planoudes and Holobolos do in their Greek translations of Latin literary texts.[40] A practice customary in chancery translation evidently influenced the style of these pioneering literary translators.

Sometime around 1283 Manuel Planoudes became a monk under the name Maximus;[41] also to the reign of Andronikos II belong two essays

---

[36]Ovid, *Metamorphoses* 13.533, processit: πρόεισι of Hecuba; and ibid., 14.46, procedit: πρόεισι of Circe.

[37]Ibid., 2.685, processisse: ἀποχωρῆσαι of cattle; ibid., 7.515, processit: προχωρησάσης of a troop of young men; and *Heroides* 9.109, procedit: προχωρεῖ of a measure of property.

[38]There is only one other theological translation in Planoudes' oeuvre, the anonymous seventh-century Irish tract *On the Twelve Abuses of the Age*, immensely popular in the middle ages. There is no evidence for the chronology or sequence of the translations, although I have followed other scholars in assuming that Planoudes' two theological translations were part of Michael VIII's project for ecclesiastical union (Rigotti, xxxiv–xlvi). For an analysis of Planoudes' translation practices in the *Metamorphoses*, see Fisher, "Ovid's *Metamorphoses*, Sailing to Byzantium."

[39]For a brief analysis of Holobolos' translation practices, see Elizabeth A. Fisher, "Manuel Holobolos, Alfred of Sareshal, and the Greek Translator of ps.-Aristotle's *De plantis*," *Classica et Mediaevalia* 57 (2006): 208–10.

[40]Gastgeber, 107–8.

[41]Rigotti, xvii–xx.

(Περὶ . . . Λατίνων and Λόγος περὶ πίστεως) written by Planoudes that attack the western doctrine of the procession of the Holy Spirit. In these essays Planoudes directly contradicted the theological position of Augustine's *De Trinitate*.[42] Moreover, Planoudes indicates his disinclination for theological topics in a letter to his friend Alexios Philanthropenos, written sometime in the 1290s, where he rehearses the annoying qualities of a mutual acquaintance who must always present himself as Planoudes' intellectual superior: "and now he is an authority on matters of the natural world and in some fashion also touches upon medical [knowledge], now he is an authority on matters of theology, which of all things I especially fear and never approach except under duress. And now he belabors a discussion of morality . . ."[43]

As an aid to understanding why Planoudes dissociated himself from Augustine's *De Trinitate* and even declared a general aversion to theology, I would like to introduce the concept of "beholder's share." The art historian Sir Ernst Gombrich coined this term to illustrate the active role a viewer necessarily takes when encountering a visual image: "Interpretation on the part of the image maker must always be matched by the interpretations of the viewer. No image tells its own story . . . the 'beholder's share' [is] the contribution we make to any representation from the stock of images stored in our mind."[44] This concept can be adapted usefully to objects other than visual images, such as music, poetry, or events in a narrative. Harry Broudy refers to the "allusionary base," a broader expression of beholder's share: "The allusionary base refers to the conglomeration of concepts, images, and memories available [to each of us] to provide meaning."[45] Planoudes' abandonment of theology may be seen as the

---

[42]Wendel briefly describes these two unpublished texts that exist only in manuscript; Wendel, "Planoudes," 2208.

[43]καὶ νῦν μὲν φυσικός ἐστι καί που καὶ ἰατρικῆς παραψαύει· (40) νῦν δὲ θεολογικός, ὅπερ ἐγὼ μάλιστα πάντων δέδοικα καὶ οὐκ ἔστιν ὅτε τούτῳ πρόσειμι πλὴν <ὑπ'> ἀνάγκης. καὶ νῦν μὲν ἠθικαῖς ἐνδιατρίβει προσλαλιαῖς· (Planoudes, *Ep.* 113, lines 40–43, ed. Leone).

[44]E.H. Gombrich, *The Image and the Eye: Further Studies in the Psychology of Pictorial Representation* (Oxford: Phaidon, 1982), 139, 145.

[45]Harry Broudy, *The Role of Imagery in Learning* (Los Angeles: Getty Center for Education in the Arts, 1987), 21.

result of conflict between two different beholder's shares at different periods in his life. As a young scholar in the 1270s he lived in a period of intense debate over theological interpretation in the eastern and western Churches. Providing an accessible version of a text central to the western concept of *filioque* seems to us and may have seemed to him an intellectually defensible activity and even a desirable means of gaining imperial favor while avoiding punishment. Some twenty years later as a mature scholar, however, Planoudes could have looked back upon the consequences of involvement in theological debate with a very different beholder's share. His translation of *De Trinitate* had not assisted the union of the eastern and western Churches, and he had subsequently contradicted and rejected Augustine's theological position in his own writings. Entering the theological discussion of the 1270s had required Planoudes to occupy an embarrassing intellectual position in later years and perhaps necessitated his monastic vocation as well. Experience would certainly have altered Planoudes' own beholder's share regarding his involvement with Augustine's *De Trinitate* and with theological controversy.

Planoudes' translation of *De Trinitate* was influential in the Greek East. Rigotti lists thirty manuscripts of the work dating from the fourteenth through the nineteenth centuries and seven Byzantine theological writers of the fourteenth and fifteenth centuries who used the translation, among them Gregory Palamas, John Cantacuzene, and Prochoros Kydones.[46] The significance of Planoudes' translation for Gregory Palamas is only now gaining scholarly recognition through the writings of Reinhard Flogaus.[47] In addition, Demetrios Kydones (c. 1324–c. 1398), Bessarion (c. 1400–1472), and Gennadios II Scholarios (c. 1400–c. 1472) offer opinions on Planoudes and his translation that were informed by contemporary discussions and by their own knowledge of both Latin and Greek. At this point, I would like to turn to their remarks.

[46]Also Gregory Akindynos, Manuel Kalekas, Joseph Bryennios, and Gregory Mamme; Rigotti, lv and note 175. For the manuscripts of Planoudes' *De Trinitate*, see Rigotti, lxxx–lxxxiv.

[47]See Flogaus' contribution in this volume.

In a refutation of Planoudes' previously mentioned essay on the procession of the Holy Spirit, the uniate Greek Cardinal Bessarion quotes Demetrios Kydones:

> One would wonder at this man who attempts through these paltry, weak arguments to undermine the book of St Augustine over which he labored greatly as he translated it into Greek. For if wishing to harm the readers he submitted to the toil of translation, he is truly unnatural and deserves great blame from the pious, in that he toiled to harm the souls of the faithful. But if knowing that the book would be beneficial to those who would read it he chose to translate it and to do his fellow Greeks a kindness, why in turn as if out of regret does he warn his readers to guard against as harmful what he translated for their benefit? The cause of this unnatural behavior was his fear of the one who was then emperor, whom he knew to be without mercy toward those who said that the Holy Spirit proceeded from the Father and the Son; he desired through these arguments to escape prison and chains.[48]

As quoted by Bessarion, the uniate Greek Kydones acknowledges the difficulty of translating Augustine's *De Trinitate* and says nothing critical of the translation itself. He traces Planoudes' overt rejection of western trinitarian doctrine to his fear of punishment by the anti-union emperor

---

[48]Demetrios Kydones quoted by Bessarion in PG 161.312.B3–C5: Δημητρίου τοῦ Κυδώνη κατὰ Πλανούδη ἐξ οἰκειοχείρων γραφέντα Θαυμάσειέ τις τὸν ἄνδρα τοῦτον, τὸν διὰ τῶν ὀλίγων τούτων καὶ ἀσθενῶν ἐπιχειρημάτων πειρώμενον τὸ τοῦ ἁγίου Αὐγουστίνου βιβλίον ἀνατρέπειν, ἐφ' ᾧ πόλλ' ἐμόγησεν ἐπὶ τὴν Ἑλλάδα μετενεγκών. Εἰ μὲν γὰρ βλάψαι βουλόμενος τοὺς ἀναγινώσκοντας τὸν ἐν τῇ ἑρμηνείᾳ πόνον ὑπέστη, ἄτοπος ὄντως καὶ πολλῆς τοῖς εὐσεβέσιν ἄξιος μέμψεως, πονεῖν ἐφ' ᾧ ταῖς ψυχαῖς τῶν ἄλλων λυμήνασθαι· εἰ δ' ἐπιστάμενος, ὠφέλιμον τοῖς ἐντευξομένοις ἔσεσθαι τὸ βιβλίον, μετενεγκεῖν τοῦτο εἵλετο, καὶ τοῖς ὁμοφύλοις χαρίσασθαι, τί πάλιν ὥσπερ ἐκ μεταμελείας, ὡς βλαβερὰ φυλάττεσθαι παραινεῖ, ἃ δ' ὠφέλειαν τῶν ἐντυγχανόντων ἡρμήνευσεν; Ἀλλὰ τῆς ἀτοπίας ταύτης αἴτιον ὁ τοῦ τότε βασιλεύοντος φόβος· ὃν εἰδὼς ἀπαραίτητον ὄντα τοῖς τὸ Πνεῦμα τὸ ἅγιον ἐκ Πατρὸς καὶ Υἱοῦ λέγουσιν ἐκπορεύεσθαι, ἠθέλησε διὰ τῶν ἐπιχειρημάτων τούτων εἰρκτῆς καὶ δεσμῶν ἑαυτὸν ἀπαλλάξαι. I am grateful to Denis Sullivan of the University of Maryland for assistance in translating the Greek passages here.

Andronikos II, implying that Planoudes' own convictions were in fact uniate, although he could not openly express them in the political climate following the death of Michael VIII.

After quoting Kydones, Cardinal Bessarion includes his own brief discussion of Planoudes' puzzling behavior in first translating Augustine's *De Trinitate* and then attacking western trinitarian views:

> And so you were going to advocate for the Latins rather than to oppose them, O best and wisest of men. For I would not accuse you of the opposite, who are so well versed in every branch of knowledge, so outstanding in philosophy and insight, so well traveled in all learning, so esteemed in everything, trained to the highest degree in the Latin language in addition to Greek, and with the abundance of your ability having translated into our language both many other marvelous things and the great work *De Trinitate* of the great and wondrous Augustine, in which in addition to many other things also the divine procession of the Holy Spirit from the Father and the Son is presented in theological terms in the best and wisest and most inspired manner. How could you yourself oppose him and words as great as his, when you were his foster child and admirer? And to do that, with these arguments (or rather puny protests) that even a child could refute? But wishing to indulge the wrath of some people, I think, or to avoid it, you took this course, both to escape the wrath and more than that to protect the truth by the weakness of your own arguments, making obvious the superiority of the truth even to those who are unable to comprehend it.[49]

[49]The most wise Cardinal Lord Bessarion, "Against the Syllogisms of the Monk Maximus Planoudes concerning the Procession of the Holy Spirit according to the Latins" (Fourth Refutation), PG 161.317.C5–D11. Καὶ οὕτω συνηγορήσων Λατίνοις ἢ ἐλέγξων ἐλήλυθας, ἀνδρῶν ἄριστε καὶ σοφώτατε. Οὐ γὰρ ἂν ἐγώ σου καταγνοίην τοὐναντίον, οὕτω πᾶσαν ἐξησκημένου παιδείαν, οὕτω δὲ διαβεβηκότος ἐν φιλοσοφίᾳ καὶ θεωρίᾳ, καὶ διὰ πάντων μὲν μαθημάτων ὁδεύσαντος, εὐδοκιμήσαντος δ᾽ ἐν ἅπασι, πρὸς δὲ τῇ Ἑλλάδι καὶ τὴν Λατίνων γλῶτταν ἐς ἄκρον ἐξησκημένου, καὶ περιουσίᾳ δυνάμεως ἄλλα τε πολλὰ θαυμαστὰ καὶ τὸ μέγα *Περὶ Τριάδος* τοῦ μεγάλου καὶ θαυμαστοῦ Αὐγουστίνου ἔργον εἰς τὴν ἡμετέραν μετενεγκόντος φωνὴν ἐν ᾧ πρὸς ἄλλοις πολλοῖς καὶ ἡ ἐκ Πατρὸς καὶ Υἱοῦ τοῦ ἁγίου Πνεύματος θεία ἐκπόρευσις ἄριστά τε καὶ σοφώτατα θεολογεῖται καὶ

Like Kydones, Bessarion brings a pro-western beholder's share to a sympathetic assessment of Planoudes' translation. He does not criticize its quality or accuracy but commends Planoudes' skill as a translator and returns to the theme of coercion exerted on Planoudes by the threat of imperial wrath, ingeniously asserting that Planoudes actually promoted a pro-western viewpoint by offering only feeble arguments in opposition to it.

An anonymous Dominican at Constantinople expressed a very different assessment of Planoudes' translation at the time of the translator's death. A reference to John XII Kosmos (1294–1303) as the "recently deposed" patriarch of Constantinople dates the Latin treatise to c. 1305[50] and places it in the context of virulent dissension between Greeks and Latins in the city.[51] With marked sarcasm the anonymous author complains:

> And in order to be able to defend the errors in which (how sad!) they obstinately had persisted, some of them misrepresent texts, as did the "venerable" (ha!) monk named Maximus, who died recently in Constantinople. For he translated from Latin into Greek the book *On the Trinity* by the great doctor St Augustine, whom the Fifth Ecumenical Council included among the Doctors of the Church, and yet the aforementioned "venerable" (ha!) monk passed over in silence and suppressed the procession of the Holy Spirit from the Son as transmitted in that work, thus operating as a forger and not as a translator, and telling a lie not only to mankind but even to God.[52]

ἐνθεώτατα· ᾧ καὶ τοῖς τοσούτοις αὐτοῦ λόγοις πῶς ἂν αὐτὸς ἐναντιοῦσθαι δύναιο, τρόφιμος ὢν ἐκείνῳ καὶ ἐραστής· καὶ ταῦτα τούτοις τοῖς λόγοις, ἢ ῥηματίοις, ἃ κἂν παῖς ἐξελέγξειεν· Ἀλλ' οἶμαι τῷ τινων θυμῷ χαρίσασθαι, ἢ ἐκκλῖναι βουλόμενος, ταύτην εὗρες ὁδόν, ἐκεῖνόν τε φυγεῖν, καὶ τῇ ἀληθείᾳ μᾶλλον ἀμῦναι τῇ ἀσθενείᾳ τῶν λόγων, τὴν ἐκείνης περιουσίαν καὶ τοῖς μὴ συνορᾶν δυναμένοις ἀνακαλύπτων.

[50]Antoine Dondaine, "'Contra Graecos.' Premiers écrits polémiques des dominicains d'Orient," *Archivum Fratrum Praedicatorum* 21 (1951): 419, n. 72.

[51]See John J. Boojamra, "Athanasios of Constantinople: A Study of Byzantine Reactions to Latin Religious Infiltration," *Church History* 48 (1979): 27–35.

[52]"Et ut defendere possint errores in quibus pertinaciter, proch dolor (!) perseverant, quidam eorum scripturas corrumpunt, sicut fecit kalogerus nomine Maximus, qui nuper obiit in Constantinopoli. Nam de latino in grecum transtulit librum De trinitate magni doctoris sancti Augustini, quem quinta ycumenica synodus connumerat doctoribus ortho-

The charge that Planoudes falsified the contents of *De Trinitate* in his translation is puzzling. The translation as it survives is accurate.[53] Dondaine suggests that the anonymous critic may have known Planoudes' text only from excerpts, or in a revised version produced for the anti-union emperor Andronikos II. If such a revision existed, however, why is there no evidence of it in the substantial manuscript tradition of the Greek text? Did third-party reports, rumor, and gossip in the Latin community promote a prejudicial and inaccurate picture of Planoudes' translation accepted by this author as his beholder's share without direct knowledge of the Greek text? Perhaps the acute political tensions of the time disposed this anonymous Dominican to accept a prejudiced and inaccurate view of Planoudes' activities.

Gennadios II Scholarios, Patriarch of Constantinople immediately after the fall of the city to the Turks (1454–1456, 1463, 1464–1465), is the last and most substantial critic of Planoudes' *De Trinitate* to be examined here. He directly addresses the theological problem presented by Planoudes' translation of the Latin verb *procedere*, first surveying the vocabulary used in an acceptable Orthodox statement of the procession of the Holy Spirit and then continuing:

For the assemblage of our teachers proclaims aloud that the Spirit both is of the Son and goes forth [προϊέναι] from the Son, being made manifest and being given to the apostles through him [i.e., the Son], and in this way the Spirit is of the Son just as of the Father, and in addition his [i.e., the Spirit's] first cause [αἰτίας] is from there [i.e., from the Father], in his eternal existence [τῇ ἀϊδίῳ ὑπάρξει] not set apart from the Son, but remaining in him by nature although distinguished from him in hypostasis [καθ᾿ ὑπόστασιν] and thus said to "go forth" [προϊέναι] through him [i.e., the Son]. Therefore Augustine speaks

doxis; processionem vero Spiritus Sancti a Filio in eodem libro traditam, dictus kalogerus subticuit et suppressit, profecto falsarii et non translatoris functus officio, et non solum hominibus mentitus sed Deo." Text from Dondaine, 421–22. I am grateful to Frank Mantello of the Catholic University of America for advice and assistance with the translation and interpretation of this passage.

[53]As demonstrated by Dondaine, 422, n. 76.

very well in agreeing with them in respect to this understanding. He agrees well in everything, except if *procedere* is always translated with "proceed" [ἐκπορεύεσθαι]; but when it [i.e., *procedere*] is applied to the Father alone, it should be translated with "proceed" [ἐκπορεύεσθαι] and when applied to the Son, or to the Father and the Son, with "go forth" [προϊέναι]. And thus that wise Planoudes should have translated his [i.e., Augustine's] words in *On the Trinity*. But he, who always translated *procedere* with "proceed" [ἐκπορεύεσθαι], either was inept in our theology and for this reason held to the teacher's [i.e., Augustine's] single expression, or he had the Latins' understanding [i.e., of the question] and corrupted his translation, thinking that everyone would attribute it to Augustine whenever they heard him say that he [i.e., the Spirit] proceeds [ἐκπορεύεσθαι] from the Son and from both [i.e., the Father and the Son].[54]

Scholarios is not unjustified in his criticism of Planoudes' translation; Planoudes does indeed translate *procedere* in the vast majority of its occurrences with ἐκπορεύεσθαι. However, it is incorrect to assert that the church fathers unanimously maintain a distinction in vocabulary,

---

[54]Gennadios I Scholarios, "Tractatus De processu spiritus sancti I," in *Oeuvres complètes de Georges (Gennadios) Scholarios,* vol. 2, ed. M. Jugie, L. Petit, and X.A. Siderides (Paris: Maison de la bonne presse, 1929), 228.34–229.14 (on-line text from *Thesaurus Linguae Graecae*).

Τὸ Πνεῦμα γὰρ καὶ τοῦ Υἱοῦ εἶναι καὶ ἐκ τοῦ Υἱοῦ προϊέναι τοῖς ἀποστόλοις δι' αὐτοῦ φανερούμενον *(35)* καὶ διδόμενον, καὶ οὕτως εἶναι τὸ Πνεῦμα τοῦ Υἱοῦ, καθάπερ καὶ τοῦ *(229.)* Πατρός, πλὴν τῆς ἐκεῖθεν αἰτίας, οὐδ' ἐν τῇ ἀϊδίῳ ὑπάρξει τοῦ Υἱοῦ διϊστάμενον, ἀλλὰ μένον μὲν ἐν αὐτῷ κατὰ φύσιν, διακρινόμενον δὲ αὐτοῦ καθ' ὑπόστασιν, καὶ οὕτω δι' αὐτοῦ λεγόμενον, προϊέναι, ὁ τῶν ἡμετέρων διδασκάλων κύκλος βοᾷ. Οὐκοῦν καὶ Αὐγουστῖνος ἄριστα λέγει, πρὸς τὴν αὐτὴν ἐκείνοις συντρέχων διάνοιαν· συνδραμεῖται δὲ καὶ ἐν πᾶσι καλῶς, *(5)* εἰ μὴ ἀεὶ τὸ προκέδερε πρὸς τὸ ἐκπορεύεσθαι μεταβάλλοιτο, ἀλλ' ὅτε μὲν πρὸς τὸν Πατέρα ἀναφέρεται μόνον πρὸς τὸ ἐκπορεύεσθαι ἑρμηνεύοιτο, ὅτε δὲ πρὸς τὸν Υἱόν, ἢ τὸν Πατέρα καὶ τὸν Υἱόν, εἰς τὸ προϊέναι. Οὕτω δὲ καὶ τὸν σοφὸν ἐκεῖνον Πλανούδην τοὺς περὶ Τριάδος λόγους ἑρμηνεύειν ἐχρῆν· ὁ δέ, τὸ προκέδερε ἀεὶ πρὸς τὸ ἐκπορεύεσθαι μεταβεβληκώς, ἢ *(10)* τῆς καθ' ἡμᾶς θεολογίας ἄπειρος ἦν, καὶ διὰ τοῦτο τῇ λέξει μόνῃ τοῦ διδασκάλου προσεῖχεν, ἢ τὰ Λατίνων φρονῶν ἐκακούργει τὴν ἑρμηνείαν, οἰόμενος πάντας τοῖς Αὐγουστίνου λόγοις ἐνδώσειν, ἐπειδὰν ἀκούωσιν αὐτὸν ἐκ τοῦ Υἱοῦ καὶ ἐξ ἀμφοτέρων ἐκπορεύεσθαι λέγοντα. For a discussion of Scholarius' views on the procession, see Rigotti, lvi–lvii.

describing the procession of the Holy Spirit from the Father alone with ἐκπορεύεσθαι and from the Father and/or the Son with προϊέναι/ προέρχεσθαι. Although a survey of entries in Lampe generally confirms Scholarios' statement, Lampe also cites several instances where forms of προϊέναι/προέρχεσθαι refer to procession from the Father alone in the writings of Gregory Nazianzen and Cyril of Alexandria.[55]

It is also inaccurate to say that Planoudes always (ἀεὶ) translates *procedere* with ἐκπορεύεσθαι. In closing, we may return to the brief passage from Planoudes' *De Trinitate* cited above (50), for it illustrates the translator's apparent desire to vary for stylistic effect the equation *procedere*: ἐκπορεύεσθαι. The passage suggests that Planoudes was indeed "theologically inept," if one uses Scholarios' criterion. In its first occurrence, *procedit* (line 62) in Augustine's text refers to the procession of the Holy Spirit from the Father only, ". . . [and there is no one] from whom the Word was begotten and from whom the Holy Spirit proceeded principally except the God and Father;" Planoudes translates here with the appropriate Greek verb ἐκπορεύεται (line 61). In the third occurrence, *procederet* (line 66) refers to procession from the Son and the Father, ". . . thus then he begot him so that also from him the common gift goes forth and the Holy Spirit is [Spirit] of both;" Planoudes translates appropriately here with προέρχεσθαι (line 67). In the second occurrence, however, *procedere* (line 63) refers to procession from the Son only, ". . . since also from the Son [of God] the Holy Spirit is found to proceed;" in this case, Planoudes translates with ἐκπορευόμενον (line 64), which is theologically incorrect according to Scholarios' criterion and illustrates Scholarios' complaint exactly. Were Planoudes to hear this criticism of his *De Trinitate* translation today, I suspect that he would say, after a long and thoughtful silence, "I fear theology most of all and never approach it except under duress."[56]

---

[55]See G.W.H. Lampe, *A Patristic Greek Lexicon* (Oxford: Clarendon Press, 1961), s.v. πρόειμι (ibo) 2.

[56]Cf. Planoudes, *Ep.* 113.40–41.

Inspiration–Exploitation–Distortion: The Use of St Augustine in the Hesychast Controversy

Reinhard Flogaus

When first invited to give a paper at this international conference on "Orthodox Readings of Augustine," I originally had in mind to present exclusively Gregory Palamas' reading of this Latin church father. The triad of "inspiration," "exploitation," and "distortion" appealed to me as a suitable heuristic instrument to describe how the fourteenth-century Byzantine archbishop used the Greek translation of Augustine's *De Trinitate* (*On the Trinity*) in his own works. However, while looking through the publications that had appeared since the publication of my own contributions to this topic, I suddenly realized the extent to which these three keywords were also appropriate to describe the contemporary scholarly discussion about Augustine in the hesychast controversy. I therefore decided to give not only a short account of the various ways Palamas read Augustine, but also a brief survey of the more recent publications on this subject.

Inspiration, Exploitation, and Distortion in the Modern Scholarly Discussion

It was thirteen years ago, in the spring of 1994, that, while reading Augustine's *De Trinitate*, I suddenly realized that I had recently come across very similar passages. These were, however, in the writings of a completely different author, i.e., in the *Capita 150* (*150 Chapters*) of Gregory Palamas (1296–1359). A thorough comparison of these two works very quickly revealed that the most obvious parallels to Augustine could be found in chapters 125 to 135 of Palamas' work, which deal with the problem of categories, a subject the bishop of Hippo had treated in books 5 and 15 of his famous *De Trinitate*. A closer look at the only manuscript of the 1281 Greek translation of *De Trinitate* by Maximus Planoudes (c. 1255–1305)[1] held by a German library, i.e., the sixteenth-century Codex Monacensis gr. 54, revealed that the passages in question proved to follow rather closely Planoudes' translation. Given these obvious parallels, could then the surprising description of the Holy Spirit as the common love of the Father and the Son in chapters 36 and 37 of Palamas' work, of which scholars had long been aware, not also have been inspired by Augustine?[2]

Whereas Roman Catholic scholars, such as the French Assumptionist Martin Jugie (1878–1954), have always been quick to suggest a direct or indirect influence on Palamas by Augustine's *De Trinitate*,[3] the most eminent Palamas scholar in the twentieth century, Fr John Meyendorff (1926–1992), who had, in fact, called Palamas "one of the most Augustinian authors of the Christian East,"[4] remained more reluctant and only

---

[1]This text was edited for the first time in 1995. Αὐγουστίνου περὶ Τριάδος βιβλία πεντεκαίδεκα ἅπερ ἐκ τῆς Λατίνων διαλέκτου εἰς τὴν Ἑλλάδα μετήνεγκε Μάξιμος ὁ Πλανούδης. Εἰσαγωγή, ἑλληνικὸν καὶ λατινικὸν κείμενον, γλωσσάριον, ed. M. Papathomopoulos, I. Tsavari, G. Rigotti, 2 vols. (Athens: Kentron Ekdoseos Ergon Hellenon Syngrapheon, 1995).

[2]Gregorios Palamas, *Cap.* 36 (Γρηγορίου τοῦ Παλαμᾶ Συγγράμματα [hereafter, PS], ed. P. Chrestou, et al., vol. 5 [Thessaloniki: Kyromanos, 1992], 54.25–55.57). Still unaware of this passage, Vladimir Lossky, *Essai sur la théologie mystique de l'Eglise d'Orient* (Paris: Aubier, 1944), 78 and 210, had declared that in eastern theology the Holy Spirit has never been described as the mutual bond of love of the Father and the Son.

[3]Martin Jugie, "Palamas," *Dictionnaire de théologie catholique*, 11.1766; see also Gerhard Podskalsky, *Theologie und Philosophie in Byzanz. Der Streit um die theologische Methodik in der spätbyzantinischen Geistesgeschichte (14./15. Jh), seine systematischen Grundlagen und seine historische Entwicklung* (München: Beck, 1977), 177. Jugie assumed a possible dependence from Aquinas' *Summa contra gentiles*. However, the translation of this work into Greek by Demetrios Kydones (1324–1397/98) was completed around Christmas 1354, i.e., after the composition of Palamas' *Capita 150*.

[4]John Meyendorff, *Introduction à l'étude de Grégoire Palamas* (Paris: Éditions du Seuil,

admitted a "close similarity" between the two on this point.[5] In his 1988 edition of the *Capita*, the Basilian father Robert E. Sinkewicz still strongly rejected this kind of dependence and suggested other possible sources.[6] A closer look at the passage in question, however, showed that also in the surrounding chapters 34, 35, and 37 Palamas was obviously making use of some reflections and distinctions set forth by Augustine mainly in book 15 of *De Trinitate*.[7] Furthermore, the explanation in chapter 27 that the image of God is found in man's νοῦς, as well as Palamas' reasoning about the death of the soul and the death of the body, found in chapter 45 and in the somewhat earlier *Ad Xenam monialem*, apparently also derived from passages in Augustine's *De Trinitate*.[8] Already on the scent of Augustine in Palamas, I kept searching and discovered another work by the defender of the hesychasts that owed a great deal to the bishop of Hippo. The work in question is Palamas' *Treatise on the Economy of the Incarna-*

1959), 175. This has been rejected by John Romanides, "Notes on the Palamite Controversy and Related Topics," *Greek Orthodox Theological Review* 6 (1960/61): 196–205.

[5]Meyendorff, *Introduction à l'étude de Grégoire Palamas*, 316; cf. also Boris Bobrinskoy, *Le Mystère de la Trinité. Cours de théologie orthodoxe* (Paris: Editions du Cerf, 1986), 304.

[6]Whereas Edmund Hussey, "The Palamite Trinitarian Models," *SVTQ* 16 (1972): 83–89, had still reckoned with Didymus' *De Spiritu Sancto* as a possible *alternative* to Augustine, R.E. Sinkewicz, in his edition of the text (*Saint Gregory Palamas: The One Hundred and Fifty Chapters. A Critical Edition, Translation and Study* [Toronto: Pontifical Institute of Medieval Studies, 1988]), categorically denied any Augustinian influence on Palamas (18) and tried to detect a possible link between the passage in question and Theoleptos of Philadelphia or Gregory the Sinaite (25–34). Four years later, in his edition of the *Capita* (see n. 2), Chrestou did not even mention this topic or scholarly discussion. Another two years later, Constantine Tsirpanlis, "Epistemology, Theognosis, the Trinity and Grace in St. Gregory Palamas," *Patristic and Byzantine Review* 13 (1994): 9, pointed out that "Palamas totally avoided the 'Augustinian temptation' and its trinitarian analogies," but instead "clarified the orthodox analogy of the Spirit as love."

[7]For the parallels, compare *Cap.* 34 (PS 5.52.24–53.9) with *Trin.* 15.5.7–6.9 (865.17f, 867.35–38.43f., 867.51–869.54, 871.7–11), *Cap.* 35 (PS 5.53.22–54.6) with *Trin.* 15.11.20 (901.20–27, 903.43–49) and 15.15.25 (923.37–50), *Cap.* 36 (PS 5.54.25–55.15) with *Trin.* 6.5.7 (399.4–10, 401.21), 6.10.11 (413.30–37), 15.17.27 (929.8–11), 15.17.29 (933.69–73), and 15.19.37 (951.145–48), and *Cap.* 37 (PS 5.55.16–22) with *Trin.* 9.12.18 (549.63–78) and 15.26.47 (979.84–88). All reference numbers in parentheses following citations of *Trin.* refer to Planoudes' translation, as it appears in the critical edition identified in n. 1.

[8]Compare *Cap.* 27 (PS 5.50.1–6) with *Trin.* 14.8.11 (803.6–9), and *Cap.* 45 (PS 5.61.7–24) and *Ad Xenam* 8f (PS 5.196.17–197.9) with *Trin.* 4.3.5 (269.11–15, 271.31–40).

tion, a work commonly counted as number 16 of his numerous *Homilies*.[9] In this work, which in the past has been regarded as a major witness for the great importance attributed by Palamas to Christ's person and work,[10] almost the entire train of thought can be traced back to the christological passages of books 4, 13, and 14 of Augustine's *De Trinitate*.

In November 1996, I first published these findings in my book *Theosis bei Palamas und Luther. Ein Beitrag zum ökumenischen Gespräch,* in which all the parallels I had discovered so far were extensively documented.[11] In January 1997 a shorter article followed in the *Jahrbuch der Österreichischen Byzantinistik*.[12] Finally in 1998 I published an article in English in *St Vladimir's Theological Quarterly* about the use of St Augustine in the hesychast controversy.[13] I eagerly awaited an Orthodox reaction to these findings, which in some sense were able to disturb the hitherto largely accepted theological equilibrium and to overthrow some cherished ideas about East and West in the hesychast controversy.

In April 1997, the Greek philosopher John Demetracopoulos published a book in Athens about Augustine and Palamas,[14] where he meticulously reproduced practically all the parallel passages from the *Capita*

[9]Γρηγορίου τοῦ Παλαμᾶ ἅπαντα τὰ ἔργα. Εἰσαγωγή, κείμενον, μετάφρασις, σχόλια, ed. P. Chrestou, vol. 9 (Thessaloniki: Paterikai Ekdoseis "Gregorios ho Palamas" 1985), 422–80. For the parallels and quotations cf. Reinhard Flogaus, *Theosis bei Palamas und Luther. Ein Beitrag zum ökumenischen Gespräch* (Göttingen: Vandenhoeck & Ruprecht, 1997), 238–61.

[10]Cf. Meyendorff, *Introduction à l'étude de Grégoire Palamas*, 181–85, 205, 215–27, 251, 267, 320; Georgios Mantzaridis, *The Deification of Man: St. Gregory Palamas and the Orthodox Tradition* (Crestwood, NY: SVS Press, 1984), 21–28, 44–48, 52, 67.

[11]Flogaus, *Theosis*, 98–109, 140, 143–53, 155f, 238–61. Although the book was submitted to the editors in spring 1995 and appeared in November 1996, it bears the imprint "1997." However, as of February 1996, a typewritten version of my doctoral thesis was available at the university library.

[12]Flogaus, "Der heimliche Blick nach Westen. Zur Rezeption von Augustins De trinitate durch Gregorios Palamas," *Jahrbuch der Österreichischen Byzantinistik* 46 (1996): 275–97. The article was submitted to the editor in spring 1995 but volume 46 only appeared in January 1997.

[13]Flogaus, "Palamas and Barlaam Revisited: A Reassessment of East and West in the Hesychast Controversy of 14th Century Byzantium," *SVTQ* 42 (1998): 1–32.

[14]John Demetracopoulos, Αὐγουστῖνος καὶ Γρηγόριος Παλαμᾶς. Τὰ προβλήματα τῶν Ἀριστοτελικῶν κατηγοριῶν καὶ τῆς τριαδικῆς ψυχοθεολογίας (Athens: Parousia, 1997).

that were listed in my publications[15] and also pointed to the parallels found in *Homily* 16.[16] Surprisingly, Demetracopoulos quoted various German books and articles, but did not mention my publications. In another publication about Palamas from the preceding year, i.e., from 1996, he had not yet identified the Augustine connection.[17] In his 1997 publication, the only missing parallel is a passage from Palamas' *Contra Beccum*, which I had discovered only later and published in 1998 in my English article.[18] Thus, with the publication of Demetracopoulos' book we are led to conclude that shortly after the German publications of my discoveries in 1996, John Demetracopoulos discovered exactly the same parallels that I had found and published previously but did not detect a single Augustinian passage in addition to these.[19]

[15]Ibid., 183–93; cf. 13f, 52–54; 83–94. The most striking parallels to my own publications (cf. "Der heimliche Blick," 289f; *Theosis*, 143–45) can be found in Demetracopoulos' description (91–93) of the four different kinds of λόγος found in *Cap.* 35. However, there is one difference, concerning the date of composition. Demetracopoulos suggested that Palamas read the *Trin.* and wrote his *Capita* while staying on Mount Athos from September 1347 to March 1348, where he would have had access to Cod. Vatop. 28 (dating mainly from the second quarter of the fourteenth century, cf. Erich Lamberz, *Katalog der griechischen Handschriften des Athosklosters Vatopedi, vol. I: Codices 1–102* [Thessaloniki: Patriarchikon Idryma Paterikon Meleton, 2006], 126), which contains Planoudes' translation, whereas I, because of the date of composition of *Ad Xenam*, had suggested that the period of Palamas' arrest in the imperial palace, i.e. the years 1345/6, was a possible moment for his first acquaintance with the Greek version of *Trin.* I was joined in this opinion by Josef Lössl, "Augustine in Byzantium," *Journal of Ecclesiastical History* 51 (2000): 279.

[16]Demetracopoulos, 14–16, 115f. In this case, Demetracopoulos limited himself to quotations of only the beginning of the *Homily* together with its parallels in *Trin.* that I had expounded in *Theosis*, 239f. However, probably due to his different dating of Palamas' acquaintance with the *Trin.*, Demetracopoulos did not mention the passage from *Ad Xenam* (see n. above), which in fact is not a literal quotation but nevertheless may have been inspired by the reading of Augustine.

[17]See Demetracopoulos, *Is Gregory Palamas an Existentialist? The Restoration of the True Meaning of His Comment on Exodus 3,14: "Ἐγώ εἰμι ὁ ὤν"* (Athens: Parousia, 1996).

[18]Compare *Contra Beccum* 2 (PS 1.164.14–16) with *Trin.* 6.5.7 (399.19) and 15.19.37 (951.142–953.150); cf. Flogaus, "Palamas and Barlaam," 22. This discovery might have consequences for the dating of this work. Whereas normally the composition of this work is assigned to 1335, the Augustinian influence speaks in favor of the later date 1355 (cf. Sinkewicz, *Gregory Palamas*, in *La théologie byzantine et sa tradition*, vol. 2, ed. C.G. Conticello and V. Conticello [Turnhout: Brepols, 2002], 138).

[19]He did, however, detect an additional instance, where the very same Augustinian passage is quoted once more by Palamas in a later work (see n. 52 below).

After all, from this point on we were already two scholars to contend a direct influence of Planoudes' translation on Gregory Palamas. This was not unimportant, since Augustine has been for a long time and, at least for some scholars, still is the heresiarch, the chief villain, whose heretical theology led to the deviation of the West from the Orthodox East, to the negation of the distinction between God's essence and his energies, and finally gave rise to heresy, atheism, and rationalism in the West.[20] According to the Greek philosopher Christos Yannaras, the "technological rape of physical and historical reality" and the "rapid fading away of religion in the West and the appearance of nihilism and irrationalism as fundamental existential categories of western man" are further tragic results of the Augustinian theological option.[21] Other Orthodox authors, e.g., Fr Michael Azkoul, classified Augustine with Origen, Arius, and Nestorius, and ascribed his numerous heresies to his persistent cleaving to Neo-Platonism.[22] From this point of view, since Palamas and Augustine were theological antagonists, Palamas' opponent Barlaam of Calabria (1290–1348) must have been an Augustinian who had read *De Trinitate* and who therefore sought to combat the doctrine of the uncreated divine energy and light using the "Augustinian" idea of a *created grace*.[23]

This interpretation of the controversy between Palamas and Barlaam is not new. It had already been advocated in the 1960s by the late Fr John Romanides (1928–2001), who labeled Barlaam a Christian Platonist theologically schooled in the works of Duns Scotus, Thomas Aquinas, and above all in those of Augustine.[24] Romanides, thus, rejected Meyendorff's

[20]Christos Yannaras, "Orthodoxy and the West," *Eastern Christian Review* 3 (1971): 286–300; *Person und Eros. Eine Gegenüberstellung der Ontologie der griechischen Kirchenväter und der Existenzphilosophie des Westens* (Göttingen: Vandenhoeck & Ruprecht, 1982), 102f, n. 91.

[21]Yannaras, "The Distinction Between Essence and Energies and its Importance for Theology," *SVTQ* 19 (1975): 244; cf. *Person und Eros*, 71f, 107.

[22]Michael Azkoul, *The Influence of Augustine of Hippo on the Orthodox Church* (Lewiston, NY: The Edwin Mellen Press, 1991), 7f, 128–79.

[23]Azkoul, 49–51, 112f.

[24]Romanides, "Notes," 188, 192, 194. Recently, David Bradshaw, *Aristotle East and West: Metaphysics and the Division of Christendom* (Cambridge: Cambridge University Press, 2004), 222, once again construed the conflict between Palamas and his opponents as a dispute about "Augustinianism." See his contribution to this volume.

conviction that the conflict had been exclusively an intra-Byzantine controversy. To be sure, Meyendorff had also seen Barlaam as a "Nominalist,"
though a Byzantine one,[25] and therefore had excluded any direct Latin
influence on him during the time of the controversy.[26] In his later years,
Romanides bluntly declared "that the heresies of Barlaam the Calabrian
condemned at the Ninth Ecumenical Council"—he obviously meant by
this the synod held in 1351—"are those of Augustine himself."[27] The apex
of anti-Augustianism was reached by Romanides' statement that Augustine's observations in books 2 and 3 about the invisibility of the Trinity
and the created character of the visions of the prophets and patriarchs in
the Old Testament "are too silly to be called heresies," which in his view,
however, meant that they were actually much worse than heresies.[28]

In order to be quite clear on this point and to preclude any possible
bias let me say that it is not only from the Orthodox side that such harsh
criticism of Augustine can be heard. The erstwhile paramount position of
Augustine as the theological authority in the West, still undisputed during the middle ages, had already seriously suffered through the use of
Augustine in Reformation and Jansenist theology. In the twentieth century, however, this criticism has turned into an aggressive campaign of
defamation and condemnation. One of the foremost critics of Augustine
in the West is the German professor of medieval philosophy Kurt Flasch.
In his book *Logik des Schreckens* (*Logic of Terror*) of 1990, he held Augustine's doctrine of grace, his idea of original sin, and his "despotic" conception of God responsible for all the bloody violence, religious wars, and
various regimes of terror that Europe has suffered from late antiquity to
the twentieth century and sardonically called Augustine the "classical

[25]Meyendorff, *Introduction à l'étude de Grégoire Palamas*, 65, 74, 281f.

[26]Meyendorff, "Les débuts de la controverse hésychaste," *Byzantion* 23 (1953): 90–96.

[27]Romanides, "Yahweh of Glory According to the 1st, 2nd and 9th Ecumenical Councils," Θεολογία 71 (2000): 133.

[28]Ibid., 134; see also 199, where he called Augustine's thought "comical and outlandish."
It is somewhat confusing that Romanides repeatedly spoke of "1451" as the date of the
"Ninth Ecumenical Council" (134, 136). In this article, Romanides also repeated his acrid
criticism of Meyendorff and Mantzarides for their contention that the deification of man
was rooted in the incarnation of Christ, and he pointed to Palamas as a clear opponent of
this idea (for the theological background of this debate see Flogaus, *Theosis*, 262–68).

author of Christian intolerance."[29] He was followed by the French historian Jean Delumeau and others.[30] Thus, it is not surprising that the Paris-
based Fraternité Orthodoxe Saint Grégoire Palamas sought alliance with
these western voices and published works of past critics of Augustine such
as Richard Simon (1638–1712) and of contemporary critics as well in their
series "La Lumière du Thabor."[31]

Thus, the influence of Augustine on Palamas and, even more, the evidence of Palamas' citations of Augustine are extremely sensitive topics
that provoke fierce reactions and remain for some Orthodox scholars
something of a taboo.[32] Mingled with the widespread concept that the
conflict between Palamas and his opponents in the fourteenth century
was, in fact, a conflict between Orthodoxy and western Augustinianism is
the idea that in the hesychast controversy the "Greek personalism" of the
fathers had been attacked by some adherents to a "Latin essentialism"
allegedly inspired by Augustine.[33] Recently David Bradshaw has slightly
modified this view by calling Barlaam "the unwitting representative of the
West" in this "confrontation between Augustinian metaphysics of the

[29]Kurt Flasch, *Logik des Schreckens. De diversis quaestionibus I 2* (Mainz: Dieterich, 1990), 119: "Augustin wurde nach 400 zum Klassiker der christlichen Intoleranz"; cf. also 7–18 and 115–20. His last lecture at Bochum University in 1995 was therefore entitled "Why I cannot be a Christian any longer" ("Warum ich nicht mehr Christ sein kann").

[30]For an overview of these various critics of Augustine see Goulven Madec, "Augustinus—Genius malignus Europas?" in *Europa imaginieren. Der europäische Binnenmarkt als kulturelle und wirtschaftliche Aufgabe*, ed. P. Koslowski (Berlin: Springer, 1992), 302–9. To be sure, Flasch was not the first to take this direction. Already in 1966, the German theologian Dietrich Ritschl had published an essay "Die Last des augustinischen Erbes," in *Parrhesia. Karl Barth zum achtzigsten Geburtstag*, ed. Eberhard Busch (Zürich: EVZ, 1966), 470–90, in which he repudiated Augustinian theology.

[31]Patric Ranson, *Richard Simon ou du caractère illégitime de l'Augustianisme en théologie* (Lausanne: L'Age d'homme, 1990); *Saint Augustin. Dossier conçu et dirigé par P. Ranson* (Lausanne: L'Age d'homme, 1988).

[32]In some way, a historical antecedent for this ongoing discussion is the fourteenth- and fifteenth-century dispute over the correctness of Planoudes' translation, which, in fact, was nothing less than a camouflaged dispute over the orthodoxy of Augustine's *Trin.* For illuminating insights on this subject see Elizabeth Fisher's "Planoudes' *De Trinitate*, the Art of Translation, and the Beholder's Share" in this volume.

[33]For further discussion of this point see Flogaus, "Palamas and Barlaam," 29–31; *Theosis*, 220–24.

divine essence and the apophatic theology of the East."[34] However, I still do not share this view. Instead I would like to caution against a systematic *exploitation* of this historical conflict of fourteenth-century Byzantium in order to fight a very modern theological battle. Such an approach would certainly lead us neither to a candid and unbiased perception of the history of this conflict nor to a real understanding of the different theological positions behind it, but instead to severe *distortions* of the historical facts. As a result of such a blurred perspective, it may very well happen that in the end Palamas as well as Augustine resemble caricatures of themselves more than anything else.

One important contribution to overcoming these misconceptions is certainly Michel Barnes' recent study in which he abundantly proved that the alleged "personalism" or "Christian existentialism" seen first by Lossky and then later by Meyendorff in Palamas' theology, as well as their negative image of Augustine's trinitarian theology, had in fact been inspired by the French Jesuit Théodore de Régnon (1831–1893).[35] Another major work in this context is the 1998 publication of the critical edition of Barlaam's *Anti-Latin Treatises* by Antonis Fyrigos.[36] His research showed that in Barlaam's corpus of treatises there is only one rather vague reference to Augustine as a witness for the opinion that the Spirit proceeds "κυρίως καὶ ἰδίως" from the Father.[37] In Gregorios Akindynos' (c. 1300–1348) *Refutatio magna*, however, we already encounter four lit-

[34]David Bradshaw, 229f.

[35]Michel R. Barnes, "De Régnon Reconsidered," *Augustinian Studies* 26.2 (1995): 57f. Barnes mentioned only Lossky, but Meyendorff has been clearly inspired by Lossky's *Mystical Theology.* As for Meyendorff, see also Romanides, "Notes," 268f, who had suggested the Russian theologian Serge Verhovskoy as source of this concept of "Personalism." However, Demetracopoulos (*Is Gregory Palamas an Existentialist?* [see n. 17 above], 12) showed that one of Meyendorff's key witnesses for the supposed "Personalism" in Palamas is based on a wrong translation and concluded: "My view is that Meyendorff's interpretation of Palamas' thought is altogether unjustified and totally misleading," 12.

[36]Barlaam Calabro, *Opere contro i Latini. Introduzione, storia dei testi, edizione critica, traduzione e indici,* ed. A. Fyrigos (Vatican City: Biblioteca Apostolica Vaticana, 1998).

[37]Barlaam, *Syntagma* 45 (*Opere contro i Latini,* 664.387–89): "Καὶ ὁ ἅγιος δὲ Αὐγουστῖνος, ἐν βίβλῳ πεντεκαιδεκάτῃ Περὶ τῆς Ἁγίας Τριάδος οὐχ ἅπαξ, ἀλλὰ πολλάκις τὸ Πνεῦμα τὸ Ἅγιον κυρίως καὶ ἰδίως φησὶν ἐκ τοῦ Πατρὸς ἐκπορεύεσθαι." For a further discussion of this reference see Flogaus, "Palamas and Barlaam," 10–12.

eral quotations from *De Trinitate*, in most cases explicitly attributed to Augustine.[38] Even if the number of quotations found here is much fewer than the number extant in Palamas, we may conclude that apparently at that time it was not so uncommon in Byzantium to cite Augustine as a witness and authority.

Nevertheless, even ten years after the first publications discussing the quotations from *De Trinitate* found in Palamas, some authors still mention only Barlaam's possible knowledge of the Greek translation of this work and pass over the fact that it is actually in Palamas' writings that we can find numerous literal quotations from Augustine's *De Trinitate*.[39] Likewise, Norman Russell recently quoted one of Palamas' explanations of the reason for the incarnation, but he failed to mention that this passage had a literal parallel in book 13 of *De Trinitate*.[40] Other strategies lead to a similar conclusion. Jeremy Wilkins, for instance, explicitly referred to my findings but, nevertheless, left it completely to the discretion of the reader whether Palamas actually used Planoudes' translation as a source for his theological writings or not.[41] Finally, some Orthodox followers of John Romanides recently even voiced their suspicion that Palamas may

[38]Compare Gregorios Akindynos, *Refutatio magna* 1.27 (CCSG 31.33.2–4), 2.9 (96.31–35), and 3.15 (189.22–42) with *Trin.* 1.10.21 (85.72f), 6.6f.8 (403.30–9), 7.1.1 (417.20–22), and 7.3.6 (439.106–11).

[39]Bradshaw, 234, referred to my article in *SVTQ* exclusively to provide evidence for Barlaam's possible knowledge of *Trin.*, which was not exactly the main topic of this publication. Recently Ettore Perella, "Palamas, Agostino e il ondamento del sapere," in: *Rivelazione e conoscenza*, ed. Giovanni Grandi and Luca Grion (Soveria Mannelli: Rubbettino 2007), 121, bluntly declared once again: "Sicuramente Palamas non conosceva direttamente Agostino e non meno sicuramente la sua concezione della processione dello Spirito Santo è molto lontana da quella descritta nel *De Trinitate*."

[40]Norman Russell, "Theosis and Gregory Palamas: Continuity or Doctrinal Change?" *SVTQ* 50 (2006): 377. The passage in question is found in *Hom.* 16.19 (9.448.18–21); for a comparison with Planoudes, see Flogaus, *Theosis*, 249.

[41]Jeremy Wilkins, "'The Image of this Highest Love': The Trinitarian Analogy in Gregory Palamas' *Capita 150*," *SVTQ* 47 (2003): 384 and 389: "I emphatically do not intend to make any claims regarding the material sources of Gregory's ideas ... It is beyond the scope of this article to establish whether or to what extent Palamas knew and used Augustine." In contrast to his own prudent approach to this question Wilkins blames me for making "an aggressive case for Augustinian inspiration" (389).

not, after all, be the author of the *Capita*.[42] Shall we soon be confronted with the same discussion about *Homily* 16?

I think my impression is not completely erroneous that some scholars are in fact so eager to avoid any taint of Augustinian influence on Palamas and any *soupçon* of a possible Latin theological pollution that their arguments eventually become somewhat strained. Frankly, I do not see the need for such anxious endeavors to erase any Augustinian traces from the writings of the defender of the hesychasts, all the more since they are doomed to fail anyway. Palamas' immaculate Orthodoxy is certainly not at stake just because he made use of some passages of the Greek translation of *De Trinitate* in his own theological and pastoral writings. Palamas certainly did not put the case for the *filioque* or any other trinitarian concept foreign to Orthodoxy by using various passages from the Greek *De Trinitate*. I am, therefore, very grateful that one of the most eminent scholars of Greek patristic and medieval literature, Robert E. Sinkewicz, who had originally denied categorically any Augustinian impact on Palamas, has lately recognized that, in fact, there are in Palamas' writings "direct citations from Augustine's *De Trinitate* in the Greek translation by Maximos Planoudes."[43]

Nevertheless, I definitely never claimed that Palamas was an "Augustinian" theologian or that his theology was in fact "Augustinian." The Jesuit scholar Joseph Lössl, of Cardiff University, who in two English articles otherwise summarized quite faithfully my German article on this topic,[44] made this allegation and, therefore, called my conclusions

---

[42]Thus, e.g., Andrew Sopko, "Scholasticism and Orthodoxy: Some Current Observations," in *The Church and the Library: Studies in Honor of Rev. Dr. George C. Papademetriou*, ed. Dean Papademetriou and Andrew Sopko (Boston: Holy Cross Orthodox Press, 2005), 391, claimed that the Augustinian passages in the *Capita* were interpolations added by Theophanes of Nicaea (died c. 1381), but he failed to present any substantial evidence. Anthony G. Roeber, "Western, Eastern or global orthodoxy?: Some reflections on St. Augustine of Hippo in recent literature," *Pro ecclesia* 17 (2008): 222, reports that Fr Maximos Lavriotes, a radically antiphanarian monk recently expelled from Mount Athos had even suggested Gennadios Scholarios (died c. 1473) as possible compiler of the *Capita*.

[43]Sinkewicz, *Gregory Palamas*, 163, who now also admits a possible Augustinian influence behind the image of Love and Joy used for the Spirit in *Cap.* 36f (ibid., 170).

[44]Compare Lössl, "Augustine's 'On the Trinity' in Gregory Palamas' 'One Hundred and

"methodologically questionable."[45] Instead Lössl presented the position of the Belgian Dominican Jacques Lison as a more appropriate assessment of the relationship between Palamas and Augustine.[46] It was likely Lison's dissertation that caused the Pontifical Council for Promoting Christian Unity in 1995 to refer to Gregory Palamas as an eastern witness for the Augustinian interpretation of the Holy Spirit as mutual bond of love between the Father and the Son.[47] As for Lison himself, he had, in fact, repeatedly dismissed the possibility of proving any direct influence of Augustine on Palamas, but, in contrast to Sinkewicz, did not want to exclude at least some "superficial" or "indirect" influence of the bishop of Hippo in chapter 36 either.[48] One of the key testimonies for his assertion that the context of chapter 36 has absolutely nothing to do with Augustinian speculations about mental acts as analogies to trinitarian relations was chapter 35, with its above-mentioned distinction of a fourfold notion of word found in each human being.[49] Unfortunately, it is exactly this paragraph that has a quite literal correspondence in book 15 of *De Trinitate*. This brings me to the second part of my paper, i.e., inspiration, exploitation, and distortion of St Augustine in St Gregory Palamas.

Fifty Chapters,'" *Augustinian Studies* 30 (1999): 69–81, and "Augustine in Byzantium," 279–86, with my article "Der heimliche Blick," 280–97.

[45]However, he did not consider it necessary to substantiate this objection by so much as a quotation from my works. The reason for this is conspicuous—he simply would not have found any remark of this type in my writings. Lössl, "Augustine's 'On the Trinity,'" 63.

[46]Ibid., 71: "There is no need to push any further in Flogaus' direction, especially after Lison's call for caution." On the other hand he claims that "Palamas goes even further than Augustine in *On the Trinity*. For he drops the terminology of similarity (οἷον, ὅμοιον, like, similar to)—something Augustine never does . . . —and equals the human spiritual experience of loving and being loved with the Spirit himself" (ibid., 70).

[47]Cf. "Die griechische und lateinische Überlieferung über den Ausgang des Heiligen Geistes. Eine Klarstellung in Verantwortung des Päpstlichen Rates zur Förderung der Einheit der Christen," *Una Sancta* 50 (1995): 324, n. 11.

[48]Jacques Lison, *L'Esprit répandu. La pneumatologie de Grégoire Palamas* (Paris: Cerf, 1994), 89; "L'Esprit comme amour selon Grégoire Palamas: Une influence augustinienne?" *Studia Patristica* 32 (1997): 325–32.

[49]Lison, "L'Esprit comme amour selon Grégoire Palamas," 329.

Inspiration, Exploitation and Distortion of St Augustine in the Writings of St Gregory Palamas

As I said before, in contrast to Fr Meyendorff,[50] I never claimed that Palamas was an "Augustinian" theologian or that his theology as a whole could be suitably characterized as such. I do, however, believe it to be undeniable that Palamas made use of Augustine in various writings. He did so not only by letting himself be inspired by some Augustinian arguments, which he incorporated in his own writings, but also by simply exploiting Augustine's notions, ideas, and arguments for a different purpose. Finally, in some cases, he used Augustine's words in order to support a concept that was the opposite to what Augustine had originally meant. Whether or not this copying and paraphrasing should be called a "reception" of Augustine may be subject to discussion. I did, in fact, use that term but showed at the same time how eclectic and sometimes even contrary to Augustine's intentions this reception was.[51] In any case, in having recourse to the Greek *De Trinitate*, Palamas obviously was anxious not to unveil his source. So far, we know only of one instance where he introduced a quotation from Planoudes' translation with the phrase "since one of the wise and apostolic men said . . ." without, however, giving either Planoudes' or Augustine's name.[52] Nevertheless, the introduction of this quotation suggests that we may conclude that Palamas—at least partially—esteemed the books of *De Trinitate* as a patristic testimony faithful to the apostolic truth. Why else would he have repeatedly copied Augustine's words?

[50]See above, n. 5.

[51]Flogaus, *Theosis*, 109, 241, 256, 277; "Der heimliche Blick," 287, 290, 297. Lössl, "Augustine in Byzantium," 286, argued against the use of this term, following a remark of Podskalsky in his review of my book (*Byzantinische Zeitschrift* 91 [1998]: 119).

[52]Compare *Contra Gregoram* 2.43 (PS 5.296.10s): "ἐπεὶ καί τις τῶν σοφῶν καὶ ἀποστολικῶν ἀνδρῶν φησιν, ὅτι 'θέσεις καὶ ἕξεις καὶ τόποι καὶ χρόνοι καὶ εἴ τι τοιοῦτον, οὐ κυρίως ἐπὶ τοῦ Θεοῦ λέγονται, ἀλλὰ μεταφορικῶς· τὸ δὲ πρὸς τὸ ποιεῖν καὶ ἐνεργεῖν ἀνῆκον ἐπὶ μόνου τοῦ Θεοῦ ἀληθέστατα ἂν λέγοιτο' . . ." with *Trin.* 5.8.9 (363.25–31). The same quotation (which the editors of *Contra Gregoram* presented as "unidentified") is found also in *Cap.* 133 (PS 5.110.10–14). Whereas this quotations is a little longer in *Cap.* 133, it is in *Contra Gregoram* that its wording is a little more faithful to Planoudes' translation (cf. for this Flogaus, "Palamas and Barlaam," 21, n. 100).

Since the space assigned to this contribution is limited, I shall restrict myself to giving a few examples for these various modes of incorporation of bits of *De Trinitate* in Palamas. One instance in which we can clearly see that Palamas let himself be inspired by Augustine's reflections is certainly the description of the image of the Trinity in our minds with the differentiation of the four kinds of "word" that can be observed in human beings.[53] It is also quite remarkable that in the preceding chapter (34), the text of Augustine inspires the archbishop of Thessaloniki to draw conclusions that normally would not have been his: namely, that God possesses goodness, life, and other predications not as *qualities* but as his *essence* (οὐσία). This idea is actually foreign to Palamas' theology, since he would normally identify these predications with God's *energy* and consider God's essence as beyond all names and all knowledge. Augustine, on the contrary, repeatedly made such an identification in order to safeguard the divine simplicity.[54] Nevertheless, in another part of the *Capita* (chapters

---

[53]A comparison of *Cap.* 35 (PS 5.53.26–54.6): "... καὶ λόγος οὐ κατὰ τὸν ἡμέτερον προφορικὸν λόγον, οὐ νοῦ γὰρ οὗτος, ἀλλὰ σώματος νῷ κινουμένου· οὐδὲ κατὰ τὸν ἡμέτερον ἐνδιάθετον λόγον, φθόγγων γὰρ οἱονεὶ τύποις κἀκεῖνος ἐν ἡμῖν διατιθέμενος γίνεται· ἀλλ' οὐδὲ κατὰ τὸν ἡμέτερον ἐν διανοίᾳ λόγον, κἂν χωρὶς φθόγγων ᾖ, ἐπιβολαῖς ἀσωμάτοις πάντῃ συμπεραιούμενος, κἀκεῖνος γὰρ μεθ' ἡμᾶς ἐστι καὶ διαλειμμάτων δεῖται καὶ χρονικῶν οὐκ ὀλίγων διαστημάτων, διεξοδικῶς προϊών, καὶ ἐξ ἀρχῆς ἀτελοῦς πρὸς τὸ ἐντελὲς συμπέρασμα προαγόμενος· ἀλλὰ κατὰ τὸν ἐμφύτως ἡμῖν, ἐξ οὗ γεγόναμεν παρὰ τοῦ κτίσαντος ἡμᾶς κατ' εἰκόνα οἰκείαν, ἐναποκείμενον τῷ νῷ λόγον, τὴν ἀεὶ συνυπάρχουσαν αὐτῷ γνῶσιν, ..." with *Trin.* 15.11.20 (901.20–27, 903.43–49) and 15.15.25 (923.37–50) reveals that Palamas' λόγος προφορικός corresponds with the λόγος προφορικὸς ἐν φθόγγῳ in Planoudes' translation, his λόγος ἐνδιάθετος, φθόγγων γὰρ οἱονεὶ τύποις ... διατιθέμενος with the ἐνδιάθετος ἐν ὁμοιώματι φθόγγου, his λόγος ἐν διανοίᾳ with the λόγος ἐν τῇ διανοίᾳ, and the description of the λόγος ἐμφύτως ἡμῖν ἐναποκείμενος τῷ νῷ as ἀεὶ συνυπάρχουσα αὐτῷ γνῶσις corresponds with τὰ παρόντα εἰσὶ καὶ πρὸς τὴν αὐτοῦ τοῦ νοῦ φύσιν ἀνήκουσιν which are described as ἐν τῷ νοΐ ἀΐδιός τις γνῶσις. For further information see Flogaus, *Theosis*, 143–46.

[54]Compare *Cap.* 34 (PS 5.52.24–53.9): "Ὁ ἀνωτάτω νοῦς, τὸ ἄκρον ἀγαθόν, ... φανερῶς οὐ ποιότητα ἀλλ' οὐσίαν ἔχει τὴν ἀγαθότητα. Διὸ καὶ πᾶν ὅπερ ἂν ἐννοήσειέ τις ἀγαθόν, ἐν ἐκείνῳ ἐστί, μᾶλλον δὲ ἐκεῖνός ἐστι· καὶ ὑπὲρ ἐκεῖνό ἐστι ... Καὶ ἡ ζωὴ ἐν αὐτῷ ἐστι, μᾶλλον δὲ αὐτός ἐστιν ἡ ζωή· ἀγαθὸν γὰρ ἡ ζωὴ καὶ ἀγαθότης ἐν αὐτῷ ἡ ζωή. Καὶ ἡ σοφία ἐν αὐτῷ ἐστι, μᾶλλον δὲ αὐτός ἐστιν· ἀγαθὸν γὰρ ἡ σοφία καὶ ἀγαθότης ἐν αὐτῷ ἡ σοφία, καὶ ἡ ἀϊδιότης καὶ ἡ μακαριότης ... Καὶ οὐκ ἔστιν ἐκεῖ διαφορὰ ζωῆς καὶ σοφίας καὶ ἀγαθότητος καὶ τῶν τοιούτων. Πάντα γὰρ ἡ ἀγαθότης ἐκείνη συνειλημμένως καὶ ἑνιαίως καὶ ἁπλουστάτως συμπεριβάλλει ..." with *Trin.* 15.5.7–6.9 (865.17f, 867.35–38, 43f, 51–869.54, 871.7–11).

117–19), which stems from his *De citatione Cyrilli*, Palamas argues that God's attributes are not to be equaled with his essence.[55]

Another example of an Augustinian inspiration is certainly the much disputed comparison of the Spirit with the love and joy that the Father and the Son share, as found in chapters 36 and 37.[56] Even though the parallels are less literal, this particular idea as presented here by Palamas and also in his *Contra Beccum* has clearly been inspired by Augustine. Finally most of the *Treatise on the Economy of the Incarnation* (homily 16), where Palamas considers power and justice and the respective tasks of the two natures of Christ in the work of salvation, quite faithfully recounts Augustine's thoughts.[57]

As an example of those passages where Palamas made use of Augustine, i.e., exploited Augustine's writings to procure for himself some valid material to support his own case, while strongly rejecting Augustine's conclusions, I would like to point to chapter 132. Once again, this chapter is based on Augustine's deliberations about relative predications in God, which were appreciated by Palamas because they showed that there was a reality in God that was not identical with his substance. In the underlying passage from book 5 of *De Trinitate*, the bishop of Hippo had argued that the Father is referred to as Father in relation to his Son, and that he is referred to as principle in relation to the Son and to the Spirit, whereas in relation to creation, the Father, the Son, and the Spirit constitute together *one* principle.[58] The final conclusion that Augustine had drawn from this

[55]Compare *Capita* (117–19) with *De citatione Cyrilli* (PS 5.100.22–102.14). For a more detailed discussion of this topic, see Flogaus, *Theosis*, 100–18.

[56]Compare *Cap.* 36 (PS 5.55.8–15) with *Trin.* 6.10.11 (413.30–37). Note also, *Cap.* 37 (PS 5.55.22–26): "'Ἀλλ' ἐν ἐκείνῳ τῷ ἀρχετύπῳ, ἐν ἐκείνῃ τῇ παντελείῳ καὶ ὑπερτελεῖ ἀγαθότητι, . . . πάντα ἐστὶν ἀπαραλλάκτως ὁ θεῖος ἔρως ὅσα ἐκείνη. Διὸ καὶ πνεῦμα ἅγιον καὶ παράκλητος ἄλλος οὗτός ἐστί τε καὶ παρ' ἡμῶν καλεῖται . . ." The translation by Hussey, op.cit. (n. 7), 85, "Therefore the Holy Spirit is another Paraclete and is named such by us," is erroneous; the conjecture suggested by Sinkewicz in his edition "and another [name for the] Paraclete" (125) is superfluous since Palamas is referring here to Jn 14.16. Compare also *Contra Beccum* 2 (PS 1.164.15f) with *Trin.* 15.19.37 (951.142–953.150). For further evidence cf. Flogaus, "Palamas and Barlaam," 22, n. 108.

[57]For the parallels (and also the minor differences), see Flogaus, *Theosis*, 238–61.

[58]Compare *Cap.* 132 (PS 5.109.26– 110. 9): ". . . λέγεται δὲ ἀναφορικῶς, καθάπερ ἔφημεν, καὶ ὁ πατὴρ μόνος πρὸς τὸν ὁμοούσιον υἱὸν πατήρ, ὁ αὐτὸς δὲ λέγεται καὶ ἀρχὴ πρὸς τὸν

was, of course, dismissed by Palamas and passed over in silence, namely, that in relation to the Spirit, the Father and the Son also constitute one principle. Thus, Palamas used Augustine to some extent for his own purpose but was not willing to follow this church father's train of thought beyond a certain point.

Finally, let me point out one instance where a passage from *De Trinitate* actually appears somewhat distorted in its rendering by Gregory Palamas. The passage in question is chapter 125, where Palamas had used a string of arguments expounded by Augustine in book 15 of *De Trinitate* in order to refute the Eunomian claim that every predication about God concerns his substance.[59] The purpose of this argument in Palamas is,

υἱόν τε καὶ τὸ πνεῦμα, λέγεται δὲ καὶ πρὸς τὴν κτίσιν ὁ πατὴρ ἀρχή, ἀλλ᾿ ὡς κτίστης καὶ δεσπότης τῶν κτισμάτων πάντων. Ὅταν οὖν ταῦτα πρὸς τὴν κτίσιν ὁ πατὴρ λέγηται, ἀρχή ἐστι καὶ ὁ υἱός, καὶ οὐκ εἰσὶ δύο ἀρχαί, ἀλλὰ μία· καὶ γὰρ ἀναφορικῶς λέγεται καὶ ὁ υἱὸς ἀρχὴ ὡς πρὸς τὴν κτίσιν, ὥσπερ ὁ δεσπότης πρὸς τὰ δοῦλα. Οὐκοῦν ὁ πατὴρ καὶ ὁ υἱὸς μετὰ τοῦ πνεύματος ὡς πρὸς τὴν κτίσιν μία ἀρχή ἐστι καὶ εἷς δεσπότης καὶ εἷς κτίστης καὶ εἷς Θεός τε καὶ πατὴρ καὶ προμηθεὺς καὶ ἔφορος, καὶ τἆλλα πάντα. Καὶ τῶν τοιούτων ἕκαστον οὐκ ἔστιν οὐσία· οὐ γὰρ ἂν πρὸς ἕτερον ἀναφορικῶς ἐλέγετο, εἴπερ ἦν αὐτοῦ οὐσία" with *Trin.* 5.13.14f (371.4–373.17): "Λέγεται ἄρα ἀναφορικῶς ὁ Πατήρ, ὁ αὐτὸς δὲ ἀναφορικῶς λέγεται καὶ ἀρχή ... ἀλλὰ Πατὴρ μὲν πρὸς τὸν Υἱὸν λέγεται, ἀρχὴ δὲ πρὸς πάντα τὰ ἐξ αὐτοῦ ... Καὶ ἀρχὴ δὲ λέγεται ὁ Υἱός ... ὥσπερ καὶ ὁ Πατὴρ ἀρχὴ τῆς κτίσεώς ἐστιν, ὅτι δὴ ἐξ αὐτοῦ τὰ πάντα· καὶ γὰρ καὶ ὁ κτίστης ἀναφορικῶς λέγεται πρὸς τὴν κτίσιν, ὥσπερ ὁ δεσπότης πρὸς τὸν δοῦλον. Καὶ διὰ τοῦτο λέγοντες καὶ τὸν Πατέρα ἀρχὴν καὶ τὸν Υἱὸν ἀρχήν, οὐ δύο ἀρχὰς τῆς κτίσεως λέγομεν· ὁ γὰρ Πατὴρ καὶ ὁ Υἱὸς ὁμοῦ πρὸς τὴν κτίσιν μία ἐστὶν ἀρχή, ὥσπερ εἷς κτίστης καὶ εἷς Θεός ..." and (375.4–7, 377.37–41): "ὁ Πατὴρ πρὸς τὸν Υἱὸν ἀρχή ἐστι· γεγέννηκε γὰρ αὐτόν. Πότερον δὲ καὶ πρὸς τὸ Πνεῦμα τὸ ἅγιον ἀρχή ἐστιν ὁ Πατήρ, ... οὐ μικρὰ ζήτησίς ἐστιν ... ὡς ὁ Πατὴρ καὶ ὁ Υἱὸς εἷς Θεός, ... οὕτως ἀναφορικῶς πρὸς τὸ Πνεῦμα τὸ ἅγιον μία ἀρχή· πρὸς δὲ τὴν κτίσιν ὁ Πατὴρ καὶ ὁ Υἱὸς καὶ τὸ Πνεῦμα τὸ ἅγιον μία ἀρχή, ὥσπερ εἷς δημιουργὸς καὶ εἷς κύριος."

[59]Compare *Cap.* 125 (PS 5.105, 23–106, 8): "Διὰ τοὺς Εὐνομιανούς, δοκοῦντας μὴ τὴν αὐτὴν πατρὸς εἶναι καὶ υἱοῦ οὐσίας, ἐπειδὴ πᾶν τὸ περὶ Θεοῦ λεγόμενον κατ᾿ οὐσίαν λέγεσθαι οἴονται καὶ φιλονεικοῦσιν ὡς, ἐπεὶ τὸ γεννᾶν καὶ γεννᾶσθαι διαφορά ἐστι, διὰ τοῦτο καὶ οὐσίας διαφόρους εἶναι, ... δείκνυται μὴ πᾶν τὸ περὶ Θεοῦ λεγόμενον κατ᾿ οὐσίαν λέγεσθαι, ἀλλὰ λέγεσθαι καὶ ἀναφορικῶς, τουτέστι πρός τι, ὅπερ αὐτὸς οὐκ ἔστιν· ὥσπερ ὁ πατὴρ λέγεται πρὸς τὸν υἱόν· οὐ γάρ ἐστι πατὴρ ὁ υἱὸς καὶ κύριος πρὸς τὴν δουλεύουσαν κτίσιν, κυριεύει γὰρ ὁ Θεὸς τῶν ἐν χρόνῳ καὶ ἐν αἰῶνι καὶ αὐτῶν τῶν αἰώνων· τὸ δὲ κυριεύειν ἄκτιστόν ἐστιν ἐνέργεια Θεοῦ, διαφέρουσα τῆς οὐσίας, ὡς πρὸς ἕτερόν τι λεγομένη, ὅπερ αὐτὸς οὐκ ἔστιν," with *Trin.* 15.3.5 (857.23–35): "Ἐν δὲ τῷ πέμπτῳ διὰ τοὺς δοκοῦντας διὰ ταῦτα μὴ τὴν αὐτὴν Πατρὸς καὶ Υἱοῦ εἶναι οὐσίαν, ἐπειδὴ πᾶν τὸ περὶ Θεοῦ λεγόμενον κατ᾿ οὐσίαν λέγεσθαι οἴονται, καὶ διὰ ταῦτα τὸ γεννᾶν καὶ γεννᾶσθαι ἢ γεννητὸν εἶναι καὶ ἀγέννητον, ἐπεὶ διαφορά ἐστι, φιλονεικοῦσιν [καὶ] οὐσίας διαφόρους

however, a different one, namely, to defend a third eternal reality in God besides οὐσία and ὑπόστασις, i.e, ἐνέργεια. Therefore, Palamas not only skipped Augustine's remark that the predications "good" and "great" refer to God's substance but also expanded the relative predication of God's lordship over creation from the realm of temporal things to the realm of eternity by adding "καὶ ἐν αἰῶνι καὶ αὐτῶν τῶν αἰώνων" and by explaining that God's lordship is an uncreated energy. This, of course, was not at all the view of Augustine, who taught that God's lordship like his creation must belong to the realm of temporal things. Thus, we are confronted with the fact that even while he quoted large parts of Augustine's argumentation, Palamas, nevertheless, rather skillfully altered it a bit here and there and thus reached a conclusion opposite to the original passage from *De Trinitate*.

To conclude, let me say once more that Palamas was certainly not an "Augustinian theologian," but that he clearly used the Greek translation of *De Trinitate* in his writings in various ways, which, in this paper, I have tried to differentiate with the three keywords "inspiration," "exploitation," and "distortion." Some of these passages, which were obviously the fruit of a rather thorough study of *De Trinitate*, have been mentioned here, but further careful scrutiny of the sources will certainly reveal even more such instances in the works of the defender of the hesychasts. Almost as important, however, as an unprejudiced look at the sources, will be the acknowledgment, at last, of the philological evidence that has been discovered so far and of the consequences drawn from this evidence for the historiography of the hesychast controversy. The various attempts to suppress these findings, to put them in question, or simply to deny them are as little help in this regard as is the reiteration of the old stereotypes used to depict the hesychast controversy in fourteenth-century Byzantium as a clash between "theological civilizations," namely, of the Augustinian West

εἶναι, ἀποδείκνυται μὴ πᾶν τὸ περὶ Θεοῦ λεγόμενον κατ' οὐσίαν λέγεσθαι, ὥσπερ κατ' οὐσίαν λέγεται ἀγαθὸς καὶ μέγας καὶ εἴ τι ἕτερον καθ' αὐτὸ λέγεται, ἀλλὰ λέγεσθαι καὶ ἀναφορικῶς, τουτέστιν οὐ καθ' αὐτὸ ἀλλὰ πρός τι ὅπερ αὐτὸς οὐκ ἔστιν, ὥσπερ Πατὴρ πρὸς τὸν Υἱόν λέγεται ἢ [codd.: καὶ] Κύριος πρὸς τὴν δουλεύουσαν αὐτῷ κτίσιν· ἔνθα καὶ εἴ τι ἀναφορικῶς, τουτέστι πρός τι, ὅπερ αὐτὸς οὐκ ἔστι, καὶ ἐν χρόνῳ λέγεται . . . παντάπασιν αὐτὸν ἐν τῇ ἑαυτοῦ φύσει ἢ οὐσίᾳ ἀναλλοίωτον διαμένειν."

and the Orthodox East. Instead, we should look at the facts and accept that
Palamas obviously did read Augustine as a father belonging to the tradition of the Church, even if some of his reasoning was not quite in accordance with Byzantine trinitarian theology. By doing so, Gregory Palamas
proved to have had a much broader theological horizon than some of his
modern interpreters. Would this not, after all, be a promising perspective
for future research on the theology of Gregory Palamas and on the history
of the hesychast controversy?

Augustine of Hippo, Basil of Caesarea, and Gregory Nazianzen

Joseph T. Lienhard, SJ

With slight embarrassment but an Augustinian spirit, I begin by retracting the title of the paper that I originally submitted, "Augustine and the Cappadocians." There are two reasons for this retraction.

The first is that the title is an anachronism. The collective title "the Cappadocian fathers" for Basil of Caesarea, Gregory Nazianzen, and Gregory of Nyssa has been in use only since the mid-nineteenth century. Augustine probably never knew of Gregory of Nyssa at all, except to confuse one fact about him: he once calls Gregory Nazianzen Basil's brother—which, of course, he was not; Gregory of Nyssa was.[1]

The second reason for the retraction is that Augustine generally did not think of Basil and Gregory Nazianzen as belonging together, distinct from other Greek bishops. As we shall see, late in his life, he does institute a sort of argument from tradition by listing Christian bishops (and even, quite generously, one presbyter[2]) as Orthodox authorities who agree with himself. Only once does he join Basil and Gregory as a distinctive pair.

Right at the outset I need to acknowledge that one important topic cannot be treated here because the literature on it is so great and the con-

---

[1]"Duo isti tam insignes viri . . . sicut fertur, etiam carne gemani" (*Contra Jul.* 1.5.19 [PL 44.652]). See Berthold Altaner, "Augustinus und Basilius der Große," *Kleine patristische Schriften,* ed. Günter Glockmann (Berlin: Akademie Verlag, 1967), 269–76. Altaner assumes that Augustine had Jerome's *De viris illustribus* and Rufinus' Latin translation and continuation of Eusebius' history available to him as sources of information on the Greek fathers but made little use of them.

[2]Jerome; see Augustine, *Contra Jul.* 2.10.33 (PL 44.697).

clusions drawn are so divergent: namely, Augustine's knowledge of Greek. On one end of the spectrum, the passage from the *Confessiones* (*Confessions*) in which Augustine complains about the poor pedagogy of his teachers of Greek is well known. On the other end of the spectrum, by the end of his life he could translate some sentences from Greek, and does so accurately. But still, how much Greek he really knew, and whether he could read Greek easily, remains a matter of speculation.

* * *

There are three possible approaches to the topic of Augustine and the Greek fathers Basil and Gregory. The first we might call impressionistic; the second, a sort of census approach or name-count; and the third, a search for sources. In every instance, the starting point in modern studies of Augustine and the eastern fathers must be the work of Berthold Altaner, whose series of articles on this topic is foundational,[3] although other studies have followed.[4]

<hr/>

[3]Altaner, "Altlateinische Übersetzungen von Basiliusschriften," *Kleine patristische Schriften,* 409–15 (orig. publ. *Historisches Jahrbuch* 61 [1941]: 208–26); Altaner, "Augustinus und Basilius der Große," ibid., 269–76 (orig. publ. *Revue bénédictine* 60 [1950]: 17–24); Altaner, "Augustinus und die griechische Sprache," ibid., 129–53 (orig. publ. *Antike und Christentum,* Ergänzungsband 1 [1939]: 19–40); Altaner, "Augustinus, Gregor von Nazianz, Gregor von Nyssa," ibid., 277–85 (orig. publ. *Revue bénédictine* 61 [1951]: 54–62); Altaner, "Die Benützung von original griechischen Vätertexten durch Augustinus," ibid. 154–63 (orig. publ. *Zeitschrift für Religions- und Geistesgeschichte* 1 [1948]: 71–79); Altaner, "Eustathius, der lateinische Übersetzer der Hexaemeron-Homilien Basilius des Großen," ibid., 437–47 (orig. publ. *Zeitschrift für die neutestamentliche Wissenschaft* 39 [1940]: 161–70).
    [4]Pierre Courcelle, *Les lettres grecques en Occident,* 2d ed. (Paris: E. de Boccard, 1948); English trans. *Late Latin Writers and Their Greek Sources* (Cambridge: Harvard, 1969); Maria-Barbara von Stritzky, "Beobachtungen zur Verbindung zwischen Gregor von Nyssa und Augustin," *Vigiliae christianae* 28 (1974): 176–85; Waclaw Eborowicz, "Saint Basile et Saint Augustin," *Vox Patrum* 3 (1982): 285–97; Gerard J.M. Bartelink, "Die Beeinflussung Augustins durch die griechischen Patres," *Augustiniana Traiectina: Communications présentées au Colloque International d'Utrecht, 13–14 novembre 1986,* ed. J. den Boeft and J. van Oort, 9–24 (Paris: Études augustiniennes, 1987); Andrew Louth, "Love and the Trinity: Saint Augustine and the Greek Fathers," *Augustinian Studies* 33 (2002): 1–16.

The Impressionistic Approach

The impressionistic approach was often employed in the earlier twentieth century. In the impressionistic approach, a scholar read Augustine, and read Basil or Gregory; seeing similar ideas, he concluded that the Greek father must have influenced Augustine, but supplied little or no textual evidence. In these passages, of course, Augustine does not name his source—if he is using one. Practitioners of the impressionistic approach were, for example, Jean Chevalier and John F. Callahan. Chevalier, writing on trinitarian relations in Augustine, asserted that Augustine read Basil's works against Eunomius and on the Holy Spirit, as well as his letters and his homilies, but offered no documentary evidence.[5] John F. Callahan discussed Basil of Caesarea and Gregory of Nyssa as sources of Augustine's theory of time; but, again, the conclusions he reached are impressionistic.[6]

Before I leave the impressionistic approach, however, I would like to indulge in an exercise parallel to it: pointing out two passages in which a parallel can be seen between Augustine and the Cappadocians, without claiming any direct dependence.

The first point is the so-called Cappadocian settlement. This phrase is scholarly shorthand for four Greek words, μία οὐσία, τρεῖς ὑποστάσεις (one essence, three hypostases), which are supposed to sum up the Cappadocian fathers' doctrine of the Trinity. But the phrase never occurs in precisely that form in their writings, nor is it found verbatim in other Greek writers of the time, although Didymus the Blind comes closest.[7] The Cappadocian settlement was in fact formulated by Augustine. He

[5]Jean Chevalier, *Saint Augustin et la pensée grecque: Les relations trinitaires,* Collectanea Friburgensia 33 (Fribourg: Librairie de l'Université, 1940). For criticism of Chevalier see Gerard J.M. Bartelink, "Basilius," *Augustinus-Lexikon* 1 (1994): 614–17.

[6]John F. Callahan, "Basil of Caesarea: A New Source for St. Augustine's Theory of Time," *Harvard Studies in Classical Philology* 63 (1958): 437–54; Callahan, "Gregory of Nyssa and the Psychological View of Time," *Proceedings of the XIIth International Congress of Philosophy,* vol. 11: *History of Ancient and Medieval Philosophy* (Florence: Sansoni, 1960), 59–66.

[7]See Joseph T. Lienhard, "*Ousia* and *Hypostasis*: The Cappadocian Settlement and the Theology of 'One Hypostasis,'" in *The Trinity: An Interdisciplinary Symposium on the Trinity,* ed. S.T. Davis, D. Kendall, and G. O'Collins (Oxford: Oxford University Press, 1999), 99–121.

writes it once in Greek, in book 5 of the *De Trinitate* (*On the Trinity*), in a famous sentence: "They [the Greeks] also say *hypostasis*; but I do not know what distinction they intend between *usia* and *hypostasis*, so that many of our people, who treat this matter in the Greek language, are accustomed to say μία οὐσία, τρεῖς ὑποστάσεις, which in Latin is 'one *essentia*, three *substantiae*.'"[8] Augustine goes on to say that, to the Latin ear, *essentia* and *substantia* mean the same thing. In book 7, Augustine repeats the formula of the Greeks twice more, this time in Latin.[9] Thus, the crisp formula known as the Cappadocian settlement comes, ironically enough, from Augustine.[10]

The second impressionistic passage is, perhaps, less well known. In his fifth theological oration, Gregory Nazianzen has a famous statement about his inability to define the procession of the Holy Spirit. "What then is procession?" he writes. "Do you tell me what is the unbegottenness of the Father, and I will explain to you the physiology of the generation of the Son and the procession of the Spirit, and we shall both of us be frenzy-stricken for prying into the mystery of God."[11] In other words, he is at a loss to define procession. There is a strangely similar passage in a late work of Augustine's, *Contra Maximinum* (*Against Maximinus*),[12] where Augus-

---

[8] *Trin.* 5.8.10 (CCSL 50.216–17): "Dicunt quidem et illi ὑπόστασιν, sed nescio quid uolunt interesse inter οὐσίαν et ὑπόστασιν ita ut plerique nostri qui haec graeco tractant eloquio dicere consuerint μία οὐσία, τρεῖς ὑποστάσεις, quod est latine, unam essentiam, tres substantias."

[9] Ibid., 7.4.7 (CCSL 50.255): "Itaque loquendi causa de ineffabilibus ut fari aliquo modo possemus quod effari nullo modo possumus dictum est a nostris graecis *una essentia, tres substantiae*, a latinis autem *una essentia* uel *substantia, tres personae* quia sicut iam diximus non aliter in sermone nostro, id est latino, essentia quam substantia solet intelligi." Ibid., 7.4.8 (CCSL 50.259): "Quod enim de personis secundum nostram, hoc de substantiis secundum graecorum consuetudinem ea quae diximus oportet intelligi. Sic enim dicunt illi *tres substantias, unam essentiam*, quemadmodum nos dicimus *tres personas, unam essentiam* uel *substantiam*."

[10] See also Jean Plagnieux, "Les formules trinitaires grecques vues par saint Augustin," in *Saint Grégoire de Nazianze théologien* (Paris: Éditions franciscaines, 1952), 405–6.

[11] Gregory Nazianzen, *Orations* 31.8, trans. in *Christology of the Later Fathers*, ed. Edward R. Hardy (Philadelphia: Westminster, 1954), 198.

[12] In 427 or 428 the Gothic Count Segisvult sent Maximinus to Hippo Regius "with a view to peace." There Maximinus first debated the priest Heraclius, but Heraclius became angry and summoned Augustine. Augustine debated with Maximinus for one day; the

tine, too, is trying to define procession. He writes several times in the *Contra Maximinum* of the procession of the Holy Spirit, stating explicitly the notorious *filioque*: "The Holy Spirit proceeds from [the Father] and from the Son,"[13] and "He proceeds from both of them."[14] Yet when it comes to defining procession, Augustine throws up his hands: "That much I know; but how to distinguish between generation and procession I do not know, I am not able, I cannot do it"[15]—"nescio, non valeo, non sufficio," he groans in desperation. All he can say is that begetting and procession are distinct, and that begetting is a narrower category than procession; whatever is born proceeds, but not everything that proceeds is born.[16] Procession is not birth; hence the Holy Spirit is not a son.[17]

Thus the impressionistic approach: the most intriguing, perhaps, but also the least trustworthy.

The Census Approach

Another interesting indicator, but not an absolute one, is how often Augustine mentions Basil of Caesarea and Gregory Nazianzen by name. This approach is made easier, and more certain, by the possibility of electronic searches.

The results are easy enough to tabulate. Augustine never mentions Gregory of Nyssa, but he does name Basil of Caesarea and Gregory Nazianzen, about a dozen and a half times each.

debate is recorded in the *Conlatio cum Maximino Arianorum episcopo* (*Discussion with Maximinus the Arian Bishop*). Because Maximinus spoke too long, Augustine had no time to answer him and later wrote a refutation of what Maximinus had said, in two books (*Contra Maximinum*).

[13] *Contra Max.* 2.5 (PL 42.761): "De illo et Filio . . . procedit Spiritus sanctus."

[14] Ibid., 2.14.1 (PL 42.770–71): "De utroque procedit."

[15] Ibid., 2.14.1 (PL 42.770): "Haec scio: distinguere autem inter illam generationem et hanc processionem nescio, non valeo, non sufficio." Roland J. Teske's translation is: "These things I know; I do not know, I cannot, I am unable to distinguish that generation from this procession." See *Arianism and Other Heresies,* trans. Roland J. Teske, in The Works of Saint Augustine, I/18 (Hyde Park, NY: New City, 1995), 280.

[16] *Contra Max.* 2.14.1.

[17] Ibid., 2.15.2.

Most of the places where Augustine mentions Basil and Gregory are in his two works against Julian of Eclanum, *Contra Julianum* (*Against Julian*, written in 422), and *Opus Imperfectum contra Julianum* (*Unfinished Work against Julian*, written in 428). Most of these instances occur in lists of Orthodox bishops. Augustine is trying to defend the thesis that his teaching, including his teaching on original sin, is the Church's teaching as well. Hence he several times provides a list of bishops, eastern and western, who agree with him.

In book 1 of *Contra Julianum*, Augustine gives the same list twice: Basil and Gregory, "two distinguished men," he writes—and here, Basil and Gregory form a distinct group—followed by a list of fourteen other bishops from the East[18]—those fourteen bishops who took part in the Synod of Diospolis in 415, which, ironically, found Pelagius Orthodox. But the fourteen bishops would have condemned Pelagius, Augustine assures his readers, if Pelagius himself had not condemned some theses from his own writings.

Apart from these two lists, there are fifteen other lists of authorities in the two works against Julian. Assuming that the Gregory mentioned in these lists is Gregory Nazianzen, as Augustine established in book 1 of the work *Contra Julianum*, Augustine names Basil eleven times and Gregory thirteen times. These occurrences of the two names are about as frequent as those of the most-named western fathers: Cyprian is named thirteen times, Ambrose and Hilary twelve times each. Another Greek, John of Constantinople—that is, John Chrysostom—is named eleven times. These six are the most frequent of the twelve names.[19] In all these instances, Augustine names Basil or Gregory without quoting their writings.

The conclusion must be simple: Augustine knew of Basil and Gregory Nazianzen, held them and their writings in high esteem, and invoked them—along with other fathers, Greek and Latin—as authorities who agreed with him against Julian of Eclanum and other opponents.

---

[18] *Contra Jul.* 1.5.19, 1.6.22.

[19] For the sake of completeness, the rest are these: Irenaeus (six times), Innocent, the presbyter Jerome, Olympius and Reticius (each four times), and Theodore (once).

The Textual Approach

The surest—if not the most fruitful—approach to the question of Augustine's relation to Basil and Gregory is a consideration of the passages from their writings that Augustine quotes while naming them as the authors. It must be said at the outset that the results are, in one sense, curiously disappointing. Augustine does not quote the great doctrinal works of Basil, such as *De Spiritu Sancto* (*On the Holy Spirit*) or *Contra Eunomium* (*Against Eunomius*), or Gregory's theological orations. But then, modern emphasis on these great dogmatic works is precisely a modern prejudice. It was, to a large extent, German history of dogma from the late nineteenth and early twentieth centuries that focused attention, rather narrowly, on a fairly limited selection of dogmatic writings of the great fathers and tried to see a pattern of continuity running through them: often a pattern of two opposing schools or traditions,[20] or a pattern of decline from biblical truth and a growing turn to philosophy or Catholicism.[21] But the fathers of the Church had their own interests and, if Basil's or Gregory's comments on the human condition are what interested Augustine most, then that fact needs to be recognized.

As his controversy with Julian of Eclanum began, Augustine appears to have devoted himself to a research project, trying to find passages in other Christian writers, western and eastern, that demonstrated his thesis: his teaching on the fall and its effects, and on baptism, were not his own invention but the common property of the Church. He began the project around 422, when he wrote his work *Contra Julianum*. In the case of Basil and Gregory, book 1 of Augustine's *Contra Julianum* marshals most of the quotations he will use;[22] another, extensive quotation from Gregory is found in book 2 of that work. Augustine comes back to these

---

[20]Théodore de Régnon's writings on the distinction between eastern and western trinitarian doctrine provide a classic example of misleading or mistaken categories, although de Régnon was not a Protestant.

[21]Often enough, these categories constitute a search for the Deformation that justifies the Reformation.

[22]For Gregory, see *Contra Jul.* 1.5.15; for Basil, ibid., 1.5.18 (and 1.5.16–17 for a quotation wrongly attributed to Basil).

quotations later in the same work, in the *Opus Imperfectum,* and in *De dono perseverantiae* (*On the Gift of Perseverance*).

BASIL OF CAESAREA

When the question of Augustine's quotations of Basil of Caesarea's words in his writings is asked, the results are thin. There are only two examples in Augustine's writings of verbatim citations of Basil's works with the author's name—and, in one of the two cases, Augustine gets the author's name wrong.

The one instance in which Augustine quotes Basil as Basil has its own intrinsic interest. In the course of an extended argument about original sin, Augustine quotes a passage from Basil's homily 1 on fasting. But, he writes to Julian of Eclanum, although a Latin translation exists,[23] he has translated the passage afresh from Greek, word for word, in order to get the exact point. The passage reads:

> But hear what pertains to the present matter, what that holy Basil says without any ambiguity about the sin of the first man, which also pertains to us. And even though I found the passage translated, still, for the sake of more careful fidelity to the truth, I preferred to translate it from the Greek word for word. In his sermon about fasting he says: "Fasting was established in paradise by law. For Adam received the first commandment: 'You shall not eat of the tree of the knowledge of good and evil' (Gen 2.17). But 'You shall not eat' is fasting, and the beginning of the establishment of law. If Eve had fasted from the tree, we would not need this fast. For 'healthy people do not need a doctor, but the sick do' (Mt 9.12). We have grown sick through sin; let us be healed through penance. Penance without fasting is empty. 'The accursed earth shall bring forth thorns and thistles' (Gen 3.17–18). You have been commanded to grieve, not to indulge yourself." And, a little later in the

[23]See *Clavis Patrum Graecorum* §2845. The translator may have been Rufinus, but the attribution is not certain. The translation has been printed only in part, in *Maxima Bibliotheca Patrum,* vol. 3 (Lyon, 1677), 404–5.

same sermon, he also says: "Because we have not fasted, we fell from paradise. Hence we should fast, so that we might return there."[24]

Augustine again quotes the last sentence just cited in the *Opus Imperfectum*.[25] Augustine's literal translation of Basil's Greek is quite accurate, with perhaps some slight adaptation to Latin style. This passage makes three interesting points, one linguistic and two theological. First, Augustine can in fact translate Basil's Greek. And then, he uses the passage to make two points that support his teachings: fasting existed in paradise before the fall, and penance reverses the effects of sin.

In another instance, Augustine cites Basil's homily 13 on baptism, but he attributes the text to John Chrysostom.[26] The passage, in which Basil is encouraging his hearers to come forward for baptism and not postpone it, reads:

[24]*Contra Jul.* 1.5.18 (PL 44.652): "Sed audi quod ad rem praesentem spectat, quid de peccato primi hominis ad nos etiam pertinente dicat iste sanctus sine ulla ambiguitate Basilius. Quod etsi reperi interpretatum, tamen propter diligentiorem veri fidem, verbum e verbo malui transferre de graeco. In sermone de ieiunio: 'Ieiunium,' inquit, 'in paradiso lege constitutum est.' Primum enim mandatum accepit Adam: 'A ligno sciendi bonum et malum non manducabitis' (Gen 2.17). 'Non manducabitis' autem, ieiunium est, et legis constitutionis initium. Si ieiunasset a ligno Eva, non isto indigeremus ieiunio. Non enim opus habent valentes medico, sed male habentes (Mt 9.12). Aegrotavimus per peccatum, sanemur per poenitentiam. Poenitentia vero sine ieiunio vacua est. 'Maledicta terra spinas et tribulos pariet' (Gen 3.17–18). Contristari ordinatus es, numquid deliciari? Et paulo post in eodem sermone, idem ipse: 'Quia non ieiunavimus,' inquit, 'decidimus de paradiso. Ieiunemus ergo, ut ad eum redeamus.'" Basil wrote in *Homilia 1 de ieiunio* 3 (PG 31.168A): νηστεία ἐν τῷ παραδείσῳ ἐνομοθετήθη. Τὴν πρώτην ἐντολὴν ἔλαβεν Ἀδαμ· Ἀπὸ τοῦ ξύλου τοῦ γινώσκειν καλὸν καὶ πονηρὸν οὐ φάγεσθε. Τὸ δὲ, οὐ φάγεσθε, νηστείας ἐστὶ καὶ ἐγκρατείας νομοθεσία. Εἰ ἐνήστευσεν ἀπὸ τοῦ ξύλου ἡ Εὖα, οὐκ ἂν ταύτης νῦν ἐδεόμεθα τῆς νηστείας. Οὐ γὰρ χρείαν ἔχουσιν οἱ ἰσχύροντες ἰατροῦ, ἀλλ' οἱ κακῶς ἔχοντες. Ἐκακώθημεν διὰ τῆς ἁμαρτίας· ἰαθῶμεν διὰ τῆς μετανοίας, μετάνοια δὲ χωρὶς νηστείας ἀργή. Ἐπικατάρατος ἡ γῆ ἡ κάνθας καὶ τριβόλους ἀνατελεῖ σοι. Στυγνάζειν προσετάχθης, μὴ γὰρ τρυφᾶν. The next sentence quoted is from *Homilia 1 de ieiunio* 4 (PG 31.168B): Ἐπειδὴ οὐκ ἐνηστεύσαμεν, ἐξεπέσομεν τοῦ παραδείσου· νηστεύσωμεν τοίνυν, ἵνα πρὸς αὐτὸν ἐπανέλθωμεν.

[25]*Opus imp.* 1.52 (CSEL 85.1.47): "Meus est Basilius, qui cum ageret de ieiunio, 'Quia non ieiunavimus,' inquit, 'decidimus de paradiso, ieiunemus ut ad eum redeamus.'" = Basil, *Homilia 1 de ieiunio* 4 (PG 31.168B).

[26]The *Clavis Patrum Graecorum,* §2857, lists this *Homilia exhortatoria ad sanctum baptisma* but does not mention any Latin translation.

Rightly does the same blessed John himself, like the martyr Cyprian, take the circumcision of the flesh that was commanded as a sign of baptism. He says: "And see how the Jew does not postpone circumcision because of a threat, because every soul that is not circumcised on the eighth day will be cut off from his people (Gen 17.14). But you," he continues, "put off—not circumcision done with the hand, which is accomplished in the removal of flesh from the body, but you hear the Lord saying: 'Amen, amen, I say to you, unless a man is born again of water and spirit, he will not enter into the kingdom of heaven'" (Jn 3.5).[27]

In one other case, Julian of Eclanum cites, as Basil's work, a book that is not his, and Augustine accepts the attribution. In the first book of *Contra Julianum*, in a passage that Augustine cites from Julian of Eclanum, Julian had written that he was quoting Basil,[28] whereas, in fact, he quoted ps-Basil, *Contra Manichaeos*.[29] Basil, Julian maintained, wrote about original sin, but he did not say that the will is corrupted. Augustine does not contest Julian's attribution; he was apparently unfamiliar with the work. The argument continues into the passage cited above,[30] where Augustine

[27]*Contra Jul.* 2.6.18 (PL 44.685–86): "Merito idem beatus Ioannes, etiam ipse, sicut et martyr Cyprianus [see Cyprian, *Ep.* 64] circumcisionem carnis in signo praeceptam commendat esse baptismatis. 'Et vide quomodo Judaeus,' inquit, 'circumcisionem non differt propter comminationem, quia omnis anima quaecumque non fuerit circumcisa die octavo, exterminabitur de populo suo' (Gen 17.14). 'Tu autem,' inquit, 'non manufactam circumcisionem differs, quae in exspoliatione carnis in corpore perficitur,' ipsum Dominum audiens dicentem, 'Amen, amen dico vobis, nisi quis renatus fuerit ex aqua et spiritu, non introibit in regnum coelorum' (Jn 3.5)." = Basil, *Homilia 13 exhortatoria ad sanctum baptisma* 2 (PG 31.428A): Ὁ Ἰουδαῖος τὴν περιτομὴν οὐχ ὑπερτίθεται διὰ τὴν ἀπειλήν, ὅτι πᾶσα ψυχή, ἥτις οὐ περιτμηθήσεται τῇ ἡμέρᾳ τῇ ὀγδόῃ ἐξολοθρευθήσεται ἐκ τοῦ λαοῦ αὐτῆς· σὺ δὲ τὴν ἀχειροποίητον περιτομὴν ἀναβάλλῃ ἐν τῇ ἀπεκδύσει τῆς σαρκὸς ἐν τῷ βαπτίσματι τελειουμένην, αὐτοῦ τοῦ Κυρίου ἀκούσας. Ἀμην, ἀμην λέγω ὑμῖν, ἐὰν μή τις γεννηθῇ δι' ὕδατὸ καὶ Πνεύματος, οὐ μὴ εἰσέλθῃ εἰς τὴν βασιλείαν τοῦ Θεοῦ.

[28]*Contra Jul.* 1.5.17 (PL 44.651).

[29]See Nello Cipriani, "L'autore dei testi pseudobasiliani riportati nel *C. Iul.* (1.16–17) e la polemica agostiniana de Giuliano d'Eclano," *Congresso internazionale su s. Agostino nel XVI centenario della conversione: Atti* (Rome: Istituto Patristico Augustinianum, 1987) 1.439–49. Cipriani identifies Serapion of Thmuis as the author of the work against the Manichees.

[30]*Contra Jul.* 1.5.18.

quotes Basil's homily on fasting, and he adds that Julian should read Basil more carefully.[31]

Gregory Nazianzen

Augustine quoted Gregory Nazianzen more often than he quoted Basil, perhaps because he had Rufinus' Latin translation of nine homilies available to him.[32] In the first book of his work *Contra Julianum*, Augustine has great—if generic—praise for Gregory Nazianzen. He writes of Gregory's great name and most celebrated reputation; Gregory's eloquence, he writes, has the merit of great grace, and his works have been translated into the Latin language.[33] Shortly thereafter Augustine again praises Gregory's authority, for this reason: what Gregory says is known to all as the Christian faith.[34]

Augustine cites passages from five of Gregory's homilies. In each instance, he is citing Rufinus' Latin translation of those homilies. The citations are virtually verbatim; they differ from the current critical edition only by a single word here or there.[35]

---

[31]One further instance, which perhaps belongs under the category of impressionistic, is this: according to Altaner (see n. 3), Augustine, *De Gen. ad lit.* 1.18.36, derives from the Latin version of Basil's *Hexaemeron* 2.6, translated by Eustathius. See the critical edition of Eustathius' translation of Basil, E. Amand de Mendieta and S.Y. Rudberg, eds., *Eustathius: ancienne version latine des neuf homélies sur l'Hexaéméron de Basile de Césarée* (Berlin: Akademie Verlag, 1958).

[32]Rufinus made his translation in 399/400.

[33]*Contra Jul.* 1.5.15 (PL 44.649): "Sed non tibi deerit magni nominis et fama celeberrima illustris episcopus etiam de partibus Orientis, cuius eloquia ingentis merito gratiae, etiam in linguam latinam translata usquequaque claruerunt. Sedeat ergo cum istis patribus etiam sanctus Gregorius, et cum eis tuae criminationis inanem patiatur invidiam: dum tamen cum eis contra novitiam pestem vestram, medicinalem proferat et ipse sententiam."

[34]*Contra Jul.* 1.5.16 (PL 44.650): "An tibi parva in uno Gregorio episcoporum orientalium videtur auctoritas? Est quidem tanta persona, ut neque ille hoc nisi ex fide christiana omnibus notissima diceret, nec illi eum tam clarum haberent atque venerandum, nisi haec ab illo dicta ex regula notissimae veritatis agnoscerent."

[35]The critical edition is *Tyranii Rufini orationum Gregorii Nazianzeni novem interpretatio*, ed. Augustus Engelbrecht, CSEL 46 (Vienna: Tempsky, 1910).

Apology for His Flight

Of the passages that Augustine cites from Gregory Nazianzen, the most extensive is one from near the end of Gregory's *Apologia de fuga* (*Apology for his Flight*), which he wrote on his return to Nazianzus after his father had ordained him a priest and he had fled back to Basil. The first time Augustine quotes the passage is in book 2 of his work *Contra Julianum*; this is also the most extensive quotation. In this passage Gregory writes at length of the struggle within a man, which can be won only by a long philosophical—he means ascetical—training. Gregory is saying that he is not yet ready to be a priest. Augustine used the passage to illustrate the effects of original sin.

> In his book, *In Self-Defense,* he says, "I do not as yet make mention of those blows by which we are attacked within ourselves by our own vices and passions and are day and night oppressed by the burning temptations of the body of this lowly state and of the body of death. In it the snares of visible things entice and arouse us at times in a hidden way and at other times quite openly, and the clay of these dregs to which we cling breathes forth the foul odor of its filth through its larger passages. The law of sin which is in our members resists the law of the spirit, as it strives to take captive the royal image which is within us so that all that has been poured into us by the gift of our original and divine creation becomes his booty. From there, though they govern themselves with a long and uncompromising pursuit of wisdom and gradually recover the nobility of their soul, hardly any summon back and turn back to God the nature of the light which is joined in them to this humble and dark clay. Or if they do this with God's help, they will call both of them back equally, if by long and constant meditation they become used to always looking upward and to pulling up by tighter reins the matter bound to them that always wrongly drags them downward and weighs them down."[36]

[36]Roland J. Teske, trans., *Answer to the Pelagians* 2, The Works of Saint Augustine, I/24 (Hyde Park, NY: New City, 1998), 341–42. *Contra Jul.* 2.3.7 (PL 44.677): "In libro quippe Apologetico: 'Illorum vero,' inquit, 'verberum nondum facio mentionem, quibus intra nos-

In the same paragraph, Augustine repeats phrases from Gregory to explain the point he is trying to make:

> When the blessed Gregory says, "We are attacked within ourselves by our own vices and passions, and, day and night, we are hard pressed by the burning goads of this body of humility and this body of death," he is speaking as one baptized, and he is speaking about the baptized. When he says, "by the law of sin that is in our members, fighting against the law of the spirit," he is speaking as one baptized, he is speaking about the baptized.[37]

Augustine repeats most of this quotation three more times: twice in the first book of the *Opus Imperfectum*[38] and once in the sixth book of the

metipsos propriis vitiis ac passionibus impugnamur, et die noctuque ignitis stimulis corporis humilitatis huius et corporis mortis urgemur, nunc latenter, nunc etiam palam provocantibus ubique et irritantibus rerum visibilium illecebris, luto hoc faecis cui inhaesimus, coeni sui fetorem venis capacioribus exhalante; sed et lege peccati, quae est in membris nostris, legi spiritus repugnante; dum imaginem regiam, quae intra nos est, captivam ducere studet: ut spoliis eius cedat, quidquid illud est quod in nos beneficio divinae ac primae illius conditionis influxit: unde vix aliquis fortasse longa se et districta regens philosophia, et paulatim nobilitatem animae suae recolens, naturam lucis quae in se est humili huic et tenebroso luto coniuncta, revocet ac reflectat ad Deum: vel si certe propitio Deo agat, utrumque pariter revocabit; si tamen longa et assidua meditatione insuescat sursum semper aspicere, et deorsum male trahentem ac degravantem materiam sibimet astrictam frenis arctioribus sublevare.'" = Gregory, *Apologetica*, oration 2.91 (PG 35.493); in Rufinus' translation, *Apologeticus*, oration 1.91 (CSEL 46.67–68).

[37]*Contra Jul.* 2.3.7 (PL 44.678): "Cum dicit beatus Gregorius, 'Intra nosmetipsos propriis vitiis ac passionibus impugnamur, et die noctuque ignitis stimulis corporis humilitatis huius et corporis mortis urgemur'; baptizatus loquitur, de baptizatis loquitur. Cum dicit, 'lege peccati quae est in membris nostris legi spiritus repugnante'; baptizatus loquitur, de baptizatis loquitur."

[38]*Opus imp.* 1.67 (CSEL 85.1.71–72): "Audi non Caelestium, sed Gregorium: 'Intra nosmet ipsos,' inquit, 'propriis vitiis ac passionibus impugnamur et die noctuque ignitis stimulis corporis humilitatis huius et corporis mortis urgemur nunc latenter, nunc etiam palam provocantibus ubique et irritantibus rerum visibilium illecebris luto hoc faecis, cui inhaesimus, caeni sui fetorem venis capacioribus exhalante, sed et lege peccati, quae est in membris nostris, legi spiritus repugnante.'"

Opus imp. 1.69 (CSEL 85.1.77): " 'Legem peccati, quae est in membris nostris, legi spiritus repugnare, dum imaginem regiam, quae intra nos est, captivam ducere studet, ut spoliis eius cedat, quidquid illud est quod in nos beneficio divinae ac primae illius condi-

same work.[39] In this passage, Gregory writes at length of the internal warfare within a man, vividly depicting the struggle with passions, night and day, secretly and openly. Augustine then insists to Julian that Gregory is speaking as one who is baptized, and about the baptized: that is, the struggle remains after baptism.

Oration on the Nativity of Christ

A shorter passage, one from Gregory's oration on the nativity of Christ, is another favorite of Augustine's. The key sentence of Gregory's, which Augustine cites five times, is, "Venerate the nativity, through which you are freed from the bonds of an earthly nativity." Augustine cites it in the first book of his work *Contra Julianum*,[40] where he continues and cites the following sentence also, the only time he does so; the sentence reads: "Honor Bethlehem, weak and small, through which the way back to paradise was laid open for you." He paraphrases the first sentence a few para-

---

tionis influxit. Unde vix aliquis,' inquit, 'fortasse longa se et districta regens philosophia et paulatim nobilitatem animae suae recolens naturam lucis, quae in se est humili huic et tenebroso luto coniuncta, revocet ac reflectat ad deum; vel si certe propitio deo agat, utrumque pariter revocabit, si tamen longa et assidua meditatione insuescat sursum semper aspicere, et deorsum male trahentem ac degravantem materiam sibimet astrictam frenis arctioribus sublevare.' Haec dicebat beatus Gregorius non inter principia emendationis suae, sed iam episcopus, volens exponere vel potius quae nota sunt admonere, in quali quantoque certamine cum vitiis interioribus, propter corpus quod aggravat animam, constituti sint sancti."

[39] *Opus imp.* 6.14 (PL 45.1528): "Iam vero beatus Gregorius hoc certamen, quod habemus in corpore mortis huius, sic ante oculos ponit, ut nullus sit huius agonis athleta, qui non se in verbis eius tanquam in speculo recognoscat. 'Intra nosmetipsos,' inquit, 'propriis vitiis et passionibus impugnamur, et die noctuque ignitis stimulis corporis humilitatis huius et corporis mortis urgemur: nunc latenter, nunc etiam palam provocantibus ubique et irritantibus rerum visibilium illecebris, luto hoc faecis cui inhaesimus coeni sui fetorem venis capacioribus exhalante; sed et lege peccati, quae est in membris nostris, legi spiritus repugnante, dum imaginem regiam quae intra nos est, captivam ducere studet; ut spoliis eius cedat, quidquid illud est, quod in nos beneficio divinae ac primae illius conditionis influxit.'"

[40] *Contra Jul.* 1.5.15 (PL 44.650): "Idem rursus: 'Venerare,' inquit, 'nativitatem, per quam terrenae nativitatis vinculis liberatus es. Honora Bethlehem pusillam et minimam, per quam tibi regressus ad paradisum patefactus est.'" = Gregory, *In Theophaneia, sive Natalitia Salvatoris,* oration 38.17 (PG 36.330–31); in Rufinus' translation, *De epiphaniis,* oration 2.17 (CSEL 46.105).

graphs later.[41] He cites the same sentence three times more in the first book of the *Opus Imperfectum*.[42]

In the same first book of his work against Julian, Augustine also quotes another passage from Gregory's oration on the nativity:

> "Just as in Adam," he says, "all of us died, so too in Christ all of us will be brought to life" (1 Cor 15.22). Hence let us be born with Christ, and let us be crucified with Christ, and let us be buried with him in death, so that we may also rise with him unto life. For it is necessary for us to suffer this useful and necessary change: that, just as we lapsed from good things to sad ones, so too we are restored from sad things to better. For where sin abounded, grace abounded all the more (Rom 5.20), so that those whom the taste of the forbidden tree condemned, the cross of Christ might justify with a more abundant grace."[43]

[41] *Contra Jul.* 1.7.32 (PL 44.663): "Sanctus Gregorius dicit, melius fuisse non excidere a ligno vitae gustu amarissimo peccati, sed emendari nos debere post lapsum. Dicit, nos ex bonis ad tristia devolutos, et vult a tristibus ad meliora reparari; ut quos gustus ligni vetiti condemnavit, Christi crux gratia largiore iustificet. Dicit, venerandam esse nativitatem, per quam terrenae nativitatis vinculis liberamur. Dicit, regeneratione ex aqua et spiritu purgari maculas primae nativitatis, per quas in iniquitatibus concipimur."

[42] *Opus imp.* 1.52 (CSEL 85.1.47): "Meus est Gregorius, qui cum de baptismo loqueretur, 'Venerare,' inquit, 'nativitatem, per quam terrenae nativitatis vinculis liberatus es.'"

Opus imp. 1.53 (CSEL 85.1.50): "Hoc igitur de ista gratia dicite, ut offensione Christianorum de qua conquerimini, careatis, quod dixit catholicus doctus doctorque Gregorius: 'Venerare nativitatem, per quam terrenae nativitatis vinculis liberatus es.' Nullo itaque modo ad istam gratiam pertinere parvulos confitemini, quamdiu negatis eos nativitate coelesti a terrenae nativitatis vinculis liberari."

Opus imp. 1.70 (CSEL 85.1.79): "Itane vero Gregorius, quando dicebat, 'Venerare nativitatem, per quam terrenae nativitatis vinculis liberatus es.'"

[43] *Contra Jul.* 1.5.15 (PL 44.649–50): "'Sicut in Adam omnes,' inquit, 'mortui sumus, ita et in Christo omnes vivificemur. Cum Christo ergo nascamur, et cum Christo crucifigamur, et consepeliamur ei in mortem, ut cum ipso etiam resurgamus ad vitam. Necesse est enim nos perpeti utilem hanc et necessariam vicissitudinem: ut sicut ex bonis ad tristia devoluti sumus, ita ex tristibus ad meliora reparemur. Ubi enim abundavit peccatum, superabundavit gratia: ut quos gustus ligni vetiti condemnavit, Christi crux gratia largiore justificet.'" = Gregory, *In Theophaneia, sive natalitia Salvatoris,* oration 38.4 (PG 36.315); in Rufinus' translation, *De epiphaniis,* oration 2.4 (CSEL 46.89–90).

Oration on Pentecost

A third passage, from Gregory's *De Pentecoste et de Spiritu Sancto* (*Oration on Pentecost*), is cited by Augustine in his work *De dono persever-antiae* (*On the Gift of Perseverance*), written in 428/29. The passage deals with trinitarian theology. It reads:

> But to these two,[44] who should suffice, we also add holy Gregory, a third, who attests that, both to believe in God, and to confess what we believe, is a gift of God, when he says: "Confess a Trinity of one Divinity, I ask you. If you wish it otherwise, say a Trinity of one nature; and God will be invoked, so that a voice might be given to you by the Holy Spirit . . . for he will give it, I am certain. He who gave what is first, will give what is second; he who gave the ability to believe, will also give the ability to confess [the faith]."[45]

The point that Augustine makes with the quotation is to reinforce his argument about predestination: both interior belief and external confession are the work of God's grace, not of human effort.

Augustine quotes one further passage from oration 41 on Pentecost in the first book of his *Opus Imperfectum*. The passage reads: "Through him the stains of the first birth are purged, through which we are conceived in iniquity, and our mothers bore us in sin."[46]

---

[44] Augustine has just quoted Cyprian and Ambrose.

[45] *De dono pers.* 19.49 (PL 45.1024–25): "Sed his duobus, qui sufficere debuerunt, sanctum Gregorium addamus et tertium, qui et credere in Deum, et quod credimus confiteri, Dei donum esse testatur, dicens: 'Unius deitatis, quaeso vos, confitemini Trinitatem: si vero aliter vultis, dicite unius esse naturae; et Deus vocem dari vobis a sancto Spiritu deprecabitur': id est, rogabitur Deus, ut permittat vobis dari vocem, qua quod creditis, confiteri possitis. 'Dabit enim, certus sum; qui dedit quod primum est, dabit et quod secundum est; qui dedit credere, dabit et confiteri.'" = Gregory, *In Pentecosten*, oration 41.8 (PG 36.440); in Rufinus' translation, *De Pentecoste et de Spiritu Sancto*, oration 4.8 (CSEL 46.150).

[46] *Opus imp.* 1.70 (CSEL 85.1.79): "Itane vero Gregorius, quando dicebat . . . de Christo loquens vel de spiritu sancto 'Per hunc primae nativitatis maculae purgantur, per quas in iniquitatibus concipimur, et in delictis genuerunt nos matres nostrae.'" = Gregory, *In Pentecosten*, oration 41.14; in Rufinus' translation *De Pentecoste et de Spiritu Sancto*, oration 4.14 (CSEL 46.158).

On the Devastation from Hail

Augustine also quotes another homily of Gregory's, *De grandinis vastatione* (*On the Devastation from Hail*), in the first book of his work against Julian. The passage reads:

> "Let the image," he says, "of God wash away the stain of bodily drowning, and let it lift up the flesh joined to itself on the wings of the word of God. And, although it would have been better not even to have needed a cleansing of this sort, but to have remained in that first dignity, to which we also hurry back after our present correction, and it would have been better not to fall from the tree of life by the most bitter taste of sin; still, in the second state, it is fitting to be improved and corrected after the fall rather than to remain in our sins."[47]

To the Citizens of Nazianzus Stricken with Grave Fear

Once, in book 2 of *Contra Julianum*, Augustine quotes another oration of Gregory's: "For when the soul is in labors and trials, when it is hostilely attacked by the flesh, then it takes refuge in God and knows whence it should beg for help."[48]

The pattern already seen continues: Augustine finds passages in Gregory that support his teaching on the effects of original sin and show that it is the teaching of all the Orthodox fathers. In summary, Augustine uses Basil to show that the sin of Adam and Eve affected all their descendants,

---

[47]*Contra Jul.* 1.5.15 (PL 44.649) "'Imago,' inquit, 'Dei labem corporeae inundationis expurget, et conjunctam sibi carnem verbi Dei sublevet pennis. Et quamvis melius fuisset, ne egere quidem hujuscemodi expurgatione, sed in illa prima dignitate permansisse, ad quam et refestinamus, post praesentem emendationem, et melius fuisset non excidere a ligno vitae gustu amarissimo peccati; tamen in secundo loco expedit emendari et corrigi post lapsum, quam in nequitiis permanere.'" = Gregory, *De grandinis vastatione*, oration 16.15 (PG 35.953–56); in Rufinus' translation, *De grandinis vastatione*, oration 8.15 (CSEL 46.253–54).

[48]*Contra Jul.* 2.3.7 (PL 44.677): "His et sanctus Gregorius attestatur dicens: 'Anima namque cum in laboribus fuerit et in angustiis, cum hostiliter urgetur a carne, tunc ad Deum refugit, et cognoscit unde debeat auxilium poscere.'" = Gregory, *Ad cives Nazianzenos gravi timore perculsos*, oration 17.5.2 (PG 35.971–72); in Rufinus' translation, oration 5.1 (CSEL 46.199).

and that the effect of baptism, even in infants, is the forgiveness of sin. Augustine uses Gregory Nazianzen more extensively, to refute the charge that he, Augustine, had returned to Manicheism: rather, in baptism, sins are forgiven but concupiscence, the effect of sin, remains. Further, Gregory—Augustine contends—wrote clearly of the fall, and of the subsequent need for conversion, new birth in Christ, and baptism.

Conclusion

We have seen three approaches to Augustine and the Greek fathers. The impressionistic approach is the most wide ranging, but it cannot offer clear historical certitude. The census approach is textually certain, but it yields little useful knowledge. The textual approach is the most useful starting point, even though the results are disappointing.[49]

What are the results?

Augustine knew Basil and Gregory mostly through Latin translations. This is clearest from his citations of five of the nine homilies of Gregory's that Rufinus translated in 399/400. He did what many scholars have done before and after: he read through the nine homilies and marked passages that he found useful, and that reinforced his own thought—thus his use of Gregory on the effects of original sin, and on predestination. When Augustine wanted to make a precise point, however, he could translate a sentence or two from Greek.

The works Augustine quoted are not Basil's or Gregory's central works, at least according to modern perceptions. From Basil he quoted a homily on fasting, and one on baptism, which he attributed to John Chrysostom. From Gregory Nazianzen, Augustine cited an extended passage from Gregory's *Apologia de fuga*, which he used four times. From another work, Gregory's *Oration on the Nativity of Christ*, Augustine cited a short sentence five times; he used it as an aphorism. He also cited three other

---

[49]A fourth possible approach, that is, a study of the indirect influence of Greek fathers on Augustine through Latin writers, such as Hilary and Ambrose, has not been considered here.

homilies of Gregory Nazianzen's. In each case, the passages quoted are intended to show that aspects of Augustine's doctrine are the teachings of the whole Church, East and West.

Preparing this paper brought home to me again another fact: many of us assume that we know who the fathers of the Church are, and in a good sense we do. We have read Quasten, and Altaner-Stuiber, and understand the big picture. We know which works are really important—generally, doctrinal or dogmatic works—and which can easily be passed over—often enough, exegetical and homiletic works and ascetical treatises. However, Augustine and other fathers did not see things that way. Augustine quoted Basil and Gregory, and other Greek fathers, not because they were Greek but because they taught the catholic truth. Augustine, especially in the late works against Julian, made frequent use of the argument from authority. "Basil is mine," he can boast to Julian. Augustine quoted Basil and Gregory to reinforce his teaching on sin and grace, because that is what he was debating with Julian of Eclanum; in other circumstances, he might well have quoted other passages. Perhaps Augustine's way of reading other fathers on sin and grace might invite all of us to a broader consideration of these teachings.

In any case, just as Augustine wanted Jerome to translate the Septuagint and not the Hebrew text of the Old Testament, so that East and West would read the same Bible, so he invites us to see what East and West have in common, which is surely far more than what divides them. I, for one, am grateful for that invitation.

Making a Human Will Divine: Augustine and Maximus on Christ and Human Salvation

BRIAN E. DALEY, SJ

How much St Augustine may have influenced the theology of St Maximus the Confessor is an open question; the short answer is that we have virtually no direct evidence that there was any influence at all. In many ways, they lived in different worlds. Augustine of Hippo (354–430) was a classic by-product of late Roman Africa: superbly educated in Cicero and Virgil; a professional rhetorician, a public figure—first as a well-connected professor on the rise, later as an endlessly busy bishop, sought after by people from all over the West to help them deal with the burning issues of a Latin Christian empire in a moment of late bloom and imminent decay. Maximus (c. 580–662) came from the other, Greek- and Syriac-speaking portion of the Roman world, some two and a half centuries later; his education, too, seems to have been outstanding for its time, but was more strictly philosophical—scholastic, we might say, in the style of the sixth century's philosophical "schools" at Athens and Alexandria, rather than literary. (Anyone who has tried to read Maximus' works in Greek knows he was *not* an accomplished rhetorician!) His Greek lives say he served in the Byzantine imperial administration as a young man, and rose to be first secretary to the Emperor Heraclius at his accession in 610; but they tell us that Maximus soon left the court to become a monk, and spent the rest of his life— despite a wide range of connections of his own—anchored in the ascetical solitude of a monastic community.[1] In the face of the siege of Constantinople by the Persians and Avars in the spring of 626, Maximus and many of his Greek monastic confreres migrated to safety in the West; although the steps of his journey are unclear, he seems to have arrived in North Africa—since 534 a part of the (now Greek-speaking) Roman empire once again, after a century of domination by the Vandals—and to have eventually settled in a Greek monastery near Carthage.[2] From there, apparently while remaining a simple unordained monk, Maximus became increasingly involved in the politico-religious debates then polarizing the eastern part of the old Roman empire, writing from a base in Carthage, Sicily, or Italy until his return to Constantinople for controversy, trial, and eventual punishment in 652 or 653. Maximus, like Augustine—or like Bernard or Thomas Merton in later centuries—was clearly a "monk of the world": well read and well informed, an international figure. But we do not know much about his reading, or even how good his Latin was, and we have no sure evidence that he looked for local theological inspiration in his land of exile.

Nonetheless, given the breadth of Maximus' knowledge, and the theological themes that engaged him, some fairly profound contact with the thought of Augustine does seem an inviting hypothesis. In a brief essay published in 1982, George Berthold pointed broadly to a number of theo-

---

[1] For details of Maximus' life, see Pauline Allen and Bronwen Neil, eds., CCSG 39 (Turnhout: Brepols, 1999); Greek text and translation in *Maximus the Confessor and his Companions: Documents from Exile* (Oxford: Oxford University Press, 2002). Other biographical material has been edited by S.L. Epifanovich in *Materialy k izučeniju žizni i tvorenij prep. Maksima Ispovědnika* (*Materials to Help the Study of the Life and Works of Maximus Confessor*) (Kiev, 1917), 1–25; in English, *The Life of our Holy Father Maximus the Confessor,* trans. C. Birchall (Boston: Holy Transfiguration Monastery, 1982). See also Polycarp Sherwood, *An Annotated Date-List of the Works of Maximus the Confessor,* Studia Anselmiana, vol. 30 (Rome: Orbis Catholicus, 1952), 1–22. Most other modern biographical treatments rely on Sherwood, but see also the Syriac *Vita* referred to in n. 2.

[2] According to the hostile but carefully detailed Syriac life of Maximus by George of Resh'aina, probably a Syrian or Palestinian contemporary and member of Sophronius' clergy, Maximus and his disciple Anastasius first stayed at a monastery of Syrian monks opposed to the regnant neo-Chalcedonian theology, at Hippo Diarrhytus, a port some fifty miles northwest of Carthage; see Sebastian Brock, "An Early Syriac Life of Maximus the Confessor," *Analecta Bollandiana* 91 (1975): 317, 326, and below, 120.

logical subjects for which Maximus showed sympathy to what one might think of as typically Augustinian positions—a general sense of the importance of the Roman Church as an unbroken witness to orthodoxy; a sense of the importance of time and history as the locus of human growth, by God's grace, toward freedom and rest; an appreciation of the sin inherited through generation by all the descendants of Adam; even a willingness to explain the western, Augustinian idea of the *filioque* in positive terms[3]— and asks simply, "Would it not have been natural for this thoroughly Eastern doctor in his 23–25 years' residence in the West to have read and studied the greatest of the Latin doctors?"[4] For those who admire the achievement and the influence of both thinkers, the strong temptation is to answer yes, but corroborating argument must reach deeply into the thought of both of them to explain why.

The world of the seventh-century monk Maximus was still Roman, in name and even—for much of his life—in geographical location; but the ideas that engaged him, and the culture in which they found their relevance, were clearly Greek. For the century that followed the Council of Chalcedon (451), the empire's officially endorsed version of the Christian confession was summed up in that council's comprehensive profession of faith, incorporating the earlier, essentially trinitarian creeds of Nicaea and Constantinople I, and adding—as a kind of hermeneutical lens for interpreting the "faith of Nicaea"—the famous, carefully crafted affirmation that the one Jesus Christ "must be acknowledged in two natures, without

---

[3]In *Opusculum* 10 (PG 91.133–38), excerpted by his disciple Anastasius from a letter of Maximus to Marinus, presbyter of Cyprus, Maximus attempts to give a favorable interpretation of two points in the current pope's "synodical letter" that had been criticized by "those in the imperial city" (Constantinople): that the Holy Spirit proceeds also from the Son, and that the Word was made flesh "as man apart from the ancestral sin" (PG 91.133D9–136A7). Maximus says the second charge, Jesus' freedom from original sin, needs no refutation, presumably because its orthodoxy is obvious, and that the first point, on the origin of the Spirit, is supported by *testimonia* from the Latin fathers and from Cyril of Alexandria's *Commentary on John*. He goes on to argue that everyone can only explain such difficult matters of faith within the terms of their own tradition (ibid., 136B12–C9). It is not clear, however, which pope or which synodical letter Maximus is referring to here. It seems not to be any of the documents collected by the Lateran Synod of 649.

[4]George C. Berthold, "Did Maximus the Confessor Know Augustine?" *Studia Patristica* 17 (1982): 14–17.

confusion or change, without division or separation—the distinction between the natures having never been abolished by their union, but rather the character proper to each of the two natures being preserved, as they came together in one person and one hypostasis . . ."[5] But despite the fact that the Chalcedonian formula of faith was constructed to represent terms and conceptions from the two main theological traditions then disputing the identity and ontological structure of Jesus—the followers of Cyril of Alexandria and those who admired Theodore of Mopsuestia and his intellectual heirs—it was, as a vehicle of compromise, more or less dead on arrival. The large, earnestly devout mass of monks and ordinary faithful in Egypt, Palestine, Syria, and Mesopotamia saw in its balanced turns of phrase simply learned equivocation, a way of avoiding the full confession that Christ our Savior is God in flesh, which had been engineered by Pope Leo and the secular-minded West.[6] Within ten years, competing hierarchies had begun to take root in Egypt and Syria; the unity of Greek Christendom had been broken, and with it the social and political unity of the whole eastern empire.

Throughout the rest of the fifth and sixth centuries, emperors tried various approaches to build a new basis for unity in faith among the traditionally Christian peoples of the East: Zeno's *Henotikon* (474), which implicitly passed over the Chalcedonian formula as a norm of faith; Anastasius I's promotion of anti-Chalcedonian theologians like Severus of Antioch to major episcopal sees; Justinian's more patient and sophisticated attempt—through his own writing as well as through political appointments and legislation—to develop new terminology for the mystery of Christ that would preserve the Chalcedonian formula as the foundation of imperial religious policy, but interpret it in a way that emphasized the Cyrillian side of its ancestry, and made clear that the "one

    [5]See Norman P. Tanner, ed., *Decrees of the Ecumenical Councils,* vol. 1 (London/Washington: Sheed and Ward/Georgetown, 1990), 86.
    [6]For a description of the popular reaction to the Chalcedonian formula in the eastern empire, see especially W.H.C. Frend, *The Rise of the Monophysite Movement* (Cambridge: Cambridge University Press, 1972), especially 50–142. For a description of the period after Chalcedon that is more focused on theological debates, see Patrick T.R. Gray, *The Defense of Chalcedon in the East, 451–553* (Leiden: Brill, 1979).

hypostasis" of Christ who subsists simultaneously "in two natures"—the personal or grammatical subject of all his acts—is indeed God the Logos, the second person of the Trinity. This new, clarifying reading of Chalcedon, which twentieth-century scholars have come to call "neo-Chalcedonianism," gradually became the dominant model for christological thinking among those groups and social classes who remained in cultural and political contact with the capital, and was officially received as church doctrine—as yet another lens for interpreting "the faith of Nicaea," a codicil to Chalcedon—at the Second Council of Constantinople in 553. But as a means of reunifying the empire in a single faith, it also failed; those faithful and bishops who rejected Chalcedon found even this rereading of its formula untrustworthy and refused to budge from their nonconformity.

When the magnetic young general Heraclius, son of the Byzantine exarch of Africa, moved east with his fleet in 610 to oust the ineffective Emperor Phokas, himself both a usurper and a Chalcedonian sympathizer, the empire was ready for new, concerted efforts at reunification.[7] Emperor from 610 until 641, Heraclius devoted most of his energies in the first two decades of his rule to military campaigns, and managed to push back the Persians to their borders, and for a few years even to hold the forces of the expanding Arab Muslims to a standoff. But if the eastern empire was to stay together more or less within its old Roman borders, from Mesopotamia west to Egypt, Libya, and North Africa and from the Arabian peninsula north to the Caucasus, it was essential that its peoples reclaim the dominant religious unity that had been lost at Chalcedon. With the help of his ecclesiastical advisors in Constantinople, notably the Patriarch Sergius and his theological allies, Heraclius was ready, by the late 620s, to make one more try to achieve what emperors since Zeno had failed to accomplish, by finding a formula for speaking of Christ on

[7]The most recent and authoritative biography of Heraclius in English is Walter E. Kaegi, *Heraclius, Emperor of Byzantium* (Cambridge: Cambridge University Press, 2003). On seventh-century Byzantine history, see also A.M. Stratos, *Byzantium in the Seventh Century*, vols. 2–4, trans. Harry. T. Hionides (Amsterdam: A.M. Hakkert, 1972, 1975, 1978); J.F. Haldon, *Byzantium in the Seventh Century* (Cambridge: Cambridge University Press, 1990); Averil Cameron, *Changing Cultures in Early Byzantium* (Aldershot: Variorum, 1996), esp. articles IV, V, VII, VIII, X.

which all could agree, and by suppressing any analysis or debate that probed too deeply beneath the surface of the new terminology. The result was "monenergism," the theory that the single divine activity or energy of God the Word, even in the incarnation, was the origin of all Jesus' thoughts and acts, human or divine. In a somewhat later form, this morphed into "monotheletism," which expressed the same dynamic unity in terms of the single divine will of God the Word, which formed all his actions, as God and as human, into expressions of divine love. Understood in this way, even talk of the two distinct and functioning natures Chalcedon ascribed to Jesus might seem unthreatening to a traditional eastern piety.[8]

This was the ecclesiastical and political setting in which the monk Maximus lived and worked. According to his Greek biography, he had been born about 580 of aristocratic parents in the capital, and lived there until, around 613, he became a monk at Chrysopolis, across the Bosporus from Constantinople—the monastery where his opponent, the future patriarch Pyrrhus, would later be abbot. His more recently published Syriac life, written in a hostile vein by a theological critic named George of Resh'aina, tells us a different story: that Maximus was a Palestinian originally named Moschion, the illegitimate son of a Samaritan father and a Persian slave girl; and that after his parents' deaths, Moschion was brought up from the age of ten in the Old Lavra (or Souka), one of the fourth-century monastic foundations of Abba Chariton in the Judean desert south of Bethlehem, where he received the name Maximus. George tells us that Maximus' spiritual father and teacher was an Origenist monk named Pantoleon; in the language of the lives of the Palestinian monks from the sixth and seventh century, "Origenism" seems to have been a code word for the theological style of strict Chalcedonians, who insisted on discussing the mystery of Christ with relentless philosophical subtlety.[9] Maximus

[8]For a useful summary of the present state of scholarship on the monenergist and monothelite controversy, with an exhaustive catalogue of documentary sources, a prosopography, and date-lists, see Friedhelm Winkelmann, *Der monenergetisch-monotheletische Streit,* Berliner Byzantinische Studien, vol. 6 (Berlin: Peter Lang, 2001).

[9]See my articles, "The Origenism of Leontius of Byzantium," *Journal of Theological Studies* 27 (1976): 333–69; and "What Did 'Origenism' Mean in the Sixth Century?" *Origeni-*

learned to do this, but he also absorbed the ascetical tradition of the fourth-century Origenist Evagrius Ponticus, and the speculative style of spirituality identified with the Origenists, which appears especially in his earlier ascetic "Centuries."[10] Whatever his origins may have been, Maximus seems to have had lifelong sympathies with Chalcedonian christology and the language of the Aristotelian schools, and to have reacted allergically to the new, monenergist line. He also seems to have spent time as a monk in the environs of the capital, first at Chrysopolis and later at Cyzicus, further west on the Sea of Marmara. During those early years he was joined by a disciple, Anastasius, who remained his companion and amanuensis until the end of his life, and who later became his biographer.

The details of Maximus' activities in the next two decades are complex and unclear. His ancient Syriac biographer suggests that he remained based in the East until the death of Heraclius in 641, and that he lived for several of those years as a hermit in Palestine, until the Muslim invaders conquered the land in 638. Modern scholars like Devreesse and Sherwood, drawing on the Greek lives and on Maximus' correspondence, agree in placing his emigration to North Africa considerably earlier, at the time of the Persian and Avar invasion of 626, when many of the monasteries near the capital seem to have been emptied. From his letters, we know that Maximus originally hoped to return to his monastery at Cyzicus,[11] and that he was at least briefly in Crete, where he held a disputation with some anti-Chalcedonian bishops;[12] his correspondence with the deacon Marinus and other ecclesiastical figures in Cyprus suggests he may have stopped off on that island as well. He also may have spent some time in

ana Sexta: Proceedings of Sixth International Conference on Origen Studies (Chantilly, France; August 30–September 3, 1993) (Leuven: Peeters, 1995), 627–38.

[10]See his *Four Centuries on Love,* ed. A. Ceresa-Gastaldo (Rome: Verba Seniorum 3, 1993), and especially his two *Gnostic Centuries* (PG 90.1084–1173); as well as his brief commentary on the Lord's Prayer, all translated with comments by George Berthold, *Maximus Confessor: Selected Writings* (New York: Paulist, 1985), 33–180. For a detailed analysis of Origenistic themes and parallels in the *Gnostic Centuries,* see Hans Urs von Balthasar, *Kosmische Liturgie,* 2d ed. (Einsiedeln: Johannes-Verlag, 1961), 482–643.

[11]See his letters to Bishop John, the abbot of Cyzicus: *Ep.* 8 (PG 90.440–46) and 30–31 (PG 90.623–26); Sherwood, 6.

[12]Maximus, *Opusculum* 3 (PG 91.49C); see Sherwood, 5.

Alexandria, since he seems to have had personal contacts in the Egyptian metropolis.[13] Whatever his route, Maximus' letters suggest he was already in the neighborhood of Carthage, living in a Greek monastic community, by the late 620s,[14] and to have lived there—perhaps with some journeys back east in the 630s—until 645, the year of his famous *Dialogue with Pyrrhus*: studying, reflecting deeply on the mystery of Christ, and corresponding energetically with Greek-speaking church leaders throughout the Mediterranean, to encourage them to resist the new imperial attempts to reconceive the christology of Chalcedon.

In the context of seventh-century imperial policy, Maximus was a rebel and a troublemaker. Although he had assimilated the "neo-Chalcedonian" perspective of the Council of 553 on the key issue of the hypostatic identity of Jesus as trinitarian Logos, his style of argument and theological sympathies lay closer to the more balanced, clearly two-nature approach of Leontius of Byzantium, a "strict Chalcedonian" writer from the sixth-century controversies whom he never mentions by name but whose thought he had clearly assimilated.[15] Yet for Maximus and his friends—leaders like the aged Patriarch Sophronius of Jerusalem and his suffragan bishop Stephen of Dor—the new attempts to reread Chalcedon in terms of a single divine operation and a single divine will in Christ

---

[13]In *Ep.* 14 (PG 90.533–44), for instance, to the general Peter, who has just moved from Proconsular Africa to Alexandria, Maximus recommends making contact with the deacon Cosmas. Sophronius, the future patriarch of Jerusalem and an early opponent of the monenergist christology sponsored by the emperor, had been head of the Greek monastery in Carthage himself in the 620s, and spent some time in Alexandria before returning to Palestine. Maximus may have accompanied or visited him at this point. The Syriac life, however, tells us that Maximus had known Sophronius as a young monk in Palestine, and that he later urged Sophronius—perhaps shortly after his becoming Patriarch of Jerusalem—to call for a synod of bishops in Cyprus, contesting the new christological movement, a step that led to the *Psephos* of Sergius of Constantinople prohibiting further discussion of the energies and wills of Christ: see cc. 7–15, Brock 315–17.

[14]See Sherwood 5–7; also Robert Devreesse, "La fin inédite d'une lettre de s. Maxime," *Revue des Sciences Religieuses* 17 (1937): 25–35.

[15]Maximus' letter 15 (PG 90.543–76), a short treatise on christology addressed to the Alexandrian deacon Cosmas, which Sherwood plausibly dates to the years 634–640, is really a digest of Leontius' christological terminology and arguments, directed against the opponents of Chalcedon who drew their arguments from Leontius' nemesis Severus of Antioch.

were simply a revival of the christology of Apollinarius in slightly altered terms.[16] Whatever its possibilities for promoting political rapprochement, it was clearly a regressive step in terms of theology.

After the death of Emperor Heraclius in February 641, followed within a few months by the death of his sickly son and successor Constantine III, rule of the empire passed into the hands of an eleven-year-old minor, Heraclius' grandson Constans II, and was administered for several years by regents. Pyrrhus, Maximus' former confrere, who had been Patriarch of Constantinople since Sergius' death in December 638, had backed the wrong successor in Heraclius' younger son Heracleonas; shortly after Constans' accession, Pyrrhus was banished from the capital on charges of corruption, without being canonically deposed, and was succeeded as patriarch by Paul. Pyrrhus made his way west to Carthage as well, and there joined the growing, increasingly discontented group of Greek émigrés who longed for a new imperial order. It was there, in July 645, that Maximus and Pyrrhus publicly debated the issue of the wills and energies of Christ, in the presence of Gregory, imperial exarch of Africa, who was soon to lead an abortive rebellion of his own. The transcript of their highly technical dialogue, which has all the marks of being authentic, shows Pyrrhus as well informed in all the contemporary arguments for seeing the two natures of Christ as animated by a single divine energy and ruled by a single divine will; yet Maximus, drawing on his stunning abilities of analysis and argument, as well as a peerless mastery of earlier patristic tradition, clearly wins the day. Pyrrhus ends by conceding the inadequacy of the imperial position promoted by his predecessor and himself and memorialized over Heraclus' name in the imperial *Ekthesis* of 638.

---

[16]See, for instance, the comments attributed to Pope Martin on excerpts from the "monenergist" writings of Theodore of Pharan, at the third session of the Lateran Synod of 649: *Acta Conciliorum Oecumenicorum*, 2d series, vol. 1, ed. Rudolf Riedinger (Berlin: De Gruyter, 1984), 118–33. For Maximus' awareness that the origins of monenergism lay in Apollinarius' understanding of Christ, see Demetrios Bathrellos, *The Byzantine Christ: Person, Nature, and Will in the Christology of St. Maximus the Confessor* (Oxford: Oxford University Press, 2004), 128, 144–45. On the life and theology of Sophronius, see Christoph von Schönborn, *Sophrone de Jérusalem: Vie monastique et confession dogmatique*, Theologie Historique, vol. 20 (Paris: Beauchesne, 1972).

The long-standing imperial policy of seeking a "soft" reading of the two-natures christology of Chalcedon, in the interests of eastern Christian reunion, seemed to be fatally shaken. Maximus, now the intellectual leader of the opposition, apparently realized that the Latin Church, which had long resisted any modifications to the christology of Leo and Chalcedon, could play a major supporting role in his agenda, even though the current debate over energies and wills had originally found little resonance, positive or negative, in the West. What Maximus' role was in stirring up western opposition to the imperial christology is not entirely clear. The bishops of the African provinces of Numidia, Mauretania, and Proconsular Africa seem to have taken up the subject in synods during the months that followed Maximus' disputation; letters from the metropolitan bishops of those provinces to the pope, the emperor, and the new patriarch of Constantinople, as well as a letter of Victor, the metropolitan of Carthage, all confirming the necessity of affirming the distinctness of human and divine energies and wills in the incarnate Word, form part of the dossier of documents received in Rome by the Lateran Synod in 649. At some time before that synod, possibly as early as 646, both Maximus and Pyrrhus seem to have gone to Rome themselves: Pyrrhus to assert his Chalcedonian credentials in the hope of winning the support of the Greek-speaking Pope Theodore, Maximus to press the Roman authorities to lend their weight to his own anti-monothelite campaign.

In a series of articles connected with the *acta* of the Lateran Synod,[17] Rudolf Riedinger—who edited the text of the *acta*, together with those of the Third Council of Constantinople of 680/681, for the series *Acta Conciliorum Oecumenicorum*—has developed the hypothesis, based on his own painstaking philological analysis of the Latin and Greek texts of the Lateran Synod and enhanced by computerized statistics, that these are not simply minutes of oral discussion, enriched by a series of relevant documents from the papal archives. Riedinger argues rather that the original text of the *acta* was Greek, using Greek documents and the Greek text of the Bible as its basic point of reference, and that the Latin version, except

---

[17]Riedinger's articles, spanning a period from 1976 to 1996, are collected as *Kleine Schriften zu den Konzilsakten des 7. Jahrhunderts* (Turnhout: Brepols, 1998).

for a few Latin documents derived from outside sources, is largely the work of a single translator, with his own somewhat idiosyncratic approach to Latin style. Riedinger's hypothesis is that Maximus himself was very probably the author of the synodal acts; that he had likely been asked by Pope Theodore, in the years between 646 and Theodore's unexpected death in May 649, to prepare documents on the monenergist/monothelite controversy that would enable the Roman Church to take a definitive, solidly informed position against the imperial policy; and that when Theodore was succeeded by an Italian, the former nuncio to Constantinople Martin of Todi, the new pope—without waiting to be officially confirmed in office by the emperor—accepted the throne of Peter, and convoked a synod of Latin-speaking bishops from Italy, North Africa, and the Western Islands, for the following October, to affirm Maximus' doctrinal dossier in traditional conciliar form. Despite division into speeches by leading bishops and several magisterial papal allocutions, despite the apparent drama of five sessions of debate and judgment, Riedinger argues that the *acta* of that synod are essentially a composition of Maximus himself from the years before Martin became pope. Though he suggests in later essays that the bishops who signed the *acta* may have done so after listening approvingly to the Latin translation of Maximus' work, Riedinger has remained hesitant to go much beyond the conclusion he offers in his first piece on the subject:

> Today [i.e., in 1976, after editing the text of the *acta*] we must conclude from this detailed work that the whole set of *acta* (except for the originally Latin letters [of Victor of Carthage and Pope Felix II] read in the second session) were composed before the synod began, by Greeks, and afterward translated into Latin. How one then should imagine the events of the synod itself—their historicity—is a question for which my imagination provides no answer. But that the *acta* handed down to us are a purely literary product (and therefore allow no direct conclusion about the reality that lies behind them) can be concluded from observations . . . that can be simply and exactly represented.[18]

[18]"Aus den Akten der Lateransynode von 649," *Byzantinische Zeitschrift* 69 (1976): 37

Until now, we have been mainly occupied with Maximus' own life and career as a christological rebel—a prophet, perhaps, proclaiming the full richness of the Nicaean and Chalcedonian faith, in terms that left him, like Jeremiah of old, swimming against the ecclesiastical stream of his day. Our initial question, however—the question that brings us to this conference—of how much he was influenced by the thought of Augustine in this challenging project, is more difficult to answer. Augustine's christology is not likely, in itself, to have influenced Maximus' thinking in a major way, if only because Augustine's historical position in the development of the Church's christological tradition lay precisely between the first theological resistance to Arianism and Apollinarianism, in the work of the great Cappadocians, and the outbreak of Cyril's controversy with Nestorius in 429, the year before Augustine's death. Although the person and saving mystery of Christ is never far from Augustine's thoughts[19]—although, Christ, as the embodiment of grace and the living way of humility and service, Augustine reminds us in book 7 of the *Confessiones*, is the boundary line between the satisfactory resolution of philosophical difficulties about God and direct, fruitful access to God in the Church[20]—still Augustine's formulation of the ontological and personal structure of Christ tends to be expressed in rhetorical rather than technical or philosophical terms. He only begins to use the vocabulary of "person," "substance," and "nature" after 410, mainly as a result of his growing contact with Latin Arians, and then only sparingly.[21] Nevertheless, Augustine assures us in

[*Kleine Schriften* 23]. In a monograph discussing at length Riedinger's hypothesis and the evidence he presents, papal historian Pietro Conte suggests the leading bishops mentioned in the *acta* of 649 may actually have read their own translated speeches at the October gathering, in a carefully scripted dramatization of Maximus' theological argument: *Il Sinodo Lateranense dell'ottobre 649* (Vatican City: Pontificia Accademia Teologica Romana, 1989), at 142–48.

[19]For more on this theme, see David Tracy's essay in this volume.

[20]See especially *Conf.* 7.9.13–15 (CCSL 27.101–03), 7.18.24 (ibid., 108), 7.20.26–21.27 (ibid., 109–12).

[21]See my article, "A Humble Mediator: The Distinctive Elements in Saint Augustine's Christology," *Word and Spirit* 9 (1987): 100–17; also "Christology" in Allan D. Fitzgerald, ed., *Augustine through the Ages: An Encyclopedia* (Grand Rapids: William B. Eerdmans Publishing Co., 1999), 164–69, for further references.

book 7 of the *Confessiones* that he always believed in the full humanity of Jesus, even in his pre-baptismal years, although "the mystery of the Word made flesh I had not begun to guess."

> I had only realized from the writings handed down concerning him that he ate and drank, slept, walked, was filled with joy, was sad, conversed, knew that his flesh was not united to your Word without a soul and a human mind . . . To move the body's limbs at will at one moment, not another, to be affected by an emotion at one time, not another, to utter wise judgment by signs at one moment, at another to keep silence: these are characteristic marks of the soul and mind with their capacity to change. If the writings about him were wrong in so describing him, everything else would be suspected of being a lie, and there would remain no salvation for the human race based on faith in these books. So because the scriptures are true, I acknowledged the whole man to be in Christ, not only the body of a man, or soul and body without a mind, but a fully human person.[22]

In his *Epistle* 137, to Volusianus—a little treatise on the central paradoxes of the mystery of Christ as faith apprehends it, written in 411 or 412—Augustine emphasizes that the very heart of the redeeming grace claimed by the Christian community is not the suggestion that God has appeared among us as a superman, but the proclamation of Jesus' ordinariness as well as his deity, the joining of two complete, wholly unlike realities, the divine and the human, in a single agent:

> He contains in himself the deep treasures of wisdom and knowledge and fills minds with faith in order to bring them to the eternal contemplation of the immutable truth. Imagine if the almighty did not create the man, wherever he was formed, from the womb of his mother, but thrust him suddenly before our eyes! Imagine if he went through no ages from infancy to youth, if he took no food and did not

---

[22] *Conf.* 7.19.25 (CCSL 27.108–09; Henry Chadwick, trans. [Oxford: Oxford University Press, 1991], 128–29).

sleep! Would he not confirm the opinion of that error, and would it not be believed that he did not in any way assume a true man, and would it not destroy what he did out of mercy if he did everything as a miracle? But now a mediator has appeared between God and human beings so that, uniting both natures in the unity of his person, he may raise up the ordinary to the extraordinary and temper the extraordinary to the ordinary.[23]

For Augustine, as for none of the classical philosophers before him, the will is a distinctive, characteristic feature of the human person: the self-determining source of motion and action within each of our conscious selves that is intrinsically linked to our intelligence and ability to evaluate the situation in which we live, yet that has an unpredictable dynamic of its own.[24] So it was essential, in his view, that Christ, as Son of God made flesh, have both a complete human will and a complete divine will, different as those may be from one another in natural terms, yet that his human will freely obey the divine. So Augustine writes, in his little treatise *Contra sermonem Arianorum* (*Against an Arian Address*) from 417–418:

When we obey God and are said to do his will by that obedience, we do not do it unwillingly, but willingly. Hence, if we do it willingly, in what sense do we not do our own will, unless in the language of Scripture that will is called ours, which is understood to be our own as opposed to the will of God. Adam had such a will, and as a result, we died in him. Christ did not have such a will so that we might have life in him . . . In terms of the Son's divinity, the Father and the Son have

[23]*Ep.* 137.3.9 (CSEL 44.108; The Works of St. Augustine: A Translation for the 21st Century, II/2, trans. Roland Teske, SJ [Hyde Park, NY: New City, 2003], 217).

[24]See especially the treatment of Albrecht Dihle, *The Theory of Will in Classical Antiquity* (Berkeley: University of California Press, 1982), 123–32. Dihle writes: "St Augustine interpreted freedom of choice, traditionally attributed to all rational beings, as the freedom of will . . . The direction of the will, however, is thought and spoken of as being independent of the cognition of the better and the worse. This indeed supersedes the famous Socratic problem of οὐδεὶς ἑκὼν ἁμαρτάνει, no one does wrong on purpose. It is not surprising that everything, in the view of St Augustine, depends on *voluntas* in religious and moral life" (128–29).

one and the same will, nor can it be different in any way where the nature of the Trinity as a whole is immutable. But so that the mediator of God and man, the man Jesus Christ, would not do his own will, which is opposed to God, he was not only man, but God and man. And through this marvelous and singular grace human nature could exist in him without any sin.[25]

In his *Explanation* (*Enarratio*) of Psalm 93, probably preached in 414, as the Pelagian controversy was just beginning, Augustine presents the two wills that Christ reveals in Gethsemane and on the cross as part of the larger economy of salvation, in which our own wills are healed:

How did our Lord marry two wills (he asks) so that they became one in the humanity he bore? In his body, the Church, there would be some people who, after wanting to do their own will, would later follow the will of God. The Lord prefigured these people in himself. He wanted to show that though they are weak, they still belong to him, and so he represented them in advance in his own person. He sweated blood from his whole body, as a sign that the blood of martyrs would gush from his body, the Church ... He revealed the human will that was in him, but if he had continued to insist on that will, he would have seemed to display perversity of heart. If you recognize that he has had compassion on you, and is setting you free in himself, imitate the next prayer he made: "Yet not what I will, but what you will be done, Father" (Mt 26.39).[26]

The Pelagian controversy, in fact, which would begin with the visit of Pelagius and Celestius to Africa in 411, and which would preoccupy Augustine for much of the rest of his life until his death in 430, was really a controversy about the will: about the ability of the human person, act-

[25]*Contra serm.* 6.7 (CSEL 92.56–7; The Works of Saint Augustine: A Translation for the 21st Century, I/18, trans. Roland J. Teske [Hyde Park, NY: New City Press, 1995], 145).
[26]*En. in Ps.* 93.19, (CCSL 39.1319; The Works of Saint Augustine: A Translation for the 21st Century, III/18, trans. Maria Boulding [Hyde Park, NY: New City Press, 2002], 395).

ing independently, to become good and holy by a disciplined use of his or her own intelligence and powers of choice. And while Augustine always continued to maintain that we bear full responsibility for the good and the evil we do, and genuinely merit reward or punishment for ourselves through our conscious human acts, he also argued, more and more insistently, that the human will itself needs to be liberated by God's free act of mercy and rejuvenation, by God's sharing his own life and freedom with us through the actions of Christ and the gift of his Holy Spirit: that we need to be divinized, enabled, remade in the image of Christ who has become one of us, if we are to share in the holiness of God. In the end, the model for this restored freedom is the person of Christ himself, whose human freedom is utterly perfect because it has been created in the very act of that humanity's being gratuitously and fully assumed by the Son of God.[27] So Augustine writes, in a powerful and significant passage from his late work *De praedestinatione sanctorum* (*On the Predestination of the Saints*), that Christ personally reveals to us what grace is:

> The most striking light of predestination and grace is the Savior himself, the very "mediator of God and the human race—the man Christ Jesus" (1 Tim 2.5). What previous merits, from works or from faith, did the human nature which is in him acquire, that he might be this? Let someone tell me: that man—on what basis did he merit to become the unique Son of God, taken up by the Word who is co-eternal with the Father in a single person? What good deed of his, what kind of action went before this? What did he do beforehand, what faith did he have, what did he pray for, that he might come to this unspeakable degree of excellence? ... Let that fountain of grace be revealed to us, then, in our head, from which it has made itself flow through all his members, according to the measure of each of us. By that grace, by which that human being from his beginning was made the Christ, every single

[27]So *Contra serm.* 6.8, (CSEL 92.58): "The one Christ, then, is both Son of God by nature, and Son of Man, who was assumed in time, by grace. He was not assumed in such a way that first he was created and then assumed, but he was created in the very act of being assumed [*ipsa assumptione creatur*]."

person is made a Christian from the beginning of his life of faith; from that Spirit, by whom he was born, the Christian too is reborn; by that same Spirit, by which he was so made as to have no sin, there is in us the remission of sins. Clearly God knew in advance that he would do this. This, then, is the predestination of the saints, as it is most obvious in him who is the Saint of saints.[28]

There are clear parallels here, for anyone who reads widely in the works of both theologians, between Augustine's christocentric under-standing of God's sovereign grace and Maximus' identification of human salvation with the mystery of Christ's person. Maximus uses, of course, the clearly defined ontological categories of substance and nature, hypostasis and persona, which were so laboriously defined in the course of the controversy before and after Chalcedon; he speaks of human salva-tion and perfection in the classic Greek patristic language of the "deifica-tion" of the activities and faculties of the human person, rather than of grace—a concept Augustine occasionally touches on, but does not develop at such length.[29] So Maximus, for instance, writes in 642 to the Cypriot deacon Marinus in *Opusculum 7*:

If, then, as man, [Christ] has a natural will, he certainly wills in reality those things that, as God by nature, he has fashioned and introduced naturally into his own constitution. For he did not come to debase the nature which he himself, as God and Word, had made, but he came that that nature might be thoroughly deified which, with the good

---

[28] *De praed. sanc.* 15.30–31 (PL 44.981–82).

[29] See, for instance, the discussion of the eschatological fulfillment of the human pil-grimage in *Trin.* 14.12.15 (CCSL 50A.442–443) and 14.19.26 (ibid., 457–58), where Augustine speaks of the mind's promised participation in the life and wisdom of God; also 14.14.20 (ibid., 448–49), where this is called "cleaving to God," and 14.17.24–19.25 (ibid., 455–57), where Augustine describes it as the perfection of the image of God in the human person; and cf. *Ep.* 140.4.11–12 (CSEL 44.162–64); *Serm.* 192.1.1 (PL 38.1011–12); *En. in Ps.* 49.1.2 (CCSL 38.875–76), 58.1.7 (CCSL 39.733–35), 146.5.11 (CCSL 40.2129–30). See Gerald Bonner, "Augus-tine's Conception of Deification," *Journal of Theological Studies* 37 (1986): 369–86; J. Oroz Reta, "De l'illumination à la deification de l'âme selon saint Augustin," *Studia Patristica* 27 (1993): 364–82.

pleasure of the Father and the co-operation of the Spirit, he willed to unite to himself in one and the same hypostasis, with everything that naturally belongs to it, apart from sin.[30]

And in the twenty-second of his *Quaestiones ad Thalassium*, composed probably in the early 630s when Maximus was still a relative newcomer in Africa, he speaks in his own terms of the divine predestination Paul and Augustine identify with God's economy of salvation, which he too sees as fulfilled in the incarnation:

> Since, therefore, ages predetermined in God's purpose for the realiza-tion of his becoming human have reached their end for us, and God has undertaken and in fact achieved his own perfect incarnation, the other "ages"—those which are to come about for the realization of the mystical and ineffable deification of humanity—must follow hence-forth . . . For if he has brought to completion his mystical work of becoming human, having become like us in every way save without sin (cf. Heb 4.15), and even descended into the lower regions of the earth where the tyranny of sin compelled humanity, then God will also com-pletely fulfill the goal of his mystical work in deifying humanity in every respect, of course, short of an identity of essence with God; and he will assimilate humanity to himself and elevate us to a position above all the heavens.[31]

The question we must ask—without hope of a clear answer—is whether Maximus' clear identification of the Chalcedonian, two-natured Christ, who is personally and exclusively a divine person yet expresses his personality fully in two unadulterated, operative natures, and who embodies and begins the work of grace in us, is influenced by what he

---

[30]Maximus, *Opusculum* 7 (PG 91.69–89; *Maximus the Confessor,* trans. Andrew Louth [London: Routledge, 1996], 185 [altered]).

[31]Maximus, *Quaestiones ad Thalassium* 22 (CCSG 7.157–59; *On the Cosmic Mystery of Jesus Christ,* trans. Paul M. Blowers and Robert Louis Wilken [Crestwood, NY: SVS Press, 2003], 116).

may have known of Augustine's pre-Chalcedonian approach to the same mystery. Latin theology from the fifth century on, even into the high middle ages, continued to live in Augustine's intellectual and rhetorical shadow. Pope Leo, whose understanding of Christ set the standard for later western adherence to the Chalcedonian formula, cites Augustine verbatim several times in his *Tome to Flavian*; Prosper Tiro, the monk from Marseilles who worked in Leo's curia as a theological consultant, was a correspondent with Augustine and a strong supporter of his doctrine of grace in his own early years. Latin theology, in something of a decline for several decades after Chalcedon, went through a new flowering in North Africa in the sixth century, after the reconquest of the province for the empire by Belisarius in 534. As David Maxwell has lucidly shown in his recent dissertation,[32] the early focus of this sixth-century African theology, reflected above all in the works of Bishop Fulgentius of Ruspe (468–533), combined the emerging "neo-Chalcedonian" understanding of the person of Christ—promoted in the west by John Maxentius and the "Scythian monks" who joined in John's crusade—with an Augustinian understanding of humanity's total dependence on the grace of the Holy Spirit for conversion and perseverance. In his later works, especially his epistle 17, addressed to the Scythian monks in the name of the African bishops exiled with him in 523, Fulgentius not only affirms clearly that the single person of Christ, who died on the cross, *is* the second person of the Trinity, as Maxentius and the Scythians did, but also echoes Augustine in seeing in the incarnation a model for the gratuitous transformation of human nature by the personal presence of the Word, which we call grace.[33]

As the sixth century continued, however, African theology became less focused on the problem of grace and increasingly resistant to Justinian's neo-Chalcedonian christology, especially to his campaign to condemn the leading figures of the fifth-century school of Antioch (the *Three Chapters*), as ratified by the Council of 553. Facundus of Hermiane wrote his

---

[32]David R. Maxwell, "Christology and Grace in the Sixth-Century Latin West: The Theopaschite Controversy" (diss., Notre Dame, 2003).

[33]See especially Maxwell, 217–41.

"Defense of the Three Chapters" between 546 and 548, in response to an imperial decree against the Antiochenes issued in 543; his contemporary, Liberatus, archdeacon of Carthage, composed his *Breviarium* in the early 560s, narrating the history and implications of the christological debate for Latin readers, and Victor of Tunnuna, an African bishop exiled by Justinian, wrote another *Chronicle* narrating the events of the controversy around 566. In 550, a synod at Carthage excommunicated Pope Vigilius, then virtually a prisoner of Justinian's in Constantinople, for caving in to the emperor's program of reshaping official imperial orthodoxy. An African layman named Junilius or Junillus, who had gone to Constantinople to serve as *quaestor* (treasury official) to Justinian in the mid-540s, translated into Latin a Greek textbook on theology by Paul of Nisibis, an open admirer of Theodore of Mopsuestia, at the request of Bishop Primasius of Hadrumetum. Clearly, there was vivid sympathy for Antiochene theology in sixth-century Africa. So when George of Resh'aina, Maximus' critical biographer, tells us a century later that Maximus and his disciple Anastasius made contact with a group of Syriac "Nestorian" monks on their arrival in Africa, the detail rings true:

> They arrived [George writes] at a monastery at the upper tip of Africa, called in Latin Hippo Diarrhytus, where some students from Nisibis were living. The abbot of the monastery was Esha'ya, and there was his son, called Isho'. There were about eighty-seven monks there, and they were Nestorians; and when they found that Maximus and Anastasius also agreed in their teaching with Nestorius their master, they received them and agreed with their doctrine. Thus they led astray the whole of Africa . . .[34]

In fact, Latin Africa had been astray, in this sense, for almost a century.

By the end of the sixth century, Latin education and theological learning seem to have been in decline throughout much of the west. When Heraclius, Patriarch Sergius, and their colleagues tried once again to find

[34]Brock, "An Early Syriac Life," 19, 317–18, and above, n. 2.

common ground with the opponents of Chalcedon in the language of "one theandric energy" and "one will," the debate—unlike the furor over the "Three Chapters" a century before—was now clearly centered in the Greek-speaking world, carried on by Greek disputants, couched in the terms of Greek philosophy, and argued through the proto-scholastic methods of Greek dialectics. One of Maximus' great achievements was to have marshaled the Latin Church, centered in the see of Rome, in support of the Chalcedonian cause, and to have made clear the dire consequences of the new imperial policy for the Church's faith in Christ.

In this campaign, it seems obvious that to the degree he was aware of Augustine's theological positions, Maximus would have found encouragement and even ammunition in them. In many ways, Augustine was a kindred theological spirit, despite the very different ways in which they approached and articulated problems. Like Augustine, who saw the foundation of Jesus' freedom from original sin and its effects in the fact that he was conceived by a virgin, in a way free from concupiscence,[35] Maximus also sees the sinlessness and perfect freedom of Jesus as rooted in his virginal origin, which parallels the creation of Adam in being free from sexual passion.[36] Augustine describes the first sin of Adam and Eve as their "evil will," their inner choice to be guided by their own desires rather than God's commands, which led them to external transgression and to loss of integrity for their descendants.[37] Maximus, too, sees "the first sin" as "the fall of free choice (προαίρεσις) from good into evil," and the "second sin," which followed it, as the "innocent" or unintended corruption of human nature for its subsequent history.[38] And just as Augustine speaks of the remedy of this inherited sin and corruptibility in terms of the incarnation

[35]E.g., *Serm.* 214.6 (PL 38.1069); *De pecc. merit.* 2.24.38 (CSEL 60.110–11). Augustine describes the effects of Adam's sin as a loss of freedom and self-control handed on by the inescapably passionate character of sexual procreation: *De civ. Dei* 14.15–19 (CCSL 48.436–42).

[36]Maximus, *Quaestiones ad Thalassium* 21 (Laga and Steel, 127–29); *Ambigua* 31 (PG 91.1273D–76D); *Ambigua* 42 (PG 91.1313CD). See Blowers and Wilken, 109–11. Jesus is, however, in Maximus' view, still subject to "natural passions," which here presumably means vulnerability and human limitation of knowledge.

[37]*De civ. Dei* 14.13–14 (CCSL 48.434–36).

[38]*Quaestiones ad Thalassium* 42 (Laga and Steel, 285; Blowers and Wilken, 119).

in human flesh of the unchanging, incorruptible Word,[39] Maximus explains Paul's phrase that Christ "became sin" (2 Cor 5.21) as indicating the reversal, in the person of Christ, of a destructive instability, an inherited sin, which began in Adam.[40] Both theologians see in the Church, as the concrete, sacramental community of faith united in the eucharist, the full present reality of Christ in the world, leading us to the Father. The Church, as Augustine so often puts it in his preaching on the Psalms, is the *totus Christus*; or, as Maximus suggests in his *Mystagogy*, "to be and to appear as one body formed of different members is really worthy of Christ himself, our true head . . . "[41] Both have a positive, if moderately critical, understanding of the leadership the bishop of Rome can offer in solving doctrinal and disciplinary controversies in the wider church.[42] Both Augustine and Maximus are respectful, too, but restrained in their attitudes to

[39]See, for instance, *De civ. Dei* 21.15 (CCSL 48.781): "God's only Son by nature was made the Son of Man for us by compassion, so that we who by nature are sons of men might become sons of God through him by grace. He, as we know, while continuing changeless, took our nature to himself from us so that in that nature he might take us to himself; and while retaining his divinity he became partaker of our weakness. His purpose was that we should be changed for the better, and by participation in his immortality and his righteousness should lose our condition of sinfulness and mortality, and should retain the good that he did in our nature . . . " Henry Bettenson, trans. (London: Penguin, 1972), 992. This pattern of salvation by "typological exchange" is a favorite *topos* in Augustine's preaching and writing; see also *De cat. rud.* 4.8 (PL 40.315).

[40]So *Quaestiones ad Thalassium* 42 (Laga and Steel, 285; Blowers and Wilken, 120): "Just as through one man, who turned voluntarily from the good, the human nature was changed from incorruption to corruption to the detriment of all humanity, so too through one man, Jesus Christ, who did not voluntarily turn from the good, human nature underwent a restoration from corruption to incorruption for the benefit of all humanity."

[41]Maximus, *Mystagogy* 1 (ed. Charalambos Soteropoulos [Athens, 1978], 199; Berthold, trans., op. cit., 187). For further references to the Church as Christ's body in Maximus, see Adam Cooper, *The Body in St. Maximus the Confessor: Holy Flesh, Wholly Deified* (Oxford: Oxford University Press, 2005), esp. 168. For a full discussion of Augustine's use of the notion of the *totus Christus* as the hermeneutical key to interpreting the Psalms, see Michael Fiedrowicz, *Psalmus Vox Totius Christi* (Freiburg: Herder, 1997).

[42]For Augustine's approach to the legitimate and illegitimate uses of papal authority in his day, see my article, "Universal Love and Local Structure: Augustine, the Papacy, and the Church in Africa," *The Jurist* 64 (2004): 39–63. On Maximus' relationship to the Roman papacy and the Latin Church, see the excerpts in *Opusculum* 10 (above, n. 3), where he attempts to explain certain accepted Roman doctrines that raised eyebrows in the Greek Church, and *Opusculum* 11 on the importance of Rome as maintaining the apostolic tradi-

civil officials, and saw even the Christian emperors not as priests but as secular rulers, called to maintain the civil order with justice and humility, and when necessary to accept the legitimate judgments of the Church.[43]

If Maximus in fact read widely in Augustine's work during his time of exile in North Africa, or even learned of Augustine's classical positions on the person and natures of Christ, on original sin and redeeming grace, on the Church and the eucharist, the significance of time and history, or the Christian hope for eschatological peace and rest as a Church in God, it seems puzzling that he never alludes to him as an authority, never attempts to interpret his thought as he does that of the Cappadocians or Dionysius the Areopagite, never simply adopts his arguments wholesale as he does with Leontius of Byzantium and other Greek writers of the sixth century. Augustine seems always close, always standing in the wings; but like most ancient authors, Maximus never seems constrained to acknowledge this kinship. Perhaps, since the reading public of his works was mainly Greek, he did not need to do so. But if Maximus is indeed the original author or at least the animating spirit of the *acta* of the Lateran Synod of 649, as Rudolf Riedinger argues, it is interesting that even there, in a document prepared for the official use of the Roman Church, Augustine is mentioned seldom, and the florilegium of texts supporting the

---

tion. Bathrellos (above, n. 16), 79, suggests that Maximus' attempts to defend the orthodoxy of Pope Honorius after his death are essentially diplomatic gestures. Hans Urs von Balthasar, on the other hand, in *Cosmic Liturgy,* trans. Brian Daley (San Francisco: Ignatius, 2003), 44–50, sees Maximus as a figure who genuinely strove to unite the eastern and western Christian traditions structurally as well as intellectually.

[43]See, for instance, Augustine's notable reflections on the propriety of giving a Christian emperor the title "happy" (*felix*), in *De civ. Dei* 5.24 (CCSL 47.200): "We Christians call rulers happy, if they rule with justice; if amid the voices of exalted praise and the reverent salutations of excessive humility, they are not inflated with pride, but remember that they are but men; if they put their power at the service of God's majesty, to extend his worship far and wide . . ." (Bettenson, trans., 220). One of the notable examples of an emperor's Christian virtue that he offers here is Theodosius' humble acceptance of temporary excommunication after he had massacred the citizens of Thessaloniki: ibid., 5.26 (ibid. 202). Maximus' *Ep.* 10, to John the Chamberlain (PG 91.449–54), which he may have written before leaving Cyzicus in 626, also reflects on the providential reasons that some human beings rule over others, when all are created equal in nature and worth; he insists that the emperor is not a priest in any sense.

synod's argument for two natural operations and wills in Christ relies much more on Greek patristic authorities than on Latin ones. Significantly, among the five brief excerpts from Augustine that the *acta* do offer, to certify the tradition of recognizing two natural wills in Christ, there appears a section of Augustine's *Ep.* 140 to Honoratus, which Augustine himself entitled *De Gratia Novi Testamenti Liber* (*On the Grace of the New Testament*), a passage that one might mistake for Maximus' own if one did not have the full text elsewhere. Augustine here interprets John's saying that "the Word was made flesh" as promising us a future:

> O men and women, do not cease to hope that you can become children of God, because the very Son of God—that is, God's Word—has been made flesh and has dwelt among us. Make your return to him; become spirit, and dwell in him who has become flesh and dwelt among you. For we have no reason not to hope that by participating in the Word, we humans can become children of God, since the Son of God, by participating in our flesh, has become a son of man. We changeable beings, therefore, transformed into something better, become participants in the Word. For the unchangeable Word, not at all transformed for the worse, was made a sharer in flesh through the mediation of a rational soul.[44]

Both our authors realized that what is at stake in our understanding of Christ, as one person living and acting as Son of God in two natures and substances, characterized by two unmixed sets of operations and determining his behavior by two unmixed wills, is nothing less than the news of our salvation. Christ reveals in himself what Maximus calls "divinization," and what Augustine calls grace: God's sovereign intervention in our history of sin to change the direction of our lives, to sanctify and liberate our wills that we might choose only the good, to form us into sharers of Christ's body and make us, in his Spirit, sons and daughters of God.

---

[44]Augustine, *Ep.* 140, *to Honoratus* 4.11–12 (CSEL 44.163).

In 1952, Vitalien Laurent, the distinguished French Assumptionist authority on Byzantine lead seals, published a small study on a seal he had recently catalogued in the Vatican Museum (seal 92), which he dated to the second quarter of the seventh century.[45] On one side of the small lead wafer, the size of a quarter, is an inscription in Greek: Πέτρου ἀπὸ ὑπάτων πα(τρ)ικίου καὶ δούκος: "(The seal of) Peter, ex-consul, of patrician rank and general." Fr Laurent argues, mainly from the titles, that this can only refer to the Peter who was general of the Greek army in Numidia in North Africa during the 630s and 640s, and whose most notable act was refusing to comply with a command from the emperor, in 632 or 633, to move with his troops to Egypt to resist the sudden tide of Muslim invaders from Arabia.[46] Maximus, we know, was well acquainted with this General Peter of Numidia, who seems to have consulted the monk on matters both of doctrine and of ecclesiastical politics; we have two letters from Maximus to him from the mid-630s on the developing crisis in the eastern Church, plus excerpts from a longer treatise, written probably in 642 or 643 and discussing Rome's reaction to the exile of Patriarch Pyrrhus.[47] Maximus also dedicated to Peter his *Computus ecclesiasticus*, on the liturgical seasons. In the account of Maximus' trial in 655, Peter's former treasurer comes forward to accuse the aged monk of influencing the general, twenty-two years earlier, not to lead his army against the Muslims: "and he wrote to you as if he were speaking to a servant of God, having confidence in you as a holy man to inquire whether you would advise him to set out. And you wrote back to him and said not to do such a thing since God was not pleased to lend aid to the Roman state under the emperor Heraclius and his family."[48] Maximus strenuously denies that he ever gave

[45]Vitalien Laurent, "Une effigie inédite de Saint Augustin sur le sceau du dux Byzantin de Numidie Pierre," *Cahiers de Byrsa* 2 (1952): 87–95. Laurent later confirmed his identification and dating, in his full catalogue of the Vatican seal collection: *Les sceaux Byzantins du médailler Vatican,* Medagliere della Bibliotheca Vaticana, vol. 1 (Vatican: Bibliotheca Apostolica Vaticana, 1962), 85–87.

[46]Walter E. Kaegi, *Heraclius* (above, n. 7), argues from this incident that Heraclius' strategic opportunities were fairly limited, as the Muslim conquest gained momentum: see 225, 233.

[47]*Ep.* 13, *Opusculum* 12. See Sherwood, 39–40, 52.

[48]*Relatio Motionis* 1 (Allen and Neal [above, n. 1], 48–51; cf. 52–53; Berthold, trans., 17; cf. 18).

such advice, and calls for either other witnesses or documentary proof to sustain the charge. He never denies, however, that he had been the general's spiritual advisor.

On the other side of this same seal is a head of St Augustine, labeled *Sanctus Augustinus* in Latin and depicted not as the lean, intense teacher of the famous sixth-century Lateran fresco in Rome, but as a fairly anonymous bishop: gazing at the viewer, round-cheeked and wearing a soft cap, something like a Renaissance pope. That a Greek general in Maximus' day, commanding imperial troops in the province where Augustine had lived two centuries before, would have a picture of St Augustine on one side of his official seal, probably ought not to surprise us; it might be a sign of personal interest and devotion toward the saint, or simply an emblem of cultural adaptation. Still, if we remember that Peter and Maximus were friends and confidants, and that Maximus treats Peter as someone who shares his own views on christology and the Church, it could well be that Augustine symbolized for both men, if not a source of ideas, at least a locally cherished model of faithful, patient, philosophically enlightened witness to the full richness of the mystery of Christ—the other side, one might say, of their own coin. Only in Byzantine Africa could these two worlds have come together so closely, while remaining so far apart.

Sempiterne Spiritus Donum: Augustine's Pneumatology and the Metaphysics of Spirit

LEWIS AYRES

Introduction

There is, I suggest, something of a tension between two central themes of recent Catholic writing about the relationship between Orthodox and Catholic pneumatologies. On the one hand, a significant body of historical scholarship has attempted to undermine the idea that the debate between Orthodox and Catholic theologies is one between unchanging trinitarian logics fixed in the earliest centuries of Christianity. Instead, such scholarship suggests, it is essential to explore how this dispute (or this series of different disputes) has taken form in different historical contexts.[1] In the case of the fourth and fifth centuries in particular, one common feature of such scholarship has been the undermining of overly simplistic categories developed in later or modern polemical contexts and used to interpret the theological texts of the first

---

[1] The best summary in English of where such scholarship has led is Brian Daley, "Revisiting the 'Filioque': Roots and Branches of an Old Debate: Part One," *Pro ecclesia* 10 (2001): 31–62; and Daley, "Revisiting the 'Filioque': Part Two: Contemporary Catholic Approaches," *Pro ecclesia* 10 (2001): 195–212. See also Henry Chadwick, *East and West: The Making of a Rift in the Church: From Apostolic Times until the Council of Florence* (Oxford: Oxford University Press, 2003). Chadwick's book does not focus on theological analysis, but it is extremely helpful as an account of the changing shape and focus of the conflict within which the pneumatological disputes considered here are located.

centuries. Deconstructing such categories has enabled a new attention to
the theological dynamics and even experiments of an age before later disputes between East and West began to govern how theologians understood their own traditions. The late André De Halleux's work is, for me at
least, seminal in such scholarship.[2] A number of De Halleux's papers from
the 1970s and 1980s deconstruct some of the basic categories used to
describe patristic pneumatologies—categories such as "personalism,"
"apophaticism," and "essentialism"—but such deconstruction is done
always in the service of a renewed attention to the common sources of
East and West.

On the other hand, some Catholic theologians for whom dialogue
with the Orthodox churches (rightly) holds a high priority have devoted
much energy to finding formulae that interpret the *filioque* such that the
Father's *monarchia* is clearly upheld and formulae that speak about the
Spirit's relationship to the Son in ways that reflect what are taken to be the
common concerns of Greek and Latin patristic theologians.[3] The results
have been received well by some Orthodox theologians—perhaps one
might say by those who stand (consciously or unconsciously) in the tradition of Bolotov's remarkable pneumatological theses from 1898—but
badly received by others, who see any interpretation of the *filioque* as
merely overly subtle justifications for that which remains fundamentally
unacceptable.[4]

[2]See especially André de Halleux, "Du Personnalisme en Pneumatologie," in *Patrologie et Oecuménisme. Recueil d'Études* (Leuven: Leuven University Press/Peeters, 1990), 396–423; "Personnalisme ou Essentialisme Trinitaire chez les Pères Cappadociens?" *Patrologie et Oecuménisme*, 215–68. Readers without French should consult his "Towards an Ecumenical Agreement on the Procession of the Holy Spirit and the Addition of the *filioque* to the Creed," in *Spirit of God, Spirit of Christ: Ecumenical Reflections on the* Filioque *Controversy*, ed. Lukas Vischer (SPCK: London, 1981), 69–84.
[3]The legacy of such work is perhaps best seen in a number of recent documents. I think especially of "The Greek and Latin Traditions Regarding the Procession of the Holy Spirit," issued by the Pontifical Council for Promoting Christian Unity in 1995; and the "The Fil-ioque: A Church-Dividing Issue?: An Agreed Statement of the North American Orthodox-Catholic Theological Consultation," issued on October 23, 2003.
[4]V.V. Bolotov, "Thesen über das Filioque von einem russischen Theologe," *Revue internationale de théologie* 6 (1898): 671–712 (French trans., "Thèses sur le 'Filioque' par

It is here that the tension of which I spoke appears. The search for ecumenically acceptable formulae always to some extent forecloses debate on the character of patristic pneumatology because it is predicated upon a certainty about the character and intention of that pneumatology—and it seems to me that the scholarship mentioned in my first paragraph suggests that there remains considerable uncertainty about precisely this character and intention. I suggest, then, that our common discussion needs continued opening up and exploration of patristic pneumatology just as much as it needs a focus on the search for new or revised formulae (and there is, of course, no reason why we cannot have both). Within this common exploration I think it important for Catholic theologians to show how "filioquist" pneumatologies may themselves not just escape the charges frequently laid against them, but even offer considerable resources for thinking beyond the simplifications bred of our mutual and deeply ingrained polemic. Perhaps nowhere is this more so than in the case of Augustine; even as a growing body of scholarship has shown the extent to which Augustine does not fit his characteristic presentation in modern summary, his pneumatology is still frequently misinterpreted. And so, following a phrase used in the literature for this conference, my aim will be to discuss "possibilities for Augustine's thought to unite rather than divide."

My argument will be that Augustine offers an extraordinarily sophisticated account of the Father as *principium* of the trinitarian communion of Father, Son, and Spirit as irreducible persons who together constitute (as he says) the *Trinitas quae est Deus*. Augustine's vision of the Spirit as the active giving love breathed by the Father as the foundation of the trinitarian communion provides, I will suggest, the wider and essential context within which we must consider those aspects of his pneumatology that are easily taken out of context and used as the basis for unhelpful polemic.

un théologien russe," *Istina* 17 [1972]: 261–92). For rejection of these moves see especially Jean-Claude Larchet, "La Question du 'Filioque'," *Le Messager Orthodoxe* 129 (1998): 3–58.

Commending the Source

I want to begin with Augustine's famous account of divine *missio* as divine *revelatio*.[5] While this may surprise, it is, I suggest, one of the best points of departure for considering Augustine's understanding of the relations between Father and Spirit. Augustine's discussion of what it means to speak about a divine person being sent is founded on the observation that although scripture attributes to the Word the language of moving from place to place, we misunderstand how scripture speaks and draws if we take this language literally. The omnipresent Word is, as Wisdom 8.1 and Psalm 138.8 tell us, always already anywhere that scripture presents as its "destination."[6] Augustine thus argues that each act of "sending" is actually an act of revealing. The sending of the divine persons is a sending intended to move people beyond attention only to what is visible and toward attention to "the hidden eternity of him who is forever present."[7] Augustine later clarifies the idea of sending as revealing by arguing that while the Son can be said to have been sent in a number of ways, he is only truly "sent into the world" (Jn 17.3) when he becomes man in order to save; true sending into the world is a revelation that effects salvation.[8]

Augustine also insists that the missions of Son and Spirit reveal not a divine person *per se*, but that each divine person comes from the Father:

> Just as being born means for the Son his being born from the Father, so his being sent means his being known to be from him. And just as for the Holy Spirit his being the gift of God means his proceeding from the Father, so his being sent means his being known to proceed from him.[9]

---

[5] Among recent literature on this topic I have found particularly helpful Luigi Gioia, "God Loved and Known through God in Augustine's *De Trinitate*" (DPhil diss., Oxford University, 2005), ch. 4.

[6] *Trin.* 2.5.7.

[7] Ibid., 2.5.9.

[8] Ibid., 4.20.28.

[9] Ibid., 4.20.29 (CCSL 50.199): "Sicut enim natum esse est filio a patre esse, ita mitti est filio cognosci quod ab illo sit. Et sicut spiritui sancto donum dei esse est a patre procedere,

Thus, the missions of Son and Spirit reveal the persons in their interconnection with the Father as source; the "hidden eternity" of him who is forever present is the hidden eternity of the Father. The revealing of Son and Spirit as being from the Father may be understood as a revealing both of the goal of our contemplation and of the nature of salvation toward that goal. This may become a little clearer if we turn to a text from the very end of *De Trinitate* (*On the Trinity*), book 4. Here Augustine summarizes a long discussion of why the sending of Son and Spirit does not imply their ontological subordination:

> Whether for the sake of the visible creature or, better, for the sake of commending to us the source [*principium*], it was not on account of inequality or difference or dissimilarity of substance that these [testimonies to the sending of the divine persons] are understood to have been put in the scriptures, for even if God the Father had willed to appear visibly through a creature subject to him it would be simply absurd if he were said to have been sent by the Son whom he generated or by the Spirit who proceeded from him.[10]

In revealing that they are "from" the Father, Son and Spirit reveal not just that the Father is the *principium*, but the sort of *principium* that he is. The Father is the source of two who are in no way different from the Father in what they are; the Father is the source of two with whom he acts inseparably. In the first place this is a revealing of that which will be the object of our contemplation when faith is replaced by sight.[11] In the second

ita mitti est cognosci quod ab illo procedat." My translations are based on that of Stephen McKenna in Fathers of the Church, vol. 45, although I have adapted his version where I felt it necessary.

[10]Ibid., 4.21.32 (CCSL 50.205): "Sive enim propter visibilem creaturam sive potius propter principii commendationem, non propter inaequalitatem vel imparilitatem vel dissimilitudinem substantiae in scripturis haec posita intelleguntur, quia etiam si voluisset deus pater per subiectam creaturam visibiliter apparere, absurdissime tamen aut a filio quem genuit aut ab spiritu sancto qui de illo procedit missus diceretur."

[11]For contemplation as the goal of Christian life see ibid., 1.10.20. It is important to note that Augustine understands this vision as one of Christ in union with the Father in the Spirit. See e.g. ibid., 1.12.30–31.

place, it is a revealing of the structure of salvation itself; to accept salvation for Augustine is to grasp in humility (whether or not this is understood at the level of explicit cognition) that God acts without mediation through Son and Spirit to enable our return. Thus, in *De Trinitate* book 4, Augustine argues that Christians must understand the sending of the Son as resulting not from the Son's subordination, but from the Father's care for us in the Son so that we may be drawn into the communion of Father and Son, a communion that is an eternal association of love (*dilectionis societatem*).[12]

And so, while Augustine's strong insistence on the role of the Father as *principium* here is of importance, it is of greater importance that this account of divine mission sets an agenda for the rest of our discussion; the task of understanding Augustine's mature pneumatology may be cast as a task of understanding how he sees scriptural testimony to the Spirit as revealing the Father as *principium* of the trinitarian communion and life into which we are drawn.

"... the essence is nothing other than the Trinity itself"

Before we can turn directly to Augustine's mature pneumatology we need to explore Augustine's understanding of how Father, Son, and Spirit constitute the divine essence. This discussion will then provide a backdrop to the specific treatment of the Spirit's role in the remainder of the paper. Books 5 to 7 of the *De Trinitate* offer just about the only extended discussion in Augustine's corpus of whether we can apply genus and species terminology to the Trinity. In a close study of Augustine's argument, Richard Cross has recently argued that Augustine understands the structure and implications of such language well, but consciously rejects its usefulness. Augustine does so because he assumes that the use of any specific noun (such as "person") implies the possibility of also using a generic noun (such as "animal").[13] Thus "essence" cannot function as a generic term

---

[12]Ibid., 4.9.12; cf. ibid., 4.19.25–20.27.
[13]Richard Cross, "*Quid tres?* On What Precisely Augustine Professes Not to Understand

and a "person" specifically; we cannot, for example, say that there are three essences because there are three persons, although we can say that Peter, James, and John are also three animals. Alternatively, "essence" is not a species term because the divine essence is not divisible into individuals. For Augustine the divine essence simply does not admit of such division.

Now, Augustine's strong insistence on the indivisibility of the divine essence travels along with, and in part results from, his description of each divine person as the fulness of God as well as being the fulness of God with the other divine persons. In *De Trinitate* book 6 Augustine writes:

> (7.9) Nor since he is a Trinity [*trinitas*] is He, therefore, tripartite [*triplex*]; otherwise the Father alone or the Son alone would be less than the Father and the Son together. Although, to tell the truth, it is difficult to see how one can speak of the Father alone or the Son alone, since the Father is with the Son and the Son with the Father always and inseparably, not that both are the Father or both the Son, but because they are always mutually in one another and neither is alone . . . (8.9) In God himself, therefore, when the equal Son adheres to the equal Father, or the equal Holy Spirit to the Father and the Son, God does not thereby become greater than each one separately, for there is nothing whereby that perfection can increase. But he is perfect whether the Father, or the Son, or the Holy Spirit; and God the Father, the Son, and the Holy Spirit is perfect, and, therefore, he is a Trinity rather than tripartite.[14]

in *De Trinitate* V and VII," *Harvard Theological Review* 100.2 (2007): 215–32. Cross refers to Irénée Chevalier's *Saint Augustin et la pensée grecque. Les relations trinitaires* (Fribourg: Collectanea Friburgensia, 1940) to justify the idea that Augustine's rejection of this terminology is based on an actual knowledge of Cappadocian discussion. Berthold Altaner's refutation of Chevalier (see the series of short papers collected in his *Kleine patristische Schriften* [Berlin: Akademie Verlag, 1967]) shows the great unlikeliness of this possibility, but Cross' main point still stands: Augustine understands such language and rejects it. Whether any of the Cappadocians endorses such language without reservation is a distinct question; my own sense is that their significant qualifications of the language are consistently underplayed in the scholarship.

[14] *Trin.* 6.7.9–8.9 (CCSL 50.237–8): "Nec quondam trinitas est ideo triplex putandus est; alioquin minor erit pater solus aut filius solus quam simul pater et filius–quamquam non

The unity of God is here understood by reflecting on what it must mean for the Father (who is wisdom and justice and goodness itself) to beget one who has "life in himself" (to use the terms of Jn 5.26). This cannot mean that the Son (or the Spirit) has anything of what it is to be God by participation; the Son no more "shares" in the Father's essence than the three persons "share" in a common essence if "share" indicates a mode of participation. The Father generates the Son as one who is irreducibly all that it is to be God and thus is necessarily perfect God in himself, and necessarily "person" or "agent," not "thing" (I will return to this emphasis shortly).[15]

Yet, to speak in these terms is, as Augustine recognizes in the middle of this passage, ridiculously artificial because the Father generates Son and breathes Spirit such that there is an irreducible unity. This we know because the Bible tells us so, but it also seems, for Augustine, to fit well with what the language of divine simplicity demands of us. In generating a Son who fully "shares" his simple perfect essence, the Father generates one who is both fully all that he is and yet, paradoxically, the Son is *necessarily* at one with the Father in the simplicity of that essence.[16] Augustine

invenitur quomodo dici possit aut pater solus aut filius solus cum semper atque inseparabiliter et ille cum filio sit et ille cum patre, non ut ambo sint pater aut ambo filius, sed quia semper in invicem neuter solus . . . In ipso igitur deo cum adhaeret aequali patri filius aequalis aut spiritus sanctus patri et filio aequalis, non fit maior deus quam singuli eorum quia non est quo crescat illa perfectio. Perfectus autem sive pater sive filius sive spiritus sanctus, et perfectus deus pater et filius et spiritus sanctus, et ideo trinitas potius quam triplex." Cf. ibid., 15.17.28.

[15]For these connections, other than the material in *Trin.* already quoted, see also *Civ.* 11.10 (CCSL 47.330): ". . . et utrumque hoc cum spiritu suo unus Deus est, qui spiritus Patris et Filii Spiritus sanctus propria quadam notione huius nominis in sacris litteris nuncupatur. Alius est autem quam Pater et Filius, quia nec Pater est nec Filius, sed alius dixi, non aliud, quia et hoc pariter simplex pariterque incommutabile bonum est et coaeternum."

[16]I have explored this particular point at greater length in my *Nicaea and Its Legacy: An Approach to Fourth-Century Trinitarian Theology* (Oxford: Oxford University Press, 2004), ch. 15. In his paper in this volume, Fr John Behr also notes the same distinctive feature of Augustine's theology. He claims also that Greek Nicaeans are consistent (and more biblical) in seeing the Father as the one true God. I would suggest, first, that this clear opposition remains to be proven: it may well be so, but I would want to see a far more extensive study to demonstrate that this is so and that this is not at all compromised by the insistence in Gregory of Nyssa and Gregory Nazianzen that terms which describe the essence must be

was the first pro-Nicaean to argue that each of the persons is the fulness of God as well as that fulness with the others, and it constitutes one of the most important of his contributions to the theology of the Trinity.[17]

Thus, in his mature writing Augustine neither views the mystery of the Trinity being both three and one by imagining the Trinity as an intelligible simple reality who must somehow be also divided, nor by imagining the Trinity as (in the terms of many modern critics) a simple reality with "internal" divisions constituted by relations. The first option would destroy the unity of the divine essence and miss the point that each irreducible divine person is the fulness of the indivisible God. The second option simply does not reflect Augustine's language. Whatever a doctrine of "subsistent relations" implies or does not imply, the language of persons *as* relations is alien to Augustine.[18] Augustine certainly emphasizes that the *names* of Father and Son, for example, are spoken relative (*relative*) to one another, but this is only to emphasize a pattern of scriptural predication. Augustine, in fact, states clearly that "every essence which is spoken of in relation is certainly something besides that relation."[19]

---

used univocally of God. At the same time, however, it is clear enough that Orthodox liturgical practice of a later era certainly permits prayer addressed to the Trinity as a whole. No doubt we will take up these questions again in a future debate. For the moment, see our exchange in *Harvard Theological Review* 100 (2007).

[17]Showing that other pro-Nicaeans do not use a given argument is always difficult. But to see some of the different tactics that pro-Nicaeans used to answer the charge that they were teaching three gods—one context where Augustine's argument might have been deployed—see for example Basil, *De Spiritu Sancto* 18.44–45; Gregory Nazianzen, *Or.* 31.13–20, Gregory of Nyssa, *Abl.* In none of these texts do we find Augustine's tactic.

[18]This does not mean that I think the notion of "subsistent relations" itself falls prey to the charges sometimes leveled against it. For an excellent discussion of the doctrine as found in Thomas Aquinas see Gilles Emery, "Essentialisme ou personnalisme dans le traité de Dieu chez saint Thomas d'Aquin?" *Revue Thomiste* 98 (1998): 5–38 (English trans. in *The Thomist* 64 [2000]: 521–63).

[19]*Trin.* 7.1.2 (CCSL 50.247): "Omnis essentia quae relative dicitur est etiam aliquid excepto relative." Included in this discussion should also be *Tract. Ev. Jo.* 39.4 (CCSL 36, 347): ". . . videte enim si non quasi apparet numerus, pater et filius et spiritus sanctus trinitas. Si tres, quid tres? Deficit numerus. Iita deus nec recedit a numero, nec capitur numero. Quia tres sunt, tamquam est numerus; si quaeris quid tres, non est numerus . . . hoc solo numerum insinuant quod ad invicem sunt, non quod ad se sunt . . . non est quid dicam tres, nisi patrem et filium et spiritum sanctum, unum deum, unum omnipotentem. Ergo

Instead of these options, Augustine imagines the *Trinitas quae est Deus* as the one God constituted by Father, Son, and Spirit, each of whom is perfectly God in themselves. As he writes in *Ep.* 120: "[h]old with unshakable faith that the Father and the Son and the Holy Spirit are a Trinity and that there is, nonetheless, one God, not that the divinity is common to these as if it were a fourth, but that it is itself the ineffably inseparable Trinity . . ."[20] Or: "[i]t remains, then, that we should believe the Trinity is of one substance, in the sense that the essence is nothing other than the Trinity itself."[21] For Augustine, then, there is nothing in God other than the three persons. But this is the same as saying that there is nothing other than the divine essence, because the persons eternally constitute the divine essence as one.

Although Augustine is resistant to the use of genus and species terminology for the persons, he does accord each of the persons, as fully God, something analogous to the rational and desiring life that constitutes the human being as *imago Dei*. Thus, even the two sections of *De Trinitate* book 15 that attempt to show by analogy how *intellegentia* helps us reflect on the Son and *voluntas* on the Spirit are both prefaced by an extended insistence that each divine person is its own memory, intelligence and will.[22] Yet, Augustine is equally clear that we fail to understand how this language can be applied to Father, Son, and Spirit unless we see both that divine persons experience no lack in their desiring and knowing—they are the good itself and for them knowing and being are the same—and that the divine persons are united such that they constitute one substance and will, and that they act inseparably.

While it is important to see how thoroughly Augustine sees the persons as constituting the divine essence, much is missed if we do not also

unum principium." There is no count-noun applicable to the three; only the referential terms Father, Son, and Spirit allow us to use number in this context.

[20] *Ep.* 120.2.12 (CSEL 34/2.715): "nunc vero tene inconcussa fide patrem et filium et spiritum sanctum esse trinitatem et tamen unum deum, non quod sit eorum communis quasi quarta diuinitas, sed quod sit ipsa ineffabiliter inseparabilis trinitas . . ."

[21] Ibid., 120.3.17 (CSEL 34/2.719): "restat itaque, ut ita credamus unius esse substantiae trinitatem, ut ipsa essentia non aliud sit quam ipsa trinitas."

[22] *Trin.* 15.7.12, 15.17.28.

explore how Augustine envisions this "constituting" to be the product of the persons' acts toward each other. One of the most important developments in his mature theology is an increasingly thoroughgoing interpretation of scriptural passages that appear to describe acts of the persons toward each other as descriptions of constitutive acts by which the persons are what they are. In other words, intra-divine "acts" are intrinsic to the act by which the Father constitutes the communion of Son and Spirit. One of the clearest examples of such exegesis is provided by his mature reflection on John 5.19 ("the Son can do nothing of his own accord, but only what he sees the Father doing"). The text is a puzzling one for pro-Nicaeans both because it seems to provide evidence against a conception of inseparable operation and against the idea of the Son's equality of power with the Father. In his mature interpretation of the passage Augustine argues that we must move beyond the material and spatial imagery used by the text and grasp that the Son's "seeing" of the Father is his being; the Son sees not as an accidental act, but that eternal act of seeing constitutes what it is to be the Son.[23] Because the persons are unchangeable there cannot be a literal sequential seeing of a succession of acts performed by the Father; the Son's seeing is necessarily essential to the Son's being.[24] Moreover, this seeing *is identical with* his eternal generation from the Father. Such exegetical moves complement Augustine's insistence that each of the persons is the fulness of God as well as being that fulness with the others because they deepen Augustine's account of how the communion of the persons is constituted by their mutual acts. The persons exist only in relation, and not as sharers in a common stuff, but through the act(s) of origination that give(s) rise to their *propria* as acts. Once again, however, it is intrinsic to Augustine's argument that the scriptural material he uses to explore these acts both enable our growth in knowledge and yet, at the same time, indicate to us where we fail in under-

[23]We should, at this point, remember Augustine's insistence that there is no passive potency in God. Talking of the Aristotelian categories, he writes at *Trin.* 5.8.9 (CCSL 50.216): "Quod autem ad faciendum attinet fortassis de solo verissime dicatur; solus enim Deus facit et ipse non fit, neque pattitur quantum ad eius substantiam pertinet qua Deus est."

[24] *Tract. Ev. Jo.* 18.10; 20.8 (CCSL 36.208): ". . . videre Filii, hoc est natum esse de Patre." See also the extensive discussion at *Tract. Ev. Jo.* 21.4.

standing; that which we might see as accidental in human life is simply essential to what it is to be a divine person.

In the following passage from book 15 Augustine brings together his insistence that the persons must each be their own memory, intelligence, and will with his account of the persons as defined by their acts toward each other:

> The Word, therefore, the only-begotten Son of God the Father . . . is wholly the same as the Father, and yet is not the Father, because this is the Son, and that is the Father. And, therefore, he knows all that the Father knows; but for him to know is of the Father, as also to be is of the Father . . . And therefore, the Father, as though uttering himself, begot the Word, equal in all things to himself . . . [commenting on Jn 5.19] God the Father, therefore, knows all things in himself, and he knows all things in his Son, but in himself as himself, and in the Son as his word, the word which is spoken concerning all those things which are in himself. In like manner, the Son also knows all things, namely, in himself, as those which were born from those which the Father knows in himself, but in the Father, as those from which were born, what the Son himself knows in himself. The Father and the Son, therefore, know each other mutually, but the former by begetting, the latter by being born. And all the things that are in their knowledge, in their wisdom, in their essence, each of them sees simultaneously, not partly or singly, . . . and nothing is there which he does not see.[25]

[25] *Trin.* 15.14.23 (CCSL 50.495–7): "Verbum ergo dei patris unigenitus filius . . . est hoc omnino quod pater, non tamen pater quia iste filius, ille pater. Ac per hoc novit omnia quae novit pater, sed ei nosse de patre est sicut esse. Nosse enim et esse ibi unum est. Et ideo patri sicut esse non est a filio ita nec nosse. Proinde tamquam se ipsum dicens pater genuit verbum sibi aequale per omnia. Nouit itaque omnia deus pater in se ipso, novit in filio, sed in se ipso tamquam se ipsum, in filio tamquam verbum suum quod est de his omnibus quae sunt in se ipso. Omnia similiter novit et filius, in se scilicet tamquam ea quae nata sunt de his quae pater novit in se ipso, in patre autem tamquam ea de quibus nata sunt quae ipse filius novit in se ipso. Sciunt ergo invicem pater et filius, sed ille gignendo, ille nascendo. Et omnia quae sunt in eorum scientia, in eorum sapientia, in eorum essentia unusquisque eorum simul videt, non particulatim aut singillatim . . . nullum est quod non semper videt." For a direct statement of the failure of any analogy between human and divine persons see ibid., 15.13.22.

This passage adds one further layer to Augustine's exegesis of John 5.19: Son and Spirit can only be likened to *intellectus* and *voluntas* if we remember that they are also irreducible persons constituted by their mode of relationship to the Father. Thus, here, the Son is not understood as the act of *intellectus* within the Trinity, nor as the Father's own wisdom or knowledge (as is the case in some earlier Nicaean theologies and in Augustine's earliest work). The Son's being and being from the Father is still identical with his seeing of the Father, but Augustine also wishes to say that the Son knows all things in himself as a gift from the Father and in the Father as the source of all he knows. Similarly, the Father eternally knows himself as the source of all that he eternally chooses to know in the Word. This modification to his reading of John 5.19 is shaped by the necessity of predicating on each of the divine "persons" the rational qualities we take to mark our own status as *imago Dei*, if the persons are to be understood as truly irreducible. Interestingly, the passage is also important in showing us how far Augustine is from conceiving of the persons as notional acts within the divine life. Each divine "person" must be their own intellectual life—understood as an immediate presence, not as a sequential movement into knowledge—constituted by the mutual knowledge of Father, Son, and Spirit.[26] This knowledge is, to emphasize one of the key points of the last two paragraphs, also an ordered knowledge, in the sense that the patterns of mutual knowing are those established from eternity by the Father.[27]

[26] For further discussion of ibid., 8–15, see my "Memory, Intelligence and Will in Augustine's Trinitarian Theology," in *The Mystery of the Trinity in the Fathers of the Church,* ed. Lewis Ayres and Vincent Twomey (Dublin: Four Courts Press, 2007), 37–64.

[27] André de Halleux has offered an extensive critique of the idea that Augustine and the Cappadocians can be encompassed under a division between "essentialism" and "personalism." I hope this section of my argument has further indicated the uselessness of the distinction by emphasizing that Augustine's own account of the trinitarian communion established from eternity by the Father itself bears many of the hallmarks that supposedly mark the Cappadocians as "personalist." I hope it is clear, however, that Augustine's focus on the trinitarian persons as constituting the divine essence and as themselves possessing (or rather, being) the attributes of rational, desiring life is always analogical or perhaps anagogical: the discussion of the three as agents is always accompanied by emphasis on ways in which they transcend that which we know in ourselves of the personal. Andrew Louth, "Love and the Trinity: Saint Augustine and the Greek Fathers," *Augustinian Studies* 33

The examples I have given in this section of the paper to establish Augustine's account of the trinitarian communion have mostly concerned the relationship between Father and Son; it is time now to see how Augustine's mature pneumatology completes his account of this communion as eternally established by the persons' mutual relationships.

Sempiterne Spiritus Donum

I want to begin with two texts, separated by around a decade. In book 6 of *De Trinitate*, Augustine writes as follows:

> Whether [the Holy Spirit] is the unity between [Father and Son], or their holiness, or their love, or whether the unity because he is the love, it is obvious that he is not one of the two. Through him both are joined together; through him the begotten is loved by the begetter, and in turn loves him who begot him; in him they preserve the unity of spirit through the bond of peace, not by a participation, but by their own essence, not by the gift of anyone superior to themselves but by their own gift . . .[28]

In book 15 of the same work, we find:

(2002): 1–16, is one of a very small number of modern scholars—especially Orthodox scholars—to read Augustine as in any sense a "personalist" (though see the conclusion to this paper). I disagree with his reading, however, because he does not take sufficient account of this analogical or anagogic quality, and because he does not give sufficient weight to the way in which Augustine understands the mutual relationships of the three as an ordered mutuality described in scripture. See also, below, n. 35. I discuss the question of Augustine's "personalism" in some detail in my *Augustine and the Trinity* (Cambridge: Cambridge University Press, 2009).

[28] *Trin.* 6.5.7 (CCSL 50.235): "Sive enim sit unitas amborum sive sanctitas sive caritas, sive ideo unitas quia caritas et ideo caritas, quia sanctitas, manifestum est quod non aliquis duorum est quo uterque coniungitur, quo genitus a gignente diligatur generatoremque suum diligat, sintque non participatione sed essentia sua neque dono superioris alicuius sed suo proprio servantes unitatem spiritus in vinculo pacis. . . . Spiritus ergo sanctus commune aliquid est patris et filii, quidquid illud est, aut ipsa communio consubstantialis et coaeterna . . ."

Nor because they give and he is given is he, therefore, less than they, for he is so given as the gift of God that he also gives himself as God. For it is impossible to say of him that he is not a master of his own power, of whom it was said: "the Spirit breathes where he will"... there is no subordination of the Gift and no domination of the givers, but the concord between the gift and the givers.[29]

Before we come directly to the character of the trinitarian communion discussed here, it will be helpful to think for a moment about the exegetical foundations of Augustine's paralleling of the titles "love" and "gift." Augustine's mature account of the Spirit's *proprium* is shaped by a complex exegetical matrix. The best way to examine that exegesis is via Augustine's reflection on the Spirit as the Spirit of Father and the Spirit of Son. This theme takes on importance in Augustine's corpus for the first time in books 5 to 7 of *De Trinitate*, and it does so there as Augustine reflects on the oddity of the name Holy Spirit.[30] Because Father, Son, and Spirit are all holy and all spirit, scripture must use these terms in two distinct ways. In the first place, the terms are individually used to designate each person of the Trinity, and thus the Trinity itself can be called "Holy Spirit." In the second place, scripture speaks of the Holy Spirit in particular by this combination of terms, inviting us into reflection on one of the most complex of trinitarian mysteries. The name "Holy Spirit" is important, Augustine argues, because it draws our attention to the fact that the Holy Spirit is also the Spirit of both Father and Son. Nevertheless, neither the name "Holy Spirit," nor the parallel designation "Spirit of" reveals to us the sort of relationship implied between the Father and his Spirit or the

---

[29]Ibid., 15.19.36 (CCSL 50.513): "Nec quia illi dant, ipse datur, ideo minor est illis. Ita enim datur sicut dei donum ut etiam se ipsum det sicut deus. Non enim dici potest non esse suae potestatis de quo dictum est: Spiritus ubi vult spirat ... Non est illic conditio dati et dominatio dantium sed concordia dati et dantium."

[30]Ibid., 5.11.12. This focus on the Spirit being "of" Father and "of" Son is not evident in the summary of trinitarian theology at ibid., 1.4.7–6.13. The statement (without any supporting exegesis) that the Spirit is the Spirit of the Father and of the Son first appears at ibid., 4.29. Discussion of the relevant texts first occurs at ibid., 5. The first statement of the summary principle or extended exegesis outside ibid., appears to be at *Tract. Ev. Jo.* 9.7, although this text may slightly pre-date or post-date the composition of *Trin.* 4–7.

Son and his Spirit. That relationship only becomes clear when we reflect on the title "gift." The distinction between "giver" and "gift," however, alongside the description of the Spirit as the Spirit "of Father" and "of Son," lets us know that we are talking about the relationship between three irreducible realities, Father, Son, and Spirit; Spirit does not refer merely to an aspect or intrinsic property of Father and Son.[31]

While, as Augustine himself knows full well, the title "gift" itself is used by scripture of that which is given to Christians for their salvation,[32] Augustine contends that the Spirit is eternally gift on the basis of further links that he suggests scripture invites us to draw.[33] These links are stated with greatest clarity in book 15 of *De Trinitate*, and it may be only in writing this book that he finally saw the full matrix of links he wishes to draw. The term "gift" is used, Augustine tells us there, *because* the Spirit is also love.[34] That which the Father gives us is the Spirit of his Son (Gal 4.6), but the gift *of* the Spirit *is* the Spirit, and the Spirit is love (Rom 5.5).[35] "Love," like "Spirit," is a term that may be predicated of all three persons, but which, Augustine argues, scripture uses so that when we grasp that the love which the Spirit gives is the Spirit, we will understand that the love which we receive is the love with which Father and Son love each other. The clarity that we find in book 15 over the hesitancy of book 5 probably resulted from an increasingly strong commitment to this exegetical link; we are seeing Augustine's pneumatology still in the course of development.

---

[31]Again, ibid., 5.11.12.

[32]See ibid., 15.19.35.

[33]See e.g. ibid., 5.16.17 (CCSL 50.224): . . . *sempiterne Spiritus donum.*

[34]See ibid., 15.18.32. The linking of love, Spirit, and gift is first discussed extensively in *De fide et symb.* 9.19 (AD 393).

[35]Louth, "Love and the Trinity," sees Augustine as arguing that the Spirit is a uniting love *because of* his conception of the role of love among Christians. This then enables him to see Augustine's procedure as a misuse of *oikonomia* as *theologia*. Such a reading seems to me to miss the complexity of Augustine's arguments that the salvific actions of the persons are also a revealing of their eternal natures. At the same time I would suggest there is far more to draw our attention in Augustine's understanding of the complex ways in which scripture speaks of the Spirit, inviting us to make connections that only become apparent as we are drawn into the process of sanctification.

This exegetical structure is complex, but it is so for Augustine *because* scripture invites Christians into a meditation on the Spirit that takes them to the heart of their faith. As I suggested in the first section of the paper, Augustine sees the revelation of the Spirit's role in the economy as an invitation for us to reflect on the character of salvation as the process of being drawn into the divine communion itself; what it is to be given the gift of the Spirit is most deeply understood when that act of giving is seen as a sharing in the love that constitutes the trinitarian communion. Augustine knows full well that here we are straining the eyes of faith toward the outer rim of what may be seen of the divine communion this side of the judgment, but such straining is itself essential to the life of faith.[36]

This exegetical excursus sets the stage for us to examine how Augustine envisages the Spirit not only as bond and love but also as personal. Let me quote again:

> Through him both are joined together; through him the begotten is loved by the begetter, and in turn loves him who begot him; in him they preserve the unity of spirit through the bond of peace, not by a participation, but by their own essence, not by the gift of anyone superior to themselves but by their own gift . . .

Father and Son maintain their "unity of spirit" and "bond of peace" not through any participation in an underlying reality nor by receiving a gift of unity from above (the reference here being, I think, to the unity of Christians in the body of Christ). Rather they maintain this unity by their *acts* of giving and loving; the Father giving and loving as the one who begets, the Son giving and loving the one who begot him. The mutual love of which Augustine speaks is thus a love identical with the eternally constitutive acts that are what it is to be Father and Son; their love is their essence because in God there is nothing accidental. When Father and Son give this love, what they give is what it is to be Father and Son; it is their

---

[36]See my "Augustine on the Rule of Faith: Rhetoric, Christology, and the Foundation of Christian Thinking," *Augustinian Studies* 36 (2005): 33–49; see also the paper by Carol Harrison in this volume.

own gift and (being God) necessarily a gift of themselves. And so, if the Spirit is love, that love must be the fulness of God, fully wisdom and truth and life and power; that love must, hence, be an active giving gift, it must be an irreducible divine "person."[37]

When Augustine writes that Father and Son preserve their unity through their own substance, he most emphatically does not mean that Father and Son are one because they both participate in a common essence mistakenly identified with the Spirit; he means that Father and Son are one in communion through the personal reality of the Spirit given in the begetting of the Son and returned by the Son as an act constitutive of what it is to be Son. But even this sentence does not capture Augustine's point because it misses his emphasis on the Spirit as both gift *and* giver; we can also say that Father and Son are one because the Spirit gives himself in the begetting of the Son and gives himself as the Son's love for the Father.

In the thirty-ninth of Augustine's *In Evangelium Johannis tractatus* (*Tractates on the Gospel of John*), probably written in the same few years as he was finishing the *De Trinitate*, we find:

> ... [if] many souls through love are one soul, and many hearts are one heart, what does the very fountain of love do in the Father and the Son? ... If, therefore, "the love of God [which] has been poured forth in our hearts by the Holy Spirit who has been given to us" makes many souls one soul and many hearts one heart, how much more does [the Spirit] make the Father and the Son and the Holy Spirit one God, one light, one *principium*?[38]

[37]My language here owes something to Rowan D. Williams, "*Sapientia* and the Trinity: Reflections on the *De trinitate*," in *Collectanea Augustiniana: Mélanges T.J. Van Bavel*, ed. B. Bruning, et al. (Leuven: Leuven University Press, 1990) =*Aug(L)* 40–1 (1990–91), vol. 1, 317–32, at 327–28: "The Spirit is 'common' to Father and Son not as a quality characterizing them equally, an impersonal attribute, but as that active divine giving, not simply identical with the person of the Father, which the Father communicates to the Son to give in his turn ... the Father, in eternally giving (divine) life to the Son, gives that life as itself a 'giving' agency, for there is no pre-personal or sub-personal divinity; he gives the Son the capacity to give that same giving life ..." I am less convinced by Williams' applying to the Spirit as such than by his account of *dilectio* as always love in search of an object.

[38]*Tract. Ev. Jo.* 39.5 (CCSL 36.348): "si ... multae animae per caritatem una anima est,

Only in his mature writing does Augustine make this specific link between the function of the Spirit in the Christian community and the Spirit's function within the communion of the Trinity. He does so three times in his *In Evangelium Johannis tractatus* and a few more times, mostly in directly anti-Arian contexts, although not in the *De Trinitate* itself.[39] The infrequency of its use perhaps belies its significance in grasping the central theme of Augustine's mature pneumatology; the Father breathes the Spirit as the one who actively constitutes Father, Son, and Spirit (note, not merely Father and Son) as the one God.

Whether we use the term "substance" or "essence" in contrast to person in trinitarian discourse, our implicit assumption is all too easily that essence names something non-personal; for Augustine, this cannot be because the essence *is* the communion of persons. It is at this point that I think we see to the heart of how Augustine envisages the Father as *principium*. It is not simply that the Father gives rise to a communion of three who are equal. The Father gives rise to a communion constituting the essence of God and defined by his act or acts of generation and spiration. The Father breathes the Spirit in the same act in which he generates the Son, and the Son is the Son because the Spirit is the essence of Father and Son as active giving love.[40] The Father is eternally the fulness of God—on

---

et multa corda unum cor; quid agit ipse fons caritatis in patre et filio? nonne ibi magis trinitas unus est deus? Inde enim nobis caritas venit, de ipso spiritu sancto, sicut dicit apostolus: caritas dei diffusa est in cordibus nostris per spiritum sanctum qui datus est nobis. Si ergo caritas dei diffusa in cordibus nostris per spiritum sanctum qui datus est nobis, multas animas facit unam animam, et multa corda facit unum cor, quanto magis pater et filius et spiritus sanctus, deus unus, lumen unum, unumque principium?"

[39] *Tract. Ev. Jo.* 14.9, 18.4; *Serm.* 47.21, 229G.5.6 (*s. Guelf.* 11); *De symb. ad cat.* 2.4; *Ep.* 170.5, 238. 2. 13 and 16. For discussion see M.F. Berrouard, "La première communauté de Jérusalem comme image de l'unitéde la Trinité. Une des exegeses augustiniennes d'Act 4, 32," in *Homo Spiritalis. Festgabe für Luc Verheijen* (Würzburg, 1987), 207–24.

[40] This sentence finds an interesting parallel in Thomas Weinandy, *The Father's Spirit of Sonship: Reconceiving the Trinity* (Edinburgh: T&T Clark, 1995), 69. See also 50: "If the Spirit is the love in whom the Father begets the Son and so conforms himself as Father and conforms the Son as Son, then to say 'God is Love' is not a statement about God's generic nature, but specifies the very heart of the Trinitarian life and designates that it is the Spirit that makes the life of God Trinitarian." My account of Augustine parallels this account even if Augustine does not offer discussion of the Father "conforming himself" in any way.

this as we have seen Augustine is clear—but the Father is also the fulness of God with Son and Spirit.

To what extent can we say that the generation of Son and spiration of Spirit determines the being of the Father? If the Father's essence is the love he shares with the Son and which is returned by the Son, then surely something along these lines must be said? But I do not know of a text in Augustine's corpus that even broaches this possibility. I suspect that, for Augustine, beginning such a discussion would allow a certain temporal dimension to insinuate itself into our conception of the Trinity; there is no act of generation followed by a secondary consequence. The best we can say is that the Father from eternity *is* the fulness of God and is so *as* the act of giving rise to Son and Spirit as the communion that is the fulness of God.

Filioque

After all this delay, we come to what many readers may have expected to be the main act of the show. In book 15 of the *De Trinitate*, Augustine famously writes:

> Only he from whom the Son was begotten and from whom the Spirit principally [*principaliter*] proceeds, is God the Father. I have added principally therefore because the Holy Spirit is also found to proceed from the Son. But the Father also gave this to him, not as though he already existed and did not yet have it, but whatever he gave to the only-begotten Word, he gave by begetting him. He so begot him, therefore, that the common gift should also proceed from him, and that the Holy Spirit should be the Spirit of both.[41]

Augustine, I suspect, would endorse much of what Weinandy intends by arguing for the thesis that the Father begets the Son in the Spirit.

[41] *Trin.* 15.17.29 (CCSL 50.503): "Et tamen non frustra in hac trinitate non dicitur verbum dei nisi filius, nec donum dei nisi spiritus sanctus, nec de quo genitum est verbum et de quo procedit principaliter spiritus sanctus nisi deus pater. Ideo autem addidi, princi-

It is, of course, commonly remarked that this passage offers us an archetypal statement of Augustine's insistence that his account of double procession finds at its core a restatement of the Father's *principium* within the Trinity. But I think it equally important that we see the extent to which this passage is simply an extension of the ideas we have explored so far. Exegetically the foundation of Augustine's discussion of procession is the matrix of texts drawn together by his mature consideration of why the Spirit is the Spirit of the Father and the Son. Ontologically, his understanding of the Spirit's procession rests on his sense of the character of the divine persons as each the fulness of God and the atemporality of the divine being. The Father's begetting of the Son is identical with the establishment of the communion of Father, Son, and Spirit because in the begetting of the Son the Father gives his love (or substance), thus eternally establishing the Son as lover of the Father and the Spirit as the personal giving love of Father and Son.

His argument is further refined a little later in book 15:

And he who can understand in that which the Son says: "as the Father has life in himself, so he has given to the Son to have life in himself," that the Father did not give life to the Son already existing without life, but so begot him apart from time that the life which the Father gave to the Son by begetting is co-eternal with the life of the Father who gave; let him understand that, just as the Father has in himself that the Holy Spirit should proceed from the Father, it is so to be understood that his proceeding also from the Son comes to the Son from the Father. For if whatever he has, the Son has from the Father, then certainly he has from the Father that the Holy Spirit also proceeds from him.[42]

---

paliter, quia et de filio spiritus sanctus procedere reperitur. Sed hoc quoque illi pater dedit (non iam exsistenti et nondum habenti), sed quidquid unigenito verbo dedit gignendo dedit. Sic ergo eum genuit ut etiam de illo donum commune procederet et spiritus sanctus spiritus esset amborum." For a seminal discussion of pneumatology in book 15 see, Basil Studer, "Zur Pneumatologie des Augustinus von Hippo (*De Trinitate* 15.17.27–50)," in *Mysterium Caritatis: Studien zur Exegese und zur Trinitätslehre in der Alten Kirche*, Studia Anselmiana, vol. 127 (Rome: Pontifico Ateneo S. Anselmo, 1999), 311–27.

[42] *Trin* 15.26.47 (CCSL 50.528): "Et qui potest intellegere in eo quod ait filius: Sicut habet

At the end of book 15, Augustine quotes from his own ninety-ninth tractate on John a passage that draws out a further consequence:

> But of him, of whom the Son has it that he is God, he has it, of course,
> that the Holy Spirit also proceeds from him. And because of this the
> Holy Spirit has it from the Father himself that he proceeds also from
> the Son, just as he proceeds from the Father.[43]

Together these passages only reinforce what we have seen, but they do
perhaps also show that in his final extensive attempt to develop this theme
Augustine emphasizes that the communion established comes into being
at all stages through the Father's eternal act.[44] The constitution of the Son
as image, truth, wisdom, and power *is* the constitution by the Father of the
Son as the one who sees all in the Father and of the Son as the one who
loves the Father in the Spirit. For the Spirit to proceed from the Son is for
the Father to establish the Spirit as the active giving love that joins the
three from eternity in a consubstantial union.

In the atemporal context of the divine communion, questions of
whether the Son mediates the Spirit or acts as secondary cause become
extremely difficult to pose, and it is perhaps no accident that Augustine
offers no discussion of the question. The Father generates the Son in the
act to which he gives rise to the trinitarian communion in the Spirit, the
Spirit is given to the Son in order that the Spirit will come forth from the
Son; but this both gives and does not give the Son a role in the constitution of the Spirit. It does give because the Father does not give to the Son
a Spirit as it were "fully formed" who then comes in some subsequent act

---

pater vitam in semetipso sic dedit filio vitam habere in semetipso non sine vita exsistenti
iam filio vitam patrem dedisse sed ita eum sine tempore genuisse ut vita quam pater filio
gignendo dedit coaeterna sit vitae patris qui dedit, intellegat sicut habet pater in semetipso
ut et de illo procedat spiritus sanctus sic dedisse filio ut de illo procedat idem spiritus sanctus et utrumque sine tempore, atque ita dictum spiritum sanctum de patre procedere ut
intellegatur quod etiam procedit de filio, de patre esse filio. Si enim quidquid habet de patre
habet filius, de patre habet utique ut et de illo procedat spiritus sanctus."

[43]Ibid., 15.27.48 and *Tract. Ev. Jo.* 99.8.
[44]I say "final" because we do not find extensive attempts to explore this theme in the
late anti-"Arian" works.

from the Son; the Spirit is eternally breathed as the love who eternally comes into being as the love given and returned. And yet, the Spirit comes from the Father as personal and active giving love who gives himself in the Son to the Father and does so at the Father's breathing. If, and here I suspect Augustine would say that the eyes of faith simply fail, the Son forms the Spirit's hypostatic existence, he does so because this is the manner in which the Father breathes forth the Spirit.[45]

Thinking with Professor Ratzinger

In a *festschrift* article from 1974, the then Professor Ratzinger expands on some implicit themes in his 1953 dissertation to offer an account of the ways in which he sees Augustine's pneumatology contributing to the emergence of a fully trinitarian and Christian metaphysic.[46] Ratzinger argues first that the identification of the Spirit as shared by Father and Son

[45]It is, I suggest, instructive to note a hiccup in Augustine's treatment of the Father as *principium* in the Trinity. In his discussion of the Spirit in the *De fide et symb.* of 393 Augustine remarks that we say the Spirit is from the Father so that we are not seen to introduce more than one *principium* in the Godhead. *Principium* here seems fairly clearly to mean an active causal source. At the same time, from early on Augustine insists that the Trinity must be one *principium* in relationship to creation. But in book 5 of *Trin.* we find a fairly convoluted discussion of the use of the term in the intra-trinitarian relations. The Father is *principium* of the Son as his begetter, and of the Spirit as his giver—proceed here being interestingly interpreted as meaning giver. Because the Son gives the Spirit as his own essence, and because he has "life in himself," the Son must also be described as the Spirit's *principium*. But in the same way as Father and Son are one God we must say they are the one *principium* of the Spirit. The most interesting aspect of this passage is that it is *not* repeated: by book 15, around ten to fifteen years later, Augustine resorts to the language we saw above: speaking of the Father as *principium*, and of the Spirit as proceeding from the Father *principaliter*, and emphasizing that the Father gives it to the Son that the Spirit proceeds from him also. This choice seems intentional. See also *Contra Max.* 2.5: "dicis vos spiritum sanctum competenter honorare ut doctorem, ut ducatorem, ut illuminatorem, ut sanctificatorem; Christum colere, ut creatorem; patrem cum sincera devotione adorare, ut auctorem. Si auctorem propterea dicis patrem, quia de ipso est filius, non est autem ipse de filio; et quia de illo et filio sic procedit spiritus sanctus, ut ipse hoc dederit filio gignendo eum talem, ut etiam de ipso procedat spiritus sanctus . . ."

[46]Joseph Ratzinger, "The Holy Spirit as Communio: Concerning the Relationship of Pneumatology and Spirituality in Augustine," *Communio* 25 (1998): 324–37.

and as irreducible person affirms the fully personal nature of the Trinity as communion:

> The mediation of Father and Son comes to full unity not when it is seen in a universal ontic *consubstantialis* but as *communio* . . . The dyad returns into unity in the trinity without breaking up the dialogue. Dialogue is actually confirmed in this way. A mediation back into unity which was not another person would break up the dialogue. The Spirit is Person as unity, unity as Person.[47]

Ratzinger then argues that this clarity affects a shift in the "metaphysics of Spirit." Describing God as Spirit (Jn 4.24) is no longer to describe an opposition between spirit and matter, but between the Spirit within the trinitarian community and the world. Describing God thus both personalizes the nature of Spirit and results in the consequence that to know the nature of Spirit one must know the Holy Spirit:

> Only one who knows what "Holy Spirit" is, can know what Spirit means. And only one who begins to know what God is, can know what spirit means. Furthermore, only one who begins to have an idea of what Holy Spirit is, can begin to know who God is.[48]

Professor Ratzinger was, I think, partly right. Augustine not only offers one of the most sustained attempts in this period to conceive of the Trinity as irreducible unity without resorting to notions of an underlying "stuff," but also one of the most sustained pro-Nicaean attempts to understand the communion of the three persons as the result of the Father's eternal act. Augustine's trinitarian vision suggests ways of understanding the Father's role as *principium* that penetrates to the heart of what it means to speak of God as love; from eternity the Father gives fully of himself to establish a communion in the Spirit of love.[49] I think we can also

---

[47]Ibid., 326.
[48]Ibid., 327.
[49]Here we see a good example of the tension with which I began. In the interests of ecu-

say that in Augustine's mature texts the hard work of divine metaphysics is done through trinitarian categories. It is not that we no longer find *en passant* discussion of what it means for God to be immaterial, non-spatial, and so forth, but that the discussions that seem to have the most profound ramifications for how we understand the divine being focus on how we understand the divine life to be shared by the divine persons.

And yet a corrective must, I suggest, be offered.[50] Professor Ratzinger is willing at least to allude to personalist language to describe Augustine's trinitarianism, and it might seem that much of my own argument is consonant with his fundamental picture. However, even as it is certainly true that Augustine offers an account of the inter-personal constitution of the trinitarian communion very different from what modern summary accounts would lead one to expect, it is also the case that Augustine sees good application of personal and agential language to Father, Son, and Spirit as inseparable from a growing attention to the ways in which the divine "persons" transcend human personhood. Because the Father has established a communion of true unity in which the Trinity is one substance, will, and power, and because of the character of the communion established from eternity by the Father, in which all that is essential to the persons is shared, we are unable to understand the character of a divine person in the abstract. Augustine's "personalism" is always analogical or anagogical; and for him this approach is demanded of us by the most basic dynamics of pro-Nicaean theology. Indeed, the very character of divine love itself is unknown to us; the more we allow our trinitarian faith to guide our interpretation of that which we think we experience, the more the eternal presence that is divine love is seen to transcend all that

menical rapprochement Catholic theologians have, rightly, come to emphasize that the Latin *procedere* encompasses two Greek terms that Orthodox theologians wish to keep separate: ἐκπορεύω, used for the Spirit's coming from the Father and προΐημι, used to describe the Spirit's mission and eternal manifestation from the Son. And yet too much focus on such terminology draws our attention away from considering what we mean when we assert the Father's *principium* in the Trinity. Augustine may well find himself dealing with an ambiguous term in *procedere*, but his use of it enables one of the most suggestive theologies of the Father's *principium*.

[50]I would not also want to speak quite so easily of "an" ancient metaphysic, but that is a separate question.

we thought we knew.[51] The character of the communion that is the Trinity is the object of our contemplation and yet—for now—constantly beyond us.

This is not to deny that the divine life is, for Augustine, fundamentally intelligible. That it is so quite probably has its origins in his early anti-Manichean and anti-skeptical reception or appropriation of Platonic themes. For Augustine the intelligibility of the divine life guarantees that the created order is itself intelligible and that there may be progress in knowledge of God. This last point is of great importance here; God's intelligibility does not guarantee that God may be comprehended in this life, but that the possibility of growth *toward* vision, growth toward the point at which faith is replaced with sight, is possible. Appropriate exploration of the trinitarian communion is, for Augustine, always experienced as an awareness of the failings of the progress we have made, but that awareness is its most productive when it is also an awareness of our need for grace if we are to traverse the route of Christ's person and come to understand his human nature as a revealing of the Word through whom and in whom all things were created. Our not knowing thus receives a peculiarly Christian cast, and we are returned to the connections between Augustine's mature pneumatolgoy and his account of Christian life as one given shape through the Spirit's gift.

---

[51]The bounds of discussion about whether Augustine can fairly be described as "apophatic" have been set by Vladimir Lossky's "Les éléments de 'Théologie négative' dans la pensée de saint Augustin," in *Augustinus Magister,* vol. 1 (Paris: Études Augustiniennes, 1954), 575–81 (English trans., "Elements of 'Negative Theology' in the Thought of St. Augustine," *SVTQ* 21 [1977]: 67–75). Lossky argues that ultimately Augustine is not fully an "apophatic" theologian because he does not yet understand God to be beyond being. This is fine as far as it goes and certainly gives a technical sense to the term desperately lacking from much modern usage. Lossky does not, however, ask whether the variety of rhetorical techniques used by pro-Nicaeans in the late fourth and early fifth centuries (*none* of whom I suspect, pace David Bradshaw, are at all consistent in their reading of *Republic* 509B) to undermine the certainties of predication that scripture sometimes seems to allow prefigure much of what comes, with Ps.-Dionysius, to define the apophatic.

Calling upon God as Father: Augustine and the Legacy of Nicaea

John Behr

The past century was not a good one for Blessed Augustine: during its course, he was subject to increasingly severe criticism for his trinitarian theology. This misfortune occurred as the so-called "de Régnon paradigm"—that the Greeks began with the three and moved to the unity, while the Latins began with the one before treating the three—migrated from a temporal to a spatial horizon. What was, for Théodore de Régnon himself, a diachronic development—from the patristic period, culminating in the Cappadocians, to the scholastic period, beginning with Augustine—became, at least in English-speaking scholarship, a geographic distinction pitting the Greek East against the Latin West,[1] and in so doing assumed features characteristic of broader concerns in the twentieth century, especially the primacy of the "person": the personalism of the Greeks emphasized the priority of the person over nature, while Latin essentialism subjugates the person to nature. That Augustine admitted bewilderment, whether real or rhetorical, at the Greek distinction between *ousia* and *hypostasis*, seems only to confirm this picture, even if it has been drawn as a result of other considerations.[2]

Arriving in the West in the early part of the century, it is perhaps not surprising that Russian Orthodox émigré theologians, wanting to empha-

---

[1] Cf. Michel R. Barnes, "De Régnon Reconsidered," *Augustinian Studies* 26.2 (1995): 51–79.

[2] That this bewilderment might be rhetorical, as Augustine reflects on the applicability of analogies for the Trinity, is suggested by R. Cross, "*Quid tres?* On What Precisely Augustine Professes Not to Understand in *De Trinitate* V and VII," *Harvard Theological Review* 100.2 (2007): 215–32.

size the distinctiveness of their own theological tradition and its superiority to that stemming from Augustine, had recourse to this framework. Vladimir Lossky, explicitly basing himself on de Régnon, argued that the *filioque* formula was but the necessary outcome of the Latin approach to the Trinity, although his main foil was not Augustine himself but the Aquinas of neo-scholasticism.[3] More recently, Metropolitan John (Zizioulas) has claimed that this approach makes οὐσία rather than ὑπόστασις the ultimate reality and causal principle in the being of God, so betraying the insight of the Cappadocians that it is the *person*, specifically the Father in a trinitarian communion with the Son and the Spirit, who is the ground of all being.[4]

Nor are such claims limited to Orthodox theologians. Following the lament of Karl Rahner that most Christians are "mere monotheists" and his call to pay closer attention to the economic dimensions of trinitarian theology, and therefore also to its scriptural groundings, the last decades of the past century saw a renaissance of interest in the Trinity.[5] Such works have invariably taken their lead from Rahner to return to a "Greek" approach, which, it is believed, does more justice to the scriptural account of salvation history and opens up a horizon in which the value of the person can become fully apparent, in a social model of trinitarian communion.[6] With this agenda driving inquiry, Augustine has inevitably faired poorly. In one popular account, the reader is informed already in the opening pages, before any serious work is done, that "Augustine inaugurated an entirely new approach. His starting point was not the creedal and biblical sense of the monarchy of the Father, but the divine essence shared

    [3]Vladimir Lossky, *The Mystical Theology of the Eastern Church*, trans. Fellowship of St Alban and St Sergius (London: James Clarke, 1957), 58. For Lossky's use of de Régnon, see Barnes, "De Régnon Reconsidered," 57–58, although his claims about the extent of Lossky's dependence on de Régnon have since been challenged by Aristotle Papanikolaou, *Being with God: Trinity, Apophaticism, and Divine-Human Communion* (Notre Dame: University of Notre Dame Press, 2006), 181 n.101.
    [4]John D. Zizioulas, *Being as Communion* (Crestwood, NY: SVS Press, 1985), 88.
    [5]Karl Rahner, *The Trinity*, trans. J. Donceel (Tunbridge Wells, UK: Burns and Oates, 1970), 10.
    [6]For the problems inherent in this social model, see Karen Kilby, "Perichoresis and Projection: Problems with the Social Doctrine of the Trinity," *New Blackfriars* 81 (2000): 432–45.

equally by the three persons."[7] The familiar lineaments are starkly drawn, only the details need to be shown. Arguing against a similar popular supposed opposition, this time between Greek and Semitic patterns of thought, James Barr cautioned that the very simplicity of such caricatures, which are readily understandable before one acquires any serious knowledge of either Greek or Semitic literature (or in our case, the writings of the Cappadocians and Augustine), should give us pause before assuming that these are either self-evidently true or have any basis in historical reality. He further notes that the effect of this caricature is that students are less likely to study the Greeks for themselves with any seriousness, instead simply finding in them the straw-man that they have been led to expect.[8] In our case, however, it is the Greeks who are being studied (though one would often do well to question the results), while Augustine's trinitarian theology has yet to be seriously explored by any twentieth-century Eastern Orthodox writer.

Against this general tendency, nevertheless, there have appeared more recently new voices arguing that the situation is, if truth be told, not so bleak. Michel Barnes and Lewis Ayres, in particular (though there are others), have argued that Augustine, in fact, shares many features of trinitarian theology with the Cappadocians, so that there is a generally recognizable "pro-Nicaean" trinitarian theology common to both Greek and Latin traditions, despite the variations not only between them but also within them.[9] Augustine's contribution, therefore, is not a radically new

---

[7]Catherine Mowry LaCugna, *God for Us: The Trinity and Christian Life* (San Francisco: HarperSanFrancisco, 1991), 10.

[8]James Barr, *Old and New in Interpretation* (New York: Harper and Row, 1966), 34–38.

[9]In addition to Barnes, "De Régnon Reconsidered," see also his "Rereading Augustine's Theology of the Trinity," in *The Trinity: An Interdisciplinary Symposium on the Trinity*, ed. S.T. Davis, D. Kendall, and G. O'Collins (Oxford: Oxford University Press, 1999), 145–76. From Lewis Ayres, see "The Fundamental Grammar of Augustine's Trinitarian Theology," in *Augustine and His Critics: Essays in Honor of Gerald Bonner*, ed. R. Dodaro and G. Lawless (London: Routledge, 2000), 51–76; "'Remember That You Are Catholic' (Serm. 52.2): Augustine on the Unity of the Triune God," *Journal of Early Christian Studies* 8.1 (2000): 39–82; and *Nicaea and Its Legacy: An Approach to Fourth-Century Trinitarian Theology* (Oxford: Oxford University Press, 2004). For other voices questioning the supposed opposition between eastern and western trinitarian theology, see Rowan Williams, "*Sapientia*

turn, but a deepened, more clearly articulated expression of a common body of inherited belief.

Two constant elements of this reassessment are Augustine's deployment of the doctrine of inseparable operations and a more complete understanding of the simplicity of God. Ayres has pointed to the importance of a usually ignored early text, Augustine's letter to Nebridius (from AD 389, three years after Augustine's conversion), which attempts to answer the question why it was that the Son alone, and not the Father or the Spirit, is said to have become incarnate. Augustine's answer is to point to how the Catholic tradition teaches the inseparability of the three persons:

> For the union of persons in the Trinity is, in the catholic faith, set forth and believed, and by a few holy and blessed ones understood, to be so inseparable that whatever is done by the Trinity must be regarded as being done by the Father and the Son and the Holy Spirit together; and that nothing is done by the Father which is not also done by the Son and the Holy Spirit together, and that nothing is done by the Holy Spirit which is not done by the Father and by the Son, and nothing is done by the Son which is not also done by the Father and the Holy Spirit.[10]

Augustine does not argue for the inseparability of the activity of the three persons, but simply assumes it as part of the inherited tradition. One can indeed find many earlier writers, eastern and western, from Ambrose to Gregory of Nyssa, who state this principle explicitly.[11] Regarding the question that then arises—why do we speak, as we indeed do "in our mysteries and sacred rites," of the Son becoming incarnate, and not the Father or the

and the Trinity: Reflections on *De trinitate*," in *Collectanea Augustiniana: Mélanges T.J. van Bavel*, ed. B. Bruning, M. Lamberigts, and J. van Houlin (Leuven: Leuven University Press, 1990), 317–22; David B. Hart, "The Mirror of the Infinite: Gregory of Nyssa on the *Vestigia Trinitatis*," in *Re-thinking Gregory of Nyssa*, ed. S. Coakley (Oxford: Blackwell, 2003), 111–31.

[10]*Ep.* 11.2.

[11]Cf. Ayres, "Remember That You Are Catholic," 46–49.

Spirit—Augustine admits that it is a subject so vast "that it is impossible either to give a sufficiently clear statement or to support it by satisfactory proofs."[12] Ayres suggests that Augustine's answer involves reformulating the question so that it becomes not "why the Son became incarnate," but "why we must speak *as if* the Son alone works in the incarnation," shifting the focus from "a consideration of God to a consideration of how God may inculcate knowledge of God in us."[13] Using the analogy of the three aspects of any given thing—that it is, that it is this or that, and that as far as possible it remains as it is—Augustine argues not that each person can be aligned to any of these aspects but that "there is nothing in which all have not a part."[14] What appears initially as the work of the Son alone is, upon further reflection, the revelation of the Father in the Son through the Spirit who guides us into this truth. In this way, as Ayres puts it, the incarnation is "the basic plot of a divine action or drama in which the Father, as the one principle, sends the Son to provide knowledge or under- standing and the Spirit to provide a lasting delight in that understand- ing."[15] This is a dispensation aimed at educating our fallen minds, moving them to the perception of the inseparable action of the Trinity as under- stood by the holy and blessed ones.

This doctrine of the inseparability of operations, a fixed part of Augus- tine's early theological apparatus, is itself inseparably bound up with the doctrine of divine simplicity. In his treatise *De fide et symbolo* (*On the Faith and Creed*), written four years after his letter to Nebridius, Augus- tine asserts we must believe that:

> The Trinity is one God, not that the Father is the same as the Son and the Spirit, but that the Father is Father, the Son is Son, and the Holy Spirit is the Holy Spirit, and this Trinity is one God, as it is written: "Hear, O Israel, the Lord your God is one Lord" (Deut 6.4).[16]

[12] *Ep.* 11.2.
[13] Ayres, "Remember That You Are Catholic," 50, 51.
[14] *Ep.* 11.3.
[15] Ayres, "Remember That You Are Catholic," 53–54.
[16] *De fide et symb.* 9.16.

While calling upon the Trinity as the one God, we are also to affirm that each is God. As he puts it a little later:

> We should call the Father God, the Son God, the Holy Spirit God; not three gods, but that the Trinity is one God, neither diverse in nature but of the same substance; neither that the Father is sometimes the Son, and sometimes the Holy Spirit, but that the Father is always Father, the Son is always Son, and the Holy Spirit always the Holy Spirit.[17]

Each is truly God; this is to be maintained against all attempts at subordinationism. Yet the three are the one God, the bedrock of scriptural monotheism, while remaining what they are, so avoiding any suggestion of modalism.

How this is to be understood is explained most fully in the account of divine simplicity presented in books 5 to 7 of *De Trinitate* (*On the Trinity*). The central point of this doctrine is that in God all qualities are identical with his essence—it is not one thing for him to be and another thing for him to be wise: "in God to be is the same as to be wise."[18] But, lest we end up concluding that the Son, as begotten, is necessarily other in essence than the unbegotten Father, Augustine points out that not everything said of God is directly predicated of his substance, for besides talking about God according to substance, we may also talk about him according to relation: when we speak of the Father, the Son, and the Holy Spirit, we are speaking in terms of how they relate to each other, a mode of speech other than asserting that God is good, great, wise, and so on.

Even with this distinction, there remains the question, however, of whether each person is called "God" singly, or whether the term should only be used when speaking of the three together. In answering this conundrum, Augustine points out that "every being which is spoken of relatively, is something apart from that relation": in his example, a master is still a man even when deprived of his possessions.[19] It is, therefore, not

---

[17]Ibid., 9.20.
[18]*Trin.* 7.1.2.
[19]*Trin.* 7.1.2.

sufficient to say that the Father is God only by virtue of the presence of the
Son, which would seem to be implied by analogy to how some understood
1 Cor 1.24 ("Christ, the power and wisdom of God"), that the Father was
wise only by virtue of the presence of his eternal Wisdom.[20] Rather, we
must assert the Father *is* God in himself, and "Father" by virtue of his relation to his Son. Likewise the Son also, begotten from the Father, *is* God—
not by a division of the essence of the Father nor by participation in the
Father, but simply by being what he is: he is wise, good, great, and God in
himself. And yet, as there are not two or three instances of what it is to be
God, for the divine essence is simple, there is only one God: the Father,
Son, and Holy Spirit. A distinction can be made that the Father is God
"principally"—as Augustine notes earlier in the work, "the Father is from
no one"[21]—while the Son receives what he is from the Father; yet this der-
ivation is such that, as Christ says, "The Father has given the Son to have
life in himself" (Jn 5.26).[22]

Summing up his conclusions at the beginning of book 8, Augustine
puts it thus:

> Those things which are predicated relatively the one to the other—as
> Father and Son, and the gift of both, the Holy Spirit—are predicated
> specially in the Trinity as belonging severally to each person, for the
> Father is not the Trinity, nor the Son the Trinity, nor the gift the
> Trinity:
>> But that whenever each is singly spoken of in respect to themselves,
>> then they are not spoken of as three in the plural number, but one, the
>> Trinity itself, as the Father God, the Son God, and the Holy Spirit God;
>> the Father good, the Son good, and the Holy Spirit good; and the
>> Father omnipotent, the Son omnipotent, and the Holy Spirit omnipo-
>> tent: yet neither three Gods, nor three goods, nor three omnipotents,

---

[20] *Trin.* 6.

[21] *Trin.* 4.29.28.

[22] Cf. Basil Studer, *The Grace of Christ and the Grace of God in Augustine of Hippo: Christocentrism or Theocentrisim?*, trans. M.J. O'Connell (Collegeville, MN: Liturgical Press,
1997), 104–9, 138–45.

but one God, good, omnipotent, the Trinity itself, and whatever else
said of them, not relatively with respect to each other, but individually
in respect to themselves.[23]

That is to say, to state that God *is* something is to say that this property is
essential to what the Father, Son, and Holy Spirit each *are*, without, however, implying that there is more of it in two or three together than in one
alone, nor suggesting that the essence is something apart from that which
the three are or from which they derive. While, on the other hand, to speak
of the Father and the Son and the Holy Spirit is to talk about how the three
are related to each other, without implying that they are distinct substances or that these are only secondary, accidental properties, separable
from what it is to be God. Thus, the divine essence should not be thought
of as being logically prior to the persons, nor are the persons merely internal divisions within the essence.

In this way, by starting with the inseparability of divine operation and
paying close attention to the grammar of divine simplicity, we arrive at a
much more sensitively drawn picture of Augustine's trinitarian theology,
and one which seems to render all the criticisms leveled against him as
baseless. As Ayres puts it:

> In using the grammar of simplicity to articulate a concept of Father,
> Son, and Spirit as each God and as the one God, we find that the more
> we grasp the full reality of each person—the full depth of being that
> they have from the Father—the more we are also forced to recognize
> the unity of their being . . . The triune communion *is* a consubstantial
> and eternal unity: but there *is* nothing but the persons.[24]

[23] *Trin.* 8.Pr.1: "Diximus alibi ea dici proprie in illa trinitate distincte ad singulas personas pertinentia quae relative dicuntur ad invicem sicut pater et filius et utriusque donum
spiritus sanctus; non enim pater trinitas aut filius trinitas aut trinitas donum. Quod vero
ad se dicuntur singuli non dici pluraliter tres sed unum ipsam trinitatem sicut deus pater,
deus filius, deus spiritus sanctus; et bonus pater, bonus filius, bonus spiritus sanctus; et
omnipotens pater, omnipotens filius, omnipotens spiritus sanctus; nec tamen tres dii aut
tres boni aut tres omnipotentes, sed unus deus, bonus, omnipotens, ipsa trinitas, et
quidquid aliud non ad invicem relative sed ad se singuli dicuntur."

[24] Ayres, "Fundamental Grammar," 66–67; *Nicaea*, 379–80.

The real distinction of the persons is not subjugated to the divine essence: as Augustine says elsewhere, "the Trinity is of one substance and the essence is nothing else than the Trinity itself."[25] Neither the three nor the one are primary, person against nature or nature over person, but the simultaneity of both, the one in three and three in one, the triune communion of the trinitarian God. This, it is claimed, is a theological grammar common to pro-Nicaeans east and west.[26]

While the two alternatives of the so-called "de Régnon paradigm" may have been reconciled, there nevertheless remain some fundamental questions—questions not so much of the grand order of metaphysical or ontological claims regarding the ultimate ground of reality, nor even the grammar by which we speak of such things, but, much more prosaically, concerning the employment of the term "God." St Gregory the Theologian knew that he was on unchartered, and even unscriptural, territory in using the term "God" of the Holy Spirit, even if it can be argued that scripture does so in other words.[27] Augustine, on the other hand, does not seem to be aware that he is using the term "God" of the Trinity in a radically new manner, one that is not only different but also problematic. The concern of the Cappadocians, following Athanasius, Origen, and Irenaeus, was not the implications of how one affirms that each divine person is God and the one God, singularly and collectively, but the reverse: to affirm that the one God is Father. As Gregory of Nyssa wrote to Peter, "The identifying sign of the particularity with respect to hypostasis" of the Spirit "is to be made known after the Son and with him, and to subsist from the Father"; the particularity of the distinguishing marks of the Son is that he "alone shines forth in an only-begotten mode," while "the God over all alone has as the special property of his hypostasis that he is the Father and subsists from no cause."[28] Two centuries earlier Origen also had argued that the very name of God is "Father"—a fatherhood defined

---

[25] *Ep.* 120.3.17: *ut ipsa essential non aliud sit quam ipsa trinitas.*
[26] Ayres, "Fundamental Grammar," 59.
[27] Gregory Nazianzen, *Or.* 31.1.
[28] Gregory of Nyssa, *Ep. Pet.* 4. Cf. J. Behr, *The Nicene Faith* (Crestwood, NY: SVS Press, 2004), 415–27.

not by the more general relationship of this God to creation, but by virtue of his relationship to the only-begotten Son, Jesus Christ, the one who reveals the name of God as Father.[29] The relationship to the Son is constitutive of the one God being the Father. This continual emphasis on the one God as Father goes back to the Pauline assertion that formed the architecture of later creeds: for Christians, he says, "there is one God and Father . . . and one Lord Jesus Christ" (1 Cor 8.6). The one God confessed by Christians in the first article of the creeds of Nicaea and Constantinople is unambiguously the Father.

It is necessary to be clear and precise about what is being asserted here: it is not the claim that the Father is God only by virtue of the presence of the Son. This would be the *reductio ad absurdam* to which Augustine reduces his opponents' exegesis of 1 Cor 1.24.[30] But Augustine himself overlooks the fact that in this verse Christ is said to be the power and wisdom not of the Father but *of God*, just as Christ is the Son of God, not simply of the Father. It is this fatherhood of God to his Son, Jesus Christ, that is being pondered by the earlier writers and enshrined in the creeds. God is who he is by virtue of his relation to his Son. Another way of putting this would be to say that the monarchy that is so frequently spoken about with regard to Cappadocian trinitarian theology is not simply the monarchy of the Father, but the monarchy of the one God as Father, the Father of an eternally present Son, consubstantial with him, and the Spirit who proceeds from him, without whom he cannot even be thought let alone addressed.

These two ways of approaching the Trinity have resulted in very different theological idioms. We have become so accustomed to speaking of "the triune God" or "the trinitarian God"—the one God who is three— that we find it difficult not to think of the Trinity whenever we read the word "God," despite the fact that such terms are simply not found within the Greek writers of this period (and it is difficult to think how to construe "triune" in Greek). Later Byzantine writers do come to speak of "the

[29]Origen, *ComJn* 19.28; Cf. J. Behr, *The Way to Nicaea* (Crestwood, NY: SVS Press, 2001), 171, 185.
[30]*Trin.* 6.1.1.

trihypostatic God," for reasons that have yet to be explored; but even then, they remain committed to the monarchy of the one God as Father. Likewise with regard to our tendency to speak of "God the Father, God the Son, and God the Holy Spirit, the one God": this might be possible in Latin, given the ambiguity resulting from the absence of an article; Greek writers, on the other hand, from the time of Philo were very much concerned with the distinction between the articular and inarticular θεός, as a key feature of the scriptural grammar, as Rahner himself noted.[31]

The usual Greek idiom is to speak of ὁ θεὸς καὶ πατήρ (the God and Father), the Son of God or the Word of God, or equally ὁ θεὸς λόγος (not God the Word but "the" God-Word) and the Spirit of God. In each case, the referent for the term "God" is clear: the one of whom Jesus is the Son and Word, as fully divine as the Father so that he can also be called upon as God (ὁ θεός, even, cf. Jn 20.28), "true God of true God," and likewise for the Holy Spirit, who is the Spirit *of God*, and, as the one received through Christ, he is the Spirit of Christ (following the language patterns of scripture) whose work, pro-Nicaeans hold, reveal him as fully divine (though not called "God" by scripture or the creed). To speak of "the triune" or "trinitarian God," the one God who is three, Father, Son, and Spirit, sounds not only odd, but distinctly modalist. The Greek idiom no doubt sounds equally odd to the Latin ear, but for appearing to be tritheist and subordinationist. Yet the word "God" *is* being used in a new manner by Augustine; the approach and framework *has* changed. The legitimacy of this development (and how one might even address such a question) cannot be sidestepped by overlooking this very real difference. This difference, however, is not that of the so-called "de Régnon paradigm," which alternates between starting with the one substance or the three persons, even if we bring both poles together to affirm that the one God is the Trinity, that "the essence is nothing else than the Trinity itself." It is rather the difference between starting from the one God who is Father, and beginning with the Father, Son, and Spirit who are each, and together, the one God.

---

[31]Cf. Philo, *On Dreams* 1.229; Origen *ComJn* 2.17; Rahner, "Theos in the New Testament," in *God, Christ, Mary and Grace*, Theological Investigations, vol. 1, trans. C. Ernst (Baltimore: Helicon, 1965), 79–148.

The consequences of this development also need to be seriously explored—for instance, in the way in which Augustine subtly revises, in accordance with his understanding of God as Trinity, the principles of scriptural interpretation in the opening books of *De Trinitate* dealing with the Old Testament theophanies, and elsewhere. For instance, in his treatment of Christ's words in John 17.3, "that they may know you, the only true God, and Jesus Christ whom you have sent," Augustine comments that we "are to understand that [Christ] too is the one true God because the Father and the Son are one true God. The meaning, then, is 'that they may know the one true God, that is, you and the one you sent, Jesus Christ.' "[32] This is, to say the least, rather strained.

Perhaps the most serious consequence arises with regard to the question of whom it is that Christians call upon as Father. Augustine suggests an answer to this when he considers whether the names Father, Son, and Spirit can be used of the Trinity together. The term Spirit is used of God more generally (cf. Jn 4.24), and so the Trinity as a whole can be called "spirit." On the other hand, the Trinity can in no way at all be called "son." But regarding the term Father, Augustine states:

The Trinity cannot in the same way be called Father, except perhaps metaphorically, in respect to the creature, on account of the adoption of sons. For that which is written, "Hear, O Israel; the Lord our God is one Lord" [Deut 6.4] is not understood as excluding the Son or excluding the Holy Spirit, and this one Lord we rightly call our Father as well because he regenerates us by his grace.[33]

Although it is qualified as metaphorical, the fatherhood of the Trinity is not simply that of the Creator to the created, but of the Trinity with respect to those adopted as sons, regenerated by his grace. Augustine cer-

[32] *En. in Ps.* 85.21 (cited in Studer, *Grace of Christ*, 139).

[33] *Trin.* 5.11.12: "non sic dici potest trinitas pater nisi forte translate ad creaturam propter adoptionem filiorum. Quod enim scriptum est: Audi, Israhel: dominus deus tuus dominus unus est, non utique excepto filio aut excepto spiritu sancto oportet intellegi, quem unum dominum deum nostrum recte dicimus etiam patrem nostrum per gratiam suam non regenerantem."

tainly knows that the addressee of liturgical prayer is the Father.[34] But if his account of divine simplicity drives us to call upon the Trinity as "Father" when saying the Lord's Prayer, rather than addressing the one God, the God of Abraham, Isaac, and Jacob, the Holy One of Israel, as "Father," adoptively in the Son by the power of the Spirit, then there is something seriously amiss; Christians would indeed be "mere monotheists" despite the "triune" nature of the one God they call upon. There is something seriously difficult and troublesome about Augustine's trinitarian theology from an Eastern Orthodox perspective. But perhaps what is needed is not simply a return to the supposedly "Greek" pole of the so-called "de Régnon paradigm," nor to bring together its alternatives, as if these were the only possible options, but to reach back to the scriptural grammar, preserved in the creeds, which precedes such oppositions and defies being bound by them.

[34]Cf. Studer, *Grace of Christ*, 143–44.

Idipsum: The Name of God according to Augustine[1]

JEAN-LUC MARION

The Question of the Names of God

No Christian theologian can escape the question of the names of God. Whether one addresses it explicitly (in the footsteps of several Cappadocian fathers and, above all, Dionysius) or implicitly (as did the defenders of orthodoxy against Arianism) is not of great importance. What matters is facing the difficulty itself: to name the unnamable, and to name it *as such*. But since, by definition, one cannot name the unnamable by using *a* name, it must be acknowledged, right from the outset, that in a sense all names are suited to name God, precisely since no name can adequately name him. The endless multiplying of divine names represents the first, indispensable step in establishing them.

Even though he is not considered a major theoretician of the divine names, there can no longer be any doubt that St Augustine was perfectly aware of the issue and did not avoid the question.[2] "Deus vero multipliciter quidem dicitur, magnus, bonus, sapiens, beatus, verus et quidquid

---

[1]The editors would like to thank Dr Christophe Chalomet, who provided an English translation of Professor Marion's essay prior to the conference.

[2]This was demonstrated if only by Vladimir Lossky, "Les éléments de 'Théologie négative' dans la pensée de saint Augustin," *Augustinus Magister,* vol. 1 (Paris: Études Augustiniennes, 1954); and Deirdre Carabine, "Negative Theology in the Thought of Saint Augustine," *Recherches de Théologie Ancienne et Médiévale* 59 (1992) (against, among others, Raoul Mortley, *From Word to Silence. II. The Way of Negation. Christian and Greek,* Theophaneia [Bonn: Hanstein, 1986]).

aliud non indigne dici videtur" (There are multiple ways of speaking of God, [as] great, good, wise, blessed, true and anything else which does not appear to be said in an unworthy manner).[3] What is remarkable about this sentence is that, beyond the enumeration of names, it provides the very principle for that enumeration and for its indefinite character (*indéf-inition*): since no name can express God *as such*, all names—each in its own way—are suitable, only as long as they name him in a worthy manner. But how is this *worthy manner* determined? What is its scope and, more importantly, what hierarchy is established between the names it generates?

These questions arise clearly in the great, solemn invocation of God and his names at the beginning of the *Confessiones* (*Confessions*):

> Summe, optime, potentissime, omnipotentissime, misericordissime et justissime, secretissime et praesentissime, pulcherrime et fortissime, stabilis et incomprehensibilis, immutabilis, mutans omnia, numquam novus, numquam vetus, innovans omnia et "in vetustatem perducens superbos et nesciunt" [Job 9.5]; semper agens, semper quietus, colligens et non egens, portans et implens et protegens, creans et nutriens et perficiens, quaerens cum nihil desit tibi . . . Et quid diximus, Deus meus, vita mea, dulcedo mea sancta, aut quid dicit aliquis, cum te dicit? Et vae tacentibus de te, quoniam loquaces muti sunt.

> (Supreme, utmost in goodness, mightiest, all-powerful, most merciful, and most just, most secret and most present, most beautiful and strongest, ever enduring and incomprehensible, unchanging and changing everything, never new, never old, making all things new and "guiding the proud to old age, and they do not know about it" [Job 9.5]; always active, ever at rest, gathering without needing anything, supporting, filling, and protecting, creating, nourishing, and perfecting, seeking even though you lack nothing . . . And what have we thus said, my God, my life, my holy sweetness, or what says anybody who

---

[3] *Trin.* 6.7.8 (BA 15.488).

says something about you? Yet woe to those who are silent about you, for they remain silent even as they chatter.)[4]

This extraordinary text shows first, with utter precision, the definite characteristics of any speculative theology worthy of its name: (a) The divine names can be said according to both the positive way (*kataphasis*–predication) and the negative way (*apophasis*–negation); (b) but neither the apophatic nor the cataphatic way is valid in itself, for God transcends the negation as well as the predication; (c) a new kind of enunciation, a new language game must therefore be chosen, which no longer consists in affirming or negating something (the names) about something (God)—since neither one nor the other is a "thing"—but which consists in saying *to* God the names with which *we* can aim at him (*le viser*), positively or negatively; this game only takes place in praise, with its invocation (in the vocative case) of God *as* . . . Without this final way, which neither merely names (*nomme*) nor negates (*dénie*) but which de-nominates (*dé-nomme*), we do not know, as St Augustine explicitly concludes, what we say when we say whatever we say "about you" (*de te*).[5] With regard to God, in order to speak of him it is not sufficient to affirm or to deny something about him. What matters is to speak *to* him, and thus to speak in the mode of praise. The *Confessiones,* thus, begin with praise: "'Magnus es, domine, et laudabilis valde . . .' Et laudare te vult homo, . . . et tamen laudare vult te homo" ("You are great, Lord, and truly worthy to be praised . . ." And man wishes to praise you, . . . and nevertheless man wishes to praise you).[6] Similarly, the *Confessiones* end in the mode of praise: "Laudant te opera tua, ut amemus te, et amemus te, ut laudent te opera tua" (Your works praise you so that we love you, and we love you

[4]*Conf.* 1.4.4 (BA 13.278ss).

[5]See my "In the Name: How to Avoid Speaking of Negative Theology," in *God, the Gift and Postmodernism,* ed. John D. Caputo and Michael J. Scanlon (Bloomington: Indiana University Press, 1999); also *In Excess: Essay in the Saturated Phenomena,* trans. R. Horner (New York: Fordham University Press, 2003).

[6]*Conf.* 1.1.1 (BA 13.272), quoting Ps 47.1, 95.4, 44.3. It is, in fact, a sort of third-degree praise: a praise that quotes a psalm, which praises God by declaring him worthy to be praised.

so that your works praise you).[7] In that precise sense, the *Confessiones* represent, from beginning to end, a tremendous treatise of speculative theology.

It should also be noted that the list of names selected for this praise reveals two other decisions made by St Augustine. Right from the beginning, it is clear that God cannot be named by one single name. Why so? Because praising God means praising him *as* . . . and this "as" implies a distance, so that there can be no pretension of having reached a univocal conceptual definition; but also, more importantly, this praise is directed to God who, by definition, transcends all definitions and is indeed praised as *incomprehensibilis*. Second, we should note that, in such a lengthy praise, not only is God never understood as "being," in one way or another, but even the very term "being" is absent.[8] Yet the majority of commentators do not hesitate to state that St Augustine defined God through *esse*, in other words that he led to the "discovery of God-Being," of "God the absolute Being," or even to one of "the Christian ontologies of being."[9] Could it be that St Augustine himself was not fully coherent, that he did

---

[7] *Conf.* 13.38.48 (BA 14.516).

[8] St Augustine always rejected the idea that God may be determined by substance: "Manifestum est Deum abusive substantiam vocari, ut nomine usitatiore intelligatur essentia, quod vere et proprie dicitur; ita ut fortasse solum Deum dici oporteat essentiam," *Trin.* 7.5.10 (BA 15.538), quoting Ex 3.14. For ". . . nihil in eo [Deo] secundum accidens dicitur, quia nihil ei accidit; nec tamen omne quod dicitur, secundum substantiam dicitur. In rebus enim creatis atque mutabilibus, quod non secundum substantiam dicitur, restat ut ut secundum accidens dicatur. [. . .] In Deo autem nihil quidem secundum accidens dicitur, quia nihil in eo mutabile." *Trin.* 5.5.6 (BA 15.432). It is thus not possible, *stricto sensu,* to speak of a *substantia* in relation to God, but it is perhaps possible to speak of his *essentia*: "substantia, vel, si melius dicitur, essentia Dei." Ibid., 3.10.21 (BA 15.318), see also ibid., 5. 2.3 (BA 15.428).

[9] See, respectively, Emily Zum Brunn, "L'exégèse augustinienne de 'Ego sum qui sum' et la 'métaphysique de l'Exode'," in *Dieu et l'être. Exégèses d'Exode 3.14 et de Coran 20.11–24* (Paris: Études augustiniennes, 1978), 142; Goulven Madec, *Saint Augustin et la philosophie notes critiques.* Collection des études augustiniennes, vol. 149 (Paris: Institut d'études augustiniennes, 1996), 39; and Étienne Gilson, *L'être et l'essence* (Paris: J. Vrin, 1948, here 1962), 45. Despite the care with which the first two scholars distance themselves from the third on the topic of the "metaphysic of Exodus," the three of them remain in complete agreement in attributing to Augustine the naming of God as being. See also David Bradshaw's book *Aristotle East and West* (Cambridge: Cambridge University Press, 2004) and his contribution to this volume.

not successfully harmonize the primacy of being in God with the de-nomination of God through divine names? Or is it rather the expression of a constant difficulty among modern readers, who do not hesitate, even with regard to St Augustine, to locate the de-nomination of God within the horizon of being and even within the metaphysics of being *qua* being?

The Usual Answer

It cannot be denied that St Augustine often links God and being. He does so on the basis of at least three arguments.

The first one comes from scripture: St Augustine is part of a tradition, since Justin, which favors the name that God gave to Moses: "Sum qui sum," according to Exodus 3.14.[10] Among the many uses of this verse it is possible to emphasize one that gave to it a clear philosophical thrust: "Cum ad sanctum Moysen ita verba Dei per angelum perferantur, ut quarenti quod sit nomen ejus . . . respondeatur 'Ego sum qui sum' . . . tan-quam in ejus comparatione, qui vere est quia incommutabilis est, ea quae mutabilia facta sunt non sint, vehementer hoc Plato tenuit et diligentis-sime commandavit" (When the words of God reach holy Moses through the angel, so that to his question concerning his name . . . the answer was "I am who I am" . . . , as if, when compared to him who truly is because he is immutable, the things which do change were not, this was vigorously defended and recommended with the greatest possible care by Plato).[11] St Augustine underlines the fact that the expression of Exodus 3.14 becomes all the more a proper name since no attribute is added to complete the tautology: "Non ait et ibi: *Ego sum Deus*; aut: *Ego sum mundi fabricator,* aut: *Ego sum omnium rerum creator,* aut: *Ego sum ipsius populi liberandi propagator;* sed hoc tantum *Ego sum qui sum*" (He does not say here, *I am*

[10]See M. Harl, "Exode 3.14 chez les Pères Grecs des quatre premiers siècles," in *Dieu et l'être*, 87–106.

[11]*Civ.* 8.11 (BA 34.270–72). See also another perfect echo of this argument: "Sed haec omnia terrena, volatica, transitoria, si comparentur illi veritati, ubi dictum est 'Ego sum qui sum', totum hic quod transit, vanitas dicitur." *En. in Ps.* 143.11 (PL 37.1863) and *De vera rel.* 97 (BA 8.168).

God; or, *I am the maker of the world*; or, *I am the creator of all things*; or, *I am the leader of the liberation of the people.* He only says, *I am who I am*).[12] The tautology of being becomes, in its singularity and rarity, something akin to the proper name, or at least the name par excellence, of God: "Quae vero proprie de Deo dicuntur, quaeque in nulla creatura inveniuntur, raro ponit Scriptura divina; sicut illud quod dictum est ad Moysen: *Ego sum qui sum* et *Qui est misit me ad vos.* Cum enim esse aliquo modo dicatur et corpus et animus, nisi proprio quodam modo vellet intelligi, non id utique diceret" (For scripture does not often say things that are properly said of God and which cannot be found in any creature, like this, which is said to Moses: *I am who I am*, and *The one who is has sent me to you.* Since, in fact, being also pertains in a sense to the body and the soul, scripture would not have spoken in that way if it had not intended it to be understood in the proper sense).[13] However, since this name is primarily a biblical name, even if it acquires an ontological meaning in relation to Plato or Aristotle, that should not be a sufficient argument to impose on Augustine being itself as a divine name.

This is especially clear when we consider that St Augustine favors the naming of God through the proclamation of being and brings it to an extreme expression: "Bonum est, quidquid aliquo modo est: ab illo enim est, qui non aliquo modo est, sed est *est*" (Everything that is in one way or another is good: for it is from him who is not in a certain way, but who is *is*).[14] Here, undoubtedly, God is, if not being, at least the fact that he is,

---

[12] *Tract. Ev. Jo.* 38.8 (PL 35.1679). For a list of the forty-seven passages in which St Augustine comments on Exodus 3.14, see A.-M. La Bonnardière, reprinted in Brunn, 164.

[13] *Trin.* 1.1.2 (BA 15.90). See also, with the same interpretative line, *En. in Ps.* 49.14 (PL 37.575) and 82.14 (PL 37.1055).

[14] *Conf.* 13.31.46 (BA 16.514). I follow the edition by Knöll and Skutella, also used by the BA. Augustine, *Confessions,* trans. J. O'Donnell (Oxford: Oxford University Press, 1997), 3.411, who assumes this reading refers to St Paul according to *De Magistro* 5.14 (BA 6.48): "Ergo, ut ea potissimum auctoritate utamur, quae nobis carissima est, cum ait Paulus apostolus 'Non erat in Christo *est et non,* sed *est* in illo erat' (2 Cor 1.19), non opinor, putandum tres istas litteras, quae enuntiamus cum dicimus *est,* fuisse in Christo, sed illud potius quod istis tribus litteris significatur." Gilson based his interpretation on this text. See his "Notes sur l'être et le temps chez Saint Augustin," in *Recherches Augustiniennes* 2 (1962): 205–23. As early as 1932, Gilson took this non-biblical expression to be a "Nom divin que nous a enseigné Dieu lui-même." *L'esprit de la philosophie médiévale* (Paris: J. Vrin, 1932)

and he alone is this fact of being. This identification is sometimes reinforced through the addition of *ipsum esse* to *esse*: "Considera igitur, quantum potes, quam magnum bonum sit ipsum esse, quod et beati et miseri volunt" (Consider therefore, as much as you are able, to what extent being itself is a great good, since both those who are happy and those who are unhappy want it).[15] In other words: "Sic sum quod sum, sic sum *ipsum esse,* sic sum cum ipso esse ut nolim hominibus deesse" (In this way I am who I am, in this way I am being itself, in this way I am with being itself, so that I do not want human beings to be without it).[16] Clearly the *ipsum esse* seems here to be above all the object of desire of those who are not themselves being. It seems to be the figurative expression of *Sum qui sum* when it becomes the object of desire among those who are not God. But what manifests itself as desired precisely belongs to being, to being itself. More than that: there is, beyond this first emphasis from *est* to *ipsum esse,* a further emphasis from *ipsum esse* to *idipsum esse*: "Deum ergo diligere debemus, . . . quod nihil aliud dicam esse, nisi *idipsum esse*" (therefore we must love God, . . . of whom I will say nothing else than that he is being itself).[17] Or: "Cum ab ea [i.e. immutabilis res, veritas] est aversus [i.e. animus], *idipsum esse* minus habet" (And when the spirit turns away from it [i.e. the immutable reality, truth] it possesses less being itself).[18] What characterizes the One whose name consists only in the name of Exodus 3.14 is being or, better, being itself. Thus it seems not only legitimate but even necessary to interpret this *ipsum esse* (especially when it is empha-

(the quote comes from 1943/1969, 53, n. 2). This rather surprising double *est* could be compared to another: "Est enim est, sicut bonorum bonum, bonum est" *En. in Ps.* 134.4 (PL 37.1741).

[15]*De lib. arb.* 3.7.20 (BA 6.362). St Augustine writes about "id quod summe est" shortly after this quote.

[16]*Serm.* 7.7 (PL 38.66). See also: "Deus . . . , cui profectio *ipsum esse*, unde essentia nominata est, maxime ac verissime competit" (God . . . to whom it is suitable in the greatest and truest way to assign *being itself,* from which essence receives its name). *Trin.* 5.2.3 (BA 15.428). Also: "Et non est ibi aliud beatum esse, et aliud magnum, aut sapientem, aut verum, aut bonum esse, aut omnino ipsum esse" (And in this case [i.e. God], being happy is nothing else than being great, or wise, or true, or good, or quite simply being itself). *Trin.* 6.7.8 (BA 15.488).

[17]*De mor. ecc.* 1.14.24 (BA 1.172).

[18]*De immor. an.* 7.12 (BA 5.190).

sized through the *idipsum esse*) by way of anticipation, in a Thomistic way: the name *Who is* could not have become the "most proper name of God" (*maxime proprium nomen Dei*) if being itself was not his essence in the first place (*essentia Dei est ipsum esse ejus*).[19]

Why not then conclude, with Maritain, that "these texts contain *virtually* the whole Thomist doctrine of divine names and of analogy"[20] and therefore that, after St Augustine, the most appropriate name of God is *ipsum esse, idipsum esse*?

Influence and Presuppositions in the Translation of *Idipsum*

This conclusion needs, however, to be rejected. Not that the authenticity of the Augustinian use of *ipsum esse* or of *idipsum esse* must be challenged. Rather, we must inquire further about the relation between these expressions and the term that is most peculiarly Augustine's in his attempt at denominating God, *idipsum*: "*idipsum quod Deus est, quidquid illud est*" (that itself which is God, whatever it is).[21] This is indeed the word that is the most peculiar to Augustine, since he uses it to designate nothing less than what he is aiming at in his contemplation at Ostia: "*erigentes nos ardiore affectu in idipsum*" (lifting ourselves up by a more ardent affect toward the thing itself).[22] But that is not simply the expression of a private experience (that of Augustine and his mother), since we find the exact same term in the rewording of the liturgical praise of the *Sanctus*: "Itaque, tu Domine, qui non es alias aliud et alias aliter, sed *idipsum* et *idipsum* et

---

[19]Thomas Aquinas, *Summa Theologiae* Ia, respectively q.13, a.11, resp. and q.12, a.2, resp. See *Summa Theologiae* Ia, q.3, a.4, resp., *Contra gentes* 2.54.

[20]Jacques Maritain, "La sagesse augustinienne," *Mélanges augustiniens* (Paris: Riviere, 1931), quoted in Gilson, *L'esprit de la philosophie médiévale*, 53.

[21]*Trin.* 2.18.35 (BA 15.268).

[22]*Conf.* 9.10.24 (BA 14.116). We modify *id ipsum* according to O'Donnell's *idipsum*; *Confessions*, 1.113. One finds the very same expressions in the commentary of Psalm 121: "Jam ergo, fratres, quisquis erigit aciem mentis, quisquis deponit caligem carnis, quisquis mundat oculum cordis, elevet et videat *idipsum*." *En. in Ps.* 121.5 (PL 37.1622). As we shall see, this is no coincidence.

idipsum, 'sanctus, sanctus, sanctus, dominus Deus omnipotens'" (Therefore you, O Lord, are not different here and again different there but you are *the thing itself* [*la chose même*] and *the thing itself* and *the thing itself,* [in other words] "holy, holy, holy, Lord God almighty").[23] As much as *idipsum* undoubtedly is the central term (for the individual as for the liturgical community), it immediately appears that it is difficult to translate it: it can be understood as that which the thing is, thus as the thing itself, but also as what remains the same. Most translators do not seem to see this problem and very often translate the term with "being itself."[24] And this is not an oversight, but a clear pattern, which comes from the fact that they do not translate *idipsum* but rather what they spontaneously read instead of it: *ipsum esse.*

Examples of such unconscious substitutions are unlimited and are not only found in French translation. We will only mention a few. Consider *Confessiones* 9.4.11, "'O in pace! O in idipsum!' [Ps 4.9] . . . tu es idipsum valde, quia non mutaris," which should be translated like this: "'O in peace, O in the thing itself' . . . you are the thing itself, you who never change," and which has now become: "'Oh! in *Being* itself' . . . you are *Being* itself, unchangeable," or, also, "Oh! Dans *l'être* même . . . tu es toi, cet être même par excellence" (Oh! In *being* itself . . . you are yourself, this being itself par excellence).[25] Or consider *Confessiones* 12.15.21: "ita est [sc. mens] abs te, Deo nostro, ut aliud sit plane quam tu et non *idipsum,*" in

---

[23] *Conf.* 12.7.7 (BA 14.352). With J. O'Donnell, despite Skutella and the French edition in the BA, I maintain the third *idipsum,* following the manuscripts and the Maurists. O'Donnell, *Confessions,* 3.308.

[24] This is the case for the last two quotes, in BA 14.117 and 353 (trans. E. Tréhorel and G. Buissou). The two principal translators in English made the same decision: Henry Chadwick, *Saint Augustine: Confessions* (Oxford: Oxford University Press, 1991); and Maria Boulding, *The Confessions* (New York: New City Press, 1997). For *Conf.* 9.10.24, Chadwick has "towards eternal *Being*" (171) while Boulding chooses "towards that which *is*" (227). For *Conf.* 12.7.7, Chadwick translates like this: "the selfsame *very being it self*" (249: this is in fact *two* translations, juxtaposing what is written in Augustine's text and what is present only in the mind of the translator); and Boulding has: "Being it self" (315). Both translators omit the third mention of the term, and they overlook the repetition of the triple liturgical *Sanctus* by the triple *Idipsum.*

[25] Respectively Boulding, 217 and BA 14.91. Here Chadwick accurately translates with "the selfsame" (169).

other words: "it is through you, our God, so that it is wholly other than you and not this itself," has now become: "un être tout autre que toi, et non *l'être* même" (a being wholly other than you, and not *being* itself), or ". . . it is not *Being itself*."[26] And again, when *Confessiones* 13.11.12 seeks to define "illud, quod supra ista est" as "sibi notum est et sibi sufficit incommutabiliter *idipsum*" (literally, "that which is above these things" as "*that itself* which knows itself and is self-sufficient without change"), it is translated in the following way: "the immutable being" defines itself as "l'Être meme," or as "the ultimate being," or even as "Being-Itself."[27]

How can we explain this persistent mistranslation, which leads to a radical misinterpretation of what the text means? Obviously *idipsum* primarily means "the same, the same thing,"[28] and if one wished to transform it into a noun in French it would have to be *l'identique,* i.e., *the identical.*[29] There should thus be no difficulty in translating this term, if one were willing to translate it. But the fact is that some end up translating *another* text, *unwritten* but dominant, which nevertheless superimposed itself on Augustine's text and fused with it. Take for example: "summe esse ac summe vivere *id ipsum est.* Summus enim es . . ."[30] This obvious text can and should be translated: "to be supremely and to live supremely are the same thing. For you are supremely . . ." But what happens is that, after having accurately translated the text in this way: "the supreme degree of being and the supreme degree of life are one and the

---

[26]Respectively BA 14.375 and Boulding, 323 (see also: "not *Being itself*," Chadwick, 25).

[27]We prefer here again *idipsum* (following O'Donnell, 1.188) to *id ipsum* (BA 14.444). Respectively BA 14.445; Chadwick, 280; Boulding, 350. See also *Conf.* 12.17.21: "ex nihilo cuncta facta sunt, quia non sunt ipsum quod Deus" becomes "de rien toutes les choses ont été faites, car elles ne sont pas l'être même comme Dieu" (BA 14.382 and 383), or "because they are not *Being itself* as God is" (Chadwick, 258), or "they are not *Being-Itself* like God" (Boulding, 325).

[28]*Trin.* 1.8.17 (BA 15.132): "nondum intellexerat [sc. Philippe], eo quoque modo *idipsum* se potuisse dicere 'Domine, ostende nobis te et sufficit nobis'" (a correct translation would be "in the same way," 133).

[29]Madec translates this as "hasarde 'l'Identique" and thus provides an accurate correction to Aimé Solignac's translation, which is influenced by Thomism (*Le Dieu d'Augustin* [Paris: Desclée de Brouwer, 2000], 129). For a similar move, see Brunn ("tu es l'identique," 158).

[30]*Conf.* 1.6.10 (BA 13.290 and the translation on 291).

same thing," the following is added: "You are indeed *Being* in its supreme degree." How can we explain this addition of *Being* to the simple Latin words *summum es*? The fact is, the translator understands *idipsum* so resolutely in the sense of *ipsum esse* that, even when constrained by philology to translate it literally as *the same thing*, or *the same*, that is, without any ontological import, the ontological claim remains intact and, to complete itself, is added in the following sentence, so that it may be maintained at all cost and survive. It is thus subtly reintroduced in the invocation of God, as an *additional* epithet *Being* for the otherwise self-sufficient *Summe enim es* . . . ("For you are supremely . . .").

These slips in translations are, of course, not purely fortuitous, nor are they caused by inattention on the part of the translators, who are otherwise consistently excellent. On the contrary, they result from too much earnestness, not on the philological but on the conceptual level: the (neo-)Thomist de-nomination of the most proper name of God determines their understanding of the Augustinian de-nomination of God's name in such an indelible way that they do not refrain from correcting the latter through the former. And they do so with a perfectly clear conscience, as one of the best among them unambiguously admits: "It was our conscious decision to leave in the translation the Latin expression *Idipsum*. This, as we obviously see, is the technical term similar to the *Ego qui sum* and the *Who I am* of *Exodus*, a term which, understood in a *metaphysical sense*, defines God as he defines himself: being in the fullest sense, immutable, eternal being. The best translation in French thus seems to be: *Being itself*."[31] It is quite clear: the translation of *idipsum* that conflates it with *ipsum esse* is not based on the text nor on St Augustine's theology but on an interpretation[32] of the term "in a metaphysical sense." The whole

[31] These words are from Aimé Solignac as he was translating a fragment of *En. in Ps.* 121.5 (on which I comment *infra* IV, n. 36) in his note on the *Idipsum* in *Conf.*, BA 14.550 (my emphasis). See the reservations made by Madec (n. 29), who nevertheless imagines that there is "a passion for Being which Augustine seeks to share with the Christian community" (*Saint Augustin et la philosophie*, 75). One can hope that St Augustine had other, more important passions to share: for instance, the passion for the Passion.

[32] See for instance M.-F. Berrouard (in an otherwise useful note on "Idipsum" in BA 71 [Paris: Desclée de Brouwer, 1993], 845): "Augustin qui avait médité sur ce mot [*idipsum*] dès

problem now is to know what "metaphysical" means here, since St Augustine (as well as all the philosophers who preceded him) obviously did not know its usage and meaning; one then needs to identify which one of the *metaphysics* that emerged after him could serve as a paradigm—and ask, in connection with this, whether what is called a little bit too easily *the* Thomist system allows for or requires the qualification of *metaphysica*, or whether one has to move further into the modern era in order to find its true paradigm; finally, and most importantly, one needs to ask whether this way of using retrospectively a "metaphysical" interpretation of the *idipsum* (and, thus, of the Augustinian de-nomination of God) can claim to have any legitimacy. The fact is, this seemingly innocuous translation, whether vaguely tainted by scholasticism or devotedly neo-Thomist, distorts St Augustine's thought by substituting a metaphysical concept of being (which, luckily, as it turns out, is not without its problems even from a metaphysical standpoint) for a radically biblical and apophatic de-nomination.

But this suggestion—that the *idipsum* should not be understood as a metaphysical and ontological statement—may look rather obvious, since "being/*esse*" refers to what these two expressions—namely Thomas Aquinas' *Ipsum esse* (*actus essendi*) and St Augustine's *Idipsum*—do *not* have in common, for *esse* is precisely missing in the *Idipsum*. On the contrary, the whole issue consists in knowing whether the de-nomination *idipsum* (meant here without *esse*) must still be, or rather must *already* be, understood "in a metaphysical sense," or whether, against this interpretation, it should resolutely not be understood within the horizon of metaphysics. For, as we have suggested, the metaphysical and ontological interpretation of *idipsum* may owe everything to the posterior and, in fact, modern Thomist tradition, and, as such, contradicts what St Augustine meant to say.

sa retraite à Cassiciacum (*Conf.* 9.4.11) le rapproche de la révélation de l'Horeb (Ex 3.14) et l'interprète comme l'expression du mystère de l'Être même de Dieu."

The Apophatic Acceptation of *Idipsum*

There is a powerful argument that can be raised to suspend the metaphysical interpretation of the expression *idipsum*: its biblical origin. Indeed, this expression does not have anything to do directly with being, as it stems from Psalm 121(122).3, a psalm that celebrates the act of entering Jerusalem: "Hierusalem quae aedificaris est civitas / cujus participatio idipsum."[33] What makes this translation a bit awkward is that it renders literally the Septuagint: Ἰερουσαλὴμ οἰκοδομουμένη ὡς πόλις, ἧς ἡ μετοχὴ αὐτῆς ἐπὶ τὸ αὐτό.[34] The verse describes the solidity and the coherence of Jerusalem and concludes that taking part in it, participating in it,[35] constitutes the thing itself—what one desires, what needs to be achieved. And therefore, by isolating αὐτό, translated as *idipsum*, St Augustine is able to understand this "thing itself in which one must participate" as a de-nomination of God. Therefore "idipsum quod Deus est— that itself which God is"[36] becomes the "that itself" which God is: "Deus . . . idipsum est."[37] Far from being a "misinterpretation,"[38] the Augustinian expression is directly based on a biblical exegesis (that of Ps 121), which

[33]This is the Latin verse that Augustine cites in his sermon. The Vulgate reads: "Hierusalem quae aedificaris ut civitas / Cujus participatio ejus simul." Lemaître de Sacy has: "Jérusalem, que l'on bâtit comme une ville, et dont toutes les parties sont dans une parfaite union entre elles," but the Revised Standard Version blurs the point: "Jerusalem, built a city which is bound firmly together, to which the tribes go up."

[34]The Hebrew expression *lo yahid* also indicates a relation to *the one, the only one.*

[35]In Greek, μετοχή means "the foreign" admitted to live in a city with a limited status, but not full citizenship, literally *participating in* the city.

[36]*Trin.* 2.18.35 (BA 15.268) or *Conf.* 12.17.25 (BA 14.382).

[37]*Trin.* 3.10.21 (BA 15.318).

[38]As suggested by a critic: "Ce contresens nous vaut une très belle exégèse qui rapprochera idipsum non seulement d'*Exode* 3,14, mais aussi . . . de la 'métaphysique de l'*Exode*." See Brunn, "L'exégèse augustinienne de l''Ego sum qui sum' et la 'métaphysique de l'Exode," in *Dieu et l'être*, 158. Not only is there no misinterpretation, but the "belle exégèse" in question tends to *distance* as much as possible Exodus 3.14 from the "metaphysic of Exodus." James Swetnam, in an otherwise excellent article ("A Note on '*in idipsum*' in St Augustine," *The Modern Schoolman* 30/4 [1952–53]: 328–31) also misinterprets St Augustine's text precisely by seeing it as a misinterpretation: "it seems that St Augustine did not perceive the real meaning of the phrase because of the extremely literal nature of the version he possessed."

allows Augustine to de-nominate God strictly without imposing any determination—especially any ontological or metaphysical determination—on him. The use of *idipsum* is rooted in a tradition that is *older* and more biblical than the *ipsum esse,* and yet the *ipsum esse,* among modern commentators, overshadows it. *Idipsum* cannot be equated with *ipsum esse,* nor does it anticipate it; it resists and dismisses it in advance.

Let us turn to the central text, the commentary on Psalm 121, in order to further define the characteristics of the *idipsum.*[39] We find four steps in this text, and so we make four comments. The first step is: "Quid est *idipsum*? Quomodo dicam, nisi *idipsum*? Fratres, si potestis, intelligis *idipsum.* Nam ego quidquid aliud dixero, non dico *idipsum*" (What is *idipsum,* the thing itself? How shall I say it, if not by saying *idipsum*? Brothers, if you are able, understand *idipsum.* For whatever else I will have said, I will not say the *idipsum*). The *idipsum,* thus, remains radically and definitively apophatic; it does not provide any essence, does not reach any definition, but only expresses its own inability to speak of God. Its own privilege comes, paradoxically, from this obvious lack of signification, which allows it to de-nominate without the pretension to define.

Hence a second step: "Conemur tamen quibusdam vicinitatibus verborum et significationum perducere infirmitatem mentis ad cogitandum *idipsum.* Quid est *idipsum*? Quod semper eodem modo est, quod non modo aliud, et modo aliud est. Quid est ergo *idipsum,* nisi quod est? Quid est quod est? Quod aeternum est. Nam quod semper aliter atque aliter est, non est, quia non manet; non omnino non est, sed non summe est" (Let us nevertheless strive, through various approximations of words and significations, to steer the weakness of our mind to the thought of the *idipsum.* What is the *idipsum*? It is always in the same way, it is not different here and different there. What then is *idipsum,* if not that which is? What is that which is? That which is eternal. For what is always different and again different is not, because it does not remain; not that it is absolutely not, but it is not supremely). On the basis of his definitive apophasis, the *idipsum* can nevertheless define itself, but through a strict negative defi-

---

[39] *En. in Ps.* 121.5 (PL 37.1621–22).

nition: it is in a mode that is different from ours or from any creature: it is in the mode of immutability. The difference between the *idipsum* and everything that is not the thing itself does not directly have to do with being (or non-being), but in the ways of being—mutable or immutable. As such, being does not characterize the *idipsum*, which, if it did, would be wholly reduced to an *ipsum esse*; being characterizes it only as a sign of immutability, as a name for immutability, *nomen incommutabilitatis*.[40]

And it is only in a third step (that is, with a long delay) that we come to Exodus 3.14:

> Et quid est quod est, nisi ille qui, quando mittebat Moysen, dixit illi: *Ego sum, qui sum*? Quid est hoc, nisi ille, qui cum diceret famulus ejus *Ecce mittis me; si dixerit mihi populus: Quis te misit?, quid dicam ei?*, nomen suum noluit aliud dicere quam *Ego sum qui sum*; et adjecit et ait: *Dices itaque filiis Israël: Qui est misit me ad vos.* Ecce idipsum: *Ego sum qui sum; qui est, misit me ad vos.* Non potes capere: multum est intelligere; multum est apprehendere.

> (And what is it that is, if not the one who, when he sent Moses, said to him: *I am who I am?* What is this, if not the one who, when his servant said *Behold, you send me; if the people ask me: who sent you? what shall I tell them?* I did not want to say another name than *I am who I am*;

---

[40]"Jam ergo angelis et in angelo deus dicebat Moysi quaerenti nomen suum *Ego sum qui sum. Dices fillis Israël: Qui est misit me ad vos.* Esse nomen est incommutabilitatis. Omnia quae mutantur desinunt esse quod erant et incipiunt esse quod non erant. Esse verum, esse sincerum, esse germanum non habet nisi qui non mutatur." *Serm.* 7.7 (PL 38.66). Jean Pépin develops his argument (that the *esse* means ultimately eternity vs. mutability) in the following way: "Da due brani emerge che, per Agostino, *idipsum* significa innanzitutto identità, immutabilità, permanenza; poiché sono i caratterri dell'essere, il termine designerà l'essere in possesso di questi caratteri, *ma non l'essere primo intuitu*; non tradurrei petanto 'l'essere', preferendo 'l'identico' o 'l'immutabile'. Del resto, *idipsum* non indica, in senso stretto, l'Essere, ma Dio *in quanto Bene* immutabile" (in *Sant'Agostino. Confessioni. Testo criticamente riveduto e apparati scritturistici di Manlio Simonetti* [Fondazione Lorenzo Valla, 1997], 5.181). He quotes *De vera rel.* 21.41 (BA 8.80): "idipsum, id est naturam incommutabilem" and *Trin.* 3.3.8 (BA 15.282): "Idipsum quippe in hoc loco (Ps 121.3), illud summum et incommutabile bonum intelligitur, quod Deus est."

and he added and said: *Tell thus to the sons of Israel: The one who has sent me to you.* Behold this *idipsum: I am who I am; the one who is has sent me to you.* You cannot grasp it: there is so much to understand, so much to comprehend.)

Not only does Exodus 3.14 enter the picture only after the *idipsum* and following its apophasis, so that the *idipsum* in a sense includes and gives its meaning to *Sum qui sum,* without becoming identical with it or fading away in it.[41] More importantly, translating *Sum qui sum* in the sense of an *ipsum esse,* which would make being the most proper name of God, proves no longer possible. *Sum qui sum,* therefore, does not contribute to the establishing of the "metaphysic of Exodus," by fading away in the *ipsum esse.* Rather, it characterizes the divine immutability in contrast to the finite mutability of everything else: "Et quis magis est, quam ille qui dixit famulo suo Moysi *Ego sum qui sum* et *Dices filiis Israël: qui est, misit me ad vos?* . . . Et ideo sola est incommutabilis substantia et essentia, qui Deus est" (And who is greater than the one who said to his servant Moses *I am who I am* and *Tell the sons of Israel: who is it who sent me to you?* . . . And thus the only immutable substance and essence is the one of God).[42] God is therefore not being, but the immutable one, whose immutability is characterized by an *equivocity* without measure of being.

There follows a fourth step, an even more surprising one since it refers Exodus 3.14 not only to God the creator but directly to Christ, God in *kenosis*: "Quid enim debes tenere? Quod pro te factus est Christus, qui ipse est Christus; et ipse Christus recte intellegitur: *Ego sum qui sum,* quo modo est 'in forma Dei'. Ubi 'non rapinam arbitratus est esse Deo' (Phil 2.6), ibi est *idipsum.* Ut autem efficiaris tu particeps in *idipsum,* factus est

<hr/>

[41]Another text clearly indicates this reversal of roles: "Sublatis de medio omnibus quibus appellari posset et dici Deus, *ipsum esse* se vocari respondit; et tanquam hoc esset ei nomen *Hoc dices eis,* inquit, *Qui est, misit me ad vos.* Ita enim ille est, ut in ejus comparatione ea quae facta sunt, non sint. Illo non comparato, sunt; quoniam ab illo sunt; illi autem comparata, non sunt, quia verum esse, *incommutabile esse* est, quod ille solus est." *En. in Ps.* 134.4 (PL 37.1741).

[42]*Trin.* 5.2.3 (BA 15.428). See Exodus 3.14, which is the basis for the following sentence: "Est enim vero solus, quia incommutabilis" (*Trin.* 7.5.10 [BA 15.538]).

ipse prior particeps tui, et 'Verbum caro factus est' (Jn 1.14), ut caro participet Verbum" (What must you hold [to be true]? That for you he became Christ, since he himself [the *idipsum*] is Christ; and Christ himself is rightly understood [as] *I am who I am,* in the mode in which he is "in the form of God." Where "he did not consider being equal to God as something to be exploited," there he is the *idipsum.* Therefore, so that you too are made a participant in the *idipsum,* he first made himself a participant of you, "and the Word became flesh," so that the flesh may participate in the Word).[43] If the *idipsum* is able to become incarnate and to go through the *kenosis,* if it is able to give itself, participating in the human, it becomes clear that its function and characteristic are not related to being, at least in the sense in which metaphysics later understood the term, that is, all the way to the point of including it in an ontology. Only because he had first reestablished the *sum qui sum* (and therefore also the *ipsum esse*) in its original soteriological meaning could St Augustine unfold the *idipsum* even in the person of the humiliated servant, Christ the Savior.

The most proper name of God, *idipsum,* is thus blatantly apophatic, emphasizing his transcendence through the privilege of immutability; the *ipsum esse* is interpreted by the *Sum qui sum* (and not the other way around), beyond the scope of being, but with an eye to divinization through Christ. This radical biblical exegesis confers on it a radically theological status, to the point where the *idipsum* is equated with the *Sanctus*: "idipsum et idipsum et idipsum, sanctus, sanctus, sanctus Deus omnipotens."[44]

Sum Qui Sum and God's Immutability

The essential point, thus, has to do with the status and the function of immutability. For the Augustinian *esse,* embedded as it is in the *idipsum,* is redirected so as to be of service to immutability. When the *esse* appears

---

[43]*En. in Ps.* 121.5 (PL 37.1621f). This is the text on which our four steps are based.
[44]*Conf.* 7.7.7 (BA 14.352).

in order to de-nominate God, it immediately designates him as the immutable: "Esse, nomen est incommutabilitatis."[45] The difference between the immutable and the mutable becomes, if not an ontological difference, at least a difference in the ways of being, and one that shapes everything that is (*tout l'étant*) through a distinction that is equally original, and perhaps even more original (*originaire*): the distinction between the creature and the Creator. "Cum enim Deus summa essentia sit, hoc est summe sit et ideo immutabilis sit, rebus quas ex nihilo creavit, esse dedit, sed non summe esse, sicut ipse est" (For, since God is supreme essence, that is, since he is supremely and therefore also immutably, he gave being to the things which he created from nothing, but not supremely as he himself is).[46] The hierarchy of beings (*étants*) is apparent and is expressed in the hierarchy of immutability, rather than in strict ontological terms. When compared to the *ego sum qui sum,* for all the things that are not absolutely, i.e. that are not immutably, even though they are, in the end, it is as if these things are not: "tanquam in ejus comparatione, qui vere est quia incommutabilis est, ea quae mutabilia sunt non sint."[47] A point is reached at which the *idipsum* can be designated directly through immutability, without any mediating determination coming from being. "Et tu es *idipsum* valde, quia non mutaris" (you, you are radically the thing itself, because you do not change).[48] Or: "non sunt *idipsum* quod Deus, et inest quaedam mutabilitas omnibus" (they [i.e. the created things] are not the same as God, and a certain mutability is present in all of them).[49] Or again: "non sunt *idipsum,* id est naturam incommutabilem" (the thing itself, that is the immutable nature).[50] And finally: "In *idipsum* quid ait,

<hr />

[45] *Serm.* 7.7, quoting Exodus 3.14, and continuing with: "Esse, nomen est incommutabilitatis. Omnia enim quae mutantur, desinunt esse quod erant et incipiunt esse quod non erant. Esse verum, esse sincerum, esse germanum non habet nisi qui non mutatur" (PL 38.66).

[46] *Civ.* 12.2 (BA 35.154).

[47] Ibid., 8.11 (BA 34.272).

[48] *Conf.* 9.4.11 (BA 14.90).

[49] Ibid., 12.17.25 (BA 14.382).

[50] *De vera rel.* 22.41 (BA 8.80). See the commentary on *ego sum qui sum* exclusively in temporal terms, ibid., 49.97 (BA 8.166–68). There remain, of course, some ambiguous texts, as for instance: "Sed aliae quae dicuntur essentiae sive substantiae, capiunt accidentia,

nisi quod mutari non potest?"[51] God says of himself *sum qui sum,* for he reveals himself first as eternal, and not in any other way. In other words, *aeternum* qualifies *esse,* not the other way around.[52] St Augustine thus accomplishes something very obvious: according to his reading, Exodus 3.14 does not lead to the *ipsum esse* of a "metaphysic of Exodus," because *ego sum qui sum* is understood through the *idipsum* of Psalm 121.3, i.e., through the identity of the thing itself. The *idipsum,* as seen in the *apophasis* brought forth by the difference between mutable and immutable, blurs the difference between beings (*étants*) and perhaps even delegitimizes any interpretation of the distance between creature and Creator within the horizon of being.

There remains a difficulty, however, for at least one text by Augustine clearly seems to interpret the distance between God's eternity and the mutability of creatures in terms of being.

> Aeternitas ipsa Dei substantia est; quae nihil habet mutabile; ibi nihil est praeteritum quasi jam non sit; nihil est futurum, quasi nondum sit. Non est ibi nisi Est; non est ibi Fuit et Erit; quia et quod fuit, jam non est; et quod erit, nondum est; sed quidquid ibi est, nonnisi est. Merito sic misit Deus famulum suum Moysen. Quaesivit enim nomen mittentis se . . . *Ego sum* Quis? *Qui sum.* Hoc est nomen tuum? Hoc est totum quod vocatis? Esset tibi nomen *ipsum esse,* nisi quidquid aliud,

quibus eis fiat vel magna, vel quantacumque mutatio. Deo autem aliquid ejusmodi accidere non potest; et ideo sola est *incommutabilis substantia* vel essentia, qui Deus est, cui profectio *ipsum esse,* un de essentia nominata est, maxime ac verissime competit" (But the others, which are called essences or substances, have accidents through which comes a change, great or small. But to God nothing of this kind can happen; there is thus only one substance or essence which is immutable, and it is God, God to whom belongs being itself (from which the name essence comes from) in the supreme and truest way). *Trin.* 5.2.3 (BA 15.428). Or: "Nam sicut omnino tu es, tu sis solus, qui es incommutabiliter et scis incommutabiliter et vis incommutabiliter." *Conf.* 13.14.18 (BA 14.458). On these texts and their relatively ambiguous character, see Brunn, 144–46.

[51]*En. in Ps.* 146.2.11 (PL 37.1906).

[52]There is a broad consensus on this point. Werner Beierwaltes, "Deus est esse—esse est Deus," in *Platonismus und Idealismus* (Frankfurt am Main: Klosterman, 1972), 5–82; Brunn, 150f; Madec, 72f.

tibi comparatum, inveniretur non esse vere? ... Magnum ecce *Est,* magnum *Est!* Ad hoc homo quid est? Ad illum tam magnum *Est,* homo quid est, quidquid est? Quis apprehendat illud esse? Quis ejus particeps fiat?

(Eternity is the very substance of God, there is nothing mutable about it; here nothing is past, as if it now no longer were; nothing is future, as if it could not yet be. Here there is nothing else than *Is*; here there is no Was and Will be, because what was no longer is, and what will be not yet is; but here, whatever is only is. God rightly sent his servant Moses in the following manner: For the latter asked the name of the one who was sending him ... *I am.* Who [am I]? *Who I am.* Is that your name, is that the entire way you are called? Could *ipsum esse* be your name, as if anything else, when compared to you, would not be considered truly to be? ... How great is this *Is,* how great he *Is!* What is man, compared to it? Compared to such a great Is, what is man, whatever it is? Who will apprehend this being? Who will participate in it?)[53]

Are we not bound to acknowledge that: (a) the *ipsum esse* replaces here the *idipsum,* which is not used to interpret *Ego sum qui sum*; (b) eternity, which replaces immutability, is considered to be a *substantia,* despite Augustine's reluctance to do so in the *De Trinitate*; (c) a new term is favored as a divine name: *Is*; (d) the eternity of this *Is* is described through the three dimensions of time, and time itself is understood in terms of being, as future, present, and past? Are not all the conditions required for a fully and exclusively ontological interpretation of Exodus 3.14 fulfilled here? But then what would remain of the peculiarity and specificity of the *idipsum*?

Yet, far from allowing us to see a proximity between St Augustine and St Thomas Aquinas in their reading of Exodus 3.14, this very same text leads E. Gilson to oppose them. Gilson does that at least twice in his works. First, in his *Introduction à l'étude de saint Augustin,* he uses the principle

---

[53]*En. in Ps.* 101.2.10 (PL 37.1310–11).

"aeternitas ipsa Dei substantia" in order to oppose the two doctrines: "Their conclusions, just like their starting-points, are not the same. To be sure, they are both turned toward the same God, and it is the same God which is named using the same name, but whereas St Thomas always sought to prove the existence of a supreme *Esse* or subsisting act of existence, St Augustine above all attempted to emphasize the necessity to explain the distorted *esse* which confronts us in experience through a supreme *Vere esse*."[54] Let us note: it is not certain that their starting points for the divine names were the same. Moreover, it is not certain that Augustine had any *vere esse* in mind.[55] But, in any case, Gilson's thesis clearly shows what *he* sees as the ontological inadequacy of St Augustine, since, even when St Augustine does not—as in the last quote—redirect the *ipsum esse* toward the *idipsum,* he does not reach the "supreme *Esse.*" This antagonism is explicitly confirmed in what remains Gilson's most important work, *The Philosophy of St Thomas Aquinas* (original title: *Le thomisme*). There the very same principle, an "aeternitas, ipsa Dei substantia," quoted from the same passage in St Augustine's work, is used as the clearest proof of "the ultimate limitations of his ontology," compared to the principle "Deum est suum esse" of St Thomas, who "underscored in such a clear way the decisive step which his ontology represented." Indeed, by maintaining the "varying degrees" present in the "ontology of essences," St Augustine showed himself unable "to bridge the gap separating the being of essence and the being of existence," that is, to entrust the preservation of God's immutable transcendence to the *ipsum esse* itself conceived as *actus essendi* (which is what Gilson meant by "existence"). Nowhere does he question the legitimacy of speaking about ontology in relation to St Augustine (or even, indeed, in relation to St Thomas as well),

---

[54]Gilson, *Introduction à l'étude de saint Augustin* (Paris: J. Vrin, 1st ed. 1929; 3d ed. 1949), 26–27. Brunn agrees with Gilson's conclusion: "La découverte du Dieu-Etre ne constitue encore qu'une connaissance imparfaite et éloignée," 144.

[55]Is not that something which is produced by commenting on the text but which is not present in the text? Just like the "absolute Being" that is supposed to be in *Conf.* 7.10.16 (according to Madec, 39), where in fact we see an intrinsic relation between eternity and charity (not between eternity and being): "o aeterna veritas et vera caritas et cara aeternitas!" (BA 13.616).

when in fact St Augustine does not know that word, which appeared more than ten centuries later. And indeed, St Augustine would not have used it, since even the *ego sum qui sum* is not related to a question about being. The reason for it is not that "the philosophy of Augustine lagged behind his theology,"[56] but rather because his philosophy is not separated from his theology. He does not differentiate between these two terms, since he ignores both. The ontological insufficiencies that Gilson and many others with him see in St Augustine in fact reveal the fundamental inadequacy of their ontological questioning of a thought that unfolds within a completely different horizon than the horizon of metaphysics. What is at stake for St Augustine is something very different than the *Seinsfrage*. Even when he discusses the *ipsum esse*, St Augustine is never concerned with being. It could be that he was, alongside many others, an exception to the rule that Gilson established perhaps with too little caution: "There is only one God, and this God is being; that is the cornerstone of any Christian philosophy."[57] St Augustine, a Christian par excellence and a Christian who thinks, does not think about "being" as God, so that he is able to think about God outside the realm of philosophy.

Suggestions for a Conclusion

From this short inquiry, some conclusions may be drawn, more as suggestions for further questioning than as firm statements.

St Augustine does not anticipate any ontological naming of God and, in particular, especially not on the *ipsum esse*, as seen within the "meta-

---

[56]*Le Thomisme. Introduction à l'étude de saint Thomas d'Aquin* (Paris, 1945), respectively 195, 196, 75, 127, 196.

[57]Gilson, *L'esprit de la philosophie médiévale*, 51. And if one wishes to attenuate such pronouncements by saying: "L'identification de Dieu et de l'Être est certainement un bien commun de la philosophie chrétienne, comme chrétienne. Mais l'accord des penseurs chrétiens sur ce point n'empêche pas que, comme philosophes, ils ne se soient divisés sur l'inteprétation de la notion d'être" (123), then one would rather have to say that Christian thinkers differ on the question of being only when they address it first of all *as Christians*, coming from a different starting point.

physics of Exodus." He rather refers any attempt to name God to the unnamable Name (as emphasized for instance by Gregory of Nyssa, *Contra Eunomium,* 2.14–15): the *idipsum* remains, beyond affirmation as well as negation, a pure deictic, simply referring to and aiming at the nameless and undefinable God.

Should the *idipsum* assume any content, it would be rather *bonum* than *being:* "*Idipsum* quippe in hoc loco [sc. Ps 121.3] illud summum et incommutabile bonum intelligitur, quod Deus est" (For in that place, the *idipsum* is understood to be the chief and incommutable good, which is God).[58] This suggests that St Augustine may be closer to Dionysius, electing ἀγαθός as the first (inadequate as all of them) name of God, before *being,* than to St Thomas Aquinas' emphasis on *ipsum esse.* This difference does not nevertheless become obvious without the critical reading of the usual and illegitimate reading of *idipsum,* which we have tried here to accomplish.

Would those suggestions acquire further validation, St Augustine would be recognized as one of the greatest theologians of the divine names, in line with the Cappadocian fathers as well as with Dionysius.

---

[58] *Trin.* 3.8 (BA 15.282).

The Hidden and the Manifest: Metaphysics after Nicaea

DAVID BENTLEY HART

I

This essay, I must confess, is intended only as a tentative approach to what I take to be an inherently elusive critical object; and hence the investigations it comprises are necessarily somewhat hesitant and incomplete, and may ultimately prove no more than suggestive of inquiries that might be taken up in the future. My principal interest lies in what I want to call "Nicaean ontology"; but I am aware not only of the invincible vagueness of such a concept but of the impatience I am likely to provoke from scholars who would argue that no general ontology can be extracted from Nicaean dogma, or from the theology of the Nicaean party, and that theologians such as the Cappadocian fathers, Hilary of Poitiers, and Augustine never aspired to be what we call "thinkers of Being." Even so, however, it seems undeniable to me that the early development of the Christian understanding of God implicitly involved a metaphysical revision of certain prevailing understandings of being; and that, as the trinitarian debates of the fourth century unfolded, and as dogmatic definitions took shape, and as those debates and definitions were clarified in the next century, inevitably certain elements of a Christian "narrative of being"—or narrative of the relation between the being of the world and the being of God[1]—also became clear for the first

---

[1] In phrasing the matter thus, I hope I indicate how my concerns differ from those of

time and received either explicit or implicit expression in the thought of the first generations of Nicaean theologians. This I find fascinating for a number of reasons, but most particularly because, as one considers how this new, Christian vision of reality announced itself in the thought of the greatest early champions of Nicaean theology, one begins to see that many of them were responding to the same conceptual revolution—not always consciously, and yet almost inevitably in the same way. And this, in a broad sense, is the guiding theme of my argument.

Before proceeding, however, I should pause to note that the immediate context of this essay is a conference on the Eastern Orthodox understanding of Augustine's theology, conducted by eastern and western Christian scholars together, and convoked in the hope that their shared efforts might help to dispel certain of the misunderstandings haunting relations between the "Greek" and "Latin" traditions. This is a project admirable in its ambition, obviously, but also one that innumerable obstacles conspire to thwart. In any modern engagement between Christian East and Christian West, we begin from the long history of an often militant refusal—on both sides—of intellectual reconciliation; more to the point, we begin from very different theological grammars, and with terminologies that can achieve only proximate correspondences, and from within conceptual worlds whose atmospheres are not perfectly congenial to one another's flora, and from a settled tradition of mutual (and frequently willful) incomprehension. All too often, moreover, this incomprehension takes the depressing form of a simple and deplorable failure of imagination: an inability to appreciate that, in order to understand another intellectual tradition, rooted in a different primary language, it is

Jean-Luc Marion (*intra*), and why my argument is in no way incompatible with his. The question that concerns me is not how the fathers came to "denominate" God "within the horizon of being" or "within the metaphysics of being *qua* being." Rather, my interest is in the question of how "being" had to be reconceived by Christian thinkers within the horizon of the relation between the transcendent God and creation; and my conviction is that the development of Christian thought led inevitably to the dissolution of the idea of "being" as a metaphysical "object" within the economy of beings and rendered the very idea of "being" analogical between God and creatures, and for that very reason impotent to comprise the difference dividing them.

not enough to translate its terms into one's own dialect and then proceed to interpret them according to the rules of one's own tradition. And the consequence of this is that, as often as not, "ecumenism" between East and West consists in little more than a relentless syncope of category errors: the drearily predictable alarm and indignation with which traditional Thomists find that Gregory Palamas, transposed into Thomas' Latin, is not a Thomist; the deep and slightly macabre delight with which earnest Palamites discover that Thomas, read through Palamite lenses, proves to be no Palamite; arch dismissals of eastern understandings of grace as "semipelagian" by doctrinaire Augustinians; the reckless intensity with which a particular kind of Orthodox polemicist fixes upon some single principle found somewhere in Latin theological tradition—like "subsistent relations" or "created grace"—violently misinterprets it, and then uses it to diagnose a fundamental deformity in western theology that must estrange it forever from the wellsprings of Orthodox truth; and so on. Perhaps this kind of thing is inevitable when a conversation arises between two traditions that claim to possess the sole, incontrovertible truth of things. It would be humbling indeed to discover that many of our most finely wrought systems of thought possess many accidental elements, peculiar to our particular cultural sensibilities or native tongues, or that perhaps our ways of depicting the truth to ourselves might be only partial and corrigible approximations to a truth that others, under extremely different forms, have approached with equal or better success. More terrible yet is the possibility that many of our differences will prove to be *only* differences of sensibility and language, and not of substance at all, thus reducing our systems to relative expressions of the truth, rather than the pristine vehicles of truth we wish them to be.

Whatever the case, however, an honest consideration of Augustine in relation to the eastern fathers *should* be able to provide a fairly powerful solvent, either of false distinctions or of false accords. For, whatever else may be true about Augustine, it is certainly the case that the profoundest differences between eastern and western tradition are to a very great degree the result not only of differences of language but of the uniquely pervasive influence of Augustine's theology in the Latin West, and of the almost complete absence of its influence in the Greek and Syrian East. And, of course, on some matters these differences are quite real, substantial, and irreconcilable. The theology of grace of the late Augustine, his increasingly intransigent extremism regarding the creature's "merit," his hideous theology of predestination and original guilt, his conviction that genuine trust in the purity and priority of grace obliged him to affirm the eternal damnation of infants who died unbaptized—in short, the entire range of his catastrophic misreading of Paul's theology (attributable only in part to bad Latin translations)—is all very far from what a modern Orthodox Christian is likely to recognize as the Church's faith. It imbues the works of Augustine's senescence with an inexpungible tincture of tragic moral idiocy, one that he bequeathed to broad streams of Catholic and Protestant tradition. This, however, is not really very important, since that aspect of Augustine's thought has fewer defenders than it once did; and, really, charity dictates that it should probably be disregarded as the product of intellectual fatigue. Rather, the issues that truly demand our attention are of another kind altogether, and concern areas of Augustine's thought where, in various times and places, scholars both western and eastern have believed they perceived vast and ultimately unbridgeable fissures between "Greek" and Augustinian thought—of a kind that make *rapprochement* between our traditions, theological or dogmatic, quite impossible—regarding the very nature of God as Trinity, the relation of created being to divine being, and the limits of what we can know of either. These, at any rate, are the topics that concern me here. I wish to speak of "Being" and of God, of the Trinity and of our ability to know God, in the theology of Augustine and of the Greek fathers, Gregory of Nyssa in particular. But I wish to pursue these topics very much at the margins of the debates that have often preoccupied both Catholic and Orthodox theologians in recent years, for the simple reason that I believe that very many of the large and now standard claims often advanced regarding the divergence of our traditions on these matters, in form, content, or intent, are unsustainable, in light either of history or of reason; and that our debates all too often concern only differing and frequently tendentious reconstructions of the Christian past.

Most obviously, I suppose, I shall ignore altogether the venerable notion (first advanced by Théodore de Régnon[2]) that the general tendency of Latin trinitarian reflection has always been to accord priority to the unity of God's nature or essence rather than to the plurality of the divine persons, while that of Greek trinitarian reflection has been the reverse. Not only do I find the sheer vastness of this assertion dauntingly imprecise; I find it utterly impossible to defend from the actual textual evidence of either East or West, ancient, medieval, or modern. More importantly, I think it clearly the case that the assertion made by a number of Orthodox theologians—from Vladimir Lossky to John Zizioulas—that Latin theology views not God the Father, but rather the divine "essence," in its "impersonal" primacy, as the ἀρχή or *principium* of the trinitarian *taxis*, is simply impossible to reconcile with the writings of the major figures of western theological tradition, and can be corroborated only by extremely forced readings of a few isolated texts. In both East and West, at least as far as the main currents of theological speculation are concerned, the *monarchia* of the Father—the *fons deitatis*—remains a governing premise within all serious trinitarian reflection, whatever differences in idiom there may be between Greek and Latin affirmations of the principle.[3] Even if this were not so, however, in the case of Augustine there can be no doubt that, in its basic shape, his account of the order of intra-trinitarian relations is all but indistinguishable from that of the Cappadocians: the Son is begotten directly of the Father, while the Spirit proceeds from the Father through the Son.[4] Indeed, Gregory of Nyssa, like Augustine after him—though, in fact, far less hesitant than Augustine—delineates generation from procession chiefly by reference to this order of relations, arguing that, inasmuch as the divine nature remains immutably the same in each of the divine persons, we discern the persons as distinct only by distinguishing between that which causes and that which is

[2]Théodore de Régnon, *Études de théologie positive sur la Sainte Trinité*, vol. 1 (Paris, 1892), 33.

[3]I have addressed this matter at greater length in "The Mirror of the Infinite: Gregory of Nyssa on the *Vestigia Trinitatis*," *Modern Theology* (2002): 541–61; reprinted in *Re-thinking Gregory of Nyssa*, ed. S. Coakley (Oxford: Blackwell, 2003), 111–31.

[4]See, for instance, Basil, *De Spiritu Sancto* 45–47.

caused, and then further distinguishing between "the one who arises immediately from the principle and the one who arises from this principle only *through* the one who arises immediately."[5] And, as for the accusation that Augustine's "filioquism" logically entails a belief on his part in some sort of divine essence prior to the trinitarian relations, or more original than the Father, neither in *De Trinitate* (*On the Trinity*) nor in any other of his works can one find a single sentence to justify it.[6]

I also find quite incredible the notion (which one associates with the thought of, among others, Christos Yannaras) that the Latin and Greek traditions are set radically at odds by the former's willingness to speak of God as Being and the latter's insistence that God is, properly speaking, entirely beyond being. For one thing, as a purely historical claim, this is clearly false, since both locutions are common to both traditions, and with precisely the same meanings in either case. More fundamentally, though, it is simply a false opposition, inasmuch as the word "being" is certainly

---

[5]Gregory of Nyssa, *Ad Ablabium*, 55–56.

[6]I cannot *quite* agree with John Behr (*intra*) that Augustine operates, unconsciously, with a radically new understanding of the name—and so the trinitarian nature of—"God," except in the sense that the absence of articles in Latin made it impossible for Augustine to use a special form of that name to indicate the Father. And I find Augustine's *obiter dictum* to the effect that it is perhaps licit to speak of the Trinity "metaphorically" as our father (though not in the proper nominative sense as our Father) insufficient evidence for Behr's argument. Nowhere in Augustine's thought is there any hint of a source of the trinitarian life more basic than the Father, and hence the different possibilities of usage within Greek and Latin should not distract us from the fundamental shape of his trinitarian thinking. I do, of course, agree that there was a considerable change in the way theologians used the name "God" after the fourth century; but I deny that this change was limited to the West, or that it was anything other than a healthy and necessary development of the principles established at Nicaea and Constantinople. Moreover, it seems wise to me to recall that neither scripture nor the Byzantine liturgy reserves the name ὁ Θεός exclusively for the Father, and that to a great extent it was too pronounced an emphasis upon the distinction between ὁ Θεός and θεός that made the Arian and Eunomian positions so perdurable in the East; it may be that, on this matter, Latin enjoyed a certain advantage over Greek in expressing the coequality of the divine persons. This matter of the articular and inarticular forms of θεός is, though, an excellent example of the sort of illusory univocities of meaning between different languages to which I have adverted above. There is a very real sense in which θεός and *deus* are only imperfectly convertible with one another; and so, when considering the differences between Greek and Latin tradition, one must always be careful to read either word within its native "semantic economy."

not univocal between the two usages; in fact, the word "being" does scant justice to the full spectrum of terms it is often called upon to represent: *ens, esse, essentia, existentia,* [*actus*] *essendi,* ὄν, ὤν, οὐσία, εἶναι, and so forth. When the Greek fathers spoke of God as Being—as, that is, τὸ ὄντως ὄν or ὤν (etc.)—or when Latin theologians, patristic or mediaeval, spoke of God as *ens, actus essendi subsistens,* or *esse* (etc.), they were speaking of God as the transcendent source and end of all things, whose being is not merely the opposite of nonbeing, and in whom there is no unrealized potential, deficiency, or change. But it is precisely in this sense that God is also (to use the venerable Platonic phrase) ἐπέκεινα τῆς οὐσίας: "super-essential," "supersubstantial," "beyond being." That is, he wholly transcends "beings," and discrete "substances," and the "totality of substances," and the created being in which all beings share; and no concept we possess of beings or of being makes it possible for us to comprehend him. Thus, as Maximus the Confessor says, both names, "Being" and "not-being," at once properly apply and properly do not apply to God: the one denotes that he is the cause of the being of all things, and the latter that he is infinitely beyond all caused being; but neither should be mistaken for a "description" of what he is.[7] In this, Maximus is following the Pseudo-Dionysius, who says that Being is a proper divine name insofar as God is Ἐγώ εἰμι ὁ ὤν ("He who is"), the source of all that exists, present within all things, around and within whom all being abides, in whom all things participate, and within whom the exemplars of all things eternally preexist as a simple unity; but he is not in any sense *a* being: he is not contained by—but rather contains—being, and so, with regard to his own essence, should properly be called not-being.[8] In Augustine's terms, God is the plenitude of being, without which nothing is,[9] but such is his transcendence as the One Who Is that, by comparison to him, those things that are *are* not[10] (which obviously represents only a semantic, not a conceptual, shift). It may be momentarily—but *only* momentarily—arresting to note

---

[7]Maximus, *Mystagogia* 1 (PG 91.664AC).
[8]Ps.-Dionysius, *De divinis nominibus* 5.1–8 (PG 3.816B–824C).
[9]*Sol.* 1.1.3–4.
[10]*En. in Ps.* 134.4.

that Thomas, in deference to God's own pronouncement out of the burning bush,[11] prefers to identify "Being" (or, rather, "to be," or the subsistent act "to be") as the more proper "name" of God; but, again, "being" has many acceptations and, as Thomas' metaphysical designation for God, it signifies that same perfect transcendence of and supremacy over created being that, say, Palamas describes in his remarks upon Exodus 3.14.[12] In either case, there is no *conceptum univocum entis* to span the divide between divine and created being, and thus the true distinction to be drawn is not one between two incompatible ways of naming God, peculiar respectively to West and East, but between two forms of the same name, corresponding to two distinct moments within what I would be content to call the "analogy of being" (though that is a term that frequently excites controversy).

II

I think it fairly uncontroversial to say that, in the intellectual world of the first three centuries before Nicaea, especially in the eastern half of the empire, something like a "Logos metaphysics" was a crucial part of the philosophical *lingua franca* of almost the entire educated class, Pagan, Jewish, Christian, and even Gnostic (even though the term generally preferred was rarely "logos"). Certainly, this was the case in Alexandria: the idea of a "derivative" or "secondary" divine principle was an indispensable premise in the city's native schools of trinitarian reflection, and in the thought either of "Hellenized" Jews like Philo or of the Platonists, middle or late. And one could describe all of these systems, without any significant exception, pagan and Jewish no less than Christian, as "subordinationist" in structure. All of them attempted, with greater or lesser complexity, and with more or less vivid mythical adornments, to connect the world here below to its highest principle by populating the interval

---

[11]Thomas is also, of course, following John of Damascus: *De fide Orthodoxa* 1.9.
[12]Gregory Palamas, *Triads* 3.2.12.

between them with various intermediate degrees of spiritual reality. All of them, that is, were shaped by the same basic metaphysical impulse, one sometimes described as the "pleonastic fallacy": the notion that, in order to overcome the infinite disproportion between the immanent and the transcendent, it is enough to conceive of some sort of *tertium quid*—or of a number of successively more accommodating quiddities—between, on the one hand, the One or the Father or ὁ Θεός and, on the other, the world of finite and mutable things. In all such systems, the second "moment" of the real—that which proceeds directly from the supreme principle of all things: *logos*, or *nous*, or what have you—was understood as a kind of economic limitation of its source, so reduced in "scale" and nature as to be capable of entering into contact with the realm of discrete beings, of translating the power of the supreme principle into various finite effects, and of uniting this world to the wellspring of all things. This derivative principle, therefore, may not as a rule properly be called ὁ Θεός, but it definitely is θεός: God with respect to all lower reality.[13] And this inevitably meant that this secondary moment of the real was understood as mediating this supreme principle in only a partial and distorted way; for such a Logos (let us settle upon this as our term) can appear within the totality of things that are only as a restriction and diffusion of—even perhaps a deviation or alienation from—that which is "most real," the Father who, in the purity of his transcendence, can never directly touch this world. For Christians who thought in such terms, this almost inevitably implied that the Logos had been, in some sense, generated *with respect to* the created order, as its most exalted expression, certainly, but as inseparably involved in its existence nonetheless. Thus it was natural for Christian apologists of the second century to speak of the Logos as having issued from the Father in eternity shortly before the creation of the world. And thus the irreducibly Alexandrian theology of Arius inevitably assumed the metaphysical—or religious—contours that it did: the divine Father is absolutely hidden from and inaccessible to all beings, unknowable even to the heav-

---

[13]This, of course, is why Augustine, in *Conf.* 7.9, quite properly credits the Platonists with having taught him the truths revealed in John 1.1–3 (though, of course, a modern scholar would prefer to say that the prologue of John is a "Middle Platonic" text).

enly powers; and only through the mediation of an inferior Logos is any-thing of him revealed. What, of course, was distinctive in Arianism was the absence of anything like a metaphysics of participation that might have allowed for some sort of real ontological continuity (however indetermi-nate) between the Father and his Logos; consequently, the only revelation of the Father that Arius' Logos would seem to be able to provide is a kind of adoring, hieratic gesture toward an abyss of infinitely incomprehensi-ble power, the sheer majesty of omnipotent and mysterious otherness.[14] The God (ὁ Θεός) of Arius is a God revealed *only* as the hidden, of whom the Logos (θεός ὁ λόγος) bears tidings, and to whom he offers up the liturgy of rational creation; but, as the revealer of the Father, his is the role only of a celestial high priest, the Angel of Mighty Counsel, the coryphaeus of the heavenly powers; he may be a kind of surrogate God to the rest of creation, but he too, logically speaking, cannot attain to an immediate knowledge of the divine essence.

Even, however, in late-antique metaphysical systems less ontologically austere than Arius', in which the economy of divine manifestation is understood as being embraced within some sort of order of μετοχή or μετουσία, the disproportion between the supreme principle of reality and this secondary principle of manifestation remains absolute. Hence all rev-elation, all disclosure of the divine, follows upon a more original veiling. The manifestation of that which is Most High—wrapped as it is in unap-proachable darkness, up upon the summit of being—is only the para-doxical manifestation of a transcendence that can never become truly manifest: perhaps not even to itself, as it possesses no Logos immanent to itself. It does not "think"; it cannot be thought. This, at least, often seems to be the case with the most severely logical, and most luminously unclut-tered, metaphysical system of the third century, that of Plotinus. For the One of Plotinus is not merely *a* unity, not merely solitary, but is oneness as such, that perfectly undifferentiated unity in which all unity and diver-sity here below subsist and are sustained, as at once identity and differ-ence. Plotinus recognized that the unity by which any particular thing is

<hr/>

[14]I am largely persuaded by the portrait of Arius that Rowan Williams paints in his *Arius: Heresy and Tradition*, 2d ed. (Grand Rapids: William B. Eerdmans Publishing Co., 2002).

what it is, and is at once part of and distinct from the greater whole, is always logically prior to that thing; thus, within every composite reality, there must always also be a more eminent "act" of simplicity (so to speak) that makes its being possible. For this reason, the supreme principle of all things must be that One that requires no higher unity to account for its integrity, and that therefore admits of no duality whatsoever, no pollution of plurality, no distinction of any kind, even that between the knower and the known. This is not, for Plotinus, to deny that the One is in some special and transcendent sense possessed of an intellectual act of self-consciousness, a kind of "superintellection" entirely transcendent of subjective or objective knowledge.[15] But the first metaphysical moment of *theoria*—reflection and knowledge—is of its nature a second moment, a departure from unity, Nous' "prismatic" conversion of the simple light of the One into boundless multiplicity; the One itself, possessing no "specular" other within itself, infinitely exceeds all reflection. Nor did philosophy have to await the arrival of Hegel to grasp that there is something fundamentally incoherent in speaking of the existence of that which is intrinsically unthinkable, or of "being" in the absence of any proportionate intelligibility: for in what way is that which absolutely—even within itself—transcends intuition, conceptualization, and knowledge anything at all? Being *is* manifestation, and to the degree that anything is *wholly* beyond thought—to the degree, that is, that anything is not "rational"—to that degree it does not exist. So it was perhaps with rigorous consistency that the Platonist tradition after Plotinus generally chose to place "being" second in the scale of emanation: for as that purely unmanifest, unthinkable, and yet transfinite unity that grants all things their unity, the One can admit of no distinctions within itself, no manifestation *to* itself, and so—in every meaningful sense—*is* not (though, obviously, neither is it not *not*).

In truth, of course, even to speak of an "ontology" in relation to these systems is somewhat misleading. Late Platonic metaphysics, in particular, is not so much ontological in its logic as "henological," and hence naturally whatever concept of being it comprises tends toward the nebulous.

<hr>

[15]See Plotinus, *Enneads* 6.7.37.15–38.26; 9.6.50–55.

"Being" in itself is not really distinct from entities, except in the manner of another entity; as part of the hierarchy of emanations, occupying a particular place within the structure of the whole, it remains one item within the inventory of things that are. Admittedly, it is an especially vital and "supereminent" causal liaison within the totality of beings; but a discrete principle among other discrete principles it remains. What a truly ontological metaphysics would view as being's proper act is, for this metaphysics, scattered among the various moments of the economy of beings. One glimpses its workings now here and now there: in the infinite fecundity of the One, in the One's power to grant everything its unity as the thing it is, in the principle of manifestation that emanates from the One, in the simple existence of things, even in that unnamed, in some sense *unnoticed* medium in which the whole continuum of emanations univocally subsists. But, ultimately, the structure of reality within this vision of things is (to use the fashionable phrase) a "hierarchy within totality," held together at its apex by a principle so exalted that it is also the negation of the whole, in all of the latter's finite particularities.[16] What has never come fully into consciousness in this tradition is (to risk a graver anachronism than any I have indulged in hitherto) the "ontological difference"—or, at any rate, the *analogy* of being. So long as being is discriminated from the transcendent principle of unity, and so long as both figure in some sense (however eminently) within a sort of continuum of metaphysical moments, what inevitably must result is a dialectic of identity and negation. This is the special pathos of such a metaphysics: for if the truth of all things is a principle in which they are grounded and by which they are simultaneously negated, then one can draw near to the fulness of truth only through a certain annihilation of particularity, through a forgetfulness of the manifest, through a sort of benign desolation of the soul, progressively eliminating—as the surd of mere particularity—all that lies between the One and the noetic self. This is not for a moment to deny the reality, the ardor, or the grandeur of the mystical elations that Plotinus describes, or the fervency with which—in his thought and in the thought

---

[16]Ibid., 6.7.17.39–43; 9.3.37–40; cf. 5.5.4.12–16; 11.1–6.

of the later Platonists—the liberated mind loves divine beauty.[17] The pathos to which I refer is a sadness residing not within Plotinus the man, but within any logically dialectical metaphysics of transcendence. For transcendence, so understood, must also be understood as a negation of the finite, and a kind of absence or positive exclusion from the scale of nature; the One is, in some sense, *there* rather than *here*. To fly thither one must fly hence, to undertake a journey of the alone to the alone, a sweetly melancholy departure from the anxiety of finitude, and even from being itself, in its concrete actuality: self, world, and neighbor. For so long as one dwells in the realm of finite vision, one dwells in untruth.

III

What exactly, one might justly ask, does any of this have to do with Nicaean theology? The answer, simply enough, is that the doctrinal determinations of the fourth century, along with all of their immediate theological ramifications, rendered many of the established metaphysical premises upon which Christians had long relied in order to understand the relation between God and the world increasingly irreconcilable with their faith, and at the same time suggested the need to conceive of that relation—perhaps for the first time in western intellectual history—in a properly "ontological" way. With the gradual defeat of subordinationist theology, and with the definition of the Son and then the Spirit as coequal and coeternal with the Father, an entire metaphysical economy had implicitly been abandoned. These new theological usages—this new Christian philosophical grammar—did not entail a rejection of the old Logos metaphysics, perhaps, but certainly did demand its revision, and at the most radical of levels. For not only is the Logos of Nicaea *not* generated with a view to creation, and *not* a lesser manifestation of a God who is simply beyond all manifestation; it is in fact the eternal reality whereby God is the God he is. There is a perfectly proportionate convertibility of

[17]There are rather too many passages on this mystical *eros* in the *Enneads* to permit exhaustive citation; but see especially 6.7.21.9–22.32; 6.7.31.17–31; 6.7.34.1–39; 6.9.9.26–56.

God with his own manifestation of himself to himself; and, in fact, this convertibility is nothing less than God's own act of self-knowledge and self-love in the mystery of his transcendent life. His being, therefore, is an infinite intelligibility; his hiddenness—his transcendence—is always already manifestation; and it is this movement of infinite disclosure that is his "essence" as God. Thus it is that the divine persons can be characterized (as they are by Augustine) as "subsistent relations": meaning not that, as certain critics of the phrase hastily assume, the persons are nothing but abstract correspondences floating in the infinite simplicity of a logically prior divine essence, but that the relations of Father to Son or Spirit, and so on, are not extrinsic relations "in addition to" other, more original "personal" identities, or "in addition to" the divine essence, but are the very reality by which the persons subsist; thus the Father is eternally and essentially Father *because* he eternally has his Son, and so on.[18] God *is* Father, Son, and Spirit; and nothing in the Father "exceeds" the Son and Spirit. In God, to know and to love, to be known and to be loved are all one act, whereby he is God and wherein nothing remains unexpressed. And, if it is correct to understand "being" as in some sense necessarily synonymous with manifestation or intelligibility—and it is—then the God who is also always Logos is also eternal Being: not *a* being, that is, but transcendent Being, beyond all finite being.

Another way of saying this is that the dogmatic definitions of the fourth century ultimately forced Christian thought, even if only tacitly, toward a recognition of the full mystery—the full transcendence—of Being within beings. All at once the hierarchy of hypostases mediating between the world and its ultimate or absolute principle had disappeared. Herein lies the great "discovery" of the Christian metaphysical tradition: the true nature of transcendence, transcendence understood not as mere dialectical supremacy, and not as ontic absence, but as the truly transcendent and therefore utterly immediate act of God, in his own infinity, giving being to beings. In affirming the consubstantiality and equality of the persons of the Trinity, Christian thought had also affirmed that it is the

---

[18] *Trin.* 7.1.2. Or, as John of Damascus puts it, the divine subsistences dwell and are established within one another (*De fide Orthodoxa* 1.14).

transcendent God alone who makes creation to be, not through a necessary diminishment of his own presence, and not by way of an economic reduction of his power in lesser principles, but as the infinite God. In this way, he is revealed as at once *superior summo meo* and *interior intimo meo*: not merely the supreme being set atop the summit of beings, but the one who is transcendently present in all beings, the ever more inward act within each finite act. This does not, of course, mean that there can be no metaphysical structure of reality, through whose agencies God acts; but it does mean that, whatever that structure might be, God is not located within it, but creates it, and does not require its mechanisms to act upon lower things. As the immediate source of the being of the whole, he is nearer to every moment within the whole than it is to itself, and is at the same time infinitely beyond the reach of the whole, even in its most exalted principles. And it is precisely in learning that God is not situated within any kind of ontic continuum with creation, as some "other thing" mediated to the creature by his simultaneous absolute absence from and dialectical involvement in the totality of beings, that we discover him to be the *ontological* cause of creation. True divine transcendence, it turns out, transcends even the traditional metaphysical divisions between the transcendent and the immanent.

This recognition of God's "transcendent immediacy" in all things, it should also be said, was in many ways a liberation from a certain sad pathos native to metaphysics; for with it came the realization that the particularity of the creature is not in its nature a form of tragic alienation from God, which must be overcome if the soul is again to ascend to her inmost truth. If God is himself the immediate actuality of the creature's emergence from nothingness, then it is precisely through becoming what it is—rather than through shedding the finite *idiomata* that distinguish it from God—that the creature truly reflects the goodness and transcendent power of God. The supreme principle does not stand over against us (if secretly within each of us) across the distance of a hierarchy of lesser metaphysical principles, but is present within the very act of each moment of the particular. God is truly Logos, and creatures—created in and through the Logos—*are* insofar as they participate in the Logos' power to manifest God. God is not merely the "really real," of which beings are distant shadows; he is, as Maximus the Confessor says, the utterly simple, the very simplicity of the simple,[19] who is all in all things, wholly present in the totality of beings and in each particular being, indwelling all things as the very source of their being, without ever abandoning that simplicity.[20] This he does not as a sublime unity absolved of all knowledge of the things he causes, but precisely *as* that one infinite intellectual action proper to his nature, wherein he knows the eternal *logoi* of all things in a single, simple act of knowledge.[21] God in himself is an infinite movement of disclosure, and in creation—rather than departing from his inmost nature—he discloses himself again by disclosing what is contained in his Logos, while still remaining hidden in the infinity and transcendence of his manifestation. And to understand the intimacy of God's immediate presence *as God* to his creatures in the abundant givenness of this disclosure is also—if only implicitly—to understand the true difference of Being from beings.

One consequence of all of this for the first generations of Nicaean theologians was that a new conceptual language had to be formed, one that could do justice not only to the trinitarian mystery, nor even only to the relation between this mystery and finite creation, but to our knowledge of the God thus revealed. For, in a sense, the God described by the dogmas of Nicaea and Constantinople was at once more radically immanent within and more radically transcendent of creation than the God of the old subordinationist metaphysics had ever been. He was immediately active in all things; but he occupied no station within the hierarchy of the real. As Augustine says, he is manifest in all things and hidden in all things, and none can know him as he is.[22] He was not the Most High God of Arius, immune to all contact with the finite, for the Logos in whom he revealed himself as creator and redeemer was his own, interior Logos, his own perfect image, his own self-knowledge and disclosure; nor certainly was he anything like the paradoxical transcendence of the One of Ploti-

[19]Maximus, *Ambigua* (PG 91.1232BC).
[20]Ibid. (PG 91.1256B).
[21]See idem, *Capita Theologiae Oeconomiae* 2.4 (PG 90.1125D–1128A).
[22]*En. in Ps.* 74.9.

nus, "revealed" only as a kind of infinite contrariety. In fact, the God who is at once the Being of all things and beyond all beings, and who is at once revealed in a Logos who is his coequal likeness and at the same time hidden in the infinity of his transcendence, is immeasurably *more* incomprehensible than the One, which is simply the Wholly Other, and which is consequently susceptible of a fairly secure kind of *dialectical* comprehension (albeit, admittedly, a comprehension consisting entirely in negations). The Christian God, by contrast, requires us to resort to the far severer, far more uncontrollable, and far more mysterious language of analogy—to indulge in a slight terminological anachronism—in the sense enunciated in Roman Catholic tradition by the fourth Lateran Council: a likeness always embraced within and exceeded by a greater unlikeness. In the terms of Gregory of Nyssa, however much of God is revealed to the soul, God still remains infinitely greater, with a perfect transcendence toward which the soul must remain forever "outstretched." Or, as Maximus says, Christian language about God is a happy blending of affirmation and negation, each conditioning the other, telling us what God is not while also telling us what he is, but in either case showing us *that* God is what he is while never allowing us to imagine we comprehend *what* it is we have said.[23]

That said, in a very significant way, the fully developed trinitarianism of the fourth century allowed theologians to make real sense of some of those extravagant scriptural claims that, within the confines of a subordinationist theology, could be read only as pious hyperbole: "we shall see face to face," for instance, and "I shall know fully, even as I am fully known" (1 Cor 13.12); or "we shall see him as he is" (1 Jn 3.2); or "who has seen me has seen the Father" (Jn 14.9); or "the Son . . . is the exact likeness of his substance" (Heb 1.3); or even "blessed are the pure of heart, for they shall see God" (μακάριοι οἱ καθαροὶ τῇ καρδίᾳ, ὅτι αὐτοὶ τὸν θεὸν ὄψονται—note the definite article—Mt 5.8). In considering the God of Nicaean theology, we discover that the knowledge of the Father granted in Christ is not an external apprehension of an unknown cause, not the remote

---

[23]Maximus, *Ambigua* (PG 91.1288C).

epiphenomenon of something infinitely greater than the medium of
its revelation, and not merely a glimpse into the "antechamber of the
essence"; rather it is a mysterious knowledge of the Father himself within
the very limitlessness of his unknowability. But, then again, the God who
is the infinite source of all cannot be an object of knowledge contained
within the whole; and, if the Logos is equal to the Father, how can he truly
reveal the Father to finite minds? And if—as became clear following the
resolution of the Eunomian controversy—the Spirit too is not the eco-
nomically limited medium of God's self-disclosure, but is also coequal
with the Father and the Son, and is indeed the very Spirit by which God's
life is made complete as knowledge and love, power and life, how can he
reveal to us the Father in the Son?

These questions are made all the more acute, obviously, by the quite
pronounced apophatic strictures that all post-Nicaean theologians—
Augustine no less than his Greek counterparts[24]—were anxious to impose

[24]Here, obviously, I am in agreement with the argument of Marion (*intra*) and not with
that of Bradshaw (*intra*). I do not think, moreover, that the two positions are equally plausible. Bradshaw's argument not only misrepresents Augustine's clearly stated positions, but
involves erroneous interpretations of the few Augustinian texts that Bradshaw himself cites.
For instance, he adduces *Serm.* 117—as austerely apophatic a text as one could hope for—
as proof that Augustine believed the human mind capable of a direct knowledge and comprehension of the divine essence; but the single sentence he mistranslates from the sermon
(from 117.5) he has also removed from its context, within which it indicates exactly the
opposite of what Bradshaw suggests. What Augustine is actually saying is that "God is an
object of the mind, to be thought about, while a body is an object for the eyes, to be seen";
but this he asserts only in order then to argue that, even so, unlike some finite object of the
senses, God is forever and entirely incomprehensible and inconceivable for the finite mind,
and so the mind—and then only the *pure* mind—can do no more than stretch out to touch
him; this alone is knowledge of God. Here, as elsewhere, Augustine emphatically denies that
any creature can grasp or intuit or understand God in himself. He is, in short, saying nothing that was not also said by Gregory of Nyssa, Maximus the Confessor (*vide infra* in text),
the Pseudo-Dionysius, and a host of other eastern writers. Bradshaw's argument is remarkably similar to that of Phillip Cary in his *Augustine's Invention of the Inner Self* (New York:
Oxford University Press, 2000); in this book Cary also avers that Augustine believed the
human mind capable of comprehending God's essence as an object of cognition, and he
too cites (as his sole solid corroboration) this same sentence from *Serm.* 117, similarly
wrenched from its context—which obliges Cary then to argue that all the statements of
divine incomprehensibility in the surrounding text do not actually mean what they seem
to mean (57–67). To abstract a single "incriminating" phrase from its surroundings, how-

upon their language. As Augustine repeatedly affirms, every kind of vision of God in himself is impossible for finite creatures,[25] none can ever know him as he is,[26] nothing the mind can possibly comprehend is God,[27] God is incomprehensible to anyone except himself,[28] we are impotent even to conceive of God,[29] and so when speaking of God we are really able to do so properly only through negation.[30] And yet he also wants to say that,

ever, as a kind of counterweight not only to mountains of controverting evidence from other sources by the same author, but to the explicit argument of the very text from which it has been taken, and within which it has a different meaning than that being ascribed to it, is simply irresponsible scholarship. By the same token, Bradshaw, like Cary, not only relies preponderantly upon the *Sol.* in his exposition of Augustine's thought—a very early and in many ways unrepresentative text—but burdens Augustine's language in that text with interpretations it simply will not support. Bradshaw even appears to repeat Cary's error of reading the Latin word *intelligibilis* as having the same connotations as the English word "intelligible," which it certainly does not; *intelligibilis*, like νοητικός in Greek, primarily means "possessing a spiritual or rational nature": simple, incorporeal, immortal, and so on; hence both the Greek and Latin fathers were as one in ascribing to God a noetic or intelligible—rather than an aesthetic or sensible—nature (for "God is Spirit"). This notion that there is a greater kinship (or more perfect likeness) between rational creation and God than there is between material creation and God is simply ubiquitous in patristic sources. Basil of Caesarea and Gregory of Nyssa, for example, both rejected the existence of any genuine material substrate to the physical world, and claimed that the physical universe is a confluence of intelligible or ideal properties, because both accepted the principle that an effect must resemble its cause, and so deduced that even the sensible realm must ultimately be reducible to intelligible elements. It is true, of course, that in the *Sol.* Augustine uses the Platonic image of God as the Sun or the Light of the intelligible world and of the intellectual realm (1.1.3; 1.9.16)—which is hardly a metaphor alien to eastern patristic tradition—and says that reason can "demonstrate God to the mind as the Sun demonstrates itself to the eye" (1.6.12), and states that "God is intelligible, not sensible" (1.8.15); and it is also true that in this early text Augustine speaks of the vision and knowledge of God (those things so plentifully promised by scripture) in tones comparable in hopefulness—if not in boldness—to certain phrases from the sermons of Gregory of Nazianzus. But nowhere in the *Sol.* is there any suggestion that one can "know" God in the sense of "comprehending God in his own nature and essence," nor does the text provide any warrant for ignoring or dismissing the innumerable statements in Augustine's writings explicitly denying the possibility of such comprehension.

[25] See, for example, *Trin.* 2.16.27; *Tract. Ev. Jo.* 124.3.17; *Contra Max.* 2.12.2.

[26] *En. in Ps.* 74.9.

[27] *Serm.* 52.6; 117.5.

[28] *Ep.* 232.6.

[29] *Serm.* 117.5.

[30] *En. in Ps.* 80.12.

even in failing to comprehend God in himself, we are led by the Spirit truly to see and know and touch God. Similarly, Gregory of Nyssa denies that any creature is capable of any θεωρία of the divine essence, and yet wants also to say that, in stretching out in desire toward God, the soul somehow sees God[31] and attains to a θεωρία τῶν ἀθεωρήτων, a vision of the invisible.[32] Gregory even speaks of David as going out of himself really to *see* the divine reality that no creature *can* see, and remaining ever thereafter unable to say how he has done this.[33] Maximus, who raises the "Greek" delight in extravagant declarations of apophatic ignorance to its most theatrical pitch, nonetheless makes it clear that his is an apophaticism of intimacy, born not from the poverty of the soul's knowledge of God, but from the overwhelming and superconceptual immediacy of that knowledge. The mind rises to God, he says, by negating its knowledge of what lies below, in order to receive true knowledge of God as a gift, and to come ultimately—beyond all finite negations—to rest in the inconceivable and ineffable reality of God.[34] When the mind has thus passed beyond cognition, reflection, cogitation, and imagination, and discovers that God is not an object of human comprehension, it is able to know him directly, through union, and so rushes into that embrace in which God shares himself as a gift with the creature,[35] and in which no separation between the mind and its first cause in God can be introduced.[36]

If this language of knowing God in a condition of insuperable unknowing seems at times little more than paradox, or to promise nothing more than a (logically impossible) affective experience of God totally devoid of concepts, what we must at all costs avoid doing is allow ourselves—solely for the sake of convenience—to impose later medieval systems of thought on the patristic texts, in the hope of thereby dispelling the difficulties with which they present us: either, as was once common among Catholic scholars, to read Augustine unreflectively through

---

[31]Gregory of Nyssa, *De vita Moysis* 2 (*Gregorii Nysseni Opera* [hereafter, GNO] 7.1, 87).
[32]Idem, *In Canticum Canticorum* 11 (GNO 6.326).
[33]Ibid., 307–11.
[34]Maximus, *Ambigua* (PG 91, 1240C–1241A).
[35]Ibid., 1220 BC.
[36]Ibid., 1260D.

Thomism, or, as is now too often the case among Orthodox scholars, to read the eastern fathers unreflectively through Palamism. For one thing, especially in the context of a discussion between communions, if we retreat to the medieval syntheses we will immediately find ourselves drawn into the tedious and irresoluble "disagreement" between the two traditions concerning the eschatological knowledge of God: between, that is, the Thomistic affirmation of an ultimate vision of the divine essence by souls elevated by grace and the Palamite denial of any vision of God's οὐσία, or of any encounter with God except through his "energies." This is a sublimely pointless argument at the end of the day. For one thing, inasmuch as Thomas explicitly denies that the mind that enjoys such a "vision" can ever *comprehend* the divine essence, and even states that the mind does not actually possess an immediate intuition of the essence, but sees God only through a certain created glory instilled in the intellect by the operations of grace;[37] and inasmuch as Palamas, however much he denies that any intellect can penetrate the divine essence, also wants to affirm that God's operations communicate the real presence of God to the mind; it is not entirely clear that the two positions are divided by anything much profounder than the acceptations of their preferred metaphors ("essence," after all, is only slightly more univocal a term than "being"). Even, though, if the two traditions are finally irreconcilable, neither should be trusted as an unproblematic précis of the theologies of the patristic period. In the case of Thomistic interpretations of Augustine, Jean-Luc Marion's essay in this volume gives sufficient evidence of the precipitous misreadings toward which such interpretations can lead. As for Palamite readings of the eastern fathers, they frequently prove no less procrustean and no less deceptive. As David Bradshaw correctly notes in his essay, whatever distinction may be drawn in the thought of, say, Gregory or Maximus between, on the one hand, the divine essence and, on the other, the divine energies or processions or "things around God" (assuming these are nearly equivalent terms), it is not a fixed distinction, but a kind of receding horizon, because God, in his operations toward

---

[37]Thomas Aquinas, *Summa Th.* 1.12.7.

creatures, reveals ever more of himself and yet always infinitely exceeds what he reveals.[38] Whether, however, this is how Palamas understood the distinction between the divine essence and the divine energies is more than a little debatable.[39] What is beyond debate is that, for many contemporary Palamites—I have in mind especially Vladimir Lossky—the distinction is something altogether more (for want of a better term)

[38]This, of course, renders it rather paradoxical to claim (as Bradshaw also does) that, for Gregory, the divine names apply only to the divine energies and not to the divine essence. Logically, if the divine energies are genuine *manifestations* of God, however limited, then whatever names apply to the energies also necessarily apply to the essence, even if only defectively, immeasurably remotely, incomprehensibly, and "improperly." It is true, of course, that for Gregory our words name God only as he acts toward us, and that all of our words fall infinitely short of God (this is true for Augustine as well). But it is an oversimplification to suggest that, for Gregory, the divine names do not *refer* to God in himself, even if we can never grasp what those names properly mean, given their infinite convertibility with one another in God's transcendent being. For all of the Cappadocians, we come to know anything of God only through his operations (or energies, if one prefers the Greek word); but none of them ever suggests that what is revealed of God therein is true of the energies alone (the Cappadocians were not Nominalists.) Gregory, certainly, has no notion of the divine energies as concretely other than or really distinct from God in himself—indeed, he explicitly rejects such a notion (*Contra Eunomium* 1 [GNO 2, 87])—and I doubt it would have occurred to him or any of his contemporaries to speak of what *belongs* only to God's "energies" or "operations," even if the words we use of God are, from our side, names of those operations. And much the same is true, certainly, of eastern patristic theology in general. John of Damascus, for example, argues that, while the "names" or "attributes" proper to God himself apply to the divine essence, we must not imagine that they are true of God in a plural way, which we could then understand; in God, who is infinitely simple, all of these attributes are one and identical with one another, and if we think of them in a composite fashion then we think of them as something outside his nature or as mere energies (which they are *not*); at the same time, as discrete predications, the positive names we apply to God "describe" God's nature, but still cannot "explain" God's essence to us (*De fide Orthodoxa* 1.9). John goes on to say that those attributes proper to "the whole God" (as opposed to the trinitarian relations) are attributes *of the essence*—which, nonetheless, we never understand in itself, just as we never understand the essence of anything merely by knowing its attributes (ibid., 1.10). For the fathers of both East and West, I think it fair to say, genuine apophaticism is not reducible to the arid dialectics of "the Wholly Other," but flows from a fruitful awareness of the impotence of our words and concepts before the infinite simplicity of God.

[39]And, in fact, a question impossible to settle. If the texts attributed to Palamas are indeed all the work of his hand, then it is quite likely that no one will ever be able convincingly to explain what Palamas meant by the distinction of essence and energies in God, since it is not at all clear that Palamas himself knew what he meant.

dialectical, and altogether more inviolable.[40] Even all of this, however, is

[40]I suspect it is this tendency in modern Orthodox scholarship that has recently given rise in certain (primarily American) circles to the fanciful idea that there has always been some great difference between eastern and western patristic traditions regarding the nature of divine simplicity. In his essay (*intra*), Bradshaw chides Augustine for asserting that, in God himself, the divine essence and divine attributes are identical; but this is a point on which all of the significant eastern fathers certainly agreed (see, for instance, the passages adduced from John of Damascus in n. 38 above). The denial of such an identity would reduce any idea of divine transcendence to absurdity. That God—*in his essence*—is not merely good, but goodness itself, and is not merely true, but is truth itself (and so on), is an affirmation simply inherent in any understanding of God as the source of all contingent things, who does not participate in some source of goodness or truth (etc.) beyond himself, who is not composite, who possesses no unrealized potential, and who is all that he is of himself alone; and, as the Damascene says, it is solely *because* God's attributes are, properly speaking, convertible with one another in the simplicity of his essence that we cannot comprehend what they are in him. As for the claim that for Gregory of Nyssa the identity of God with his attributes, as well as their identity with one another, is true only at the level of the energies, it is difficult to see how this can be demonstrated from Gregory's texts or, for that matter, defended logically. And Bradshaw is making an unwarranted leap in assuming that, when Augustine affirms the identity of the divine essence and the divine will (again, an assertion with which none of the eastern fathers would disagree), he must mean that the particular determinations of God's will in time are aspects of the divine essence; this is no more an implication of Augustine's thought than it is of Maximus' belief that the eternal *logoi* of all things (which are not just forms, but creative intentions) dwell from everlasting in the Logos. Augustine's view does not differ significantly from Gregory of Nyssa's, as expressed in the first chapter of the *Oratio catechetica*: that we must assert that the divine will must be the same as divine goodness and commensurate with divine omnipotence, for otherwise we would introduce complexity and mutability *into the divine simplicity*; or, as John of Damascus says, God is one essence, one Godhead, one power, one will, etc. (*De fide Orthodoxa* 1.8). In fine, God's will is not something dependent on realities "beyond" himself or limited by finite potencies, but encompasses the whole span of his power and being, and is therefore perfectly free; all that God wills belongs naturally (though not necessarily) to that one eternal act whereby he wills his own goodness. I am unsure why Bradshaw suggests that Augustine's claim that God wills all things in a single eternal act is alien to eastern tradition (again, see John of Damascus, *De fide Orthodoxa* 1.9). And, as for whether such a belief accounts for Augustine's understanding of predestination, I tend to think just the opposite is true: that the theology of *praedestinatio ante praevisa merita* is a betrayal of the principle of the identity of divine will and essence, because at some level this theology introduces into God's determinations a purely arbitrary moment that cannot be reconciled with the idea that, in God, all acts of will are perfectly in concord with his nature. I doubt, moreover, that a close reading of the *Sophist* would have altered Augustine's thinking. In dismissing Augustine's equation of real being with perfect unity, Bradshaw is confusing a number of different issues. Again, "being" is not a univocal term; but insofar as "being" means the subsistence of a particular thing, it is an idea that certainly necessarily entails that

rather beside the point, for the simple reason that both traditions, when they talk about the knowability or unknowability of the divine οὐσία or *essentia*, are for the most part talking pious nonsense. There is no such "thing" as the divine essence; there is no such object, whether of knowledge or of ignorance. It is ultimately immaterial whether we prefer to use the term οὐσία to indicate the transcendence and incomprehensibility of God in himself or to use the term "incomprehensibility of the essence" instead. God is *essentially* Father, Son, and Spirit, and (as modern Orthodox theologians never tire of insisting) there is no other reality prior to, apart from, or more original than the paternal *arche*, which perfectly reveals itself in an eternal and coequal *Logos* and communicates itself by the Spirit who searches the deep things of God and makes Christ known to us. There is no divine essence, then, into the vision of which the souls of the saved will ultimately be admitted, nor even from the knowledge of which human minds are eternally excluded, and any language that suggests otherwise—whether patristic, Thomist, or Palamite—is an empty reification. The question of the knowledge of God, properly conceived— conceived, that is, in the terms provided by scripture and the best of patristic dogmatic reflection—is the question of how we know the Father in the Son through the Spirit, even as the Father infinitely exceeds our knowledge; it is, that is to say, an intrinsically trinitarian question, to which none but a truly trinitarian answer is adequate.

IV

The single passage from the New Testament that perhaps most perfectly expresses the answer toward which Nicaean theology, East and West, was inexorably driven is Paul's comparison, in 2 Corinthians 3.12–18, between the veiled face of Moses and the unveiled faces of those being trans-

thing's unity with respect both to its substance and to its act of existence; and insofar as "being" means the source of all things—which participates in nothing above itself and which cannot have the character of a composite event—it is an idea that necessarily entails absolute simplicity.

formed, from glory to glory, into the likeness of Christ; and perhaps no word in that passage more perfectly captures the essence of that answer than the single, somewhat amphibologous participle κατοπτριζόμενοι: either "beholding in a mirror" or "mirroring" or both—"speculating," "reflecting," "reflecting upon." At the risk of reducing an immense diversity of theological impulses and tendencies to a small set of abstract principles, I think it possible to identify two distinct but inseparable moments within Nicaean thought regarding our knowledge of the trinitarian God: first, the recognition that the interior life of this God is one of infinite and "reflective" intelligibility—from everlasting, a life that is always already Logos and Spirit—and, second, the affirmation that we know God by being admitted to a finite participation in that intelligibility, through our transformation by the Spirit into ever purer reflections of the Logos in whom the depths of the Father shine forth. That is to say, we know God by being drawn into the mystery of his own trinitarian act of self-knowledge, which yet remains ever infinitely beyond us. The medium of God's revelation, therefore, is God himself; and the site—the matter—of that revelation is the living soul. As Augustine says, what we know of God we know through an image directly impressed upon our nature.[41] Or, as Gregory of Nyssa says, human nature is a mirror, capable of bearing the impress of whatever it is turned toward,[42] created to reflect its divine archetype within itself and to communicate that beauty to the whole of creation; and the soul comes to know God only insofar as it looks to Christ and thereby becomes what he is,[43] adorned with his beauty.[44] Revelation is sanctification, and the mind knows the Father in the Son by becoming itself an ever truer image of that Image.

The indiscerptibility of these two principles, in the theologies of both East and West, can be illustrated quite vividly by a fairly straightforward comparison between the thought of Gregory of Nyssa and that of Augustine, one that comes into focus for me principally around a (so to speak)

---

[41] *Trin.* 14.15.21; *En. in Ps.* 4.8.

[42] Gregory of Nyssa, *In Canticum Canticorum* 4 (GNO 6.104).

[43] Ibid., 2 (GNO 6.68).

[44] Ibid., 15 (GNO 6.440).

matched set of quotations to which I find myself repeatedly returning. The first is from Gregory's *De Anima et Resurrectione (On the Soul and Resurrection)*: "the divine nature exceeds each [finite] good, and the good is wholly beloved by the good, and thus it follows that when it looks upon itself it desires what it possesses and possesses what it desires, and receives nothing from outside itself";[45] and this line of reflection that Gregory takes up again a few lines below: "the life of that transcendent nature is love, in that the beautiful is entirely lovable to those who recognize it (and the divine does recognize it), and so this recognition becomes love, because the object of his recognition is in its nature beautiful."[46] The second, much longer quotation is from book 6 of Augustine's *De Trinitate*:

... the Son is from the Father, so as both to be and to be coeternal with the Father. For if the image perfectly fills the measure of him whose image it is, then it is coequal to its source ... [Hilary of Poitiers] has, in regard to this image, employed the name "form" on account, I believe, of its beauty, wherein there is at once such harmony, and prime equality, and prime similitude, in no way discordant, in no measure unequal, and in no part dissimilar, but wholly answering to the identity of the one whose image it is. ... Wherefore that ineffable conjunction of the Father and his image is never without fruition, without love, without rejoicing. Hence that love, delight, felicity or beatitude, if any human voice can worthily say it, is called by him, in brief, use, and is in the Trinity the Holy Spirit, not begotten, but of the begetter and begotten alike the very sweetness, filling all creatures, according to their capacities, with his bountiful superabundance and excessiveness.[47]

[45]Idem, *De Anima et Resurrectione* (PG 46.93): "Ἐπεὶ δὲ παντὸς ἀγαθοῦ ἐπέκεινα ἡ θεία φύσις, τὸ δὲ ἀγαθὸν ἀγαθῷ φίλον πάντως, διὰ τοῦτο ἑαυτὴν βλέπουσα καὶ ὃ ἔχει, θέλει, καὶ ὃ θέλει, ἔχει, οὐδὲν τῶν ἔξωθεν εἰς ἑαυτὴν δεχομένη."

[46]Ibid. (PG 46.96): "ἥ τε γὰρ ζωὴ τῆς ἄνω φύσεως ἀγάπη ἐστίν, ἐπειδὴ τὸ καλὸν ἀγαπητὸν πάντως ἐστὶ τοῖς γινώσκουσι (γινώσκει δὲ ἑαυτὸ τὸ θεῖον), ἡ δὲ γνῶσις ἀγάπη γίνεται, διότι καλόν ἐστι φύσει τὸ γινωσκόμενον."

[47]*Trin.* 6.10.11: "Imago enim si perfecte implet illud cuius imago est, ipsa coaequatur ei, non illud imagini suae. In qua imagine speciem nominavit, credo, propter pulchritudinem,

And this, according to Augustine, leads us to say that: "In that Trinity is the highest origin of all things, and the most perfect beauty, and the most blessed delight. Therefore those three are seen to be mutually determined, and are in themselves infinite."[48]

Admittedly, Augustine is speaking here directly about the Trinity, while Gregory is merely speaking with a trinitarian grammar (to appreciate the full profundity of which one must seek supplementary arguments from other of his works). But what these passages reveal is that, for both theologians, God's one act of being God is also that one, eternal, "speculative" act by which he knows and loves the fulness of his own essence. As Augustine takes such pains to argue, it is not the case that the Father merely begets his image, wisdom, and being in the Son, while remaining something apart; he already is wisdom and being—he already knows and is—and begets his image not by reduction or alienation, but as the perfect expression of his essence: and hence he eternally begets, of his nature.[49] Or, as Gregory argues—from the opposite direction, as it were, but with the same end in view—the Son is the eternal image in which the Father contemplates and loves his essence, and thus the Father can never be conceived of without his Son, for "if ever the brightness of the Father's glory did not shine forth, that glory would be dark and blind."[50] And this "infinite speculation," if one may phrase it that way, is for Gregory that one original act of knowledge in which each of the divine persons shares: the Only Begotten who dwells in the Father, sees the Father in himself, while the Spirit searches out the depths of God.[51] God himself is, as it were, an

ubi iam est tanta congruentia, et prima aequalitas, et prima similitudo, nulla in re dissidens, et nullo modo inaequalis, et nulla ex parte dissimilis, sed ad identidem respondens ei cuius imago est. . . . Ille igitur ineffabilis quidam complexus patris et imaginis non est sine per-fruitione, sine charitate, sine gaudio. Illa ergo dilectio, delectatio, felicitas vel beatitudo, si tamen aliqua humana voce digne dicitur, usus ab illo appellatus est breviter, et est in trinitate spiritus sanctus, non genitus, sed genitoris genitique suavitas, ingenti largitate atque ubertate perfundens omnes creaturas pro captu earum."

[48]Ibid., 6.10.12: "In illa enim trinitate summa origo est rerum omnium, et perfectissima pulchritudo, et beatissima delectatio. Itaque illa tria, et ad se invicem determinari videntur, et in se infinita sunt."

[49]*Trin.* 7.1.2.

[50]Gregory, *Refutatio Confessionis Eunomii* (GNO 2.355).

[51]Idem, *Contra Eunomium* 2 (GNO 1.340).

eternal play of the invisible and the visible, the inaccessible depths and heights of the Father made radiantly manifest in the infinite impress of his beauty, God "mirroring" himself and so knowing himself by pouring himself out wholly in the Son and Spirit. And it is from the Trinity's own eternal "circle of glory"[52] that the logic of created being unfolds: creation, one could say, is another inflection of an infinite light, receiving that light as the very gift of its being. There are not, then, discrete moments of being's dispensation within a scale of which God is somehow "part": he does not lie beyond the economy of manifestation as the essentially unmanifest mystery whose solitude is inverted and so distorted in all that lies below him. Rather, God himself is the immediate source of every moment of finite reality: its hidden depths, its manifest surface, its rational structure, its beauty. Creation *is* only as the answer of light to light, a gracious "overflow" of the self-donating movement of the Trinity, existing solely as the manifestation—the reflection—of the splendor of a God whose own being is manifestation, recognition, and delight.

For Augustine, this understanding of God bears especially plentiful fruit when he (as famously he does) employs metaphors such as memory, understanding, and will, or mind, love, and knowledge, in order to understand the way in which the three persons of the Trinity are each wholly God and yet distinct within the single act of God's being. When, for instance, the mind knows and loves itself, each moment of that single act is in itself what it is, and yet each entirely indwells and reveals and is the life of each of the other two.

> But when the mind knows itself in these three, and loves itself, there remains a trinity: mind, love, knowledge; nor are they confused with one another by any sort of intermingling, even though each is single in itself and entire in the totality, either each one in the other two or the other two in each, but in any case *all in all*.[53]

[52] See idem, *Adversus Macedonianos: De Spiritu Sancto* (GNO 3.1, 109); *Contra Eunomium* 1 (GNO 1.217–18).

[53] *Trin.* 9.5.8: "At in illis tribus cum se novit mens et amat se, manet trinitas, mens, amor, notitia; et nulla commixtione confunditur quamvis et singula sint in se ipsis et invicem tota in totis, sive singula in binis sive bina in singulis, itaque omnia in omnibus."

Which is to say, with a somewhat infuriating precision, that:

> They are, moreover, within one another, for the loving mind is within
> love, and love is within the knowledge of the lover, and knowledge is
> within the knowing mind. Thus each is in the other two, because the
> mind that knows and loves itself is within its own love and knowledge,
> and the love of the mind that loves and knows itself is within the mind
> and its knowledge, and the knowledge of the mind that knows and
> loves itself is in the mind and its love, because it loves itself as know-
> ing and knows itself loving. And thus also each pair of these is within
> the third of them, for the mind that knows and loves itself is within
> love always along with its knowledge, and within knowledge always
> along with its love, and love and knowledge are simultaneously pres-
> ent within the mind that loves and knows itself.[54]

And these images acquire richer hues as Augustine attempts to form
remote analogies by which to think of the trinitarian processions from the
life of the mind. When the mind knows and approves itself, he says, this
knowledge is its "word," because it is a knowledge exactly adequate to and
identical with what it knows (*ut ei sit par omnino et aequale atque identidem*) and thus constitutes a perfect and equal likeness, for the begotten is
equal to the begetter (*et est gignenti aequale quod genitum est*).[55] And when
the mind knows and loves itself, the object of that love and knowledge—
which, like every object known or loved, "co-generates" that knowledge or
love[56]—is one with the source from which that knowledge or love flows:
"And this is a certain image of the Trinity, the mind itself and its knowl-

---

[54]Ibid.: "In alternis autem ita sunt quia et mens amans in amore est et amor in amantis notitia at notitia in mente noscente. Singula in binis ita sunt quia mens quae se novit et
amat in amore et notitia sua est, et amor amantis mentis seseque scientis in mente notiti-
aque eius est, et notitia mentis se scientis et amantis in mente atque in amore eius est quia
scientem se amat et amantem se novit. Ac per hoc et bina in singulis quia mens quae se novit
et amat cum sua notitia est in amore et cum suo amore in notitia, amorque ipse et notitia
simul sunt in mente quae se amat et novit."

[55]Ibid., 9.11.16.

[56]Ibid., 9.12.18: ". . . omnis res quamcumque cognoscimus congenerat in nobis notitiam
sui; ab utroque enim notitia paritur, a cognoscente et cognito."

edge, which is its offspring and its word concerning itself, and love then
being the third, and these three are one and are one substance."[57] Similarly, we say that memory, understanding, and will—while distinct and
complete in themselves—must still be called one mind, one life, and one
being. Each contains the other two entirely: I remember my memory,
understanding, and will; I understand that I remember, understand, and
will; I will that I remember, understand, and will; and so on; and I understand all three of these in their totality together; and what I do not understand, I do not will or remember; and what I do not remember, I do not
understand or will; and what I do not will I cannot remember or understand.[58] This is, of course, exquisitely correct (if exasperatingly repetitive).
And yet—it seems worth noting—Augustine's analogies, however sche-
matically exact they may be, never cease to function as metaphors; these
elements of the inner self as such do not yet, for him, constitute the true
image of God within us. In that sense, in fact, Augustine's position is actually more cautious than Gregory's (conceptually vaguer) suggestion that,
because God is Mind and Word, so we—in imitation of him—possess
words and understanding, and that, because God is love and beholds and
hearkens to and searches out all things, so we love and see and hear and
seek to understand.[59] That said, Gregory no more than Augustine means
to suggest that the divine image in us can be reduced to some particular
set of attributes, or even to the structure of consciousness as a whole.

I should also note that Augustine's profound sense of the simplicity of
the one "diversified" act of God's being is in no way weakened by his insistence that names like "Wisdom" are accorded to the Son only through
appropriation—that, for instance, the Son is called Wisdom because he
always reveals the Father to us. For it would be absurd to imagine that the
Father is wise only through the Son, in the sense of the Son being "that
part" of God, apart from which the Father would be devoid of Wisdom;
for "if the Father who begot Wisdom is thereby made wise, and if to him

[57]Ibid.: "Et est quaedam imago trinitatis, ipsa mens et notitia eius, et amor tertius, et
haec tria unam atque una substantia."
[58]Ibid., 10.10.13–12.19.
[59]Gregory of Nyssa, *De Hominis Opificio* 16 (PG 44.181).

it is not the same thing to be and to be wise, then the Son is one of his qualities, not his offspring, and then he will no longer be absolute in his simplicity."[60] And for Augustine it is not merely the simplicity of the divine nature, but the paternal *monarchia* that is at stake:

> if . . . it is the Son who makes the Father wise [and] if in God it is the same thing both to be and to be wise, and in him essence is Wisdom, then it would not be the Son who has his essence from the Father, which is the true state of things, but rather the Father who has his essence from the Son, which is both supremely absurd and supremely false.[61]

Gregory, admittedly, does at one point appear to argue the opposite—that the Father can never be conceived of without his Son, for were he alone he would have no light, truth, wisdom, life, holiness, or power[62]—but, read in context, this claim has nothing to do with the sort of crudely mechanical concept of the Trinity that Augustine is attacking; indeed, it is precisely such a concept that Gregory is rejecting. More importantly, Augustine is not in any way denying that there is a distinct paternal or filial or spiritual modality or idiom; Augustine is not a tritheist, who believes God to be a confederation of three individual consciousnesses, any more than Gregory imagines God to be a composite of separable functions. Both, however, find themselves on this point running up against the limits of language with particular force.[63]

In any event, for both theologians the hiddenness of God the Father—unlike the inviolable singularity of the One—is always already also a fully commensurate disclosure of the Father in the Son and Spirit. God the infi-

---

[60] *Trin.* 7.1.2: ". . . si et pater qui genuit sapientiam ex ea fit sapiens neque hoc est illi esse quod sapere, qualitas eius est filius, non proles eius, et non ibi erit iam summa simplicitas."

[61] Ibid., 15.7.12: "si . . . filius patren sapientem facit. . . . Et si hoc est deo esse quod sapere et ea illi essentia est quae sapientia, non filius a patre, quod verum est, sed a filio potius habet pater essentiam, quod absurdissimum atque falsissimum est."

[62] Gregory of Nyssa, *Contra Eunomium* 3.1 (GNO 2.32).

[63] One should perhaps, however, note the irony that, if either of these positions can be said to be more reminiscent of the Palamite position (if only obliquely), it is Augustine's.

nitely hidden is also God the infinitely manifest. Creation, moreover, belongs entirely to this mystery: not as the immeasurably remote consequence of a departure from the One, a final negation of an original negation, but as a peaceful emergence into the light of God of that which in itself is nothing, and a finite expression of and moment within God's eternal act of love and knowledge.[64] And for both Gregory and Augustine, the relationship of creatures to God—inasmuch as neither thinks in terms of some secret ground of identity along a continuum of substances, or thinks of God as some ineffably remote substance at the other end of that continuum—lies in the immediate and simple relation of the image to that which it reflects. Nor, then, are creatures images simply in the sense that they constitute mere signs of the power of God to cause finite effects. If they were, no created image would be more a likeness of God than a dissemblance, no more a participation than an alienation; creatures then would be mere univocal instances of a single creative event, and no "image" would constitute a nearer or more appropriate analogy of God's nature than another. The image of God in creation—and in rational natures in particular—must be an actual communication of the light of God's own inward life, his own eternal Image of himself within the trinitarian mystery. It is, so to speak, a created reprise of the movement of God's being as God, coming to pass within beings who have no existence apart from their capacity to reflect his presence.

It is possible, then, to affirm both that the Father infinitely exceeds all finite knowledge and that, in mirroring Christ within ourselves we are somehow being conformed to the Father's coequal manifestation of himself to himself: the very "splendor of his glory," his "form" and "impress," in seeing whom we truly see the Father. We can become images of God because God is always already, in himself, Image.[65] When either Gregory or Augustine speaks of divinization—which neither tends to do as frequently as other of the fathers—it is typically understood as a greater and

---

[64]See Gregory of Nyssa, *De Perfectione* (GNO 8.1.188–89). No theologian rang more magnificent changes on this theme, of course, than Maximus the Confessor, but that is a topic for another time.
[65]Ibid.

more perfect fulfillment of the divine image within us. For, in the infinite intelligibility of God's life, in that eternal act whereby God knows and loves himself, we *are* as known and loved by God; and so we become truly what we are the more perfectly we show forth God's beauty in ourselves— the more purely the soul reflects God's knowledge of himself, by coming to know even as it is known. As Augustine says, our enlightenment is participation in the Word who, "being made a partaker in our mortality, made us partakers in his divinity";[66] and the image of God in us will achieve true likeness to God only as it achieves the vision of God: we shall be like God only when, as scripture promises, we shall see him face to face, and shall look with face unveiled at the glory of the Lord "in a mirror," precisely by being transformed into that same image from glory to glory, and becoming like him, and thus seeing him as he is.[67] Gregory, of course, develops this theme of our transformation "from glory to glory" as no other theologian ever did: as we venture into God, we find the divine nature to be inexhaustible,[68] but so long as the soul follows after the Logos it is continuously transformed, throughout eternity, into an ever more radiant vessel of divine glory,[69] while never ceasing joyously to yearn for yet more of God's beauty[70] (and so on). By comparison, Augustine's imagery seems rather homely: Christ is for us both the way to God and also the eternal abode within the divine, and so "by walking in him we draw near to him."[71]

What both theologians have in common, however, is their obvious certainty that this awakening within us of the image—and thus the knowledge—of God is a fully trinitarian event, in two senses: it is both a real entry into the life of the Trinity, by the grace of the Spirit, and also a refashioning of the soul into an ever more faithful likeness of the trinitar-

---

[66] *Trin.* 4.2.4: ". . . factus particeps mortalitatis nostrae fecit partcipes divinitatis suae."
[67] Ibid., 14.17.23.
[68] Gregory of Nyssa, *In Canticum Canticorum* 11 (GNO 6.321).
[69] Ibid., 6.173–9; 8.246, 253; idem, *De Virginitate* (GNO 8.1.280–81); *De Perfectione* (GNO 8.1.212–14); *Contra Eunomium* 1 (GNO 1.112, 285–87); *De Mortuis oratio* (GNO 9.34–39); *In Inscriptiones Psalmorum* 1.5 (GNO 5.39–40); *De Vita Moysis* 2 (GNO 7.1.41–42, 114–18); etc.
[70] Idem, *De Virginitate* (GNO 10.289).
[71] *Trin.* 7.3.4–6.

ian *taxis*. Insofar, says Augustine, as we know God, we are made like him,
however remotely; and when we know God, and properly love this knowledge, we are made better than we were, and this knowledge becomes a
word for us, and a kind of likeness to God within us.[72] And it is only thus
that the coinherence within us of memory, understanding, and will is
raised to the dignity of the divine likeness; the mind is the image of God
not simply when it remembers and understands and loves itself, but only
when it is able to remember and understand and love him by whom it was
made; and in this way, says Augustine, the mind participates in the
supreme light.[73] And it is the Spirit who makes the Son visible in and to
us, and who through the Son reveals the Father. As Gregory writes, "there
is no means whereby to look upon the Father's *hypostasis* save by gazing
at it through its stamp [χαρακτήρ], and the stamp of the Father's *hypostasis* is the Only Begotten, to whom, again, none can approach whose mind
has not been illuminated by the Holy Spirit."[74] As Augustine says, we are
images of the Word who became flesh, created through him, and as we
become ever more resplendent likenesses of him, he reveals to us who the
Father is; he is light, born of a Father who is light, and in becoming a man
he established that perfect "exemplum" that refashions us after the divine
image; and the Spirit, as the supreme charity conjoining Father and Son,
is that love that subjoins us to the Son and Father.[75] And Gregory speaks
in nearly identical terms: when, he says, Christ prays that his followers
might be one even as he and his Father are one and coinhere in one
another, and says that he has given his followers the same glory his Father
has given him, he is speaking of the gift of the Holy Spirit; indeed, that
glory *is* the Spirit, the glory that the Son had with the Father before the
world was made,[76] the "bond of peace" or "bond of unity" (so like the

[72]Ibid., 9.11.16.
[73]Ibid., 14.12.15: "Haec igitur trinitas mentis non propterea dei est imago quia sui mem-
init mens et intelligit ac diligit se, sed quia potest etiam meminisse et intellegere et amare a
quo facta est."
[74]Gregory of Nyssa, *Ad Eustathium: De Sancta Trinitate* (GNO 3.1.13).
[75]*Trin.* 7.3.4–6.
[76]Gregory of Nyssa, *Tunc et Ipse Filius* 21–22; *In Canticum Canticorum* 15 (GNO
6.466–68).

Augustinian *vinculum pacis* or *vinculum caritatis*) by which Father and Son dwell in one another, and by which we dwell in God when the Son breathes the Spirit forth upon us.[77] And, for Gregory, this process of sanctification is one in which a kind of "trinitarian" structure intrinsic to human existence becomes an ever purer mirror of the Trinity. The Spirit meets us, successively, in our practice, word (λόγος) and thought (ἐνθύμιον), the last of these being the principle (ἀρχικώτερον) of all three; for mind (διάνοια) is the original source (ἀρχή) that becomes manifest in speech, while practice comes third and puts mind and word into action. Thus the Spirit transforms us, until "there is a harmony of the hidden man with the manifest";[78] and thus, one might say, the Spirit conducts the trinitarian glory upward into our thought, making our own internal life an ever fuller reflection of God's own "circle of glory."

Here, however, I shall draw to a close. As I announced at the beginning of this essay, my ambition has been only to make a tentative initial move in the direction of investigations that require more searching attention than I can grant them here. I can, though, offer a summary of the themes upon which such investigations, it seems to me, might proceed. First, that Christian trinitarianism as developed in the fourth century did most definitely involve, however implicitly, a new kind of metaphysics, one that was—perhaps for the first time in western thought—fully "ontological" in its structure. Second, that with this revision of prevailing models of reality came also a new understanding of the nature of divine transcendence, one that finally liberated the thought of God (and of his hiddenness) from the metaphysics of mere ontic supremacy. Third, that with the idea of God's life as truly trinitarian—in which Logos and Spirit are not secondary or lesser moments within a divine economy, but the actual being of God as God—came a new, more mysterious, but far richer understanding of the relation between God in himself and the image of God reflected in created being. Fourth, that this relation, so understood, at once promises us a far more intimate knowledge of God than previ-

---

[77]Idem, *Tunc et Ipse Filius,* 22; *In Canticum Canticorum* 15 (GNO 6.466–67).
[78]Idem., *De Perfectione* (GNO 8.1.210–12): "συμφωνίαν εἶναι τοῦ κρυπτοῦ ἀνθρώπου πρὸς τὸν φαινόμενον." Cf. idem, *Adversus Macedonianos* (GNO 3.1.98–99).

ously conceivable and also apprises us of a depth of mystery within God far greater than previously imaginable. And, fifth, that our union with God comes not through the reduction of the soul to a featureless identity more real than any image, or an asymptotic approach to such an identity, but as an ever greater fulness of the trinitarian image within us, and in the ever more expressive beauty, and splendor, and holiness by which the infinity of God—that pure, incomprehensible depth of limitless intelligibility—is reflected in the mirrors of creation and in the awakening splendor of the sanctified soul. And the reason that these investigations seem to me particularly germane to the discussions that have prompted this essay is that, taken together, these principles appear to indicate the ground of a deep and astonishingly rich unity between our traditions, a unity too easily forgotten or obscured when we devote ourselves to interpreting the past in the light of our later separation, and to inventing ever more abstract principles by which not only to explain the real differences that do exist between us, but also to justify to ourselves divisions that are really, in essence, little more than historical accidents.

Augustine the Metaphysician

DAVID BRADSHAW

My goal in this paper is to situate the thought of Augustine in relation to the tradition of classical metaphysics, particularly the thought of Plato, Aristotle, and Plotinus. In many ways this is a familiar project, for scholars have long pursued the many hints left by Augustine himself in relating his thought to these sources. However, my particular emphasis will be on the differences between the way Augustine responded to the legacy of Greek philosophy and the way the Greek fathers met the same challenge.[1] I believe that many of the theological differences between Augustine and the Greek fathers can be traced to the different ways in which they responded to this common heritage. Although they both made extensive use of classical metaphysics, they did so in different ways, which sometimes are complementary and sometimes are in conflict. Recognizing precisely where the two resulting bodies of thought mesh and where they do not is a difficult task, but surely the right way to begin is by seeing them both in relation to their common sources.

First we must have clearly in view some basic points in the natural theologies of Plato and Aristotle. Although Aristotle came second chronologically, his thought is more readily grasped than the rather fragmentary suggestions of Plato, so I shall take it first. The Prime Mover described in *Metaphysics* Lambda is a being whose οὐσία (essence) is actuality or ἐνεργεία (activity).[2] This is true in three distinct but related

---

[1] In referring to the Greek fathers throughout this paper, I shall have in mind primarily the Cappadocian fathers, Dionysius the Areopagite, Maximus the Confessor, John Damascene, and Gregory Palamas, although similar ideas can also be found in many less well-known authors.

[2] Aristotle, *Metaphysics* 12.6 1071b20.

senses.[3] First, since the Prime Mover is posited to explain motion it cannot itself be subject to motion, and thus it is pure actuality in the sense of having no potentiality to change or to be acted upon. Second, because its activity of causing motion must be continuous and eternal, it can have no unrealized capacities to act; everything it can do it already does and has done from all eternity, all at once and as a whole. Finally, the Prime Mover is self-thinking thought, a being whose "thought is a thinking of thinking."[4] This means that it is ἐνεργεία in the sense of activity as well as that of actuality, for its substance is nothing other than the self-subsistent activity of thought.

The third point is the most difficult and controversial. It is most plausibly understood as meaning that the Prime Mover's thinking embraces all possible intelligible content; after all, if it did not there would be a kind of thinking in which the Prime Mover could engage but does not, and it would in that respect fail to be fully actual. In saying that the Prime Mover "thinks itself," what Aristotle means is that, precisely because its act of thinking is fully actual, this act is identical to its object, for there is nothing other than the object—no unrealized potency—constituting the act as what it is. (The Prime Mover is in this respect sharply different from human intellects, which are distinct from both their act of thinking and their object of thought because they include a vast range of unrealized potencies.) Given the identity of the Prime Mover's thought with its object, a remarkable result follows: the Prime Mover not only *thinks* all possible intelligible content, it *is* all possible intelligible content, existing all at once as a single eternal and fully actual substance. Aristotle does not draw this conclusion explicitly, but later commentators, beginning with Alexander of Aphrodisias, did so, and it became a fundamental ingredient in the synthesis of Plato and Aristotle executed by the Neoplatonists.

This conclusion points to a further important role of the Prime Mover. For Aristotle the intelligible content of something is the cause of its being.

---

[3]For what follows see in more detail my "A New Look at the Prime Mover," *Journal of the History of Philosophy* 39 (2001): 1–22, incorporated as chapter 2 of *Aristotle East and West: Metaphysics and the Division of Christendom* (Cambridge: Cambridge University Press, 2004).
[4]Aristotle, *Metaphysics* 12.9 1074b34.

This is because the question of why something exists is, as he understands it, the question of why a given parcel of matter constitutes the item which it does, and the answer to that question is its form.[5] It would seem to follow that since the Prime Mover is the totality of all possible intelligible content, existing at the highest level of actuality, it is the cause of the *being* of all things—not as their creator, but as their formal cause. Although Aristotle says little on this point directly, that his thought leads in this direction was again recognized by Alexander, as well as by the Middle Platonist Alcinous, who began the process of incorporating Aristotle's theology within Platonism.[6] This implication was given particular emphasis by Plotinus, who took the Prime Mover as the model for the second hypostasis of his own system, Intellect. Plotinus, however, was fully comfortable (as Aristotle was not) with the Platonic distinction among degrees of reality. He typically says not that Intellect is the cause of the being of sensible objects but that it *is* being, τὸ ὄν. Its objects of thought—with which it is identical in a relationship of unity in multiplicity—he refers to not only as τὰ νοητά, the objects of intellect, but also as τὰ ὄντα, the things that are.[7]

In Aristotle, then, particularly as he was interpreted in late antiquity, we find a picture of God as fully actual and eternal intellect, one who sim-

---

[5]Aristotle, *Metaphysics* 7.17; cf. Charles Kahn, "Why Existence Does Not Emerge as a Distinct Concept in Ancient Greek Philosophy," *Philosophies of Existence: Ancient and Medieval*, ed. Parviz Morewedge (New York: Fordham University Press, 1982), 7–17.

[6]See *Aristotle East and West*, 66–72.

[7]The question of how the Prime Mover (or Intellect) can be simple, although its objects of thought are many, is another bit of unfinished business that Aristotle left for Plotinus. Aristotle remarks that the Prime Mover is "without parts and indivisible" (1073a7) and later he adds that its object of thought is incomposite (1075a5–10). Yet, as we have seen, its thinking embraces all possible intelligible content. Aristotle's solution would seem to be that its object of thought is actually one but potentially many; that is, it is one as thought by the Prime Mover, but many in that it can be resolved into a multiplicity of separate truths. See Jonathan Lear, *Aristotle: The Desire to Understand* (Cambridge: Cambridge University Press, 1988), 303–6. Plotinus adopts a similar approach in describing the relationship between Intellect (νοῦς) and its objects of thought (τὰ νοητά). He offers a number of analogies, such as that Intellect knows the intelligibles in the way that one who has mastered a science understands it as an integral whole, although it can be analyzed into a multiplicity of theorems, or that Intellect is to the intelligibles as a seed to the multiplicity of its powers (*Enneads* 5.9.6, 8). This is the relationship that I refer to as "unity in multiplicity."

ply in virtue of his activity of thought constitutes the being of the sensible world. It is not hard to recognize in this picture the source of what later came to be called cataphatic theology. If God is the intelligible structure of sensible objects, he is not only their being but also their unity, life, wisdom, beauty, and other perfections. This is a step that Aristotle did not take, but it is a reasonable extrapolation from his thought, one that again can be found in Plotinus. For Plotinus the perfections of sensible objects are simply τὰ ὄντα, the things that are. Christian thinkers would later ring many variations upon this theme. In the Cappadocians the perfections of creatures are the divine energies or the "things around God"; in Dionysius the Areopagite, the divine processions; in Augustine and Aquinas, the divine ideas; in Maximus the Confessor, they are the divine λόγοι; in Gregory Palamas, they are again the divine energies. However important the differences among these formulations, they are all recognizably ways of describing how God is present within creation as its ontological structure.

Let us turn now to Plato. If Aristotle is the father of cataphatic theology, Plato is the father of apophatic theology. Precisely how he came to be understood in this way is a complicated story, which has been well told by others.[8] At the risk of oversimplification, I shall focus on just a few key texts. The first is the Myth of the Sun in the *Republic*. There we learn that the Good is that which gives being to the Forms, although it is "beyond being in dignity and power."[9] Later Platonists read this statement in light of the close association between being and intelligibility that had been integral to Greek philosophy at least since Parmenides. They inferred that the Good must be beyond intellect (νοῦς) as well, in that it is not intelligible or an object of thought (νοητόν). Obviously this does not mean that it cannot be spoken of or thought about at all. It means that the Good is not subject to νόησις, the specific kind of thinking that "divides reality at the joints" by conforming itself to, and thereby becoming isomorphic

[8]For example, John Dillon, *The Transcendence of God in Philo* (Berkeley: Center for Hermeneutical Studies, 1975); Raoul Mortley, *From Word to Silence*, 2 vols. (Bonn: Hanstein, 1986); Deirdre Carabine, *The Unknown God: Negative Theology in the Platonic Tradition, Plato to Eriugena* (Grand Rapids: William B. Eerdmans Publishing Co., 1995).
[9]Plato, *Republic* 509b.

with, the intelligible structure of the object known. Since the Good is the source of all form, it possesses no form, and therefore cannot be an object of νόησις.

Later readers also identified the Good, so understood, with another even more enigmatic Platonic entity, the One. Actually there are two Ones that are relevant here. The first is the One of the First Hypothesis of the *Parmenides*. In this section of the dialogue Parmenides, applying the strictest possible interpretation to the notion of unity, concludes that the One has no limits or shape, is neither at rest nor in motion, is neither like nor unlike anything else or even itself, and finally that it does not partake of being, has no name, and is not an object of knowledge, perception, or opinion.[10] Although the *Parmenides* makes no reference to the Good, it did not escape later readers that such a purely negative description would be highly appropriate to that which is "beyond being." The other One is that of Plato's unwritten doctrines. Aristotle tells us in the *Metaphysics* that Plato posited a One which, in conjunction with the Indefinite Dyad, is the source of the Forms.[11] He also remarks that some in the Academy identified this One with the Good.[12] It is quite plausible to see Plato himself as among this group, for after all the Good is also the source of the Forms inasmuch as it is the cause of their being.[13] Later interpreters, putting these various fragments together, concluded that the One of the unwritten doctrines, the One of the *Parmenides*, and the Good of the *Republic* are one and the same.

Here we have, then, a first principle sharply different from that of Aristotle: unknowable, unnamable, the source of being for other things, while itself "beyond being." Yet because it is also the Good, all things in some inchoate way seek it; indeed, they have a kind of innate awareness of it as the source of their being and the object of their deepest longing. The question facing Christian philosophers would inevitably be which of these two

[10]Plato, *Parmenides* 137c-142a.
[11]Aristotle, *Metaphysics* 1.6 987b18–24, 988a10–13.
[12]Aristotle, *Metaphysics* 14.4 1091b13–14.
[13]There are also sketchy reports of a public lecture on the Good in which Plato allegedly made this identification; see Konrad Gaiser, "Plato's Enigmatic Lecture 'On the Good,'" *Phronesis* 25 (1980): 5–37.

ways of thinking about God is most adequate to biblical revelation. Is God the ultimate Mind, who knows all that can be known in a single, simple, eternal act of knowing, and thereby constitutes being itself, as well as the other perfections of creatures? Or is he rather beyond mind and beyond being, one who can be described negatively (as in the *Parmenides*) or gestured to metaphorically (as in the *Republic*), but who cannot be apprehended intellectually because he has no intelligible form? Or is it possible that somehow *both* of these descriptions are correct, so that we ought to seek some kind of synthesis between them?

Both Augustine and the Greek fathers answered this question by seeking a synthesis. In fact, by their time such an answer already had important precedents. Philo of Alexandria thinks of God as unknowable and unnamable in his essence (οὐσία), but as knowable through the divine powers (δυνάμεις) that accompany him.[14] Philo's doctrine of the divine powers owes more to Stoic theology and the pseudo-Aristotelian *De Mundo*, however, than to the sources we have examined. A nearer precedent can be found in the Middle Platonists, particularly Numenius and Alcinous, and, of course, in Plotinus. As I have mentioned, Plotinus incorporates Aristotle's Prime Mover into his own system as Intellect, disengaging it from its role as the first cause of motion and identifying its objects of thought as the "things that are," that is, Plato's Forms. He also gives an account of how Intellect originates from the One through a process of emanation and is oriented to the One in an act of return. Plotinus refers indifferently to both Intellect and the One as God, for both are immeasurably superior to all sensible or psychic being.[15] Yet Intellect is for Plotinus a subordinate God, inasmuch as it mediates between the One and Soul, which in turn mediates the content of Intellect to the sensible world.

It seems to me that the most illuminating way of viewing the difference between Augustine and the Greek fathers is to see them as pursuing

[14]See John Dillon, *The Middle Platonists, 80 B.C. to A.D. 220,* 2d ed. (Ithaca, NY: Cornell University Press, 1996), 161–66.

[15]See John Rist, "Theos and the One in Some Texts of Plotinus," *Mediaeval Studies* 24 (1962): 169–80 (reprinted in his *Platonism and Its Christian Heritage* [London: Variorum, 1985]).

different ways of adapting—while, of course, radically modifying—the Plotinian synthesis. Since our subject here is Augustine, I will describe the approach of the Greek fathers only briefly. I have mentioned that the "things that are" of Plotinus, the diversified content of the thought of Intellect, become in the Greek fathers the "things around God," the divine processions, or the divine energies. These are seen neither as creatures nor as ways in which the divine essence is diversified and grasped by our limited human understanding. The diversity among them is real and would exist even if we did not. The simplest way to describe them is to say that they are actions that God performs. (Activity is, of course, the original meaning of "energy," ἐνέργεια.) Yet in saying this, one must not assume that they are distinct from God in precisely the same way that a creature's actions are distinct from that creature. The divine processions or energies are *actions which manifest God, and in so doing constitute his presence to that which receives the manifestation.* The source of this idea lies more in the Bible than in philosophy, and particularly in the two intertwining themes of the divine glory and the divine "working" or "operation" (as ἐνέργεια in the Bible has generally been translated).[16] However, in articulating it the Greek fathers drew freely on existing philosophical vocabulary, including the resonances that ἐνεργεία had received from its use in the Plotinian theory of emanation, and later the notion of a procession (πρόοδος) as it appears in Proclus.[17]

That is the cataphatic side of their thought. They were just as emphatic in insisting that, much like the One of Plotinus, God possesses no form and is beyond any conceptual determination. Already in Clement of Alexandria, since God is infinite he is "without form or name," the names we give him being based on his powers.[18] The Cappadocians adopt this

---

[16]See my "The Divine Energies in the New Testament," *SVTQ* 50 (2006): 189–223, and "The Divine Glory and the Divine Energies," *Faith and Philosophy* 23 (2006): 279–98.

[17]The notion of the "things around God" is not philosophical but can be found in the Hermetica; see *Aristotle East and West*, 132, 166–67, as well as 182 (on πρόοδος) and 74–96 (on ἐνέργεια and emanation). I have summarized the philosophical and semantic evolution of ἐνέργεια in "The Concept of the Divine Energies," *Philosophy and Theology* 18 (2006): 93–120.

[18]Clement, *Stromata* 5.12 (PG 9.121B).

view but translate it into their own idiom, distinguishing the unnamable and unknowable divine οὐσία from the "things around God" or the divine energies. The divine οὐσία here is not simply essence or definition (although it includes that), but *God as he is known to himself*, as distinct from how he is manifested. It is important not to think of this division as a fixed and impassable boundary. On the contrary, God invites us to know him ever more deeply, and for the Greek fathers (particularly Gregory of Nyssa and Maximus) the afterlife is a kind of "perpetual progress" into God. The point of the distinction is that precisely as we grow in such knowledge, we grow in the awareness of how much more there is in God that we do not know, as well as in the desire to know him ever more fully.[19] The distinction between the divine essence and energies is thus not so much a fixed boundary as a kind of receding horizon, one that remains ever before us no matter how far we may progress.

All of this means that the Greek fathers view *both* the Plotinian description of the One *and* the Plotinian description of Intellect as suitable to God, but in different respects. The first applies to God as he is known only to himself, the second to God as he freely manifests himself and is present in his manifestation. Obviously, since these are different ways of describing the one God, they are not distinct hypostases like Intellect and the One. Trinitarian doctrine bears upon the essence/energies distinction only indirectly, in that if there is to be a real plurality of divine energies apart from the act of creation it can come about only through the mutual self-giving and glorification of the persons of the Trinity.[20] The triune character of God is thus present in the background, as it were, but not in the foreground, for there is no attempt to correlate either the essence or the energies with specific persons of the Trinity.

Turning now to Augustine, we find that he too adapts and reworks the Plotinian legacy, but in a different way. He provides an account of what he learned from the Platonists in book 7 of the *Confessiones*. There he

---

[19]The Cappadocians may have been influenced at this point by Philo of Alexandria, who found this theme in the life of Moses; see my "The Vision of God in Philo of Alexandria," *American Catholic Philosophical Quarterly* 72 (1998): 483–500.

[20]See *Aristotle East and West*, 214–20, 273–74.

explains that one of the turning points in his journey toward Christianity was his reading "some books of the Platonists." Remarkably, he claims to have learned from these books what is taught in the first verses of the Gospel of John: "In the beginning was the Word, and the Word was with God, and the Word was God. The same was in the beginning with God. All things were made by him; and without him was not anything made that was made."[21] What is there in the teaching of Plotinus, or any other Platonist, that would correspond to these words? Augustine does not say. Instead he tells us in the next chapter how he "entered into my own depths" and found there the unchangeable light of truth. "He who knows the truth knows that Light, and he who knows the Light knows eternity . . . O eternal truth and true love and beloved eternity! Thou art my God, I sigh to thee by day and by night."[22] Yet even in discovering this light, he realized that he is far from it because of his own unlikeness to it. Finally, in a climactic moment he overcomes this looming sense of despair:

> And I said "Is truth then nothing at all, since it is not extended either through finite spaces or infinite?" And thou didst cry to me from afar: "I am who am." And I heard Thee, as one hears in the heart; and there was from that moment no ground of doubt in me: I would more easily have doubted my own life than have doubted that truth is.[23]

It would seem that Augustine's existential despair at his remoteness from the light of truth, and his doubts regarding God's existence, were tightly linked. Both are resolved as he comes to realize that truth exists and is real, despite the fact that it is not an extended object. It is at this point that he realizes that existence does not require being extended in time or space. This in turn frees him to believe the Gospel of John, for the Word spoken of there, which both "was with God, and was God," is none other than the light of truth. Augustine goes on in the next chapter to add that God as

---

[21] *Conf.* 7.9.
[22] *Conf.* 7.10. Translations are from Augustine, *Confessions*, trans. F.J. Sheed (Indianapolis: Hackett, 1992).
[23] Ibid.

Truth is not only real, he is more real than other things: "Then I thought upon those other things that are less than you, and I saw that they neither absolutely are nor yet totally are not: they are, in as much as they are from you: they are not, in as much as they are not what you are. For that truly is, which abides unchangeably."[24]

One can decode and elaborate the terse account in the *Confessiones* of Augustine's encounter with Platonism by drawing upon the works he wrote shortly after his conversion. One of the first of these, the *Soliloquiorum*, identifies God as "the Intelligible Light, in, by, and through whom all intelligible things are illumined."[25] Like the Good of the *Republic*, God is "the sun of the intellectual realm."[26] Unlike the Good, however—at least in its Neoplatonic interpretation—God "belongs to the realm of intelligible things."[27] Reason, who is Augustine's interlocutor in this dialogue, promises "to let you see God with your mind as the sun is seen with the eye."[28] The only prerequisite is that the soul must be purged, through faith, hope, and charity, from its desire for mortal things. As in the *Confessiones*, Augustine closely links being, truth, and immutability. He argues that, since truth remains even when mortal things perish, it does not exist in mortal things but only in those which are immortal. From this he infers that "only immortal things are true . . . Therefore nothing which is not immortal can be said truly to be."[29]

Another early work, *De moribus ecclesiase catholicae et de moribus Manichaeorum* (*On the Catholic and Manichean Ways of Life*), goes further in explaining the close relationship between being and unity. Augustine writes, "[t]hat must be said to be in the highest sense of the word which remains always the same, is identical with itself throughout and cannot be corrupted or altered in any part, and which is not subject to

[24]*Conf.* 7.11.
[25]*Sol.* 1.1.3, *Augustine: Earlier Writings,* trans. John H.S. Burleigh (Philadelphia: Westminster Press, 1953).
[26]Ibid., 1.9.16.
[27]Ibid., 1.8.15.
[28]Ibid., 1.6.12.
[29]Ibid., 1.15.28.

time, nor different now from what it used to be."[30] Although the emphasis here is certainly on temporal homogeneity, the phrase "identical with itself throughout" indicates that Augustine also has in mind homogeneity of qualities or intelligible structure. Presumably, in an incorporeal being such as God, this would mean the absence of distinctions such as those of essence and accident or genus and differentia. A little later he goes so far as to identify being and unity. He also adds, on this basis, that things attain being insofar as they attain order:

> Those things which tend toward being, tend toward order, and in attaining order, they attain being, so far as it can be attained by creatures. Order reduces whatever it orders to a certain harmony. To be, however, is nothing but to be one. And so, to the extent that a thing acquires unity, to that extent it has being.[31]

For creatures, then, being and unity are a matter of degree, and both have to be achieved through the attainment of order.

Finally, *De vera religione* (*On True Religion*) follows up on the further association of God, as perfect being and unity, with truth. God is "the uncreated and most perfect form . . . the one truth . . . the first and highest essence."[32] As the work progresses, we find more specifically that God as Truth is the second person of the Trinity, and that the second person is not only Truth, but also Unity (or One, *unum*).[33] More precisely, the Father is Unity and the Son, as his perfect likeness, is also Unity:

> We can understand that there is something so resembling the sole Unity and principle of all unity that it coincides with it and is identical with it. This is Truth, the Word that was in the beginning, the divine

---

[30]*De mor. ecc.* 2.1.1. Translation from *The Catholic and Manichaean Ways of Life*, trans. D. Gallagher and I. Gallagher (Washington, DC: Catholic University of America Press, 1966).

[31]Ibid., 2.6.8.

[32]*De vera rel.* 11.22, trans. Burleigh, op. cit.

[33]Ibid., 31.58.

Word that was with God . . . [T]his is itself the complete likeness of
Unity, and is therefore Truth . . . Since things are true in so far as they
have being, and have being in so far as they resemble the source of all
unity, that is the form of all things that have being, which is the
supreme likeness of the principle. It is also perfect Truth because it is
without any unlikeness.[34]

We find here the explanation for why perfect being coincides with eternity
and immutability. Truth and being depend on unity. Since extension,
whether spatial or temporal, detracts from unity—as a fortiori does
change—nothing that is extended in these ways can have perfect being.
Thus to be is ultimately to be one, without extension or division of any
kind.[35]

Readers of Plotinus will recognize here a truncated form of an argument given in *Enneads* 6.9. Plotinus observes that anything which "is" is
one, and that degrees of being vary according to degrees of unity.[36] He differs from Augustine, however, in his answer to the question of whether
Being (τὸ ὄν) and the One are the same. He argues that they are not, for
anything that "is" is composite. Forms are composite insofar as they can
be defined, and even Intellect is both that which thinks and that which is

[34]Ibid., 36.66. I have slightly altered the translation by capitalizing "truth" and "unity"
and by removing a comma after "that is." For the Latin, see CCL 32 (Turnholt: Brepols,
1962), 231.

[35]See also ibid., 30.55: "Who can find absolute equality or similarity in bodily objects?
Who would venture to say, after due consideration, that any body truly and simply is one?
All are changed by passing from form to form or from place to place, and consist of parts
each occupying its own place and extended in space." Note also *Conf.* 3.7, where Augustine
describes how he did not know "that God is a spirit, having no parts extended in length or
breadth, to whose being bulk does not belong: for bulk is less in its part than in its whole
. . . and so could not be wholly itself in every place, as spirit is." Thus he did not know "that
other reality which truly is," spirit or God. The identification of being with self-identity is
the essential link needed to understand its further identification with immutability, a recur-
rent theme in Augustine which has often been noticed by commentators; see, e.g., Etienne
Gilson, *The Christian Philosophy of Saint Augustine* (London: Gollancz, 1961), 21–22; James
F. Anderson, *St. Augustine and Being: A Metaphysical Essay* (The Hague: Martinus Nijhoff,
1965), 12–18.

[36]Plotinus, *Enneads* 6.9.1.

thought.[37] He concludes that the One is formless (ἀνείδεον)[38] and that our awareness of it is not by knowledge or thought (νόησις), but by "a presence superior to knowledge."[39] Elsewhere he adds that even the name "One" ought not to be taken to indicate something like a Form of Unity, but is only a way of denying multiplicity, and must itself ultimately be negated.[40] He also explicitly distinguishes the "one" which is predicated of the Forms, inasmuch as each Form is a unity, from the One which is "beyond being."[41]

It is plain that Augustine has taken with Plotinus the first step, that of recognizing the dependence of being on unity, but that when it comes to the question of whether Being and the One are the same, he gives a different answer. Why? The reason must surely lie in the particular way in which he came to believe in the Christian God. The realization that truth exists, and exists more fully than material objects, led Augustine to two simultaneous conclusions: that God is Truth, and that being is perfect wholeness or unity. Since God is perfectly and fully real, "He Who Is," he is thus not only Truth but also Unity. Apparently Augustine believed that he had been preceded in this discovery by the Platonists—Plotinus, Porphyry, or both—whom he understood as teaching that God as Truth is Intellect, and God as Unity is the One. In Christian terms these are, respectively, the Son and the Father.[42] Augustine parted ways with the Platonists primarily in rejecting the hierarchical relationship between Intellect and the One, as well as its implication that the One is "beyond Intellect" and "beyond being." For Augustine, since the Father and the Son are consubstantial, each must be in some sense Truth, Unity, and Being, although for various reasons we may appropriate these names to one or the other.

[37]Ibid., 6.9.2.
[38]Ibid., 6.9.3–4.
[39]Ibid., 6.9.4.
[40]Ibid., 5.5.6.
[41]Ibid., 6.6.5.
[42]As an aside, we may note that Augustine also extended these metaphysical correlations to the Holy Spirit. The Father is the source of measure (*mensura*) or unity (*unum*), the Son of form (*species*), the Holy Spirit of order (*ordo*), and this triad, which is to be found in all creatures, is a vestige of the Trinity. See *De beata vita* 4.34–35; *De vera rel.* 7.13, 55.113; *Trin.* 6.10.11–12.

We have here, then, a second and quite different way of appropriating Plotinian metaphysics. This time trinitarian doctrine is present directly rather than implicitly, in the straightforward correlation of the One with the Father and Intellect with the Son.[43] The greatest change from Plotinus consists not in collapsing the distinction of hypostases, but in rejecting the hierarchical ranking that allows the One and Intellect to differ in respect to being, unity, and intelligibility. It is a highly significant corollary of this that Augustine also rejects apophaticism. As he remarks in one of his sermons, "God is for the mind to understand, as body is for the mind to see."[44] It is true that he frequently states that God exceeds the capacities of human thought or speech.[45] Nonetheless, on the key question of whether God is intrinsically an object of intellect—that is, of νόησις, understood as the kind of thinking that conforms itself to the nature of the object known—his answer is consistently affirmative.[46]

I stated earlier that the philosophical differences between Augustine and the Greek fathers help to explain many of their theological differences. In the space remaining I will focus on just one example of how this is so. It is an issue that has sometimes proven to be contentious in confrontations between the two traditions, and therefore deserves careful attention: that of divine simplicity.

There are two separate arguments in Augustine for divine simplicity. The first is that God must be identical to his perfections, for otherwise he would possess them by participation and so would be inferior to that in which he participates. This argument can be found at several points in the De Trinitate.[47] The other argument, which is in the De civitate Dei, is that

---

[43]See Civ. 10.23 and 10.28. Porphyry spoke of the One as the Father and of Intellect as νοὺς πατρικός, the Intellect of the Father. Augustine faults Porphyry not for making these identifications but for failing to leave room for the Holy Spirit. Another precedent was Marius Victorinus, although Victorinus retains Plotinian apophaticism regarding the Father (or the One) and thereby flirts with subordinationism; cf. Aristotle East and West, 108–14.

[44]Serm. 117.5.

[45]See Deirdre Carabine, "Negative Theology in the Thought of Saint Augustine," Recherches de théologie ancienne et médiévale 59 (1992): 5–22, incorporated as The Unknown God, 259–77. See also the contribution by Jean-Luc Marion to the present volume.

[46]See further Aristotle East and West, 226–29.

[47]Trin. 5.10.11, 7.1.2, 15.5.7.

since God *is* absolutely and without qualification, for him to live, to understand, to be blessed, and to enjoy his other perfections is the same as to be; thus the divine nature "is the same as itself" and "is what it has."[48] Whereas the first of these arguments is at home in any broadly Platonic metaphysics, the second depends specifically on Augustine's conception of being as undivided wholeness. Only the second leads to the distinctively Augustinian conclusion that the divine essence is identical with the divine attributes as well as with the divine *esse*, and that all of these are identical with one another. Indeed the first argument (the denial of participation) is also to be found in Gregory of Nyssa.[49] Gregory is just as emphatic as Augustine in affirming that God is Goodness, Beauty, Wisdom, and the other divine perfections; yet, since he also holds that the divine names are names of the divine energies rather than the divine essence, he must be understood as asserting these identities at the level of the energies.[50] That is, they are names for God as he is manifest in his activity. What he clearly does *not* mean is that God's attributes are identical to his essence, as is held by Augustine.

Among the identities that Augustine infers from divine simplicity is that God is identical with his own will.[51] By this he must mean God's expressed and determinate will, and not merely the will as a faculty, for to take the identity as applying only to the will as a faculty would introduce a distinction in God that would compromise his unity. This is presumably why Augustine holds that whatever God wills he wills in a single eternal and immutable act, of which divine actions occurring in time are merely the consequences.[52]

The implications of identifying the divine essence with the divine will are immense. One is that it becomes very hard to see how God could will differently than he does, for in doing so one allows that God's essence could be different. The issue here is not precisely divine freedom, for free-

[48] *Civ.* 8.6, 11.10.
[49] Gregory of Nyssa, *Contra Eunomium* 1.235, 276, 285–87.
[50] See *Aristotle East and West*, 161–65.
[51] *Conf.* 7.4, 11.10, 12.15.
[52] *Conf.* 12.15, *Civ.* 12.17, *De Gen. ad lit.* 4.23–25.

dom can be defined (as it was, for example, by Plotinus) as acting fully in accord with one's own nature. The issue is rather divine free choice, *liberum arbitrium.* Could God have chosen not to create, or could he have chosen to create things differently than he did? Augustine's answer to these questions appears to be no. In book 3 of *De libero arbitrio* (*On Free Will*) he argues that for God not to have created any of the things "necessary to the perfection of the universe"—such as souls whom he foreknew would be damned—would be a kind of "envy" that is impossible for God.[53] Augustine is so confident of this reasoning that, a bit earlier, he argues that since angels *ought* to exist we can be certain that they do.[54] Admittedly, his reasoning here pertains to divine goodness rather than simplicity. Yet surely, in being so confident that God's will must issue in one determinate action, Augustine relies upon his strong sense of the identity of God's will with his essence. His reasoning is in fact quite similar to that of Plotinus, who argues that the Good by its nature must produce all that it is capable of producing.[55]

Another important consequence is that it becomes hard to see how there can be any true interaction between God and creatures. The problem is that, given the identity of God's will with his essence, to hold that God's will is affected by creatures must be to hold that his essence is so affected. So far as I am aware, Augustine does not confront this issue directly.[56] However, he comes close in repeatedly insisting that God's will

[53]*De lib. arb.* 3.9; cf. a similar statement at *De Gen. ad lit.* 4.16. For discussion of these rather surprising texts, see Robert-Henri Cousineau, "Creation and Freedom, An Augustinian Problem," *Recherches Augustiniennes* 2 (1962): 253–71; Roland J. Teske, "The Motive for Creation according to Saint Augustine," *Modern Schoolman* 65 (1988): 245–53. Note that the denial of *liberum arbitrium* in God is perfectly compatible with holding, as Augustine does, that God's will has no cause.

[54]*De lib. arb* 3.5.

[55]*Enneads* 4.8.6, 5.12.45–48. Plotinus further identifies the will (βούλησις) of the One with its essence (οὐσία), although he uses either term of the One only reluctantly (6.8.13).

[56]Aquinas (who similarly identifies the divine will and essence) does attempt to address it directly, although to my mind not satisfactorily. See *Aristotle East and West*, 247–50, 259–62; cf. W. Matthews Grant, "Aquinas, Divine Simplicity, and Divine Freedom," *Proceedings of the American Catholic Philosophical Association* 77 (2003): 129–44.

has no cause and that God cannot be affected.[57] It seems highly plausible (although it cannot be proven) that Augustine's interpretation of the biblical texts on predestination was at least partly determined by these prior philosophical commitments.

These are a few examples of how Augustine's philosophical views spill over, as it were, into his theology. Obviously any thorough comparison of Augustine and the Greek fathers would have to take account of how similar issues are treated in the Greek tradition. That is a large project on which I have attempted to make a beginning elsewhere.[58]

Ultimately, however, in assessing Augustine's particular way of appropriating classical metaphysics, we ought to focus primarily not on its theological implications but on its intrinsic philosophical value. Here I would like to end with a simple but, as it seems to me, highly significant observation. This is that even Plato ultimately moved away from the identification of being with undivided wholeness that is typical of the middle dialogues. In the *Sophist* he argues that the Forms blend or partake of one another, so that all partake of the Form of the Different, and even non-being "is" inasmuch as each of the Forms is not the others.[59] On such a view, to be is *not* simply to be one, for each of the Forms truly is, yet its being is constituted partly by its relations to the others. Thus Plato himself provides grounds for rejecting any straightforward identification of being with unity. One can only speculate how the subsequent history of philosophy might have been different if Augustine's fertile and perceptive mind had encountered the *Sophist*.

[57]See the articles by Cousineau and Teske (above, n. 53), and for divine impassibility see *Civ.* 12.17.

[58]See, besides the book and articles referred to above, my "Time and Eternity in the Greek Fathers," *The Thomist* 70 (2006): 311–66.

[59]Plato, *Sophist* 256d–e.

Postscript

It became clear during the initial presentation of papers that David Bentley Hart and I disagreed on several aspects of the topic at hand. Since the points at issue between Professor Hart and myself are of fundamental importance, I have appended this postscript to address his concerns.

First let me mention, in order to set it aside, a point where Professor Hart seems to undermine his own position as much as my own. This is his assertion that to speak of either the knowability or unknowability of the divine essence is "pious nonsense." If this were true it would make the dispute between us largely pointless, for our dispute concerns in part the interpretation of such language, and there is little point in disputing about the meaning of nonsense. I also note that Professor Hart freely speaks of the divine essence, not only when interpreting the fathers, but also in his own voice, as in his assertion that God "in his essence" is goodness itself, truth itself, and so on. Surely it would be strange if modern theologians were to be permitted to use such language, while the fathers are not. Admittedly, however, these points are merely ad hominem. As regards the substantive issue, I do not find the reason Hart adduces for rejecting such language persuasive. In speaking of the divine *essentia* or οὐσία one certainly does not posit a "reality prior to, apart from, or more original than the paternal ἀρχή"; after all, if one did, then the very assertion that the Son is ὁμοούσιος with the Father would be suspect. The best way to take these terms is as I suggested above: as referring to God *as he is known to himself*, as distinct from how he is manifested. So far as I can see, this is a meaning equally acceptable to East and West, and neutral as regards the points at issue between Hart and myself. It also carries no anti-trinitarian implications, for God may very well (and does, in the Christian view) know himself to be Trinity. I shall therefore set aside the charge of "pious nonsense" as misguided.

Turning now to the substance of the dispute, I shall first deal with our differences regarding divine intelligibility, and then turn to some broader issues.

It is clear that Professor Hart and I do not interpret Augustine's sermon 117 in the same way. Here is the passage at issue, as translated by Edmund Hill, O.P., in The Works of Saint Augustine: A Translation for the 21st Century. Augustine has been describing how the Word, not being spatially extended like sensible objects, is "not less in his parts than in his totality." He continues:

> But you are quite unable to imagine or think of such a thing. And such ignorance is more religious and devout than any presumption of knowledge. After all, we are talking about God. It says, *and the Word was God* (Jn 1.1). We are talking about God; so why be surprised if you cannot grasp it? I mean, if you can grasp it, it isn't God. Let us rather make a devout confession of ignorance, instead of a brash profession of knowledge. Certainly it is great bliss to have a little touch or taste of God with the mind; but completely to grasp him, to comprehend him, is utterly impossible.
>
> God belongs to the mind, he is to be understood; material bodies belong to the eyes, they are to be seen [*ad mentem Deus pertinet, intelligendus est; ad oculos corpus, videndum est*]. But do you imagine you can completely grasp, or comprehend, a body with your eyes? You most certainly can't. I mean, whatever you look at, you are not looking at the whole of it. When you see someone's face, you don't see their back while you see their face; and when you see their back, you don't at that moment see their face. So then you don't see things in such a way as to grasp or comprehend them whole ... [The rest of the paragraph elaborates on this point.]
>
> So then, brothers and sisters, what can we say about that Word? Look, here we are, saying about material things staring us in the face, that we cannot take them all in, grasp them totally, by a look. So what mind's eye will be able to grasp God, take all of him in? It is enough to touch his fringes, if the mind's eye is pure. But if it does touch upon him, it does so with a kind of immaterial and spiritual touch, but still does not embrace or comprehend him all; and that too, if the mind is pure.[60]

[60]*Serm.* 117.5. The Works of Saint Augustine: A Translation for the 21st Century, part 3,

Augustine's language here is deliberately paradoxical, involving at least two sharp rhetorical reversals. First, he asserts that God cannot be fully grasped or comprehended, and then he summarizes this assertion, surprisingly enough, in the formula that God *intelligendus est*. Apparently, God is for the mind alone to understand, and *precisely for that reason* is not fully intelligible or comprehensible. That is the first reversal. Given that the rest of the sentence contrasts God as *intelligendus* with sensible body as *videndum*, one might suppose at this point that Augustine intends a fundamental contrast between the mind, which can never fully comprehend its object, and the senses, which do so. However, such a conclusion would be premature, for we quickly find that the senses do not comprehend their object either. Augustine takes this as strengthening his point: neither the mind nor the senses fully comprehend their object, so how could anyone hope fully to comprehend God? Only when it is pure can the mind aspire to "touch upon him ... with a kind of immaterial and spiritual touch."

Now if Professor Hart's point is that this passage alone does not clearly distinguish Augustine's position from that of the Greek fathers, I agree. The entire passage is reminiscent of the second of Gregory Nazianzen's theological orations, which similarly hammers home the unknowability of God by stressing the deficiencies in our knowledge of sensible beings. On the other hand, the passage does not provide particularly strong evidence for a principled apophaticism either, for it places the unknowability of God more or less on a par with that of sensible objects. To be sure, it does so for rhetorical reasons: its thrust is that, given that we do not really comprehend sensible objects, how can we hope to comprehend God, who so vastly transcends them? This argument is fine as far as it goes. But it leaves untouched the more difficult question of in precisely what sense God really is intelligible, despite the failures of our own attempts to comprehend him. In particular, it says nothing about whether the angels or the blessed in heaven, who are free from the limitations of our present earthly ways of knowing, might have a far more adequate cognition of

Sermons, vol. 4, trans. Edmund Hill, O.P. (Brooklyn, NY: New City Press, 1992), 211–12 (PL 38.663–64).

God than we do here. It is on these questions, and not the relatively uncontroversial issue of whether God can be fully comprehended by creatures, that I think there is a substantive difference between Augustine and the Greek fathers.

Perhaps I ought not to have cited the sermon at all without going into these complexities.[61] However, I did not cite it as *proof* of a substantive difference, and certainly not as my "sole solid corroboration." I cited it merely to illustrate (via the striking application of *intelligendus* to God) a difference that is clear on other grounds. To repeat what is said above, I maintain that Augustine rejected apophaticism in the specific sense of the denial that God is an object of νόησις; and I take this rejection to be simply a corollary of the particular way in which he collapses the distinction between the One and Intellect of Plotinus, so that terms such as Truth, Form, and Being, which were for Plotinus applicable to Intellect but not to the One, become for Augustine straightforwardly applicable to the divine essence.[62]

Since Professor Hart wishes for further evidence, however, I will gladly provide it, as I have already done elsewhere.[63] The clearest evidence comes from Augustine's discussion of the beatific vision. Hart seems to regard the belief in an eschatological vision of the divine essence as a specifically Thomistic doctrine, or at best as a "Thomistic interpretation" of Augustine, and therefore as belonging to those "medieval syntheses" that we ought to avoid. He says this without any reference to Augustine's actual writings on

[61]Hart also has a fair point in observing that I ought to have translated the sentence I quoted from this sermon literally rather than relying on Cary's paraphrase—although, had I done so, it would have made no difference to my argument.

[62]Incidentally, it is not true that I rely preponderantly upon the *Sol.*, as even a casual reading of my essay will confirm. It is also not true that *intelligibilis* primarily means "possessing a spiritual or rational nature." The entry for this term in the *Thesaurus Linguae Latinae* indicates that its original meaning was the same as that of "intelligible" in English, and that this meaning remained current throughout late antiquity. The sense Hart cites arose in Christian Latin in the late fourth century, so that in Augustine either meaning is possible. One could quibble over particular occurrences, but I am not sure what difference it would make, particularly since Hart himself, in the same footnote, renders the term as "intelligible."

[63]See above, n. 46.

the subject. When one turns to those writings, one finds that the essential elements of the Thomistic view are already present. Augustine regards Moses (in Exodus 33) and St Paul (when he was taken up into the "third heaven," 2 Cor 12.2) as having been granted a distinctive form of the vision of God known as "intellectual" vision. Unlike corporeal theophanies, dreams, and prophetic visions, intellectual vision has as its object "that form by which God is what he is," or equivalently, "the very substance of God."[64] Such a vision is available only to one who has been taken up out of the body, as were Moses and St Paul, presumably (although Augustine is not fully explicit about this) because the senses introduce corporeal images that would obscure or constrict the vision.[65] The angels and the blessed in heaven enjoy this sort of vision permanently, although for the blessed it will be fully complete only after the resurrection of the body.[66]

In light of these texts, I do not see how it is possible to say, as does Professor Hart, that for Augustine "every kind of vision of God in himself is impossible for finite creatures." The intellectual vision is precisely a vision of "God in himself"; that is the point of distinguishing it from visions of corporeal theophanies and the like, which Augustine regards as mediated. I also do not see how it is possible to deny that there is a real difference on this issue between Augustine and the Greek fathers.[67] It is not my purpose at present to argue that one side is more right than the other, but only to insist that their difference ought not to be glossed over or ignored.

[64] De Gen. ad lit. 12.26.54–28.56, 34.67–36.69; Ep. 147.31–32. For the quoted phrases (speciem scilicet, qua deus est quidquid est, and ipsa Dei substantia) see 12.28.56 and 147.31; cf. the discussion in Dom Cuthbert Butler, Western Mysticism (New York: Harper and Row, 1966), 55–62.

[65] De Gen. ad lit. 12.27.55, Ep. 147.31; cf. Ad Simpl. 2.1.1.

[66] De Gen. ad lit. 35.68–36.69; Ep. 147.32. The point about completion after the resurrection is a difference between Augustine and Aquinas; cf. Aristotle East and West, 256.

[67] For the classic discussion of the doctrine of the Greek fathers (including their interpretation of the biblical texts cited by Hart) see Vladimir Lossky, The Vision of God (Crestwood, NY: SVS Press, 1973). I have discussed the eschatological vision in Maximus and Palamas in Aristotle East and West, 192–95, 236. Incidentally I believe that Palamas would endorse the notion of the "receding horizon" as the boundary between the divine essence and energies, for, like Gregory of Nyssa and Maximus, he envisions the state of the blessed as one of perpetual progress; see Triads 1.3.22, 2.2.11.

I also disagree with Hart regarding what Augustine means in identifying God with his own will. I am not sure what more I can do here than repeat what I stated earlier, that to interpret the identity as applying only to the will as a faculty, and not to God's express and determinate will—which I take to be Hart's view—introduces a distinction between what God *is* and what God *has* (namely, a certain express and determinate will) of the sort that Augustine explicitly denies. Since Hart himself insists on divine simplicity in the strongest terms, I am surprised that he does not see the point. Note as well that Hart insists repeatedly that God can possess no "unrealized potential." This is the familiar doctrine of God as *actus purus*. On such a view, there is again no way to distinguish other than notionally between God's will as a faculty and the expression of that will in a particular determinate set of choices, for the simple reason that to do so would require positing choices that God could have made but did not, and these would constitute an unrealized potency.[68] Surely it is no accident that Aristotle, who originated this way of thinking about God, did not ascribe to God anything like free choice. Professor Hart seems to think that the view of God as possessing no unrealized potential was commonly held among the fathers of both East and West. Perhaps it is present by implication in Augustine, but I know of no grounds for ascribing it to the Greek fathers, and Hart provides no evidence to the contrary.

That brings me to our numerous differences regarding the Greek fathers. I cannot discuss them all here, but will limit myself to the points Professor Hart makes in response to my essay. He alleges that "logically, if the divine energies are genuine *manifestations* of God, however limited, then whatever names apply to the energies also apply to the essence," so that I am wrong to "claim . . . that, for Gregory, the divine names apply only to the divine energies and not to the divine essence." If this is indeed a logical entailment it was apparently lost on Gregory, for Gregory states explicitly that the divine names indicate or signify (σημαίνειν) the divine energies and not the divine nature.[69] Perhaps by "apply" Hart has in mind something different from what Gregory means by σημαίνειν, but if so, he

---

[68]This problem is closely related to that mentioned above, n. 56.
[69]See *Aristotle East and West*, 163–64.

should explain the difference. Hart also seems to think that I present Gregory as saying that "the divine names do not *refer* to God in himself." But I did not say this. Certainly for Gregory the divine names refer to God, and he presents a carefully reasoned analysis of the semantics of θεός to explain how this is possible. I am not sure what would be added (unless emphasis?) by saying that they refer to "God in himself."

Professor Hart also presents John Damascene as arguing that the names or attributes of God "apply to the divine essence" but are not "true of God in a plural way," since they are all "identical with one another." I find these statements confusing, partly because I am unsure what to make of the notion of applying to the essence, and partly because I do not know what it means to be "true of God in a plural way." What John actually says is that names such as "good" and "just" *follow* the nature (παρέπονται τῇ φύσει). I take this to be his way of adapting the notion, familiar from the Cappadocians, that such names signify "the things concerning the divine nature" (τὰ περὶ τὴν θειάν φύσιν).[70] It is precisely the fact that these names indicate (σημαίνειν) or reveal (δηλοῦν) only the things concerning the divine nature, and not the divine nature itself, which John cites as explaining how they are compatible with divine simplicity. He most certainly does *not* say that they are identical with one another, whether "in God" or elsewhere.

Naturally, then, I am unconvinced by the bald claim that for the Greek fathers "the divine essence and divine attributes are identical." I know of no texts where they say such a thing, and quite a few where they deny it.[71] I am also puzzled by the claim that Gregory in the *Oratio catechetica* identifies the divine will and the divine goodness, and that John Damascene identifies the divine essence, Godhead, power, and will. Gregory says nothing of the sort; he merely says that the divine will "wills whatever is good," which is hardly to say that the will is the same as the *attribute* of goodness.[72] Likewise John says only that "there is one essence, one good-

[70]See ibid., 207–8.
[71]See ibid., 161–69, 180–82, 189–91, as well as other texts discussed by Lossky, *The Vision of God*.
[72]More precisely, "whatever is good, this it also wishes, and, wishing, is able to perform, and, being able, will not fail to perform"; Gregory of Nyssa, *Oratio catechetica* 1, trans. *Nicene and Post-Nicene Fathers*, series 2, 5.476.

ness, one power, one will, one energy, one authority, one and the same, I repeat, not three resembling each other."[73] Here he merely denies that each person of the Trinity has an essence, goodness, or other attributes distinct from that of the others; he says nothing about the relationships *among* the essence and attributes.

There are many other points where Professor Hart and I disagree, but to address them all here would go too far afield. In closing let me thank Professor Hart for his stimulating remarks.

---

[73]John Damascene, *De fide Orthodoxa* 1.8, trans. *Nicene and Post-Nicene Fathers*, series 2, 9.10.

De profundis: Augustine's Reading of Orthodoxy

CAROL HARRISON

"**O**rthodoxy," either in the upper or lower case, is something of a loaded term. It is for this reason that, in the subtitle of this paper, I have deliberately attempted to turn the remit of the present volume on its head and, instead of talking about "orthodox readings of Augustine," I would like to talk about "Augustine's reading of orthodoxy." It goes without saying that this will always be in reference to orthodoxy in the lower case. By investigating what Augustine thinks orthodoxy is, I would like to ask whether he is indeed orthodox in his own terms. The title of the paper is an attempt to hint, with more than a passing nod to the Psalms, that the aspect of orthodoxy I would like to pursue, both in elucidating and then evaluating Augustine's use of the term, is what I would like to call its "dark side."

Orthodoxy—right opinion or belief—is something that has more often than not emerged, and been consciously formulated and articulated, in the context of conflict; when opinions or beliefs that have threatened to undermine it have been identified, opposed and effectively despatched, with a clear definition of what is believed to be right or true. In this sense, statements of orthodoxy often take the form of rules of faith, creedal formulas, canonical rules, or other short, memorable summaries of what is held to be the true faith against heretical misinterpretation and distortion. To ask what is orthodox is, then, in some sense, to ask for a definition, for a statement, for a clear, fixed, unmovable, and unmoving articulation of what the faith of the Church is. If we asked this question of

Augustine, we would find ample material in his works to establish a firm, clear, comprehensive answer. He spent most of his life articulating and fiercely defending orthodoxy, the true faith, against all comers—Manicheans, Donatists, and Pelagians among them. He did so convinced that the true faith was to be found in the Catholic Church,[1] founded upon the twofold authority of its divinely inspired scriptures[2] and of the divine grace, which it mediates through a tradition that originated in Christ, passed on in unbroken succession through its apostles to its bishops, is formulated in its councils, creeds, and canons, and is above all present in its sacraments. The universality of the Church, its antiquity, and the fact that it enjoyed the general consent of human beings only sealed its claim to orthodoxy—to be *the* right faith.[3]

So far so good: scripture, tradition, the Church, and its sacraments. This is what we might rightly expect as an answer to how Augustine understood orthodoxy, but neither the question of what orthodoxy is, nor the answer, is quite so straightforward. I would like to suggest that if we look, not beyond, but within the seemingly monolithic, immovable, and immutable fixity of this sort of orthodoxy we will find a darker side: an unavoidable undercurrent of ambiguity, difficulty, and obscurity; of fluidity, change, and flexibility that, unless it is acknowledged and consciously appreciated, can only lead to unexplained conflict, disagreement, and potentially dangerous fractures and divisions. The image that comes to mind is of the plates that make up the earth's surface: they seem fixed, and on the basis of that reassuring fixity we describe them, allocate names to places, create maps and atlases, identify geological characteristics, and so on. Yet we are all aware that these vast plates are slowly, inexorably, moving and changing (perhaps more aware than ever, given global warming, but that is not really my point here); that at any minute they might erupt or clash to change things forever; that the earth is temporal, mutable, and can undergo dramatic transformations. More often than not, however, we choose to ignore it.

[1] *Ep.* 164.6.
[2] *Ep.* 147.4; *Civ.* 11.3.
[3] *Ep.* 186.33; *De util. cred.* 31.

With this image in mind I would like to move on to examine the undercurrents, as it were, of Augustine's reading of orthodoxy. What we called the "dark side" of orthodoxy—its inherent ambiguity, fluidity, and potential for change—is perhaps nearest the surface in the first of the unquestioned authorities to which Augustine, like all the fathers, appeals: the scriptures. Whenever Augustine wishes to confirm or establish the truth of any belief—whether it is indeed "orthodox"—his first response is to turn to the scriptures and to defend and argue his case from them. But the truth of the scriptures is far from clear or fixed; in fact they are a prime example of what it means to have divine treasure in earthen vessels: the divine Word incarnate, eternal truth expressed in temporal, mutable, corporeal form. The truth is often found well below the surface; it is more often obscured by the words in which it is expressed than revealed by them; it needs to be sought out by means of figurative interpretation, analogy, metaphor, typology, allegory; it resists the rationalistic grasp of the proud and is accessible only to the tentative search of the humble. This is indeed shifting ground. In book 12 of the *Confessiones* (*Confessions*), Augustine admits that it is extremely difficult, if not impossible (and perhaps not desirable), to attempt to ascertain the specific truth of a particular passage, or what single meaning its author intended to convey; different individuals might find a different truth or meaning in any one passage, and each of the meanings they find is acceptable so long as they do not contradict the double commandment of love of God and neighbor.[4] The potential that each passage of scripture has for meaningful and true interpretation—or improvisation—on the basic theme of the double commandment loosens up the notion of orthodoxy as something essentially fixed and unmoving and shifts the emphasis to the very much more flexible and creative idea that, like a jazz scale, according to which the players will then improvise on a particular set of notes, there are certain "rules of thumb" or "rules of faith" that the interpreter must indeed observe, but they are rules that effectively enable him or her to freely improvise on the particular details of scripture to arrive at new, shifting, diverse meanings,

---

[4] *Conf.* 12.25.35; *De doc.* 1.39.44.

which, nevertheless, resonate with the faith and do not diverge from its truth—in other words, which are orthodox. What might emerge from these improvisations—as we all know from our reading of patristic sermons—can, at best, be exhilarating, illuminating, and surprising, and at worst, disconcerting, digressive, and depressing.

The second authority to which Augustine and the fathers appeal to establish what is orthodox is, of course, the Church and the divinely given grace and teaching, which originates in Christ and which the Church transmits through its tradition and sacraments. In many respects Augustine understands it in the same manner as the scriptures, and it shares many of the characteristics that we have described as belonging to the "dark side" of orthodoxy: the divine truth that the tradition of the Church hands on, or mediates, and the sacramental grace that it bestows are something that is given to us through temporal, mutable, corporeal means. Its truth and grace are not something we possess, but something given, which we must receive by hearing, reading, interpreting, and participating. How we do this is not always clear or straightforward. The tradition or teaching of the Church is something that is at once divine but, like scripture, is mediated to us through frail, faltering, fallible human beings. They can differ, or we can differ in our interpretation of them, but again Augustine maintains that what is important is not to diverge from Christ's teaching, summed up in the double commandment of love of God and love of neighbor. Cyprian, like the Donatists, may have erred in advocating rebaptism of heretics, but unlike them he did not break with the tradition of the Church but rather remained within the unity of charity, and therefore remained orthodox, despite his uncomfortable disagreement with the bishop of Rome. In other words, there might well be difficulties, disagreements, and differences, but so long as they resonate with the double commandment they are still comprehended by right faith, or orthodoxy.[5]

Augustine is clearly aware that, far from being fixed or unmoving, orthodoxy, or right faith, is something that, while given to us by God in

---

[5]*De bap. contra Don.* 1.18.28–19.29.

scripture, the tradition, and sacraments of the Church, is defined by its alterity; it only emerges insofar as we participate in it and receive it. We do this by listening to God in prayer, hearing him in scripture and the preacher, participating in the liturgy, receiving the sacraments, loving our neighbor, and above all loving God by confessing our complete and utter dependence upon his grace. In other words, right faith/orthodoxy is not something fixed, which we can claim to know or possess or impose, as Augustine accuses the Manichees, Donatists, and Pelagians of doing, but something that we are given and receive only through relation to, and participation in, the unity of love that constitutes the Church, where God is present and is mediated to us. Like a piece of improvisation, true faith emerges and is defined only by being performed, communicated, shared, and received by and with others. It is something of an understatement to observe that Augustine's thought is profoundly "social"; suffice it to say that for him human beings *are* only insofar as they relate to God and to one another. Human beings are by definition relational, and their life is always—from Adam and Eve in Genesis, who were intended to found a society, to the City of God in this life and the life to come—a social one.[6]

To return to our earlier analogy: like the earth's plates, human society might appear, from our perspective, to be always the same: immovably fixed, settled, and definable. But in truth it is always slowly but inexorably shifting and changing, as its members take account of the past, accommodate themselves to the present, and anticipate the future, receiving, assimilating, transposing, and improvising upon the tacit, everyday customs, habits, consensus, and traditions that make it what it is. The temporal, culturally determined nature of human society and its beliefs is something Augustine demonstrates an acute consciousness of in many of his works. Against the Manichees it allows him to understand and exonerate the behavior of the patriarchs as simply "of their time";[7] in *De doctrina Christiana (On Christian Teaching)*, it determines the way in which he thinks the Christian must approach the interpretation of scripture (conscious of the weight of pagan learning, tradition, and custom; able to

[6] *Civ.* 12.28.1, 19.5; *De bono conj.* 1.1.
[7] *Conf.* 3.7.13.

identify and use aspects of it useful to a Christian culture and reject those inimical to it);[8] it informs the way in which we articulate what we believe and understand (in a language that only succeeds in communicating anything at all because human beings agree, by custom and common consent, upon what it means);[9] in *De civitate Dei* (*City of God*) it imposes a particular understanding of the interrelation between human action and divine providence in sacred and secular history. Augustine is well aware that the constantly shifting, fluid, and flexible nature of human society means that orthodoxy or right faith must be creatively and imaginatively re-thought, reformulated, and improvised. In other words, it must be expressed in a manner in which it will resonate with its hearers—both Christian and non-Christian—if it is not to become arcane, offensive, obscure, or unintelligible.

Perhaps most important, for Augustine, is the fundamental principle that all human reality and all human belief or opinion, if they are to be rightly valued and held, must be treated as provisional and open ended, and be constantly directed toward their source and end in God. They are, by definition, signs (*signa*) or pointers to a reality or truth (*res*) that lies beyond them and must therefore never be taken as an end in themselves, or enjoyed for themselves, but must always be used and referred toward God.[10] Belief or opinion is right, or orthodox, only if it knows itself to *be* belief and opinion and not knowledge; if it is exercised in humility rather than pride; if it is oriented in hope and love toward what it does not yet see or understand. The whole thrust of Augustine's thought is eschatological. Here we have only temporal, mutable, and corporeal signs that are inevitably ambiguous, obscure, and difficult. The best we can do is rightly believe that they are created and inspired by God and, if they are thus heard and seen, they serve to inspire our love and desire for him. It is not without reason that whenever Augustine sets out to give a formal statement or description of what orthodox faith or life is—in book 1 of *De doctrina Christiana*, in *De catechizandis rudibus* (*On Teaching the Unin-*

[8]See esp. *De doc.* 2.19.29–42.63.
[9]*De doc.* 2.24.37.
[10]For a theoretical statement see book 1 of *De doc.*

structed), in the *Enchiridion ad Laurentium* (*Enchirdion*), the *Regulae (Rule for Monks)*—he does so by stressing love of God and neighbor as the only sure and certain way to hold on to the truth amid the difficulties and ambiguities of scriptural interpretation and Christian life in community, society, or the world.[11]

The problem, then, is how to hear and read orthodoxy, or right faith, as precisely that: *faith* in the temporal, mutable, corporeal signs that point toward and are given and revealed to us by God, rather than as ultimate, fixed, definitive statements of truth. Augustine's answer seems to be that faith must be directed toward God in love, a love of one's neighbor and of one's neighbor toward and in God; a love that will be satisfied with nothing else but God, and is therefore forever caught up in the eschatological tension between this world and the life to come, when he will be fully revealed and possessed. What we called the "dark side" of orthodoxy, the unavoidable undercurrent of ambiguity, difficulty, and obscurity that accompanies any encounter with the temporal, mutable, corporeal signs that mediate divine truth in this life, thus turns out to be what defines it, and without which it would cease to be right faith and become blind, proud idolatry.[12]

Should we simply conclude, then, that Augustine's reading of orthodoxy is characterized by his appreciation of its "dark side"? I think we can go a little further than that. We need to ask: what happens when those silently moving plates clash? When the slow, almost imperceptible shifting erupts into a volcano or earthquake? When the dark side comes to the surface and can no longer be overlooked or ignored? When the comfortable and comforting fixity and certainty of stable and immutable teaching is completely shaken? When this happens, should we regard what emerges as a new, offensive, and unacceptable innovation, hostile to and discontinuous with the fixed and certain we have become accustomed to, or as something that we should have anticipated and expected if we had dared to glimpse below the surface and been more aware of the fluidity

---

[11]*De doc.* 1.35.39 and 1.36.40; *De cat. rud.* 10.15; *Ench.*121; and *Reg.* 1.2 and 5.2.
[12]E.g. *Conf.* 5.3.5; 7.9.13–15; *Tract. ep. Jo.* 2.4.

and ambiguity of the tacit, unspoken, unarticulated but constant presence of divine truth, grace, and providential action?

Augustine's teaching on the fall, original sin, the effects of original sin upon the will of fallen creatures, and their need for grace to do or to will the good, might, I think, be considered as one such eruption, earthquake, or seismic shift. It is an understanding of Christian life and faith that, while it can be difficult to argue from scripture, was certainly quietly rumbling away in the western tradition, in the likes of Tertullian, Cyprian, or Ambrosiaster, and which had surfaced in a way that had already shaped the sacramental practices of the Church in infant baptism.[13] Perhaps more importantly, I would like to suggest, it represents a full and explicit outworking or bringing to the surface of what the "dark side" of orthodoxy actually represents: the unavoidable undercurrent of ambiguity, difficulty, and obscurity that accompanies any encounter with the temporal, mutable, corporeal signs that mediate divine truth in this life. Augustine's theology of the fall, original sin, and the need for grace, is, as it were, a sustained attempt to come to terms with this "dark side" theologically (or as other contributors to this volume have put it: to encounter the "Void" [Professor Tracy]; to name the un-namable God—*Idipsum* [Professor Marion]) and to think through what an orthodox theology, based on orthodox or right faith, might be. How does one make sense of the unavoidable ambiguity, difficulty, and obscurity of the revelation of divine truth in scripture, the tradition, and sacramental practices of the Church, or the divine Word incarnate? Is it simply because we are temporal, mutable, and corporeal creatures and divine truth or *res* is revealed and accessible to us only through temporal, mutable, corporeal signs (*signa*). Yes, but there is more: for Augustine it is also to be explained by the fact that, as he argued against the Manicheans, ambiguity, obscurity, and difficulty are not an inherent part of what it is to be a creature but a symptom of the creature's turning away from the truth; and as he argued against the Donatists, that while a perfect human society perhaps existed

---

[13]See Gerald Bonner, "Les origins africaines de la doctrine augustinienne sur la chute et le péché originel," *God's Decree and Man's Destiny* (London: Variorum, 1987), 8.97–116, for discussion and references.

in Eden, it is now unattainable, in the Church or elsewhere, in this life, and must be sought in faith, hope, and love for the life to come; and against the Pelagians and the philosophers, that while eternal, immutable, incorporeal truth was once accessible to us, it is no longer; that whereas we had once known and participated in the truth, this is now lost to us without God's gracious incarnation, revelation, and inspiration. Orthodoxy, or right faith, for Augustine, is a matter of faith, hope, and love for what we do not yet possess rather than the certainty of knowledge, vision, or perfection attained. Controversy certainly prompted Augustine into formulating the true faith or orthodoxy, systematically and clearly, but it is a clear and systematic statement of the ever present "dark side"—of creation's and the creature's dependence and contingency upon their Creator for their being and their continuation in being. What Augustine has done is to provide us not with a topography of the earth's surface but of the dark, shifting, and unsettling undercurrents of human sinfulness and divine grace we would rather choose to ignore.

In concluding this paper I would like, briefly, to mention one other meaning of orthodoxy that has been mentioned a number of times in this volume and which bears directly on what we have just said: orthodoxy is, of course, not only right faith (*recta fides*) but also right praise (*recta jubilatio/laus*). We have seen that the difficulty, obscurity, and ambiguity of the dark side are best encountered in faith, hope, and most especially, love. One might also add, on a rather more optimistic note, that the best and most appropriate expression of this faith, hope, and love is undoubtedly praise: the wordless praise of jubilation for that "which cannot be uttered."[14] Right faith leads inevitably to right praise.

---

[14]*En. in Ps.* 99.5. Cf. 32.i.8; 65.2; 94.4.

Augustine's Christomorphic Theocentrism

DAVID TRACY

Introduction: Augustine in Fragments?

In an essay on Wittgenstein and Nietzsche,[1] Erich Heller developed an interesting dual metaphor: understanding some thinkers is like climbing Mont Blanc; understanding other thinkers is like exploring an ancient city like Rome. First, Mont Blanc: the journey can be tedious, sometimes through detours, always tough. But once you have managed to reach the summit, you know exactly where you are. The surrounding territory lies before you as a clear, ordered, coherent panorama. Heller's philosophical examples for this mountain imagery are nicely chosen: Aristotle and Kant. One can easily add theological examples: Thomas Aquinas, Gregory Palamas, John Calvin—difficult, disciplined, deeply impressive, orderly, coherent, panoramic thinkers all.

On the other hand, a never-completed understanding of an ancient city is a good metaphor for understanding a very different kind of thinker: Plato, Pascal, Simone Weil, Wittgenstein, Nietzsche, Gregory of Nyssa, Martin Luther, and, surely, Augustine. Years of studying the texts of Augustine is indeed like getting to know an ancient, crowded, labyrinthine city—a city like Rome with layer after layer of history, with individual neighborhoods often defining an era (for example, Renaissance Rome

---

[1]Erich Heller, "Ludwig Wittgenstein," in *Encounters,* ed. Melvin Lasky (New York: Simon & Schuster, 1965), 376–92.

manifests itself in the Via Giulia and a few Renaissance palaces here and there—all surrounded by Baroque and *Risorgimento* and contemporary times). One never really knows a city like Rome. One can take walk after walk for years; one can study interminable books of history, art, philosophy, and theology; one can consult ancient, medieval, Renaissance, Baroque, *Risorgimento*, and contemporary maps. Despite all that work, any honest explorer of Rome (even a native) is always unsure if one has really understood Rome. One is never quite sure where one is in relationship to the ever-shifting whole named Rome. In my judgment, Heller's city metaphor seems particularly appropriate for those very rare thinkers who are also great artists or, if you prefer, those very rare artists who are also major thinkers: Nietzsche, Kierkegaard, Pascal, and Gregory Nazianzen, surely; but especially Plato and Augustine. The thought of these thinker-artists will never yield to a single Mont Blanc panorama.

After great and sustained labor, one may believe that one has reached something like an adequate vision of the basic set of distinctions, definitions, and ordering structures that constitute the great work of an Aristotle, a Thomas Aquinas, a Kant. But does anyone wish to announce that she has understood all the fragments, resolved all the seeming contradictions, unfolded all Augustine's tropes and topics in his often astounding late-antique Latin rhetoric? Augustine is singular: both thinker and artist, rhetorician and dialectician, at times a gently dialogical and fiercely polemical writer, a contemplative and full-time pastor. Karl Jaspers states that no great thinker was ever as busy with the world's business as Nicholas of Cusa; he forgot Augustine.

Reading Augustine will always disclose new alleys, new diggings (in Augustine's case, newly discovered sermons and letters), new readers, ever new admirers and detractors, new methods of scholarship to shift an emphasis for interpreting Augustinian texts. For example, there is an important difference in understanding Augustine on God from the emphasis (perhaps overemphasis) on Augustine's Platonism from the Courcelle period of scholarship of the 1950s[2] to the present scholarly

---

[2]Pierre Courcelle, *Recherches sur les "Confessions" de saint Augustin* (Paris: E. de Boccard, 1968).

insistence that *De Trinitate* (*On the Trinity*) can be adequately interpreted only by noting the importance of Augustine's defense of Nicaea against the Latin homoiousians.[3] As with revisions in understanding any ancient, but still thriving, city—Jerusalem, Athens, Rome, etc.—every new scholarly advance complicates but rarely effaces former readings. There is much work still to be done by scholars, literary critics and literary theorists, philosophers, and theologians on the fascinating, debatable, exact relationships of Augustine to Plotinus and/or Porphyry. In the multiple texts of Augustine as well as in the texts of his many admirers and critics from his own time until today, Augustine has always been both a famous and controversial thinker through the avalanche of conflicting receptions of fragments of his work through the centuries. The *Confessiones* (*Confessions*) is the one Augustinian text every educated person in our culture has probably read. Even those contemptuous of other Augustinian texts may well agree with Ludwig Wittgenstein that Augustine's *Confessiones* is "the most serious book we possess in our culture."

In the various texts of Augustine, we find a lasting city but not a very stable one. Which text, which fragment, of the enormous oeuvre is most worth attention now? All educated persons enter *Città Augustiana* in their youth through the *Confessiones*. Most then journey on to *De civitate Dei* (*City of God*). The more philosophically and theologically inclined eventually turn to Augustine's third classic work, *De Trinitate*. Any one of these texts is clearly worth a lifetime or two of scholarly study and hard philosophical and theological reflection. After serious study of Augustine's three great classics, however, you will still not be on a mountaintop to envisage the vast Augustinian panorama. Petrarch, after climbing Mount Ventoux with Augustine's *Confessiones* in hand, hoped that by rereading *Confessiones* on that mountaintop he might finally see clearly the Augustinian vision. In vain: Augustine, I repeat, is not a mountain but an ancient city. Like all of us, Petrarch did see a rich part of Augustine's view.[4] How-

---

[3] Inter alia, Lewis Ayres, "The Fundamental Grammar of Augustine's Trinitarian Theology," in *Augustine and His Critics,* ed. R. Dodaro and G. Lawless (London: Routledge, 2000), 51–76.

[4] Brian Stock, *After Augustine: The Meditative Reader and the Text* (Philadelphia: University of Pennsylvania Press, 2001), 71–86.

ever, again like all of us, Petrarch glimpsed only one part of that crowded city. Augustine is a teeming, overcrowded city; he is not a clean, well-lighted mountaintop.

Theological students must also labor with Augustine's polemical texts, those very influential, perhaps—dare I suggest it, too influential—texts: against the skeptics, the Manicheans, the Donatists, the Arians, the Pelagians, and, in the *De civitate Dei*, even against the formerly honored Platonists. And yet alongside these famously polemical texts there exist also the more serene, the deeply dialogical, and mostly non-polemical early writings from Augustine's leisure year at Cassiciacum. Those early dialogical writings are not only fascinating in themselves; they are also deeply suggestive of the kind of dialogues Augustine may well have continued to write if he had not been forced to leave his life of *otium* (contemplative leisure) and his companions both at Cassiciacum and in his rural retreat at his home in Thagaste. For Augustine was, in effect, coerced into a bishopric and its enormous pastoral duties. The time of dialogues with likeminded companions was over. His pastoral life as priest, then as bishop, had begun.

Once Augustine became a baptized Christian this classically trained rhetorician realized he did not know the Bible at all well. His only childhood memories here were of catechesis and Monica's lessons. As an adult he held to a dismissive "cultured despiser" view of the Bible compared to Virgil, Horace, and Cicero. The Platonist allegorical sermons of Ambrose of Milan freed Augustine to read the Bible with new and eager eyes. Moreover, the books of "some Platonists" freed Augustine from his earlier materialistic view of the world. Thus altered, the newly baptized Augustine was ready to become more and more a biblical theologian. One result of Augustine's turn to the Bible has been to lead many contemporary interpreters (I among them) to find certain of his biblical texts far more important than his more polemical works:[5] the sermons, the sermon-commentaries, initially the commentaries on Paul, then the sermon-commentaries on 1 John and the Sermon on the Mount, the commentaries on

---

[5] *Bible de Tous les Temps,* vol. 3 of *Saint Augustin et la Bible,* ed. A.-M. La Bonnardière (Paris: Beauchesne, 1986).

Genesis, and his incomparable commentary on the Psalms. In these sermons and biblical commentaries, Augustine's passionate intelligence and
full rhetorical genius are ablaze.

Augustine the thinker and artist, therefore, does not yield to a single
vision from the beginnings of his writings at Cassiciacum through his
Retractiones (*Retractions*) and his anti-Julian of Eclanum texts at the end.
In that sense, even when we possess full texts, what we possess are in fact
fragments of some larger whole, at once elusive and overdetermined. In
Augustine, the texts themselves have become fragmentary: sometimes
complementing one another; sometimes merely stranded next to one
another like sunken ruins; sometimes seeming to contradict one another.
For example, it is not easy or perhaps even desirable to try to render coherent all of Augustine's positions on free will.[6] There are still other fragments in Augustine's texts that are more like verbs than nouns. Such
fragments are not merely fragments of a larger whole by means of which,
as with the German Romantics, nostalgia is evoked for some lost whole
(in this case, some lost totality called "true" Augustinianism). Rather, as
Walter Benjamin shows with other texts[7] (in his case, principally *Trauer-
spiel*, kabbalistic texts, Kafka, nineteenth-century Paris) there are certain
texts that, even when we possess the whole text, are fragmentary in their
explosive power to shatter any temptation of totality (Augustinianism
again) or some final once-and-for-all "true" interpretation. Only period
pieces yield to a once-and-for-all interpretation—classics never. There are
Augustinian fragments (perhaps more accurately named frag-events[8])
that dissolve, implode, or explode to manifest unforeseen new meanings
not easily assimilable to other fragments. All true readers of Augustine live
for a while with one or another fragment—sentences, metaphors, images,
at times whole texts, as frag-events.

[6]Note, for example, the seeming contradictions between the early text, *De lib. arb.*, and
Retr.

[7]Walter Benjamin, *The Arcades Project*, trans. Howard Eiland and Kevin McLaughlin
(Cambridge: The Belknap Press of Harvard University Press, 1999).

[8]In a forthcoming work entitled *This Side of God*, I have a chapter distinguishing the
Romantic notion of fragment from one I defend as frag-event.

Some Augustinian images and phrases as frag-events have haunted his readers for centuries: *pondus meum, amor meus* ("my weight is my love");[9] *[s]ero te amavi* ("late have I loved you");[10] *quaerebam quod amarem, amans amare* ("I searched for something to love, in love with loving");[11] and most unforgettably the Augustinian strain that has haunted western cultures for centuries: *[t]u excitas, ut laudare te delectet, quia fecisti nos ad te et inquietum est cor nostrum, donec requiescat in te* ("you move us to delight for praising you, for you formed us for yourself and our hearts are restless until they find rest in you").[12]

If one views Augustine's texts as an ancient, layered, crowded city, one also may understand better how certain famous longtime visitors (tourists need not apply) to the *Città Augustiniana* tended to embrace one fragment, one neighborhood—the one that exploded for them as the central clue they had long sought. Thomas Aquinas loved Augustine with a purity of will peculiar to that serene thinker. As one example, Thomas sharpened brilliantly the more intellectualist moments in Augustine's trinitarian analogy of God.[13] On the contrary, Cornelius Jansen stated that he read most of Augustine several times but he read the anti-Pelagian writings thirty times! Calvin also read the anti-Pelagian writings with frightening attentiveness. Hans Urs von Balthasar read *De vera religione* (*On True Religion*) even more than *Confessiones* as a less subjective Augustinian text that discloses how Augustine found true religion in Christianity's disclosive, beautiful forms.[14] Bernard Lonergan read Augustine's early dialogues over and over before he turned to Thomas Aquinas and after that composed his own cognitional theory in *Insight*.[15] Reinhold

[9] *Conf.* 13.9.10.
[10] *Conf.* 10.27.38.
[11] *Conf.* 3.1.1.
[12] *Conf.* 1.1.1.
[13] Bernard Lonergan, *Verbum: Word and Idea in Aquinas,* ed. David B. Burrell (Notre Dame: University of Notre Dame Press, 1967).
[14] Hans Urs von Balthasar, *The Glory of the Lord: Theological Aesthetics,* vol. 2 (San Francisco: Ignatius Press, 1989), 93–112.
[15] Richard M. Liddy, *Transforming Light: Intellectual Conversion in the Early Lonergan* (Collegeville, MN: The Liturgical Press, 1993), 50–74.

Niebuhr insisted that his entire Christian theological ethics (which Niebuhr named Christian realism) was really a modern version of *De civitate Dei*. Martin Heidegger's youthful work in his Augustine seminars underlies, more than Heidegger admitted, much of the structure of *Being and Time*:[16] not only "fallenness" but *Befindlichkeit* is ultimately Augustinian *affectus*; the appeals to the cognitive power of mood (*Stimmung*) are Augustinian.

This very partial list could easily be expanded. Diverse, often conflicting receptions of Augustine in philosophy and western Christian theology are not the exception but the standard. For the moment, I cite these familiar examples only to suggest that hermeneutically the reception of Augustine, pace all pure historicists, is sometimes as important for understanding Augustine well as are readings determined solely by Augustine's historical context.[17] Furthermore, Augustine's dialectical arguments are embedded in and transformed by a rhetoric of both the topics and the tropes. Many postmodern rhetoricians (e.g., Paul de Man, Jacques Derrida, Michel Foucault, Julia Kristeva) prefer the radical unstable irony of the tropes to the more stable irony of topical arguments. All careful readers can find both kinds of rhetoric in text after text of Augustine. It is fascinating how protean the reception of Augustine continues to be: the last work of the "inventor" of postmodernity, Jean-François Lyotard, is an unfinished manuscript on Augustine;[18] the too often ignored fact that Augustine was a North African theologian writing in a colonial outpost of the Roman empire has made him newly fascinating to postcolonial critics.[19] On the other hand, despite the efforts of some contemporary inter-

[16]John Van Buren, *The Young Heidegger: Rumor of the Hidden King* (Bloomington: Indiana University Press, 1994), especially 158–96.

[17]Hans-Georg Gadamer, *Truth and Method*, 2d ed., trans. Joel Weinsheimer and Donald G. Marshall (New York: Continuum, 1989), 171–265.

[18]Jean-Françoise Lyotard, *The Confession of Augustine*, trans. Richard Beardsworth (Stanford: Stanford University Press, 2000).

[19]See the interesting essays in Pierre-Yves Fux, Jean-Michel Roessli, Otto Wermelinger, *Augustinus Afer: Saint Augustin, africanité et universalité. Actes du colloque international Alger-Annaba, 1–7 avril 2001* (Fribourg, Suisse: Editions Universitaires Fribourg Suisse, 2003).

preters, I fail to see how Augustine's usual views on women (*De Trinitate* is an exception) are anything other than a typical fourth-century masculinist ideology.[20]

When one states that Augustine was a great fragmentary writer, one means, among other things, that Augustine was not a writer with a single unchanging theological vision (as, for example, Evagrius was and Irenaeus seems to have been). Peter Brown nicely stated that even after his conversion Augustine never felt fully healed: Augustine was always a Christian in convalescence. One can justly add to Brown's apposite comment that intellectually as well Augustine, in his philosophical and theological thinking as much as in his artistic imagination, was also never at rest. He was always rethinking his theological vision, always *inquietum*. Except for *De Trinitate*, most of his writing is occasional. In the *Retractiones*, Augustine tried to render his thought more coherent than perhaps it was. The fragmentary imagination of Augustine can be viewed not as a defect but an advantage. Most major contemporary artists and thinkers build their final vision (if one emerges) by collating ever-changing fragments. Among modern poets, think of the fragmentary Emily Dickinson, Yeats, Eliot, indeed most major modern poets as distinct from the more rare modern poetic visionaries of a single commanding vision: Blake, Rimbaud, Wordsworth, Whitman. The difference between the fragmentary artist or thinker and the visionary is not a difference of quality at all. It is a difference of temperament and a difference of historical context. In fact, visionary poets of a single commanding vision often do not seem to fare too well in fragmented and fragmentary modernity:[21] Rimbaud very early abandoned poetry altogether; Wordsworth and Whitman, in later life, kept adding to and revising their original vision until they almost ruined it. Most modern thinkers have a similar fragmentary stance. That

---

[20]For a contrary view, see K.E. Borresen, *Subordination and Equivalence: The Nature and Role of Woman in Augustine and Thomas Aquinas,* trans. C.H. Talbot (Washington: University Press of America, 1981).

[21]For the concept "fragmentary" as distinct from "fragment," see Maurice Blanchot, *The Infinite Conversation,* trans. Susan Hanson (Minneapolis: University of Minnesota Press, 1993); and see Kevin Hart, *Postmodernism* (Oxford: One World Publications, 2004), 67–87.

is why, after all, we find it necessary to speak of early and late Wittgenstein; early and late Heidegger; early and late Karl Barth; early and late Karl Rahner, et al.

As contemporary receptions—often intellectual revivals—show, the thinkers of an ever-elusive fragmentary vision disclosed in a work always-in-process seem more helpful in our fragmented and fragmentary day: note the distinct philosophical retrievals of Plato's Good beyond Being in Emmanuel Levinas and Iris Murdoch; note the surprising new turn in many western theologians to Gregory of Nyssa; note new ways that Martin Luther is now interpreted—from traditional grace-sin perspectives to the *unio Christi* (even deification!) interpretations of Luther by the new Finnish School.[22] No reading of any great classic can ever prove definitive. Classic texts are fragmentary. Period pieces are all too unitary.

Augustine's Theocentrism and Christomorphism

In some event, epiphany, or manifestation or through the "hints and guesses"[23] afforded to each of us by fragments that affect our lives, one can become more receptive to naming the Real anew: the Void, the Open, the Good, God.[24] Today many major thinkers (not only Christians, Jews, and Muslims) find that the Real somehow discloses itself for our naming. The only name that we can create through reason alone for the Real is a name at the limits of the possible, i.e., at the limits of reason (e.g., God as a limit-concept for Kant). Many modern philosophers can persuasively argue for the reasonable-ness of belief in naming the Real, God. Other philosophers argue for the reasonableness of naming the Real as the impersonal Good beyond Being (Murdoch), or as the Open (Heidegger), or as the Void (Nietzsche). But very few contemporary thinkers, on the basis of reason alone, presume to name the Real. The Real must somehow disclose itself for our

---

[22] *Union with Christ: The New Finnish Interpretation of Luther,* ed. Carl E. Braaten and Robert W. Jenson (Grand Rapids: William B. Eerdmans Publishing Co., 1998).

[23] The phrase is T.S. Eliot's in *The Four Quartets* (London: Faber and Faber, 1968), 30.

[24] I analyze these four namings of the Real in the aforementioned *This Side of God.*

naming. Not only biblical thinkers realize this. For example, Nietzsche insisted that his ultimate name for the Real—will to power as eternal return—is a result, in Nietzsche's own language, of both "revelation" and "inspiration" (a word Nietzsche says he is surprised to use). Indeed, Nietzsche names the exact places (Genoa and Sils-Maria) and the exact time that the revelation of eternal return happened. It is also the case that the later Heidegger dared to name the Real as the Open by thinking meditatively, i.e., receptively, with certain thinkers (the pre-Socratics), certain works of art (Rilke, Hölderlin, the Greek temple, van Gogh's painting etc.), and, even more so, I believe, through the radical Open described in the classic way of Taoism. This listening to Other-Power revealing itself is clear as well in Plato's *The Republic*, where "the Good beyond Being" cannot be arrived at through dialectical effort alone but must happen, just as in the *Symposium* the Beautiful Itself also happens "suddenly." By means of such events or happenings, the Real manifests itself for our naming. In Augustine, as for the Jewish Platonist Philo before him and as for Thomas Aquinas and many other Christian thinkers after him, there is one great exception to the Real somehow disclosing itself as impersonal Void, or Open, or the Good followed by our philosophical labor to name that disclosure. As Philo very early claimed, the Real as God discloses Godself by name in Exodus 3.14—at least in the Septuagint Greek (Philo) and Latin (Augustine, Thomas Aquinas, et al.) translations of the original Hebrew. *Ego sum qui sum* ("I am who am") is one such Latin translation of the Hebrew *ehye asher ehye.* These Septuagint Greek and Latin translations are not errors, although they are only two possible translations of the Hebrew.[25]

The truest naming of God for Augustine, however, is not Exodus 3.14, nor the Plotinian the One or the Good. For Augustine, God reveals Godself through Christ in both creation and redemption. As Love, God is the Trinity of the loving, interrelated divine persons of Father, Son, Holy Spirit. To so name God (and therefore, the Real) occurred to Augustine not principally through personal mystical experience (with Monica)[26] but

[25]André LaCocque and Paul Ricoeur, *Thinking Biblically: Exegetical and Hermeneutical Studies,* trans. David Pellauer (Chicago: University of Chicago Press, 1998), 307–30.
[26]For a balanced account of the debate on whether Augustine had mystical experiences

through faith in the revelation of Jesus Christ. One can, I believe, refor-mulate Augustine's point this way: only by naming Jesus of Nazareth (i.e., the Jesus whose words, actions, and sufferings are narrated in the gospels) the Christ can we name God. Through faith in Christ the Christian names God as Love-Trinity in and through naming Jesus as the Christ. In Augus-tine's own words, to name God truly (i.e., as trinitarian love) is possible only by moving through Christ the man (i.e., Jesus) (*per Christum hominem*) to Christ as God (*ad Christum divinum*). In Augustinian chris-tology, the Form Christ gathers all other forms to name God: *per Chris-tum hominem ad Christum divinum.* Augustine's theology is theocentric through and through. At the same time, Augustine's theocentrism is con-stituted in and through his emphatic christomorphism.

Even those theologians who do not admire Augustine's *De Trinitate* as much as I do must admit that to understand the heart of Augustine's the-ology in its full theocentrism, we are very fortunate to possess not only the fragments of the other trinitarian reflections throughout Augustine's oeu-vre but his one fully systematic treatise: on the Real as God wherein God is Love, i.e., is Trinity. This trinitarian theocentrism is also just as pro-foundly christomorphic. For Augustine, only through the Form of forms, the incarnate Mediator, Jesus Christ, do Christians adequately learn to name God as Love, as Triune.

And yet there remains a problem in understanding Augustine's christology: viz., that unlike in his treatise on God, *De Trinitate,* Augus-tine did not write a single treatise on christology. And yet his christology, although never finalized systematically, is nevertheless the central Form that throughout his work in-forms and trans-forms all Augustine's theol-ogy: on God, on creation, on grace, on eschatology, on ecclesiology, on anthropology.

Moreover, a similar search is needed to gather all the fragmentary forms in Augustine's multiple texts on the Spirit.[27] Otherwise, we erro-

at Milan and in Ostia with Monica, see Bernard McGinn, *The Foundations of Mysticism: Origins to the Fifth Century* (New York: Crossroad, 1991), 228–38.

[27]For an example here see Eugene TeSelle, "Holy Spirit," in *Augustine through the Ages: An Encyclopedia,* ed. A. Fitzgerald (Grand Rapids: William B. Eerdmans Publishing Co., 1999), 434–37.

neously accuse Augustine (as he has been accused too often) of chris-
tomonism. It is true that Augustine, like western theology in general,
lacked a fully developed doctrine of the Holy Spirit such as one finds in
the eastern Christian tradition from Basil onward. But this typical western underdevelopment of a doctrine of the Spirit should not become an
occasion to cite Augustine as a christomonist. He was not. The Christ-
saturated Augustine, as especially his *Enarrationes in Psalmos* (*Enarrations
on the Psalms*) shows, is also a Spirit-saturated theologian. It is true that
Augustine needed to learn far more than he ever did (his Greek was not
fluent) from his Cappadocian older contemporaries for developing fuller
objective and subjective doctrines of the Holy Spirit.

This underdeveloped pneumatology is a real lack in Augustine, as in
most western theology (including my own). At the same time, one finds
in the theocentric-christomorphic Augustine one of the most impressive
christologies in all Christian theology, even if Augustine's christology
unfortunately was never expressed systematically in a single treatise. Perhaps the fact that Augustine did not devote a major single treatise to
christology as he did to the Trinity has caused his christology to be under-
valued in many histories of doctrine and histories of theology by being
read as simply one more admirable but not notably original neo-Platonic
christology of mediation. Augustine's christology is indeed a mediator
christology, but far more than that. To see how this is the case demands
appealing to several Augustinian texts, images, metaphors, arguments—
in sum, many different fragments of Augustine's christology scattered
throughout his oeuvre. Only then can one appreciate the richness and
complexity of Augustine's christology. Only then—*per Christum hominem
ad Christum divinum* and, I presume to add to render Augustine's implicit
position explicit, *per Christum divinum ad Deum Trinitatem* (through
Christ as God to God as Trinity)—can we grasp Augustine's naming of the
Real as the God who is Love and, as Love, the mutual loving relationships
of Father, Son, and Holy Spirit.

Christological Fragments

In histories of doctrine and histories of theology Augustine's christology is usually described as a traditional mediatorship christology. In terms of the person of Christ, Augustine's christology is often further described as Chalcedonian *avant la lettre*: Augustine died in 430 CE; Ephesus occurred in 431 (he had been invited); Chalcedon in 451. The descriptions of Augustine's christology as Christ the mediator are, of course, accurate. Without the technical terms of Chalcedon, Augustine's understanding of the person of Christ *was* proto-Chalcedonian (i.e., one divine person in two natures). Augustine always held to the definition of Nicaea. In fact, Augustine, in fidelity to Ambrose in his strong anti-Latin Arian position of Ambrose, also consistently (most notably perhaps in the early anti-Arian books of his *De Trinitate*) stood fast against the characteristically Latin Arian position. There can be no doubt that Augustine held a strong Nicaean christology and a strong mediator christology.

But should that be the end of a discussion of Augustine's christology? On the one hand, there is no single Augustinian treatise on christology; on the other hand, christology is the most pervasive reality in all his works. Christ the mediator for Augustine is Christ the incarnate God-man, above all Christ *the* Form of both true God and true humanity. As the Form of Forms, Christ in-forms all reality, trans-forms all theology. Christ the Form is not only incarnational but, as in Augustine's too often ignored theology of the cross (for example, in the *Enarrationes in Psalmos*), is also Christ as Cruciform Form. Augustine, in the Psalms commentary-sermons, dares to speak of *Deus crucifixus*. The cruciform Christ form not only in-forms and trans-forms all theology (in harmony with the kenotic incarnation) but shatters and fragments any christology that may be tempted to remain only a traditional mediator christology. Jesus Christ the mediator, Christ the Form of Forms, Christ the kenotic incarnate God, Christ the Fragmenting Cruciform, Christ the risen one, are the indispensable foundations of Augustine's christology. Even that complex, however, is not Augustine's whole christological edifice. His fuller christological edifice can be built up only by gathering the varied christological fragments in Augustine's oeuvre, early, middle, and late. Fortunately, Basil Studer's scholarly work[28] has gathered together the more important christological fragments to aid any theological attempt to formulate Augustine's full christology.

The exact nature of Christ as mediator for Augustine continues to attract scholarly attention. Given the Platonist understandings of the notion of mediation in Augustine, early and late, Augustine's christology of Christ as mediator is directly related to both Nicaea and to Platonism. As it happens, Augustine's largely Platonist formulation of the category of mediation is more important in the development of the pre-Chalcedonian christology of the person of Christ than earlier scholars like Adolf von Harnack (who tended to elide the christology of Christ's person as God-man mediator to the soteriological work of Christ as mediator of salvation) noticed. Indeed, in the last twenty-five years, the exact relationship of the Augustinian christology on the person of Christ as mediator to the debates within post-Plotinus neo-Platonism from Porphyry through Iamblichus as well as, post-Augustine, to Proclus in the sixth century has received renewed scholarly attention. This can be seen, for example, in the work of Professor Giovanni Reale at Milano.[29] Reale's thesis is persuasive to me: post-Plotinus, the major theoretical difficulty for all neo-Platonic thinkers was the philosophical need to determine the forms of mediation necessary to allow the Plotinian One to emanate to the many. In Reale's reading, the pagan neo-Platonists kept complicating emanation by multiplying the forms of mediation from the Plotinian One/Good to the many (including from Iamblichus forward through theurgy). On the other hand, Augustine's strategy—as an explicitly Christian Platonist—was the exact opposite: Augustine argued persuasively in Christian theological neo-Platonic terms that Jesus Christ, the God-man, as the mediator was the only mediation needed. Unlike Iamblichus and the

[28]Basil Studer, *The Grace of Christ and the Grace of God in Augustine of Hippo: Christocentrism or Theocentrism?*, trans. Matthew J. O'Connell (Collegeville, MN: Liturgical Press, 1997).

[29]Giovanni Reale, *Agostino. Amore Assoluto e 'terza navigazione'* (Milan: Vita Epensiero, 1994).

pagan neo-Platonists after Plotinus, Augustine through his christology of
Christ, the one mediator, simplified the Platonic issue of mediation rather
than complicated the neo-Platonist problem of mediation from the over-
flowing, emanating, impersonal One/Good of Plotinus. Augustine could
thus simplify the problem since, as a Christian, he held to a kenotic personal God who so loves the world that God the Father with the Spirit
sends the Son the divine love in creation (not emanation) and salvation
(by Jesus Christ as mediator). Christ bestows God's kenotic love to creatures who have soiled through sin the already gifted (kenotic) love of God
in creation. In that theological sense,[30] humans are wounded and deeply
damaged but nevertheless have not lost their essence as still *imago Dei* (an
image of God). God's love, both ecstatic and kenotic, is rendered present
in and through the ultimate, singular, sufficient mediation, viz. the personal mediator Jesus Christ, the incarnate God-man One. The "pagan"
neo-Platonists complicated the problem of mediation by ever more medi-
ations of emanation. Augustine solved the problem of mediation for
Christian Platonists through Christ the One Mediator.

As Pierre Hadot's works have demonstrated,[31] all the ancient philosophers and theologians (whether Stoic, Epicurean, Aristotelian; whether
pagan, Jewish [Philo], or Christian Platonist) held that philosophy-theol-
ogy was never a purely theoretical discipline, as it often is in modernity.
Theory and practice were rarely divorced in ancient thought, as they
regrettably still are for many, probably most, philosophers in modern
western philosophy and theology. Some scholars hold that this separation
of practice and theory (philosophy as a way of life; philosophy as a theory
of life) began when western medieval theology moved from the monasteries to the universities. Yet this claim requires more nuanced distinctions—distinctions that are not separations, as the scholastics nicely said.
For example, Thomas Aquinas, for whom Augustine always remained the
principal theological authority, developed distinctions that were not sep-

[30]Carol Harrison, *Augustine: Christian Truth and Fractured Humanity: Christian Theology in Context* (Oxford: Oxford University Press, 2000).
[31]Pierre Hadot, *Philosophy as a Way of Life: Spiritual Exercises from Socrates to Foucault*,
ed. A. Davidson (London: Blackwell, 1995).

arations, including the distinction, not separation, between theory and practice. Moreover, Thomas' great contemporary at the University of Paris, Bonaventure, can be interpreted as correlating the new Franciscan spirituality of creation to traditional Augustinian interiority as well as to the achievements of high scholasticism. As a result, in Bonaventure's more scholastic works, and even more so in his other works (especially his *Itinerarium mentis in Deum*), Bonaventure's medieval theology does not separate theory from practice, spirituality from theology. Unfortunately, however, these fatal separations occurred in western theology from the nominalists of the late medieval period through the strangely eclectic sixteenth-century univocal theoretical philosophy of Suarez to much modern philosophy, including the Suarezian Thomism of modern western neo-scholasticism. That Suarezian influence in the neo-scholastics was unfortunate. In fact, neo-scholasticism, the once all-powerful modern Catholic philosophical and theological force, seemed to believe, as Bernard Lonergan once observed, in clear and distinct ideas and very few of them.

Paradoxically, the neo-scholastics were far less interested in Augustine than Descartes was. For them Augustine was an "inspiring" but merely rhetorical thinker. As Pierre Hadot expresses it: in separating philosophy (or theology) as theory from philosophy or theology as a way of life, most modern western thought lost the concern with specific spiritual practices so characteristic of all the ancient schools. Even more importantly, "modern" theology ignored what Bernard McGinn names the third form of medieval theology—the lay theologies often written in the vernacular, especially by the medieval women mystics. By way of contrast, in eastern Christian thought, with its contemplative character and its liturgical grounding, this fatal modern western separation of theory and practice rarely occurred.[32] The sustained contemporary western Christian interest in Orthodox theology since the great Catholic theologians of *ressourcement* (Daniélou, de Lubac, Congar, von Balthasar, et al.) is partly due to the need, among western theologians, to learn how much Orthodox the-

---

[32]In Orthodox theology this separation does occur in neo-Palamite theology.

ology, even in modernity, managed not to separate theory from practice, nor theology from spirituality.

The fact of the separation of theory and practice and the attendant loss of a contemplative moment in much western theology has also occasioned, in my judgment, serious repercussions in modern western theological interpretations of Augustine's theology of Christ as mediator. For example, the problem of many modern Catholic theological readings of Augustine had the opposite difficulty to liberal Protestant near-reductions of Christ's person to Christ's work. In fact, many Catholic theologians interpreted Augustine's christology as almost exclusively concerned with Christ's person (the mediator) and its proleptic relationship to Chalcedon. Among Catholic interpreters, soteriological concerns, the main focus of liberal Protestant interpreters since von Harnack, were quietly shifted to Augustine's theology of grace.

Fortunately, what has occurred in our day is a remarkable shift of emphasis in contemporary Augustinian scholarship from Augustine's relationship to his theoretical side of neo-Platonism to his deeply doctrinal, i.e., Nicaean, concerns as well as a new emphasis on the richer christology to be found in Augustine's biblical commentaries and sermons. This new emphasis in Augustine can be found in his commentaries and sermons *De sermone Domini in monte* (*On the Sermon of the Mount*), *In Evangelium Johannis tractatus* (*Tractates on the Gospel of John*), *In epistulam Johannis ad Parthos tractatus* (*Tractates on the First Epistle of John*) as well as his christological readings of the Old Testament not only in the more familiar Augustinian readings of Paul for his theology of grace but, even more so, in Augustine's development of his fuller christology of the person and the work of Christ in, especially, his *Enarrationes in Psalmos*. In addition, the recent scholarly attention to Augustine's sermons and letters (aided, of course, by the recent discovery of further sermons and letters as well as the hope, with the aid of modern technology, for yet further discoveries) has also enriched interpretations of Augustine's christology as Christ as mediator. Christ's mediatorship in Augustine is more complex than either earlier modern Catholic or modern Protestant and modern Orthodox readings had acknowledged.

In sum, thanks to contemporary Augustinian scholarship, all theologians, even non-specialists in Augustine like myself, have been driven to reread the relevant polemical works (especially the Latin anti-Arianism works) as well as to reread with more scriptural and doctrinal eyes the three classic Augustinian texts—*Confessiones, De civitate Dei* and *De Trinitate.* Theologians are also now driven to read, often for the first time, the many letters, sermons, and the biblical commentaries to understand the fuller contours of Augustine's christology. There are multiple ways to illuminate not only Christ's person as mediator but Christ's work. In Augustine, Christ is both the way to God and the homeland longed for.[33] In still other texts we can also find Augustine interpreting Christ as both the external and the interior teacher as well as Christ as both the physician and the medicine taken. In addition, in one of Augustine's most striking metaphors for the Church, the Church is the hospital where we receive the mediator-physician's medicines (the sacraments, preaching, spiritual counseling, and actions guided by the *ordo caritatis*).

Augustine as bishop learned the Bible more fully in order to preach to his people and to trans-form himself Christianly. We should also remember that his sermons were preached to very ordinary people, the largely illiterate congregation of provincial Hippo. One can observe this busily pastoral side of Augustine in the older but still very informative work of Professor van der Meer, *Augustine the Bishop.*[34] More recently, one can also observe Augustine the pastor in the new appendix in the new edition of Peter Brown's famous biography, *Augustine of Hippo.*[35] In a characteristically modest moment of scholarly self-correction, Brown comments that the newly discovered sermons and letters of the old Augustine in his episcopal role as caring, compassionate pastor for his people calls into serious question the harsher portrait of the late Augustine that he (Peter

[33] See Christ as both way and homeland in Goulven Madec, *La Patrie et la voie. Le Christ dans la vie et la pensée de saint Augustin* (Paris: Desclée, 1989).

[34] Frederik van der Meer, *Augustine the Bishop: The Life and Work of a Father of the Church,* trans. Brian H. Battershaw and G.R. Lamb (London: Sheed and Ward, 1961).

[35] Peter Brown, *Augustine of Hippo: A Biography,* rev. ed. (Berkeley: University of California Press, 2000), 441–73.

Brown) held in the first edition. Augustine was unduly harsh and extreme in his late polemical controversies with Julian of Eclanum. Julian himself, to be sure, was just as fierce and polemical in return. In my judgment, pace Jansen and Calvin, the elderly Augustine-young Julian dispute is, on the whole, not a happy sight. In the same time period, however, in sermon after sermon, action after action for his people (including legal juridical work for a good part of his everyday life, such as judge of family disputes over property), Augustine showed his pastoral rather than polemical side. In the sermons we possess Augustine did not preach double predestination to his people. As his sermon/commentaries make clear, Augustine distinguished but never separated his understanding of Christ's person from Christ's work. The key is Augustine's almost mantra-like description of the Christian way to God: *per Christian hominem ad Christum divinum.*[36]

A typical quotation from the sermons is:

> Now because Christ is himself truth and life with the Father, the Word of God, of which it says *The life was the light of men* (Jn 1.4); so because he is with the Father life and truth, and because we didn't have any way of getting to the truth, the Son of God, who is always in the Father truth and life, became the way by taking to himself a man. Walk along the man, and you arrive at God. You go by him, you come to him: Don't look for a way to come to him by, apart from him. After all, if he had refused to be the way, we would always be going astray. So he became the way; by which you could come to him. I'm not telling you, "Look for the way"; the way itself has come to you; get up and walk.[37]

Christ as both God and human being is more and more portrayed by Augustine as radically humble, i.e., kenotic. God entered our darkness in the flesh of Jesus Christ. The great hymn of Paul in Philippians sings the

[36]Studer, 43–47.

[37]*Serm.* 141.411 (*Sermons [94A-147A] on the New Testament,* in The Works of Saint Augustine: A Translation for the 21st Century, III/4, trans. Edmund Hill [Brooklyn: New City Press, 1992]).

Word's kenotic, humble, compassionate movement, from the "form of God" to the "form of a slave." At the same time, Augustine, in his sermons and biblical commentaries deliberately traveled beyond Paul's relative lack of attention to the teachings, ministry, life, and fate of the Jesus of the four gospels.

On the doctrinal-symbolic level of theology, therefore, Augustine joined a Pauline kenotic reading of the incarnation to Paul's theology of the cross in order to articulate the central doctrinal-symbolic dialectic of Christian faith: incarnation-cross-resurrection. It is this tripartite christological doctrinal complex that led Augustine's Pauline kenotic theology to his further, more narratively detailed, christology in the gospels. We find God by following the way of the incarnate God-man, Jesus the Christ. That mediating way of Christ the mediator became clearer and clearer for Augustine through the narrated details of the life of Jesus in the gospels. Eventually, for Augustine, the gospels and the Psalms, even more than Paul, spell out how we may move *per Christum hominem ad Christum divinum.* As early as the dialogue with his son Adeodatus, *De Magistro* (*On the Teacher*), Augustine discovered one aspect of this *per-ad* motif: Jesus was the teacher who became the interior teacher of the Christian way. What is more, as the influence of Paul's Philippians imprinted itself on Augustine's mind, he increased his attention to the affections and therefore to the centrality of the Christian virtues of humility and *caritas* for the Christian way christologically construed. Augustine, unlike most Platonists, believed that the "affections" counted intellectually. Remarkably, the Platonist Augustine prayed to God not for less but for more affections!

For Augustine, if one follows the way of the narrated Jesus of the gospels, one follows the way of one "like us in all things save sin"—the Jesuanic way of compassionate suffering, joyous, vulnerable, humble, kenotic love for others. In Augustine's theology, any Christian graced by God in Christ is graced to live the way of Jesus. For Augustine, no Christian disciple should expect or desire a purely tranquil life of ancient *apatheia.* Despite a life-long commitment to contemplation, continued every evening in his small *monasterium* next to his episcopal cathedral, Augustine did not finally wish for a life of *apatheia*—that noble ancient ideal, whether for Stoic or Platonist or even for some ancient Christians. To repeat: Augustine had once hoped to live, converse, and write with his friends at Cassiciacum and at rural Thagaste. Nonetheless, after Augustine became priest and bishop, all that changed. Without abandoning the ideal of contemplative interiority, Augustine modified that contemplative ideal considerably (presumably at great personal price). He did so not for his own sake but in order to serve his people every day, all day before returning to the monastery-like companionship of his priestly colleagues. Later Christians named this now familiar Christian spiritual way "contemplation-in-action." Through his dual love of the contemplative ideal and of ceaseless pastoral activity in the world Augustine was one of the earliest Christian proponents of this option. *Pondus meum, amor meus.*

In his Psalms commentaries and sermons, moreover, Augustine states (in his commentary on Psalm 140.7)[38] that two texts provide the key for understanding all scripture: Paul, as Saul, hearing the voice "why do you persecute me?" and Matthew 25 on the test beyond all beliefs in doctrines, the final Christian test of action for others, especially the poor, the oppressed, the marginal, the hungry, the naked, the mad, the possessed, the imprisoned.

In his ever developing christology, Augustine consistently believed that we are led by Jesus Christ as mediator, teacher, and healer—not so much to become "deified" (Augustine is relatively sparse in his use of this familiar eastern Christian language) but to become adopted sons and daughters of Christ by discipleship *per Christum hominem ad Christum divinum*. There is one final, surprising, perhaps even shocking fragment in Augustine's fuller christology.[39] Augustine was often driven to dark christologi-

---

[38]*En. in Ps.* 140.7 (*Exposition of the Psalms [Enarrationes in Psalmos], 121–150*, The Works of Saint Augustine: A Translation for the 21st Century, III/20, trans. Maria Boulding [Hyde Park, NY: New City Press, 2004], 306).

[39]Inter alia, see Augustine's remarkable reflections on the difference between Paul's welcoming of death and Christ's (as God-man, not only as human) sadness and suffering in facing death in Gethsemane. Augustine's Latin has a rhetorical intensity not captured in the otherwise accurate translation. "Iste gaudet coronandus, et tristis est ille coronaturus: gaudet sic apostolus, et dicit Christus Dominus noster: *Pater, si fieri potest, transeat hic calix.* Sed tristitiam sic assumsit quomodo carnem. Nolite enim putare quia hoc dicimus, non fuisse tristem Dominum. Si enim hoc dixerimus, quia non erat tristis, cum evangelium

cal reflections. Augustine dares to speak of *Deus crucifixus*; the *Christum divinum* emerges through the afflicted, human Jesus. The form of Christ is cruciform; the cruciform shatters and fragments all Christian complacency, including Augustine's earlier more sanguine mediator christology.

Conclusion: The Unstoppable Christological Drive of Augustine

Augustine's christology—at least the very abbreviated version I formulate and articulate above—can be constituted only by gathering many Augustinian christological fragments into a tentative interpreted unity. Of course, this is only a beginning. Even if my readings are persuasive, these interpretations would, of course, only serve to initiate a study of Augustine's full christology. Above all we need extended theological reflection on how, exactly, Augustine's *per Christum hominem ad Christum divinum* christology allied to his pneumatology leads to naming of the Real as the trinitarian God who is Love.

There are some further implications of Augustine's christology for contemporary thought. Here are a few:

Augustine's christology addresses the Void named by so many contemporary thinkers as their principal concern. What other early Christian thinker was so obsessed with the void-producing question, *unde malum?*[40]

---

dicat: *Tristis est anima mea usque ad mortem,* ergo et quando dicit evangelium: Dormiuit Jesus, non dormiuit Jesus; et quando evangelium evangelium dicit: Manducauit Jesus, non manducauit Jesus . . ." *En. in Ps.* 93.19 (CCSL 39.1320–21). "Paul rejoices at the prospect of being crowned, yet Christ, who is to crown him is saddened. The apostle is jubilant, while Christ our Lord is praying, *Father, if it is possible, let this cup pass from me* [Mt 26.39]. But he had taken that sadness upon himself in the same way as he had taken flesh. I do not mean that the Lord was not truly sad: do not take my words in that way. If we were to say that his sadness was not real when the gospel testifies, *My soul is sorrowful to the point of death,* we would have to assert likewise that when the gospel says, 'Jesus slept,' he did not really sleep, and when it says, 'Jesus ate,' he did not really eat [Mt 26.38]." *Exposition of the Psalms 73–98,* The Works of Saint Augustine: A Translation for the 21st Century, III/18 (Hyde Park, NY: New City Press, 2002), 397.

[40]Gillian R. Evans, *Augustine on Evil* (Cambridge: Cambridge University Press, 1982).

Julian of Eclanum was unjust to sneer that an elderly Augustine was still a Manichean. Augustine had abandoned the idealistic Manichean anti-body, anti-marriage, anti-reproduction positions. Unlike every Pelagian, then or now, Augustine stared into the nihilistic abyss of evil, the ultimate terrifying Void. Moreover, Augustine, good Platonist as he was, interpreted evil ontologically as *privatio boni*. However, unlike some other Platonists, Augustine's incorporation of evil as *privatio boni* did not remove the existential sting of the void-abyss opened by the never-ending question for Augustine: *unde malum*.

From another angle on the Void, perhaps the endless abyss of the cavern of *memoria*—surely one of Augustine's greatest philosophical discoveries—can be read as a positive Abyss-Void, analogous to Zen Buddhism's positive portrait of the Void to which we should let go to without fear. Augustine too wants us to let go to, i.e., understand and will, the abyssal, void-like cavern of our memory. On the other hand, Augustine's increasingly angry and, at times, desperate rhetoric in his febrile exchanges with Julian of Eclanum suggest that some deep sense of the existential void of evil, and not just the ontological non-being (*privatio boni*), never left Augustine.

Indeed, Augustine's fury at the Pelagian moralistic refusal to understand the depth of the void of evil and thereby our consistent need for God's grace sounds Bolero-like, louder and louder in his final anti-Pelagian writings. Augustine has always and will always appeal to anyone who also cannot entirely silence the Void even in the midst of a strong faith in God's grace: Luther with his sense of the hidden God, Pascal with his sense of the silence of infinite space, Paul Tillich with his sense that a sense of meaninglessness, a sense of the void is now many Christians' principal question. An Augustinian sense of Void emerges both positively through his discovery of the cave-abyss of *memoria* at the heart of our inwardness (the nature-grace typology in Augustine) and negatively through his overriding sense of the power of evil in us and the ineluctable power of the question *unde malum* (the sin-grace typology in Augustine). Augustine will always be a natural conversation partner for anyone, believer or non-believer, who possesses a strong sense of the power of the Void. Augustine knew that we could be saved only by God's grace—the only

Other Power strong enough to save us from the negative Void within, that *nihil* we self-destructively seem unable not to seek (*non posse non peccare*).

Nor is Augustine irrelevant to a Heideggerian option on naming the Real as the Open. For all the Romantics and, in a strikingly new way, for the later Heidegger, the power of the Real as the Open is disclosed by every work of art. After *Being and Time* Heidegger abandoned Augustine and moved to a new mode of contemplative thinking (Heidegger called it meditative thinking as distinct from calculative thinking). Heidegger's later philosophical thought—no longer Christian but still religious through and through—certainly no longer rested in God (as the Augustinian thinking of his early seminars did), nor did his later thought rest in the Void of *Being and Time* (i.e., Death replaces God as our destiny). The Void-Death—the end of all possibility for *Dasein*—must be appropriated resolutely. The Real for the Heidegger of *Being and Time,* more than he admitted perhaps even to himself, was the Void opened up to authentic *Da-sein* to be appropriated as the Real of one's own death. After his further Void-inflected Nietzsche work, the later Heidegger emerges; his late turning to the Real as the Open manifested and hidden through the artwork, the "clearing" and ultimately, I believe, through a western Heideggerian form of Taoism and Zen Buddhism.

I cannot avoid the temptation of a brief "what if" reflection here. What if Heidegger had continued his reading of Augustine after *Being and Time* and had read, among other Augustinian texts, the Genesis commentaries for their disclosure of what he sought: an Open disclosing the goodness of infinite differences of each and every reality—for Augustine each real being created by a kenotic loving Creator God? Of course, Heidegger did not continue to read Augustine. Even if he had, he probably would not have found it persuasive at all. After all, God was dead for Heidegger from his Nietzsche interpretation forward. Nevertheless, the contemporary discussion on the best name for the Real—the Void, the Open, the Good or God—would have been greatly enhanced, I suggest, if the full complexity of Augustine's theocentrism and christomorphism were more fully comprehended by the once Augustinian Heidegger. Given the enormous influences of Heidegger (and Nietzsche behind him) in postmodern thought, a continued Augustinian moment could have been very fruitful for postmodern thought. Augustine is still present among the secular postmoderns—Lacan, Kristeva, Derrida, Lyotard—but never as deeply and pervasively as in the early Heidegger.

Despite Augustine's reputation in our culture as "pessimistic," Augustine's final word is more accurately described as hope-ful rather than either optimistic or pessimistic. Optimism and pessimism, if they are virtues at all, are purely natural ones. Optimism and pessimism are positions largely dependent less on choice than on one's temperament, one's society and one's personal and historical fate. It is perhaps impossible not to be pessimistic after the evil, the slaughters, the horrors of the twentieth century. In a natural sense, Augustine was what William James[41] named "a sick soul" (restless, conflicted, convalescent). In that sense, Augustine was a natural pessimist. But Augustine never was—save possibly at Cassiciacum—what James named the alternative human type, a "healthy-minded" optimist.

In his Christian conversion Augustine turned (or more accurately, as he would insist, was turned by God's grace) from his natural sick-souled pessimism to a faith working through love. After his acceptance of priestly and episcopal duties, whatever optimism was present at Cassiciacum retreated into the cave of his memory. Existentially, Augustine was always convalescent. Intellectually, he was restless. At the same time, Augustine discovered in Christianity what he most needed: a faith that gave, as gift, a genuine, transforming hope. Christian hope is neither optimism nor pessimism. A faith that may empower one to act compassionately for others as Jesus is narrated to have done (a major concern of Augustine's sermons) is no minor matter. A faith that grants hope on behalf of the hopeless is worth noticing after the century we have just survived and the future we cannot imagine. Augustine's hard-won hope is his greatest gift to the contemporary discussion. And yet even hope is not Augustine's final word. A large part of the greatness of Augustine's sermons and commentaries on the Psalms is that in Augustine, as in the Psalms themselves

[41]William James, *The Varieties of Religious Experience*, in *The Works of William James* (Cambridge: Harvard University Press, 1985), 71–139.

(more than any other biblical book), one finds all the affects of life itself: lamentations, jubilation, thanksgiving, praise, wonder, teaching, anger, mercy, faith, hope, love. Without his Christian conversion Augustine, the most varied, the most affect-laden of great thinkers, may have found himself torn into a thousand pieces. In the Psalms (the leitmotif of the *Confessiones* as well) Augustine found his home. There it becomes clear that Augustine's hope was accompanied by the rarest of contemporary experiences: authentic joy—not fear, not a facile happiness but inexplicable, rare joy, an experience as rare and gifted as love. Joy, like Love, cannot be achieved. It happens.

I will end with a passage from Augustine, again from his wondrous work on the Psalms. Here Augustine recalls (perhaps from memories of his own rural youth) the wordless chant of workers in the field, the chant then named *jubilum*:

> Do not worry, for he provides you with a technique for singing. Do not go seeking lyrics, as though you could spell out in words anything that will give God pleasure. Sing to him in jubilation. This is what acceptable singing to God means: to sing jubilantly. But what is that? It is to grasp the fact that what is sung in the heart cannot be articulated in words. Think of people who sing at harvest time, or in the vineyard, or at any work that goes with a swing. They begin by caroling their joy in words, but after a while they seem to be so full of gladness that they find words no longer adequate to express it, so they abandon distinct syllables and words, and resort to a single cry of jubilant happiness. Jubilation is a shout of joy; it indicates that the heart is bringing forth what defies speech. To whom, then, is this jubilation more fittingly offered than to God who surpasses all utterance? You cannot speak of him because he transcends our speech; and if you cannot speak of him, yet may not remain silent, what else can you do but cry out in jubilation, so that your heart may tell its joy without words, and the unbounded rush of gladness not be cramped by syllables? *Sing skillfully to him in jubilation.*[42]

[42]*En. in Ps.* 32 (*Enarrationes in Psalmos [Expositions of the Psalms]*, 1–32, III/15, 401). I was first alerted to this wonderful quotation some years ago in the chapter on Augustine

An amazing memory in the cavern of Augustine's *memoria*: the word-saturated rhetorician here remembers not words but a time when he is silent and listened to others' *jubilum*. He listens not only in hope but in jubilating joy. A joyful Augustine—that is a side of him that even Peter Brown did not much notice. Augustine's move in naming God is ultimately beyond all language of predication into the language of praise and ultimately jubilating wordless joy, that cicada-like humming beyond speech: *Per Christum hominem ad Christum divinum; per Christum divinum ad Deum Trinitate* (through Christ the man to Christ as God; through Christ as God to God as Trinity).

titled "The Clamour of the Heart," in Rowan Williams' *The Wound of Knowledge: Christian Spirituality from the New Testament to St. John of the Cross* (Cambridge: Cowley Publications, 1979). For another fine reflection on Augustine's spirituality, see the Introduction to *Augustine of Hippo: Selected Writings,* in The Classics of Western Spirituality, ed. Mary T. Clark (New York: Paulist Press, 1984).

"Heart in Pilgrimage": St Augustine as Interpreter of the Psalms[1]

Andrew Louth

My argument in this paper is that the obstacles to a true appreciation of St Augustine by the Orthodox are fundamentally the same as the obstacles faced by western Christians. And also that the remedy in both cases is the same. That might seem very surprising, but I hope I shall be able to convince you of its truth. The problem with understanding Augustine—both for the East and for the West—is that we think we understand him perfectly well already. Virtually no one comes to Augustine with no preconceptions: that, at least, is my conclusion after nearly forty years of teaching early Christian doctrine, including Augustine, to undergraduate students in England. For Christians of the western tradition, this is because he has been so influential. Scholasticism and the Reformation would be inconceivable without Augustine. But which Augustine? He wrote an enormous amount, so much that his biographer, Possidius, said of his works, that "there are so many that there is hardly a student who has been able to read and get acquainted with them all."[2]

The Augustine who governs our preconceptions tends to be the Augustine of the great controversies. First of all, there is Augustine the

---

[1]This essay doubled as the 2007 Orthodoxy in America Lecture and the keynote address for the conference. The mission of Fordham's annual Orthodoxy in America Lecture is to bring the insights of the Orthodox tradition to a broader, non-academic audience, which often includes Orthodox and non-Orthodox students and lay persons.

[2]Possidius, *Vita* 18.9, F.R. Hoare, trans., *The Western Fathers* (London: Sheed & Ward, 1955), 217.

"Doctor of Grace," the champion of the grace of God against the Pelagians, someone who elaborated a doctrine of grace that has left later theologians debating whether he allowed any room for human free will at all. Certainly, he is one who shored up his doctrine of grace with a doctrine of original sin, indeed of original guilt, so that all human beings come into the world worthy of damnation, forming a *massa peccati*. Augustine also pressed his understanding of the priority of grace to the point of elaborating a doctrine of predestination, even a doctrine of "double predestination," whereby human beings are created by God either for election or damnation, regardless of the kind of lives they may live. Or, secondly, there is the Augustine who opposed the Donatists, those North African Christians who maintained that the Catholic Church in North Africa had ceased to exist as a Church, owing to its collusion with bishops who had forfeited grace by their cowardly behavior during the great persecution at the beginning of the fourth century— nearly a century before Augustine's own engagement with the Donatists. This Augustine developed a doctrine of the Church that sees it as forming a mixed community of saints and sinners until the last judgment, with sacraments that are valid, whatever the moral state of the minister, for it is Christ himself who is the true minister of the sacraments. In the controversy with the Donatists, Augustine was eventually driven to accept the use of persecution against recalcitrant Donatists. And then there is the Augustine who spent the best part of a decade of his early manhood as a Manichee. Despite his eventual return to the faith of his childhood, and of his mother, there were those, even in his lifetime, who claimed that Augustine was still a covert Manichee, sharing their hatred of the body and sex. There is also the Augustine of the major works—*De civitate Dei* (*The City of God*) and *De Trinitate* (*On the Trinity*). The *De civitate Dei* is often treated as a quarry for the political ideas of the western middle ages, while it is in his treatise *De Trinitate* that many Orthodox are determined to find the Augustine who, in his doctrine of the Trinity, effectively broke the unity of the *Una Sancta*—the "One, Holy Church"—by his endorsement of the doctrine of the double procession of the Holy Spirit, the *filioque*.

It is not easy for us, Christians of either the East or the West, to get behind these enormous preconceptions, and many might ask, why should we?—Augustine *is* the doctor of grace, and that is what is important about him. But if we follow these preconceptions, we are very soon reading Augustine in the light of later theology, making him take sides in subsequent controversies that he never envisaged. If one actually starts to read Augustine, even the Augustine of the controversies outlined above, one quickly finds oneself in the presence of someone with a quick intelligence, who thought on his feet, whose ideas are more often tentative, not definitive, who was constantly exploring what it meant to confess Christ, to seek to follow him, to be a member of his body, to submit to the transforming effect of the grace of the resurrection. These controversies occupied Augustine's time, and certainly shaped his thinking, but the fundamental reality of Augustine's life as a priest and bishop was as the pastor of the Catholic Christian community in Hippo. It was there that day by day he prayed with his congregation, preached to them, celebrated the eucharist as their bishop. For roughly thirty-five years that was his principal, daily concern. Once a bishop, he never left North Africa, but spent his whole time there, mostly at Hippo, though also in Carthage; he preached several times a week, and many of those sermons have been preserved for us, though many more have been lost. It has been estimated that Augustine must have preached about 8,000 homilies, of which 546 survive; if you add to them the homilies on the Psalms, and the Gospel and First Epistle of John, the total of surviving sermons comes to a little over 1,000, which is about one-eighth of his preaching.[3] But this is a good deal, and it is here, I think, that we find the heart of Augustine. It is here that again and again scholars over the last half-century have sought to discover the "hidden Augustine," the priest and pastor.

So what I want to do in this essay is to peer behind these preconceptions, and simply listen to Augustine the preacher and pastor. In this way, Christians of both western and eastern traditions can find themselves in the presence of a father of the Church, one whose voice speaks with

[3]See Goulven Madec, *La Patrie et la voie* (Paris: Desclée, 1989), 115–16.

authority from the heart of the *Una Sancta*. In particular, it is Augustine as commentator on the Psalms that I want to explore with you, for in his *Enarrationes in Psalmos* (*Enarrations on the Psalms*), we have a complete series of reflections on the Psalms, mostly in the form of homilies given to his congregations. Here, I think, we find the heart of Augustine: a "heart in pilgrimage," to borrow a phrase from the English poet and priest, George Herbert.

Why these reflections on the Psalms? Several reasons come to mind. The first is that the psalms are fundamental to the consciousness of the Church: they are constantly quoted from the New Testament onward; they have become the backbone of the Church's regular—daily and weekly—pattern of prayer; in many contexts it came to be expected that Christians would learn the whole psalter by heart: the second canon of the Seventh Ecumenical Synod, for example, requires that any candidate for the episcopate should know the psalter by heart. Augustine shared this sense of the importance and centrality of the psalter; Possidius tells us that, on his death bed, Augustine "ordered those Psalms of David which are especially penitential to be copied out and, when he was very weak, used to lie in bed facing the wall where the sheets of paper were put up, gazing at them and reading them, and copiously and continuously weeping as he read."[4] His *Enarrationes in Psalmos*, the title given them by Erasmus, were put together by Augustine with some deliberation. Most of the homilies were actually preached to a congregation, either at Hippo or at Carthage, more than a third of them in a single year: 412. These homilies were supplemented by others that were never preached, so far as we know, but were dictated, so that, together with the preached homilies, the whole of the psalter is covered. The homilies on the first thirty-two psalms seem to have been composed as a kind of exercise in sustained reading and commentary, just after his ordination as a priest. Various others seem to have been dictated toward 420, with the explicit intention of completing the *Enarrationes in Psalmos*, including a set of thirty homilies on the long Psalm 118 (119 in the Hebrew enumeration). This evident desire to present

[4]Possidius, *Vita* 31.2 (242).

a complete set of reflections on the Psalms underlines the significance that the Psalms had for Augustine.[5]

There are various ways in which we could explore Augustine's treatment of the Psalms. We could trace the themes and images he develops, but that would require much more time than we have at our disposal. Instead, what I have decided to do is to take one of Augustine's homilies and follow it through with you. This will not exactly be a close reading, though it will include some close reading, but it is really an exercise in seeing how Augustine read one of the psalms with his congregation. I have chosen the homily on Psalm 100 (101 in the Hebrew), which begins: *Misericordiam et iudicium cantabo tibi Domine* (I shall sing to you of mercy and judgment, O Lord).[6] Various considerations guided this choice: among them, that it was actually preached by Augustine to his congregation in Hippo—in Eastertide in 395, when Augustine was on the threshold of consecration as a bishop—and that it is not too long.

Augustine's method of exegesis is always to follow the words closely, to interrogate them. This is partly a matter of his rhetorical training; such word-by-word consideration was what he had learned in his years as a student. But even more it is because these are the words of holy men inspired by the Holy Spirit: each word is significant, as are the order of the words and their meaning. So Augustine begins with what is meant by singing to God of mercy and judgment—mercy and judgment *together*:

> Let no one delude himself into thinking himself free of punishment because of God's mercy, for it is also judgment; and let no one changing for the better be terrified by God's judgment, because mercy precedes it. For when men judge, sometimes they are overcome with

---

[5]For a good introduction to the *En. in Ps.*, see the article by Michael Cameron in *Augustine through the Ages: An Encyclopedia,* ed. Allan D. Fitzgerald (Grand Rapids: William B. Eerdmans Publishing Co., 1999), 290–96, with useful bibliography. I have taken my information about the dating of the homilies from the Corpus Christianorum edition (see below, n. 6), xv–xix, which may be more positive than the evidence can sustain. See also, Rowan Williams, "Augustine and the Psalms," *Interpretation* 58 (2004): 17–27.

[6]The text, edited by E. Dekkers and J. Fraipont on the basis of the Maurist text, in CCSL 39, vol. 3, *Enarrationes in Psalmos LI–C* (Turnholt: Brepols, 1956), 1405–17.

mercy and act against justice; and there seems to be mercy in them and not judgment; sometimes, however, they want to adhere to strict judgment, and they lose sight of mercy. God, however, neither loses the severity of judgment in the goodness of mercy, nor in judging with severity does he lose the goodness of mercy.[7]

However, Augustine says we must observe the order: mercy first, and then judgment. "If we distinguish these two by times, we shall perhaps find that now—*modo,* for the time being—is the time of mercy, while the time of judgment is future." Why, he asks? First of all, look to God, the Father. Remember what the Lord has said: "Be like your heavenly Father . . . Love your enemies, pray for those who persecute you, that you may be sons of your Father who is in heaven, who makes the sun rise on both good and bad, and rain to fall on the just and the unjust."[8]

> Behold mercy. When you see the just and the unjust looking at the same sun, enjoying the same light, drinking from the same fountains, watered by the same rain, filled by the same fruits of the earth, breathing the same air, having equally the world's goods, do not think that God is unjust, who gives these things equally to the just and the unjust. For it is the time of mercy, not yet the time of judgment. For unless God first spares us in mercy, he will not find those he can crown in judgment. It is therefore the time of mercy, when the patience of God leads those who sin to repentance.[9]

This is how Augustine sets the scene for his interpretation of the psalm: we are living in the time of mercy; there awaits us the time of judgment. He continues this contrast between mercy and judgment by drawing a contrast between the Latin verbs *donare* and *reddere* (to grant and to give back, or to recompense). The time of mercy is the time of *donare,* the time of gifts; the time of judgment will be the time of *reddere,* the time of rec-

---

[7] *En. in Ps.* 100.1.
[8] Mt 5.48, 44–45.
[9] *En. in Ps.* 100.1.

ompense. Augustine illustrates this from the example of Paul, who was first a blasphemer and persecutor, but then shown mercy, so that Christ Jesus might show his long-suffering in him (cf. 1 Tim. 1.13, 16). At that time, "the Lord came to give to Paul, not to recompense him." He then goes on to quote from 2 Timothy: "For now I am being sacrificed, the time of my departure is at hand. I have fought the good fight, I have finished the course, I have kept the faith"—all this, Augustine comments, in the time of mercy. "Hear, now, of judgment: For the rest there is laid up for me the crown of justice, which the Lord, the just judge, will recompense me [*reddet mihi*] in that day. When he gives, he is merciful; when he gives back, he will be judge, because 'I will sing to you of mercy and judgment, O Lord.' "[10]

But we must not presume on God's mercy, Augustine continues:

> Therefore, brethren, because we have the time of mercy, let us not delude ourselves, let us not excuse ourselves, let us not say: God always pardons. Look, what I did yesterday, God has pardoned; what I do today, God also pardons; I shall do it tomorrow, because God pardons. You are aware of mercy, and you do not fear judgment. But if you want to sing of mercy and of judgment, understand that he thus pardons, that he may correct, not that you may remain in wickedness.[11]

And Augustine goes on to quote from Psalm 49(50), where the psalmist represents God as upbraiding humankind for all kinds of sins and cruelties, ending: "these things you did, and I kept silence [*Haec fecisti, et tacui*]." "What does this mean: I kept silence," Augustine asks. "It cannot mean: I did not rebuke, but rather: I have not judged. For how could he keep silence who day by day cries out in the scriptures, in the gospel, in his preachers? I kept silence from punishment [*supplicium*], not from words." The time of mercy is the time to learn our faults and repent, and not to presume of God's long-suffering. This is what is meant by "singing of mercy and judgment":

[10]Ibid., 100.2.
[11]Ibid., 100.3.

Because therefore mercy and judgment is sung to us, we also who act with mercy can be sure in the expectation of judgment; and let us be in his body, that we also may sing. For it is Christ who is singing this; if only the head sings, it is sung from the Lord, and is no concern of ours; if, however, it is the whole Christ who sings, that is the head and his body, it is in his members to cleave to him through faith, through hope, and through love; you both sing in him and exult in him; because he works in you, and thirsts in you, and hungers and suffers tribulation in you. Up to the present he is dying in you, and you have now been raised in him ... Therefore, my brothers, Christ is singing; but how, you know, for I know that you are not ignorant about him. The Lord Christ is the Word of God, through whom everything was made. His Word, that he might redeem us, became flesh and dwelt among us; God who is above all became man, the Son of God equal to the Father; he became man for this, that God the man might be mediator between humans and God, and reconcile those placed apart, join together the separated, recall those estranged and lead back the wanderers: for this he became man. He therefore becomes the head of the Church, having both head and members. Seek then his members; for the time being they groan throughout the whole world; then they will rejoice—at the end, at the crown of justice, with which, as Paul says, the Lord, the just judge, will reward me in that day. For the time being, therefore, we sing in hope, all gathered together into one. For clothed with Christ, we are Christ with our head.[12]

Mercy and judgment are the marks of this age and of the one to come; we live in the age of mercy, the mercy shown us in Christ. In union with him, though we groan in this present age, we can also sing—sing of mercy, but also sing of judgment, as we look to the age to come and its dawning.

Augustine has spent the first third of this sermon dwelling on this contrast between mercy and judgment. The rest of the sermon continues under this overarching theme.

[12]Ibid.

The next verse reads: "I will sing psalms [*psallam*] and understand in the way of purity [*via immaculata*], when you come to me." It is only in the way of purity, Augustine comments, that we can sing psalms and understand. "If you want to understand, sing in the way of purity, that is, work for God in gladness [*in hilaritate*]."[13] What, then, Augustine asks, is this way of purity (or "life of purity": the text now reads *vita,* instead of *via*)? He answers his question by quoting the next verse: "I walked in the innocence of my heart, in the midst of my house." "This way of purity begins in innocence, and also reaches its end in it." But what is meant by innocence, Augustine's interrogation of the text continues? The Latin word *innocentia* suggests something not harmed or not harmful: from the verb *noceo,* to harm. And, Augustine remarks, "there are two ways in which someone can cause harm: either by making someone unhappy [*miserum*], or by deserting someone in their unhappiness; for you do not want to be made unhappy by another, nor do you want to be deserted by another, if you are unhappy." There is a play of words here, very important for grasping Augustine's sequence of ideas: the play between *misericordia,* mercy, and *miser,* unhappy, pitiable, miserable. Mercy, *misericordia,* is what those who are *miseri* need: the time of *misericordia* is the time of the *miseri;* it is also the time of the *nocentes,* those who harm others and reduce them to being *miseri.* The *nocentes* do this in two ways: by active harm—by violence, oppression, robbery, covetousness, calumny— by what Augustine calls generally *studium malevolentiae;* and by neglecting the needy, despising the tears of the unhappy. Either way, the one who does this *alienat cor suum*—makes his heart strange to himself. If we ask who is innocent, the answer is: "One who neither harms another nor harms himself. For one who harms himself is not innocent." And Augustine goes on to comment, "But if someone corrupts himself, if he overthrows God's temple in himself, what do you expect, that he will be merciful to others, and spare the miserable? He who is cruel to himself, could he be merciful to another? The whole of justice therefore can be reduced to the single word: innocence." So, "the one who wants to harm

---

[13]Ibid., 100.4.

others has first harmed himself; nor can he walk about, because there is
no 'where' [*quia non est ubi*]. For all wickedness is subject to narrowness:
only innocence is broad, where it may walk about." The freedom to walk
can only be exercised in the space provided by innocence of heart; there
one is free to walk "in the midst of my house." Augustine picks up on this
and comments:

> He says the "midst of his house"—or the Church itself; for Christ
> walks about in it—or his heart, for our heart is our interior house, as
> he expressed it when he said above: "in the innocence of my heart."
> What is the innocence of his heart? The midst of his house. Whoever
> does evil in this house is driven outside it . . . Whoever does not have
> a peaceful heart cannot freely dwell in his heart . . .[14]

And Augustine goes on to cite the example of the paralytic whom the Lord
healed, telling him to "take up his bed and go into his house": "he takes up
his bed and rules his body; now he goes into his house, enters into his conscience; now he finds broad place [*latam*], where he walks around, sings,
and understands."

Note how this exegesis turns on the idea that the wicked person has
damaged himself, has driven himself out of his heart, which has become
too narrow to inhabit. In contrast, the innocent harms no one, and finds
within himself a broad space, where he can walk about in freedom.

There follows a series of verses in which the one who "sings of mercy
and judgment" expresses his attitude toward those who "work iniquity"
(*facientes praevaricationem*), the "crooked heart" (*cor pravum*), the proud,
and those whose heart is insatiable. The psalmist will have nothing to do
with them: he hates them; he will drive them away; he will not eat with
them. Augustine is at pains to make sure that such hatred is not misun-
derstood. The psalmist "hates those who work iniquity" (*facientes praevaricationem*: the Latin *praevaricatio* has a very different meaning from
our English "prevarication"—it means deeply culpable evil). "But," says

Augustine, "you must hate the prevaricators, not the men. There is one man the prevaricator, but see that he has two names—man and prevaricator: God made man, man made himself a prevaricator; love in him what God made, drive away in him what he has made of himself."[15] Or, a little later on: "Behold the good persecutor persecutes not man, but sin."[16] Mention of the *cor pravum* provokes a discussion of prayer, which is only true prayer—prayer from an "upright heart" (*cor rectum*)—if it wants what God wants. Augustine considers, briefly, Christ's prayer in the garden of Gethsemane, and his expression of "sadness, even unto death." Augustine comments, "But what was that voice, save the sound of our weakness?"—Christ, as head of the body, gives expression to the groaning of the members. When he comes to consider the psalmist's refusal to eat with the proud and those with insatiable hearts, Augustine considers the counter-example in the gospel, where Christ eats with the proud pharisee, how the prostitute wept at the Lord's feet and caused the pharisee silently to blame Christ's ignorance of the woman's nature. Augustine comments, "How did he know that Christ was ignorant, unless he suspected that he did not know, because he did not push her away? Because, if it had been him, he would have repelled her. The Lord, however, not only knew that the woman was a sinner, but as a physician saw that the wounds of that proud man were incurable." Christ could use the meal with the proud man at least to warn him of the danger of his pride. For us, Augustine warns, "Beware, lest in their banquets you are caught in the snares of the devil."[17]

Augustine finally comes to the last verse of the psalm: "In the morning I put to death all the sinners on the earth." "This is a dark saying," he remarks, "we do well to pay attention, for it is the very end of the psalm."[18] The psalmist gives his reason in the final words: "that I may utterly destroy from the city of the Lord all workers of iniquity." So, Augustine comments, there are workers of iniquity within the city of the Lord, but that is, as we

---

[15]Ibid., 100.5.
[16]Ibid., 100.8.
[17]Ibid., 100.9.
[18]Ibid., 100.12.

well know, because it is still the "time of mercy"; but the morning will be
the time of judgment; then the workers of iniquity will be destroyed. If
morning is the coming time of judgment, then the present time of mercy
is night, and the theme of night, *nox*, leads to this reflection:

> For at the present, while you do not see my heart and I do not see
> yours, it is night. You sought I do not know what from someone. You
> did not get it; you thought yourself despised, but maybe you were not
> despised; for you do not see the heart—and suddenly you blaspheme.
> In the night pardon is to be given you when you go astray. Someone
> loves you, I do not know who, and you think that he hates you; or he
> hates you, and you think that he loves you; but whatever it is, it is night.
> Do not fear, trust in Christ; in him grasp the day. You can think noth-
> ing evil of him, for we are sure and certain that he cannot be deceived.
> He loves us. Of ourselves, however, we cannot yet be certain. For God
> knows our love for one another; we, however, even if we love one
> another, who knows how such love works out among us? Why does
> no one see the heart? Because it is night. In this night temptations
> abound. It is, as it were, of this night that the psalmist says, "You have
> placed darkness and made night; in it all the beasts of the forest move.
> The young lions [*catuli leonum*] roar after their prey and they seek
> their food from God." In the night the young lions seek their food.
> Who are these young lions? The princes and powers of this air, the
> demons and the angels of the devil. How do they seek their food?
> When they tempt. But they do not come near it, unless God gives them
> power, for thus it is said: "they seek their food from God." The devil
> sought Job to tempt him. What food? The rich, the fat, the just man of
> God, to whom the Lord bore testimony and said: "a man without
> blame, he was a true worshipper of God." He sought him to tempt him,
> seeking food from God. And he accepted that he should be tempted
> but not crushed, purified but not oppressed, or perhaps not purified
> but proved. However, those who are tempted are sometimes handed
> over for some secret reason into the hands of the tempter, because,
> perhaps, they are delivered over to their desires. For the devil harms no

one, unless he receives power from God. But when? In the night. What does this mean: in the night? In this time . . .[19]

"This time," to which Augustine refers, is the time of mercy. But this time will pass, and in the morning will come the time of judgment. And what is meant by "in the morning"? Augustine ends his sermon with these reflections:

> What is: in the morning? While the night is still passing. Why does he still pardon? Because it is the time of mercy. Why does he not always pardon? Because "of mercy and judgment I shall sing to you, O Lord." Brothers, let no one delude himself: all who work iniquity will be put to death; Christ puts them to death in the morning, and destroys them from his city. But while it is still the time of mercy, let us hear him. Wherever he calls out through the law, through the prophets, through the psalms, through letters, through the gospels. See that he is not silent, that he pardons, that he distributes mercy. But beware, because the judgment is to come.[20]

The voice of Augustine the preacher is a fascinating voice. It unfolds the message of the psalm with a sense of great respect for the intelligence of his people. He does not try to fob them off with generalizing morality, nor does he make light of the difficulties of the psalm. Even in looking at a single psalm, we recognize several guiding themes: it is Christ's voice we hear in the psalm, and part of what is meant by understanding the psalm is learning how to join our voice to Christ's; the Christ singing in the psalm is Christ the head of the Church, of which we are the members; in this sense, the Church links this time of trial and temptation with the future time of glory, when Christ will be revealed as judge; finding Christ in the psalm also leads, in both minor and more important ways, to finding the gospel reflected in the psalm. Above all, perhaps, we hear in this homily, the voice of St Augustine the pastor, who had a deep understand-

[19]Ibid.
[20]Ibid., 100.13.

ing of the darkness of the human condition. This sense of the darkness of the human condition lies behind his concept of original sin, and the frailty of the human will, but here, Augustine does not systematize this insight: it remains an insight, based on human experience, an insight we find, expressed in very similar terms, in the Macarian Homilies, for instance. At this level, of pastoral concern and psychological insight, we can all—Christians of both western and eastern traditions—find a voice that has still a great deal to say to us all.

Index

Italicized titles of works in the index are Augustine's unless otherwise specified.